THE
AMERICAN EXPRESS
POCKET GUIDE TO
TOKYO

Peter McGill

PRENTICE HALL PRESS
NEW YORK

The Author
Peter McGill has lived for several years in Tokyo, where he is based as Asia correspondent for the *Observer*. His wife is Japanese. Previously he was in Hong Kong for two years, first as an administrator for the government and later as a foreign correspondent.

Few travel books are without errors, and no guidebook can ever be completely up to date, for telephone numbers and opening hours change without warning, and hotels and restaurants come under new management, which can affect standards. While every effort has been made to ensure that all information is accurate at the time of going to press, the publishers will be glad to receive any corrections and suggestions for improvements, which can be incorporated in the next edition, but cannot accept any consequences arising from the use of the book, or from the information contained herein. Dollar amounts reflect exchange rates in effect in fall 1987.

Editor Elizabeth Newman
Series Editor David Townsend Jones
Assistant Editor Alison Franks
Editorial assistants Helen Panay, Jaspal Kharay
Indexer Hilary Bird
Gazetteer Anderley Moore

Art Editor Nigel O'Gorman
Design assistant Christopher Howson
Illustrator Karen Cochrane
Map Editor David Haslam
Jacket illustration Rozier Gaudriault
Production Barbara Hind

Edited and designed by Mitchell Beazley
International Limited
Artists House, 14-15 Manette Street,
London W1V 5LB
for the American Express Pocket Travel
Guide Series

© American Express Publishing
Corporation Inc. 1988
All rights reserved including the right of
reproduction in whole or in part in any form
Published by Prentice Hall Press
A Division of Simon & Schuster, Inc.
Gulf & Western Building
One Gulf & Western Plaza
New York, New York 10023
PRENTICE HALL PRESS is a
trademark of Simon & Schuster, Inc.
Maps in 2-color and 4-color by Lovell Johns Ltd, Oxford, England
Typeset by Bookworm Typesetting, Manchester, England
Printed and bound in Great Britain by Purnell Book Production Ltd,
a member of the BPCC group.

**Library of Congress Cataloging-
in-Publication Data**
McGill, Peter.
  The American Express pocket guide
to Tokyo.
  Includes index.
  1. Tokyo (Japan)—Description—Guide book
  I. American Express Company. II. Title.
DS896.38.M34 1988 915.2'1350448 87-720
ISBN 0-13-025107-0

Contents

How to use this book

The American Express Pocket Guide to Tokyo is an encyclopedia of travel information, organized in the sections listed on the previous page. There is also a comprehensive index (pages 206-216), and there are full-color maps at the end of the book.

For easy reference, all major sections (*Sights and places of interest*, *Hotels*, *Restaurants*) and other sections as far as possible are arranged alphabetically. For the organization of the book as a whole, see *Contents*. For places that do not have individual entries in *Sights and places of interest*, see the *Index*.

Abbreviations
As far as possible only standard abbreviations have been used. These include days of the week and months, points of the compass, Avenue (Ave.), Saint (St), rooms (rms), C for century, and measurements.

Floors
American usage applies in this book: thus "first floor" refers, in European terms, to the ground floor, and so on.

Cross-references
Whenever a place or section title is printed in *sans serif italics* (for example, *Kan'eiji Temple* or *Basic information*) in the text, you can turn to the appropriate heading in the book for fuller information. Cross-references in this typeface refer either to sections in the book — *Basic information* or *Planning and walks* for example — or to individual entries in the *A-Z* of *Sights and places of interest*, such as *Tokyo Tower* or *Ueno Zoo*.

For easy reference, use the running heads printed at the top corner of the page (see, for example, *Basic information* on pages 12-13, *Ginza* on page 62, or *Ueno Zoo* on page 91).

How entries are organized

Okura Museum
2-10-3, Toranomon, Minato-ku ☎583-0781. Map 5J8 ■ & ⚞ ⚌ ☐ ☛ Open 10am-4pm (last entry 3.45pm). Closed—— Mon, year end, New Year and while changing displays. Subways: Kamiyacho, Toranomon.

It is strange how few purposeful businessmen and well-heeled —— guests ever notice this "Chinoiserie" folly, with its sweeping gabled roof, pillars, verandas and large guardian bronzes, marooned esthetically and physically in one corner of the **Okura** hotel's large front courtyard (see *Hotels*). The original museum on this site was the first private museum in Japan, opened in 1917 to house the prodigious collection of the late industrial magnate Kihachiro Okura, founder of the **Imperial** (see *Hotels*). His late son Kishichiro subsequently started the Okura hotel. Six years after it opened, the building and many items of the collection were destroyed in the Great Kanto Earthquake. The present 1928 gallery is the work of Chuta Ito, who also designed the curious Indian-style Tsukiji Honganji Temple.

The current highly eclectic collection of Japanese and Chinese paintings, bronzes, calligraphy, ceramics, masks, swords, lacquer, costumes and books, as well as the occasional Korean and Indian work, is rotated for exhibition about three times a year.

Bold type is used in the text mainly for emphasis, to draw attention to something of special interest or importance. At the same time it picks out places — temples or minor museums, for example — that do not have separate descriptions of their own.

Map references
Each full-color map at the end of the book has a page number (2-16) and is divided into a grid of squares, identified vertically by letters (A, B, C, D, etc.) and horizontally by numbers (1, 2, 3, 4, etc.). A map reference identifies the page and square in which the street or place can be found — thus *Tokyo Tower* is located in Map 5J8.

Price categories
Price categories for hotels and restaurants are denoted by the symbols □ ▮□ ▮▮□ ▮▮▮ and ▮▮▮▮ which signify cheap, inexpensive, moderately priced, expensive and very expensive, respectively. In Tokyo these correspond approximately with the following actual prices, which give a guideline at the time of printing. Although actual prices will inevitably increase, in most cases the relative price category — for example expensive or cheap — is likely to remain more or less the same.

Price categories	Corresponding to approximate prices	
	for **hotels** *double room with bath (single rooms are not much cheaper)*	For **restaurants** *meal for one with service, tax and two small bottles of sake*
□ cheap	under $70-105	$8-20
▮□ inexpensive	$105-130	$20-35
▮▮□ moderate	$130-165	$35-70
▮▮▮▮ expensive	$165-200	$70-140
▮▮▮▮ very expensive	over $200	over $140

—Bold blue type for entry headings.

—Blue italics for address, practical information and symbols.
For list of symbols see page 6 or back flap of jacket.

—Black text for description.

—San serif italics used for cross-references to other entries or sections.

—Bold type used for emphasis.

Entries for hotels, restaurants, shops, etc. follow the same organization, and are sometimes printed across a half column. In hotels, symbols indicating special facilities appear at the end of the entry, in black.

— **Keio Plaza**
2-2-1, Nishi-Shinjuku, Shinjuku-ku, Tokyo 160 ☎344-0111 ▮▮▮
●26874 ⊗ 344-0247. Map 6G3 ▮▮
1,485 rms ⇐ ⊒ AE CB ◑ ◑ VISA
JR/subway: Shinjuku.
Location: w *Shinjuku ("Skyscraper City").* The Keio Plaza (a member of the Intercontinental Hotel chain), with its 47 floors, is still the tallest hotel in Japan, but with the addition of the new **Hilton** and **Century Hyatt** nearby it can hardly be called the most glamorous or luxurious in *Shinjuku.* However, the rooftop lounge offers suitably stunning views over the metropolis.
と ⇌ ▼ ⌐ ⚓

Key to symbols

☎	Telephone	AE	American Express
IDD	International Direct Dialing (IDD)	CB	Carte Blanche
⊕	Telex	DC	Diners Club
℻	Facsimile (fax)	MC	MasterCard
★	Recommended sight	VISA	Visa
i	Tourist information	⌂	Quiet hotel
🚗	Parking	☘	Garden
🆓	Free entrance	⇌	Swimming pool
🎫	Entrance fee payable	☗	Bar
🎫	Entrance expensive	♨	Sauna
♿	Facilities for disabled people	⚬	Tennis
📷	Photography forbidden	✓	Golf
⚐	Guided tour	💪	Gym/fitness facilities
🍽	Cafeteria	♨	Onsen
✳	Special interest for children	🎤	Conference facilities
◁	Good view	🍴	Restaurant
🛏	Hotel	▭	A la carte available
🏠	Ryokan	🎴	Set (fixed price) menu available
🌸	Good value		
▭	Cheap		
▥	Inexpensive		
▦	Moderately priced		
▧	Expensive		
▨	Very expensive		

Note to readers
The following are translations of Japanese words and suffixes
used commonly in place names:

bashi bridge
dori avenue
ji temple
jinja shrine
mon gate

An introduction to Tokyo

Tokyo is both dynamic and exciting, but unlike some other great cities, many of its charms and beauties lie hidden beneath the surface. The city cannot boast wide avenues, elegant town houses and carefully laid out parks; in fact, it appears largely composed of a jumble of alleys latticed by congested traffic arteries. At first glance, visitors may be forgiven for assuming this enormous city of 11.8 million people (with a further 17 million living in outposts of greater Tokyo) is without any distinguishing or outstanding feature. Even the builders' modern blight of reinforced concrete has produced relatively few high-rise buildings to punctuate the monotonous skyline.

This, however, does not truly represent Tokyo, one of the world's most fascinating cities. Even the briefest acquaintance with the city makes one realize that behind the concrete facade its people are as "Japanese" as those in ancient Kyoto or Nara. In the city center, gleaming office buildings stand shoulder-to-shoulder with ascetically simple Shinto shrines. The people themselves, with their relentless profusion of energy, are Tokyo's hallmark, and frantic Tokyoites may sometimes appear to take their surroundings and cultural legacy for granted. Despite this, you will probably find more local pride and attachment in the typical Tokyoite than in a Londoner or New Yorker, for this is primarily a city of small villages, each with its own Shinto shrine or Buddhist temple, and neighborhood festivals.

More immediately recognizable are the different Tokyo districts: the Marunouchi-Otemachi business center, where many of the world's largest corporations have their headquarters; the internationally famous Ginza shopping mecca; the nightlife center of Roppongi; and the Harajuku teenage capital. Less easily defined are areas such as Asakusa, Ueno or Ningyocho that best preserve the history and rich popular culture of old Tokyo — or Edo, as it was called over a century ago, before the shogunate's demise.

The physical character of Tokyo *is* more amorphous than great Western capitals, but mainly for cogent historical reasons. Primarily it derives from the city's adolescence as a *joka machi*, or castle town. Most of the city has inherited the contorted street configurations intended by the shoguns to confuse invading armies, with the exception of the distinct, rectangular grids of Marunouchi, Otemachi or the Kasumigaseki government area, which are recent impositions on deliberate disorder. Traditional Japanese wooden architecture, although well suited to Japan's climate, has suffered near-extinction in Tokyo through seemingly endless disasters. Between 1603 and 1868, no fewer than 97 conflagrations swept the city, and fires were commonly called *Edo-no-hana*, or the flowers of Edo. In 1707, Mt. Fuji erupted, and in 1854 and 1855 major earthquakes that rocked the city were taken as harbingers of approaching doom. The Great Kanto Earthquake of 1923 and the subsequent fire destroyed 20-30 percent of the houses in Tokyo and killed approximately 100,000 people, finally convincing the city government of the need for stone and concrete buildings. The 1945 US firebombings claimed a similar number of human victims, but destroyed even more of the still mainly wooden city.

Tokyo's evolution

Toward the end of the 12thC, a junior member of one of the two great contending feudal clans of the time built a house and fortified compound close to the mouth of the Tone River in the Kanto plain, and named his family Edo, or estuary, after its location.

It was not until 1457 that a minor feudal captain called Dokan Ota built his castle where it is believed Shigenaga Edo had founded his house. The castle had three fortresses, the chief one also being Dokan's own residence.

During a conflict between branches of his lord's family, Dokan was falsely accused of disloyalty and consequently murdered in 1486. After being besieged in 1524, the castle fell into the hands of the Hojo family of Odawara and was held by them until Odawara Castle itself fell to the all-conquering Hideyoshi Toyotomi in 1590. Toyotomi offered the eight Hojo provinces of the East to his powerful ally Ieyasu Tokugawa, who chose to make Edo his new castle, and entered the little coastal town in Aug that same year. Dokan's fort was by then a dilapidated ruin, roofed with wooden shingles and thatch like a farmhouse, and only dry ditch and grassy embankment defenses. The land side of the castle was a wilderness of reeds and bamboo groves; today's district of Hibiya was a sea inlet where fishermen had their huts; and from Nihonbashi to Ginza and Shimbashi there were still sandbanks and tidal flats.

However, Tokugawa was quick to recognize Dokan's foresight in selecting this location. As well as its strategic potential, it more or less conformed to the four ancient directional principles of Chinese geomancy. There was a "blue dragon," or river, to the E; a "red phenix," or pond, to the S; a "white tiger," or main thoroughfare, to the W; and a "realm of the black tortoise," or mountain, to the N. In fact the mountain is W, not N, and the main Tokaido highway is S, not W, but these anomalies were cleverly bypassed by having the main gate, Otemon, to the W side of the castle instead of its classic Chinese position to the S. Thus the essential topographical features reassumed their auspicious positions on the geomantic "compass."

Tokugawa vanquished forces loyal to his former ally Toyotomi at the battle of Sekigahara in 1600, and three years later was made shogun by the emperor in Kyoto. The subdued *daimyo* (literally meaning "great name") feudal lords competed with one another in demonstrating their loyalty to the new supremo by supplying ships to transport the huge stones and thousands of laborers needed for the castle's construction. The shogun's seat, finally completed in 1640, was the largest and most magnificent castle in the land. Its total area covered 1.8sq.km (³⁄₄sq. mile), with four *maru* (circles, or enclosed fortresses), 21 *yagura* (watchtowers), 28 *tamon* (storehouses for ammunition) and 99 gates.

Instead of the conventional single moat, the castle stood at the center of a whorl of moats that wound round the town boundaries, crossed by 36 bridges, gates and their *mitsuke* (approaches). Although much of the outer swirl of moats has since been filled in, parts can still be traced along either the Chuo or Sobu JR lines from Suidobashi to Yotsuya stations, or the remnants of the moat in front of Akasakamitsuke (Akasaka Lookout) Subway Station near the New Otani and Akasaka Prince hotels.

Yamanote and Shitamachi

Edo's basic social contours — on the one hand, the Yamanote (hand of the hill) high ground, dominated by the shogun's castle, *daimyo* lords and warrior-class, and on the other, the Shitamachi (town below) area, inhabited by common townspeople — stayed intact at least until the Meiji Restoration of 1868.

In 1633, to protect himself from subversives and intrigue, Tokugawa forced the *daimyo* to leave their families and a body of retainers as permanent hostages of the shogun's Edo court. The *daimyo* themselves were required to alternate residence in Edo with their own homes every six months if their domains were nearby or every other year if from more distant areas.

The three main branches of the Tokugawa family (*gosanke*) were accommodated in the westernmost grounds of the castle (now the Fukiage Garden of the Imperial Palace where the Emperor and Empress have their private residence), and each of the other 250 or so *daimyo* in Japan were required to build a *yashiki* (residence) in Edo, positioned between the castle and the outer swirl of moats according to each *daimyo*'s degree of loyalty. *Fudai*, or hereditary *daimyo*, who had joined the Tokugawa side before the Battle of Sekigahara, were privileged by being leased land for their main *yashiki* nearest to Otemon gate, in a district called Daimyo Koji (Lane of the Lords) extending s through present-day Otemachi and Marunouchi (which means within the *maru*, or enclosure). Land for the *tozama*, or "outside," *daimyo*, who had sworn allegiance to Ieyasu only after the Battle of Sekigahara, followed the spiral of the moat farthest out in the areas of the Sakuradamon, Toranomon and Akasaka gates. It is no coincidence that these districts are the most formally laid out in present-day Tokyo, for with their confiscation after the 1868 Imperial Restoration they became the center of government and business development.

The shogun's 7,000 *hatamoto* warrior-retainers, who made up the officer corps of his fighting force and filled posts in the bureaucracy, were assigned land w and n of the castle in a broad swathe running sw from the Akasaka gate, toward the ne and Sujikaibashi gate.

The use of land beyond the outer moat was also specific, the s being reserved for *tozama daimyo* villas and warehouses, and areas from the sw to ne were used to house *hatamoto* and lesser-ranked *gokenin* (literally, "housemen"), the lowest-ranking direct retainers of the shogunate.

Near the bottom of the feudal pecking order were the townspeople: merchants and craftsmen drawn mainly from western Japan, and assorted day laborers, tinkers, hawkers, litter-bearers and the others, who settled in the lowland to the e, mostly reclaimed with earth from partially leveled Kanda Hill (an arc traced n from Shimbashi, Ginza and Kyobashi marks the moat dividing them from *yashiki* of the inner *daimyo*). Merchants congregated along the waterways near Nihonbashi Bridge, and it was here, in 1673, that the son of a founder (of the Mitsui house from Ise in w Japan) first set up a dry goods store that was the foundation of today's mighty Mitsui conglomerate.

These neat geographical distinctions were to blur somewhat over the next two-and-a-half centuries due to fires, explosive population growth, pauperization of the military and enrichment of the merchant classes. After the disastrous 1657 "Longsleeves Fire," the *gosanke* residences were moved out of the castle grounds to create a firebreak, as well as many *daimyo* buildings adjacent to the castle. All the temples and most of the shrines were also moved out to a suburban belt connecting Asakusa, Yanaka, Hongo, Yotsuya, Azabu and Shiba and to the e of the Sumida River, where they are still to be found.

It was under the repressive shogunal regime and in the Shitamachi downtown area that Edo's popular culture, known chiefly to the outside world through *kabuki* and *ukiyo-e* woodblock prints, flourished. Except for rich merchants, most of the burgeoning population of townspeople lived in slums. Here, *nagaya*, or long houses, faced 1m-wide alleys with open drains running down the middle, with a small kitchen inside leading into just one 9sq.m (97sq.ft) room; toilets were communal. By 1725, when Edo had grown into the world's largest city with a population of 1.3 million, the 600,000 townspeople were crammed into an area covering only one-tenth of the city and overcrowding was far worse than anything to be found in modern-day Tokyo.

Deriving from this period, the idealized picture of the *Edokko*, or child of Edo, has been heavily sentimentalized, but demonstrably, out of this overcrowding, communal deprivation and precariousness, a profound ethos of seeking evanescent pleasure developed. The *ukiyo-e* (a type of woodblock print, literally meaning "floating world immortalized in pictures") could be found in any of the city's hundreds of mixed public bathhouses; and watching all-day performances at one of the three licensed *kabuki* theaters, or visiting one of the many centers of geisha entertainment and prostitution, also became popular.

The overthrow of the shogunate in 1868 and the beginning of Japan's miraculous economic transformation also led to profound changes in Tokyo. One of the most noticeable was wrought by the advent of the railroads. Both Shinjuku and Shinagawa quickly developed from being mere out-of-the-city "post stations" catering to highway travelers, into major urban centers, thanks to their new strategic role as focal points of the railroad. New waves of immigrants from the provinces attracted by Tokyo's beacon have mainly chosen to live in the w and s of the city, frightened off perhaps by the entrenched community pride and spirit of the old Shitamachi that is still present, or its lingering *déclassé* image, which until now has saved much of it from overdevelopment.

Progress has robbed the Shitamachi of its role as guardian of Edo's merchant culture, except, that is, in carefully tended nurseries of tradition such as Asakusa; but any *Edokko* will instantly claim that it remains the warmest, coziest and most robust part of the great metropolis.

Before you go

Documents required
American citizens need a visa to enter Japan, as do Australian and South African visitors and holders of Hong Kong British passports. A tourist visa is valid for 90 days, and a multiple-entry visa limits each stay to this period of time. Apply to your Japanese embassy or consulate with your passport, one passport-sized photo and a round-trip ticket to Japan. Citizens of Austria, West Germany, Ireland, Liechtenstein, Mexico, Switzerland and the UK are allowed to stay in Japan for 180 days as tourists with only a passport. Tourists from most other countries are allowed 90 days. Vaccinations are not required for entry into Japan.

Travel and medical insurance
Japanese medical care is generally of a high standard. However, extended hospital treatment is expensive and medical insurance is strongly recommended. Many doctors and dentists speak English or German, and there are many English-speaking hospitals.

Money
The Japanese unit of currency is the yen (¥). Coins are ¥1, ¥5, ¥10, ¥50, ¥100 and recently ¥500. Bank notes are ¥500 (now being withdrawn), ¥1,000, ¥5,000 and ¥10,000. Any amount of currency can be imported or exported.

Cash and travelers cheques in major foreign currencies can be easily exchanged. Travelers cheques issued by American Express, Thomas Cook, Barclays, Bank of America, Citibank, Visa and MasterCard are widely recognized. Make sure you read the instructions included with your travelers cheques. It is important to note separately the serial numbers of your cheques and the telephone number to call in case of loss. Companies that specialize in travelers cheques, such as American Express, provide extensive local refund facilities through their own offices or agents. Credit cards are honored by all airlines, major hotels, department stores, and many restaurants and stores. American Express, Diners Club, MasterCard and Visa are generally acceptable. Carte Blanche has less coverage.

Japan rail pass

This ticket offers unlimited free travel within a specified period on any of the rail (including the famous Shinkansen "bullet" trains), bus or ferry services of Japanese Railways (JR). The pass is only available to tourists visiting Japan from abroad, and must be bought from an authorized agent before you enter Japan. Contact your local Japan Travel Bureau (JTB), Japanese Air Lines (JAL) office, Japanese consulate or travel agent for details. The JR counter at Narita Airport Arrival Lobby will hand over the pass when you present your Exchange Order, or you can use the voucher to obtain your pass at any of the travel service centers at Tokyo, Ueno, Ikebukuro, Shinjuku or Shibuya stations.

Customs

After clearing passport control and collecting your baggage, move on to the "Non-Resident" customs counter.

Non-residents can bring in any items for personal use duty-free, except for the following, which can be imported up to these specified amounts:

Tobacco   400 cigarettes *or* 100 cigars *or* 500g tobacco.
Alcoholic drinks   3 bottles (760cc each).
Perfume   2fl.oz.
Watches   Two timepieces each costing ¥30,000 or less, including those in current use.
Other goods   Non-residents may import ¥100,000-worth of extra goods.

Getting there

All international flights for the Tokyo area arrive at Narita's New Tokyo International Airport, built among paddy fields. It is 66km (41 miles) from the city center and at least 1hr away by bus or train. Departing passengers are required to pay a ¥2,000 tax.

Climate

Japan has four distinct seasons. Spring and autumn are the most pleasant. Mar to May are cool and dry in Tokyo. June marks the beginning of summer and the "rainy season," which lasts until early July; by Aug humidity climbs to an oppressive 80 percent and the mercury frequently hits 30°C (86°F); heat waves are common. Sept to early Oct is the "typhoon season," but it is cooler. Late Oct to Nov brings mild, temperate weather. Winters (Dec to Feb) are dry but cold, with occasional snowfalls.

Clothes

Lightweight clothes and short sleeves are appropriate for summer (jackets, if worn, should be unlined). Skimpy, revealing

11

sportswear, however, provokes giggles and sneers from conservative Tokyoites. Light sweaters or jackets are useful in autumn. Winter visitors should be well wrapped-up.

Suits and ties are universally worn by Japanese *salariman* (male office workers) during working days, but Tokyo restaurants have no dress codes. Sneakers, sandals and occasionally denims are barred by smarter discos.

General delivery

A letter marked *poste restante* c/o any Japanese post office will be held until collected. Certain commercial firms also provide a *poste restante* service for customers only:
American Express   Shuwa Kamiyacho Building, 5th floor, 4-3-13, Toranomon, Minato-ku, Tokyo 105
Central Post Office   2-7-2, Marunouchi, Chiyoda-ku, Tokyo 100

Getting around

From the airport to the city

Even the stoic Japanese find Narita's long distance from Tokyo and the relatively poor connecting transportation irritating. Express bus and train services take 1hr, and services close well before midnight. On mercifully rare occasions when freak weather delays evening arrivals, six or more plane loads of passengers are marooned for hours waiting for "emergency" transportation.

Express (limousine) buses leave Narita from 6.50am-11.30pm for Tokyo City Air Terminal (TCAT) in the center, where there is normally a line-up of taxis. Less frequent buses run to hotels in various Tokyo sub-centers: Shinjuku, Akasaka, Shiba, Shinagawa, Ginza and Ikebukuro; or directly to Haneda domestic airport and Yokohama. However, the fare is expensive.

The Keisei "Skyliner" express train is slightly cheaper, but more inconvenient: first a 5min connecting bus ride to Narita Station, then a 1hr train ride to Ueno in northern Tokyo. At both ends passengers must carry their own luggage.

JR's train service to Tokyo starts from Narita Station, a 25min shuttle bus ride from the airport, and it is more expensive and less frequent than Keisei. This is only recommended for those who wish to economize by using their newly acquired JR "Rail Pass" (see *Japan rail pass* above).

Taxis from Narita are only for the rich, and the luggage trunk is often too small for suitcases.

Cars may be rented at the airport (see the warning in *Getting around by car* first, however).

Japanese addresses

Only a very few major avenues and thoroughfares in Tokyo have names, and even fewer Tokyoites know them. A Tokyo address instead is divided into the post office zip code, the *ku* or city ward, place name, a *chome* subdivision, and numbers for the street and building (sometimes with its own name). A typical address might be 2-7-2, Marunouchi, Chiyoda-ku, Tokyo 100. The last number is the postal zip. "Chiyoda-ku" means it is in the Chiyoda ward, right in the heart of the city. Marunouchi is the business district within Chiyoda-ku. The first "2" stands for 2-chome, a subdivision of Marunouchi legible on a detailed map. "7" is the street, and the last "2" is the building.

The system is eminently logical and clear to the postman with an intimate knowledge of his small beat, but hopeless even for most ordinary Tokyoites visiting a building for the first time. Store assistants are often unaware of what *chome* they are working in and residents frequently do not know the location of the next one.

If not commonly known, the best solution is to telephone your destination beforehand to get explicit directions (often you will be told to wait at the nearest local landmark or station exit to be picked up). Taxi drivers have maps with *chome* marked but may have to ask locals for more detailed help. If possible ask hotel staff to write down instructions first for the driver.

Public transportation

Tokyo has probably the world's safest, cleanest and most efficient public transportation systems, but for a foreign visitor the maze of interconnecting subway and rail lines can be confusing and frustrating. Every station has its name signposted both in Japanese and roman letters, and all except the two municipal subway lines also have the previous and next approaching stations in roman script. Platform directions inside the stations are less dependable — at Shinjuku JR Station, one of the largest and busiest in the capital, all the signs to the various platforms are only written in Japanese. Subways and private railroads operate from early morning to midnight. JR trains run later, until 12.30-1am. Buses in Tokyo tend to be grindingly slow because of heavy road traffic, and destination signs are only shown in Japanese. (The signs, however, normally also show route numbers.)

Japanese Railways

JR's four Tokyo commuter lines each has its own color. The most convenient is the "Yamanote" loop line, which encircles the downtown area, these trains being either all green or silver with a green horizontal stripe. Buy your ticket at any of the JR ticket machines mounted on the station wall; they accept ¥10, ¥50, ¥100 coins and sometimes ¥1,000 notes. If you are unsure of the fare, buy the cheapest ticket, which is valid for the next two stops in either direction. At the gate, your ticket will be punched and handed back; keep it for collection when you get off. At your destination, if you have traveled more than two stops, hand over the ticket at the "Fare Adjustment Office" inside the station (near the exit) and pay the excess. You will be given a receipt to be handed to the ticket collector on the way out.

Subways

Buy a ticket at one of the machines on the station wall. For the seven private subways (Chiyoda, Ginza, Hanzomon, Hibiya, Marunouchi, Yurakucho and Tozai), transfers can be made at any intersection with other lines. The three metropolitan subways (Toei Mita, Toei Asakusa and Toei Shinjuku) have a separate fare system. Within the city, all subway trains stop at every station. If unsure of the fare, buy the cheapest ticket and pay the excess at the exit wicket where you get off.

Taxis

Taxis display a sign in the lower left-hand corner of their windshield that is lit red when vacant and green when occupied. Drivers are required to take passengers to any destination in the city, and every taxi has a digital meter. Tipping is never expected. The left-hand back door is opened and closed by the driver by a remote-controlled lever, so stand back from the swinging door after the taxi has stopped. There is a standard fare covering the first 2km (1 mile), with supplements for each additional 370m

(400yds) and a time charge for when the taxi is moving at less than 10kph. There is also a 20 percent surcharge between 11pm and 5am. Expressway tolls are extra. Very few taxi drivers speak English, so unless you are heading to your hotel or a famous landmark it is best to ask the hotel to write down the destination, in Japanese, before you start.

Getting around by car

Tokyo driving is little fun but far from impossible for the determined foreigner. Although traffic congestion is maddening, and traffic lights are often spaced every 50m (54yds), major routes and directions are numbered and signposted with roman script. It sometimes makes good sense to rent a car for a trip out of town (see *Excursions*). The Japan Automobile Federation (JAF) (*head office, opposite the Tokyo Tower: Kikai Shinko Kai Building, 1st floor, 3-5-4, Shibakoen, Minato-ku ☎436-2811*) supplies booklets in English on Japanese traffic laws (in Japan they drive on the left), and its nationwide free breakdown service is available through reciprocal agreements to members of the following associations: the American AAA, Canadian CAA, British AA, Dutch ANWB, German ADAC, Italian ACI, Austrian OAMTC, Norwegian NAF, Swiss TCS, Australian AAA, New Zealand AA, Hong Kong AA and the Singapore AA.

To drive in Japan, you need a Japanese or international driver's license. (Note that Japan has no reciprocal agreement to recognize international licenses from West Germany.) It is usually possible to exchange a foreign license for a Japanese one (the process takes one day) at the licensing office (*Unten Menkyo Shikenjo, 1-12-5, Higashi Oi, Shinagawa-ku ☎474-1374*).

Renting a car

Rental companies accept major credit cards. Rent-it-here-leave-it-there deals are available, and drivers can be as young as 18. Comprehensive insurance is optional, but recommended.

Domestic airlines

Nearly all domestic flights from Tokyo leave from Haneda airport, which is easily reached by monorail from Hamamatsucho Station on the JR Yamanote loop line or by taxi from central Tokyo.
All Nippon Airways (ANA) ☎552-6311
Japan Air Lines (JAL) ☎456-2111
Toa Domestic Airlines (TDA) ☎747-8111

Limousine rental

Hourly rates for private limousines (with drivers) compare favorably with taxis. Among the reputable firms are:
Hotel Okura Limousine 2-10-4, Toranomon, Minato-ku ☎583-2424 (per hour with English-speaking drivers)
Imperial Hotel Limousine Service 1-5-2, Kojimachi, Chiyoda-ku ☎264-7441 (per hour with English-speaking drivers)
Japan Travel Bureau 1-13-1, Nihonbashi, Chuo-ku ☎276-7771 (half/whole day private guided tours by car)

On-the-spot information

Public holidays

Jan 1; Adults' Day, Jan 15; Spring Equinox Day, Mar 21; Emperor's Birthday, Apr 29; Constitution Day, May 3; Children's Day, May 5; Respect for the Aged Day, Sept 15; Autumn Equinox

Day, Sept 23; Gymnastics Day, Oct 10; Culture Day, Nov 3; Labor Thanksgiving Day, Nov 23.

Business offices, schools, post offices and other government services (although not transportation) are closed on these days. Restaurants, shops and department stores usually remain open, except on New Year's Day. Many establishments close for 2-5 days over the New Year season.

Time zones
Japan is 14hrs ahead of Eastern Standard Time, from 15-17hrs ahead of the other time zones in the USA, and 9hrs ahead of GMT.

Banks and currency exchange
Banking hours are 9am-3pm Mon-Fri and 9am-noon Sat (except the second and third Sat in every month). Most bank branches in Tokyo have foreign exchange sections that have the same opening hours (except for Sat mornings when they are closed).

Shopping hours
Most department stores are open 10am-6pm weekdays and 10am-6.30pm Sat and Sun. They are closed once a week (the day differs for each). Most other stores are open 10am-8pm seven days a week. Restaurants are generally open 11.30am-11pm, but in late-night entertainment areas such as Roppongi a few stay open as late as 1am. Bars and discos do not have to close until 4am.

Rush hours
There are only a few Tokyo stations, such as Shinjuku and Ikebukuro, where staff actually push passengers into trains to close the doors, but the image of rush-hour commuters as canned sardines is otherwise correct. Between 7-9am and 5-7pm, the choice of transportation is between discomfort and frustration. Driving or taking a taxi, however, would take twice as long as the train.

Post and telephone services
Post offices are open 9am-5pm Mon-Fri, 9am-12.30pm Sat. The Central Post Office next to Tokyo Station is open 24hrs.

Public telephones can be found everywhere and are never vandalized. To operate, lift the receiver, insert ¥10 or ¥100 and dial the number. Inside the city the Tokyo code (03) is not needed. When calling an out-of-town number, first dial the code number printed in parentheses. For example, when dialing Yokohama from Tokyo ☎(045) followed by the number.

Yellow public phones accept ¥100 coins, useful for long distance calls. NTT and KDD, the international telecom company, sell "telephone cards," which can be used on green public phones for local, long-distance and some IDD international calls.

Call KDD (☎*0051*) from a private phone or a public green international-type phone for operator-assisted overseas calls. KDD has a 24hr office (*1-8-1, Otemachi, Chiyoda-ku* ☎*270-5111*) for international telephone, telegram, telex and fax calls.

Fax has become widely used in Japan, being particularly suitable for transmitting complex Japanese writing. Most Japanese offices and hotels have their own fax machines (Group 3 type).

Public rest rooms
These are usually found only at JR stations and in public parks, and are not recommended. The best solution is to use the rest room of a department store or office building. The traditional

15

seatless, squat-type Japanese toilet is increasingly rare; the vast majority are now Western-style.

Electric current
The current in Tokyo is 100-110V, 50 cycles AC. The voltage is the same in western Japan (e.g., Kyoto) but is 60 cycles AC.

Koban
Every Japanese neighborhood has its own *koban* (police box), invaluable when you are lost or seeking directions. Although the police on duty are rarely able to speak much English, they will usually draw a map for uncomprehending foreigners. If you need to report a crime, take your passport for identity, as this is required for filing a report.

Laws and regulations
Drug offenses are considered very serious in Japan. If you are found to have used, smuggled, attempted to sell, or had illegal drugs (including marijuana) in your possession, you could risk deportation, or detention, trial and imprisonment. Jaywalking (almost never practiced by Japanese) and dropping litter are both offenses that will earn police reprimands. Smoking is not permitted inside subway and commuter trains, in elevators or in most stores or theaters. Hitchhiking is illegal.

Tipping
This is not required or expected anywhere in Japan. A 10 percent government tax is levied on bills of more than ¥2,500 per person at hotels and restaurants. Hotels, *ryokan* and first-rate restaurants also charge a 10-15 percent service charge. Clubs may add a "table" or "music" charge to the bill, so inquire before entering.

Disabled travelers
Many rest rooms provide special facilities for the disabled, and hotels can often provide specially converted rooms. Tokyo streets have raised, yellow plastic markers embedded in the sidewalk at crossing points to assist the blind; JR stations have the same markers a small distance from platform edges and before stairs. Generally, however, train stations are almost impossible to negotiate without help.

Conversion tables

Length

cm	0				5				10				15				20				25				30
in	0	1	2	3	4	5	6	7	8	9	10	11	12

meters	0	0.5	1	1.5	2
ft/yd	0	1ft	2ft	3ft(1yd)	2yd

Weight

grams	0	100	200 (¼kg)	300	400	500 (½kg)	600	700 (¾kg)	800	900	1,000 (1kg)
ounces	0	4 (¼lb)	8 (½lb)	12 (¾lb)	16 (1lb)	20	24 (1½lb)	28	32 (2lb)		

Fluid measures

liters	0	1	2	3	4	5	liters	0	5	10	20	30
imp.pints	0	1	2	3	4	5	6	7	8	imp. gallons	0 1 2 3 4 5 6	
US pints	0 1 2 3 4 5 6 7 8									US gallons	0 1 2 3 4 5 6 7	

Newspapers and local publications

Japan has four daily English-language newspapers, on sale in hotels or at major railroad stations: three are English editions of vernacular newspapers (the *Asahi*, *Yomiuri*, and *Mainichi*); the fourth is the independent *Japan Times*. The monthly English-language *Tokyo Journal* gives comprehensive reviews and listings of plays, films, exhibitions, concerts, *kabuki*, ballets, festivals, restaurants, discos, nightspots and a host of other services.

Useful addresses

Tourist information

American Express Travel Service Shuwa Kamiyacho Building, 4-3-13, Toranomon, Minato-ku ☎459-6155 is a valuable source of information for any traveler in need of help, advice or emergency services.
Japan National Tourist Organization, Tourist Information Center Kotani Building, 1-6-6, Yurakucho, Chiyoda-ku ☎502-1461 (open 9am-5pm). Toll-free outside Tokyo ☎106 and tell operator, "Collect Call, TIC please."
New Tokyo International Airport Office (Narita) ☎(0476) 32-8711.
Tourist Information Service 24hr recorded message ☎503-2911 (English), 503-2926 (French).
Japan Guide Association Shin Kokusai Building, 3-4-1, Marunouchi, Chiyoda-ku ☎213-2706 (volunteer guides).

Main post offices

Tokyo Central Post Office 2-7-2, Marunouchi, Chiyoda-ku (next to s exit of Tokyo Station)
Tokyo International Post Office 2-3-3, Otemachi, Chiyoda-ku

Embassies and consulates

Australia 2-1-14, Mita, Minato-ku ☎453-0251
Austria 1-1-20, Moto Azabu, Minato-ku ☎451-8281
Belgium 5-4, Nibancho, Chiyoda-ku ☎262-0191
Canada 7-3-38, Akasaka, Minato-ku ☎408-2101
Denmark 29-6, Sarugaku-cho, Shibuya-ku ☎496-3001
Finland 3-5-39, Minami Azabu, Minato-ku ☎442-2231
France 4-11-44, Minami Azabu, Minato-ku ☎473-0171
Germany (West) 4-5-10, Minami Azabu, Minato-ku ☎473-0151
Greece 3-16-30, Minami Azabu, Minato-ku ☎403-0871
Ireland No.25 Kowa Building, 8-7, Sanbancho, Chiyoda-ku ☎263-0695
Italy 2-5-4, Mita, Minato-ku ☎453-5291
Netherlands 3-6-3, Shibakoen, Minato-ku ☎431-5126
New Zealand 20-40, Kamiyana-cho, Shibuya-ku ☎467-2271
Norway 5-12-2, Minami Azabu, Minato-ku ☎440-2611
Singapore 5-12-3, Roppongi, Minato-ku ☎586-9111
South Africa Zenkyoren Building, 2-7-9, Hirakawacho, Chiyoda-ku ☎265-3366 (consulate)
Spain 1-3-29, Roppongi, Minato-ku ☎583-8531
Sweden 1-10-3, Roppongi, Minato-ku ☎582-6981
Switzerland 5-9-12, Minami Azabu, Minato-ku ☎473-0121
United Kingdom Kinokuniya Building, 1-10-15, Kojimachi, Chiyoda-ku ☎265-4001
USA 1-10-5, Akasaka, Minato-ku ☎583-7141

Tour operators

Fujita Travel 6-2-10, Ginza, Chuo-ku ☎573-1417

Basic information

Hato Bus Travel   1-18-15, Shimbashi, Minato-ku ☎595-2811
Japan Gray Line   3-3-3, Nishi-Shimbashi, Minato-ku ☎433-5745/ 436-6881
Japan Travel Bureau   Nittetsu Nihonbashi Building, 1-13-1, Nihonbashi, Chuo-ku ☎276-7811 (Foreign Tourist Dept.)
Toppan Travel   Toppan Yaesu Building, 2-7-2, Yaesu, Chuo-ku ☎276-8111

Major places of worship
The following places of worship hold services in English:
Anglican-Episcopal   St Alban's, 3-6-25, Shibakoen, Minato-ku ☎431-8534
Baptist   Tokyo Baptist Church, 9-2, Hachiyama-cho, Shibuya-ku ☎461-8425
Catholic   St Ignatius, 6-5, Kojimachi, Chiyoda-ku ☎263-4584
Jewish   Jewish Community of Japan, 3-8-8, Hiro, Shibuya-ku ☎400-2559
Lutheran   St Paul International Lutheran Church, 1-2-32, Fujimi, Chiyoda-ku ☎261-3740

Customs and etiquette

Although outwardly Tokyo appears very Western, its internal dynamics are similar to the rest of Japanese society — in other words completely different from the West. *Gaijin* (foreign visitors) are not expected to understand the complexities of Japanese social exchange and are usually excused *faux pas*, but a basic knowledge or interest in Japanese mores and values may incur admiration and will certainly help break the ice and smooth relations.

Status and position are crucial in Japan and are intrinsic to the Japanese language with its polite forms of address: for example, different verbs are used to address strangers, customers or one's superiors. *Meishi* cards, which are *de rigueur* in business, swiftly became popular in Japan not just as useful *aide-mémoires* but to establish the relative status and positions of the different parties being introduced. The depth of one's bow, on meeting and departing, is an indication of the degree of respect to the other party (*meishi* should be proffered with a slight bow of the head).

A basic social value is *wa* (harmony), to be achieved, or its appearance at least preserved, at all times inside organizations and even between friends. In business and politics *wa* can mean endless meetings and discussions until a consensus of opinion emerges on a decision or policy. Socially, *wa* does not imply that all Japanese have the same opinions or beliefs, merely that overt, public displays of conflict are to be avoided at all costs and are regarded as deeply embarrassing.

Another related social trait is the division between *tatemae*, or surface talk, and *honne*, or inner truth (the cause of occasional outbursts by foreigners that Japanese are "two-faced"). Concerned about concealing embarrassing taboos or true feelings that if openly expressed would hurt others or damage one's standing, Japanese are far less likely to express such "truths" than foreigners, especially during a brief acquaintance. Associated with this is a preference for comfortable small talk, evidenced even on some news broadcasts, which begin with a discussion of the weather or seasonal changes.

Modern Japanese are liable to dismiss these traditional concepts as feudalistic, but the concepts of *on* (indebtedness), *giri* (social obligation) and *ninjo* (natural or personal inclination) are still very much evident. The debt of *on*, which demands repayment, might be something as universal as nurturing and care by one's parents, or a simple favor repaid with a present (which then may create another *on* requiring a present in return to the donor, starting an endless cycle of gift-giving). The sometimes intense conflict between *giri* and *ninjo* — the ethical codes of society versus one's own feelings or desires — is a recurrent theme of Japanese literature and films. In such cases, when suppression neither of *giri* nor *ninjo* is possible, Japanese may resort to suicide.

To Western eyes, Japanese children seem spoiled by lack of discipline and overindulgence by their parents. Such emotional dependence, or *amae*, during childhood is probably the biggest psychological reason why Japanese adults are less individualistic and more respectful of authority than Westerners, who established their self-identity through adolescent rebellion. An adult Japanese is prone to make a decision based on anticipation of others' feelings, rather than on abstract principle.

Alcohol has an especially important "lubricant" role in Japanese society. Foreigners are often shocked to see respectably dressed middle-aged Japanese businessmen reeling out of bars or collapsing in trains after drinking too much. Drinking serves not just as a necessary escape valve for social pressures, but as an emotional cement, an expression of solidarity. The sharing of drink — even beer — is ritualized, each person taking turns pouring drink for others, using both hands to hold the bottle.

Japanese society is undeniably sexist. Japanese women are discriminated against in employment, and for most the major goal still remains a "good marriage." Nowadays, however, *o-miai*, or traditionally arranged matches are less common. But the image of feminine submissiveness that Japanese women feign in public is countered by their strong control of the household.

Visitors may be shocked by the amount of pornography in Japan (although, paradoxically, illustration of pubic hair is censored). But it should be remembered that in Japan sex has never had the same moral and religious prohibitions as in the West.

Shibui

The adjective *shibui* (in noun form *shibumi*), denotes a subtle, unobtrusive and deeply moving beauty cherished by Japanese connoisseurs since the Muromachi period. Literally *shibui* means astringent, like the acid taste of an unripe persimmon, and opposite to *amai* (sweet). Colorful beauty (exemplified by the Yomeimon gate at Nikko) came to be associated with lack of sophistication; the *shibui* virtues of understated beauty and quietly appealing ambience were for those who asserted their refined tastes. Examples of *shibumi* abound in Japanese architecture, interior design, and art. The voice of a singer, or even a baseball player who contributes to the game without any spectacular play, may also be called *shibui* by the Japanese.

Meishi

These are name cards that have become indispensable business tools in Japan. The ideal is to have roman letters printed on one side and Japanese on the other. Some overseas branches of Japan Air Lines provide *meishi* free to travelers on first and executive classes, which can be picked up on arrival in Tokyo (but check with your local branch before departing). Otherwise, several small *meishi* shops in Tokyo offer a same-day service. Inquire at your hotel, or contact the Japan Tourist Organization for further information.

Essential Japanese

The Japanese normally take 6yrs of English in school, yet few would dare to speak even a few words to a foreigner without collapsing in giggles or turning deep crimson. A typical Japanese person may understand some simple English if spoken clearly and slowly, or preferably if it is written down. (A surprising number have mastered the complexities of English grammar and even read the "classics" in the original without being able to speak more than a few words of English.)

The following simple Japanese words and phrases will help.

Basic communication

Yes hai
No ie
Thank you (domo) arigato
Yes please hai onegaishimasu
No thank you kekko deso
I'm sorry gomen-nasai
Excuse me . . . (also used to call waiter) sumimasen . . .
Good morning o-haiyo-gozaimasu
Good afternoon konnichi-wa
Good evening konban-wa
Good night oiya-sumi-nasai
Goodbye sayonara
Excuse me, do you speak English? sumimasen, Eigo hanashimasu-ka?
Yes, just a little hai, sukoshi dake
No, I can't ie, dame desu
What is your name? o-namae wa?
My name is "Smith" watashi wa "Smith" desu
Are you Mr/Ms "Smith?" "Smith" -san desu ka?

Finding your way around

Police box koban
Where is the police box? koban wa doko desu ka?
Straight ahead masugu
Left hidari
Right migi
Map chizu
Airplane hikoki
(Narita) airport (Narita) kuko
Train densha
Bus basu
Car jidosha or kuruma
Taxi takushi
Station eki
JR station JR eki
Subway station chikatetsu eki
Where is the station? eki wa doko desu ka?
Hotel(s) hoteru
Where is the hotel? hoteru wa doko desu ka?
Telephone denwa
Excuse me, is there a telephone? sumimasen, denwa arimasu ka?
Telephone number denwa bango
Bathroom o-tearai

Food and drink

How much is it? ikura desu ka?
It is expensive takai desu
It is cheap yasui desu
Do you like it? suki desu ka?
It tastes good oishi desu
It doesn't taste good oishi-kunai desu
Menu, please menu kudasai
Bill kanjo
Bill, please kanjo onegaishimasu
Do you accept credit cards? credit cardo tsukaimasu ka?
Pub pubu
Coffee shop kissaten
Restaurant restoran
Beer biru
Japanese sake o-sake (or Nihon-shu)
Water mizu
Milk gyu-nyu (or milku)
Coffee kohee
Indian tea kocha
Japanese or Chinese tea ocha
Sugar sato
Sugar, please sato, kudasai

Shopping

Paper kami
Envelope futo
Pencil enpitsu
Department store(s) departo
Camera store kamera ya
Electrical store denki ya
Television terebi
Watch tokei
Cigarettes tabako
Matches matchi
Post office yubin kyoku
Stamp(s) kitte
Postcard ehagaki

Medical

Pharmacy yakkyoko
Medicine kusuri
Doctor isha
Dentist haisha

Emergencies

Please call an ambulance kyukyusha o yonde kudasai
Please call a policeman keikan o yonde kudasai
Fire! kaji desu!

Emergency information

Emergency services
Police ☎110
Ambulance/Fire ☎119
Press red button on telephone, then dial. No money required.
(The call will be answered in Japanese, so either ask for prior
assistance from a Japanese speaker, or see *Essential Japanese*.)

Hospitals with emergency rooms
English is spoken at the following hospitals:
Ginza area: St Luke's International Hospital (Sei Roka Byoin),
10-1, Akashi-cho, Chuo-ku ☎541-5151. *North Tokyo*: Tokyo
Sanitarium Hospital (Tokyo Eisei Byoin), Seventh Day
Adventists, 3-17-3, Amanuma, Suginami-ku ☎392-6151.
Shinjuku area: International Catholic Hospital (Seibo Byoin),
2-5-1, Naka Ochai, Shinjuku-ku ☎951-1111. *Tokyo Tower
Area*: Tokyo Medical and Surgical Clinic, No.32 Mori
Building, 3-4-30, Shibakoen, Minato-ku ☎436-3028.

English-speaking clinics
Hibiya Clinic   ☎502-2681
International Clinic   ☎582-2646
Ishikawa Clinic   ☎401-6340
King's Clinic   ☎400-7917/409-0764

English-speaking pharmacy
American Pharmacy   Hibiya Park Building, 1-8-1,
Yurakucho, Chiyoda-ku ☎271-4034/5 (open 9am-7pm
weekdays, 11am-6pm Sat, closed Sun, hols)

Help line
Tokyo English Life-line   ☎264-4347

Automobile accidents
—Call the police immediately (☎110), preferably with a
   Japanese speaker to assist you.
—If car is rented, call number in rental agreement.
—Do not admit liability or incriminate yourself.
—Ask witnesses to stay and give statements.
—Exchange names, addresses, car details and insurance
   companies with other driver(s).
—Remain to give your statement to the police.

Car breakdowns
Call one of the following from nearest telephone:
—Number indicated in car rental agreement
—Local service station of JAF (see *Getting around by car*)

Lost passport
Report the loss at the nearest *koban* (police box) and contact
the consular section of your embassy, where you will be issued
with emergency travel documents.

Lost travelers cheques
Notify the police immediately, then follow the instructions
provided with your travelers cheques, or contact the issuing
company's nearest office. Contact your embassy or American
Express if you are stranded with no money.

Time chart

1180	The first reference to Edo (the former name for Tokyo), a small coastal village in the province of Musashi.
1457	Dokan Ota, a samurai warrior, built a castle in Edo during the period of the internecine struggle for supremacy among the retainers of the effete, Kyoto-based shogun Yoshimasa Ashikaga (1436-90).
1467-1590	Rivalry between two powerful *daimyo* (feudal barons), Katsumoto Hosokawa and Sozen Yamana, reached the point of open warfare. This signaled the start of the "Age of Civil Wars" (*Sengoku-Jidai*) that was waged throughout Japan for more than a century, as rival military leaders vied for supremacy.
1590-1600	Ieyasu Tokugawa, a *daimyo*, was granted the entire Kanto plain as his fiefdom by warlord Hideyoshi Toyotomi, for help in the campaign to unify Japan and in the victorious siege of the former Kanto chieftain's castle at Odawara. Tokugawa made Edo his headquarters. After Toyotomi's death in 1598, Tokugawa became the most powerful *daimyo* in Japan.
1603	Tokugawa assumed the ancient title of *sei tai shogun* (Emperor's barbarian-subduing generalissimo) and made Edo the capital for the Tokugawa shogunate, which endured for 264yrs.
1614-15	Tokugawa annihilated the Toyotomi clan and their followers, who had made a last stand at Osaka Castle.
1635-1720	Shogun Iemitsu Tokugawa, the grandson of Ieyasu, introduced the *sankin kotai* ("alternate residence") requirement for *daimyo* to spend half their time as semi-hostages of the shogun in Edo, helping to maintain central control over the warrior-landowners. Edo's castle, the largest in the world, was completed. To the w of the castle was the samurai residential district, and to the E a commercial and residential area took root on reclaimed land. Merchants and artisans flocked to Edo, which became the world's largest city with a population of 1.2 million.
1720-1850	After its early dynamism, the shogunate stagnated into a rigid feudal society and economy, cut off from the outside world by continued self-isolation.
1853	US Commodore Matthew Perry's "Black Ships" steamed into Edo Bay and forced the shogunate to "open up," and start trading with the West.
1867	Under mounting pressure from internal forces who wanted to modernize Japan to meet the external threat from the West, the shogunate was finally overthrown. This revolution restored the Emperor to his ancient role as political head of Japan.
1868-69	Edo was renamed Tokyo (Eastern Capital) and replaced Kyoto as the nation's capital and seat of the Emperor. He took residence in the old shogun's palace.
1869-89	Reformers began to dismantle the feudal system and disarm the samurai. Japan's first railroad line was completed, which linked Tokyo with Yokohama. The Emperor "gave" his people a new, semi-democratic constitution with a parliament and cabinet system.

1923	Tokyo was devastated by the Great Kanto Earthquake and subsequent firestorm. Out of the 2.7 million population in Tokyo and Yokohama, 91,995 were killed and 1.98 million lost their homes.
1932	The assassination of Prime Minister Tsuyoshi Inukai in Tokyo, by rightist naval cadets.
1936	Right-wing army elements seized control of central Tokyo. They assassinated a number of prominent government officials, and demanded the Emperor should be restored as absolute ruler. Emperor Hirohito, however, ordered the revolt's suppression.
1941-45	Emperor Hirohito declared war on the USA, Britain and the Netherlands. Much of Tokyo was destroyed by US firebombing. Japan formally surrendered to US General Douglas MacArthur on board the battleship *Missouri* in Tokyo Bay.
1945-52	Tokyo became the US Occupation headquarters for the Supreme Commander for Allied Powers (SCAP), General MacArthur.
1952-60	Tokyo's population increased from 6.3 million to 9.7 million as the economy recovered and large companies moved their headquarters to the capital.
1964	The first Shinkansen ("bullet" train) ran from Tokyo to Osaka. A feverish building program was completed in time for Tokyo's hosting of the Olympic Games. Japan achieved the status of being a "developed nation."
1978	The New Tokyo International Airport was opened at Narita, 66km (41 miles) from Tokyo, despite a 9yr campaign of protests and often violent demonstrations by local farmers and environmentalist students. Tokyo's population reached 11 million.
1979	First Tokyo Summit of leaders of industrialized nations.
1982	The Joetsu and Tohoku Shinkansen lines were opened, connecting Tokyo with the NE and NW of the main Honshu island.
1986	Second Tokyo Summit of leaders of industrialized nations.

Periods in Japanese history

?BC-AD53	Archeological Age (Jomon ?BC-c.200BC, Yayoi c.200BC-c.AD250, Kofun c.250-538)
538-645	Asuka
645-794	Nara
794-1185	Heian
1185-1334	Kamakura (Kamakura shogunate)
1334-1573	Muromachi (Ashigaka shogunate)
1573-1603	Momoyama (but note that historians consider the Momoyama art period to extend to 1615)
1603-1868	Edo (Tokugawa shogunate)
1868-1912	Meiji (reign of Emperor Meiji)
1912-26	Taisho (reign of Emperor Taisho)
1926-	Showa (the current reign of Emperor Hirohito: Emperor Showa is his posthumous title, as with Emperors Meiji and Taisho)

Architecture

Much of Tokyo's traditional architecture has been lost over the years by a succession of disasters, but there are still a few remaining examples, scattered throughout the city.

1603-1868

The city's origins date back to the magnificent Edo Castle, which was initiated by Ieyasu (1543-1616), the first Tokugawa shogun, on the site of largely earthen fortifications erected by the "father of Tokyo," Dokan Ota (1432-86). Built in the style of the great feudal castles of Japan, it was developed in the late 16thC by warlords Nobunaga Oda (1534-82) and Hideyoshi Toyotomi (1537-98). But nothing survives of the main *tenshu* (keep) apart from its foundation, although its moats, ramparts, *yagura* (watchtowers) and *masugata* (gates), which once checked the onrush of enemy forces into Edo Castle, may still be seen in the grounds of what is now the Imperial Palace. A classic, surviving example of *tenshu* architecture is the castle of the White Heron at Himeji, w of Kobe.

Fires, earthquakes, wartime bombings and modern development have eradicated any examples of Edo houses of the warrior class, whether of the *daimyo* (barons) or the lowly *hatamoto* (guardsmen), except for the 1827 Akamon (Red Gate) remnant of the Maeda lords of Kaga's Edo residence (now sw of Tokyo University's main campus). The military aristocrats' passion for gorgeous palaces was not all-consuming. They had an equal passion for exquisite naturalness and simplicity, as can still be seen

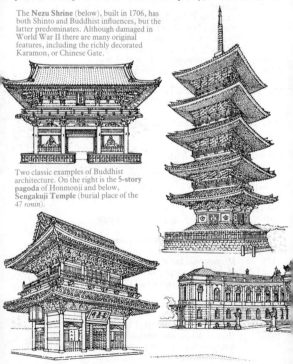

The **Nezu Shrine** (below), built in 1706, has both Shinto and Buddhist influences, but the latter predominates. Although damaged in World War II there are many original features, including the richly decorated Karamon, or Chinese Gate.

Two classic examples of Buddhist architecture. On the right is the **5-story pagoda** of Honmonji and below, **Sengakuji Temple** (burial place of the *47 ronin*).

by the humble but meticulously designed tea-ceremony cottages, in gardens such as Rikugien, Lord Mito's Korakuen, or the shoguns' (later emperors') Hamarikyu.

Temple and shrine architecture

Tokyo is much better provided with temples and shrines from the Edo era. Japanese Buddhist architecture — relatively unadorned, solemn and harmonious — can be seen at its best in the 1605 Sanmon gate of Zojoji Temple in Shiba and the 1681 Gokokuji Temple complex, with its wooden Honden (Main Hall) dominated by a sweeping gabled roof. The *Zeitgeist* that ushered in the Tokugawa shogunate (this period from 1573-1615 was known as Azuchi-Momoyama) was one of grandeur, magnificence and breadth of vision, giving rise to a renaissance in Japanese art.

Architecturally, the Momoyama style was typified by the unbridled use of brightly colored sculpture and ornamental gilt fittings. Edo peace and conservatism moved further into ornamental extravagance with the culmination of the florid, excessive mausolea at Nikko, polychromatically mirrored by the smaller Toshogu Shrine (1651) and in the hipped-gable Karamon, or Chinese-style, mausolea gates of Kan'eiji Temple (the latter two may still be seen at Ueno). The Nezu Shrine, built in 1706, is heavily of Chinese and Buddhist influence (a product of the near fusion of Buddhism and Shintoism at this time) and further illustrates this decadent exuberance. There was nationalist reaction in favor of returning to the native roots of Shintoist architecture, exemplified in the famous shrines of Ise, which found expression

The Russian Orthodox **Nikolai Cathedral** was designed by English architect Josiah Conder in an attempt to bring Western-style architecture to Japan.

The **Akasaka Detached Palace** appears to be a Japanese version of Buckingham Palace or Versailles. The present neo-Baroque building dates from 1909.

in Yoyogi's 1920 Meiji Shrine, with its traditional harmony of simple wooden buildings set in natural surroundings.

1868-1945

The Meiji Restoration of 1868 precipitated the launch of a vigorous import of Western-style architecture as Japan strove desperately to catch up with the imperialist Western powers. The English architect Josiah Conder wielded enormous influence, and surviving buildings of his design include the Russian Orthodox Nikolai Cathedral in Ochanomizu, Mitsui Club in Mita and Iwasaki mansion in Yushima. Derivative classicism, romanticism and eclecticism prevailed among his students. Although Westerners may not find anything outstanding in these buildings, in Japan they were imbued with revolutionary and symbolic importance: Tokuma Katayama's French Baroque Akasaka Detached Palace (1909) and Hyokeikan wing of the Tokyo National Museum (1909), and Kingo Tatsuno's Bank of Japan (1896) and his vaguely French-style Tokyo Station (1914), are examples.

During the militaristic 1930s, Art Deco, reinforced concrete modernism, and the Bauhaus internationalist-style (for example, the 1933 former residence of Prince Asaka with an Art Deco interior, now Tokyo Metropolitan Teien Art Museum), all reached Japan. The 1936 National Diet Building, 1937 Honkan wing of the Tokyo National Museum and 1938 Dai-ichi Life Insurance Building are prime examples of the stern leadenness then in vogue

The **Kabukiza Theater**, a 1950 reconstruction of the 1924 original, has a Momoyama-style facade inspired by 16thC castle architecture.

The 1983 **Tokyo Metropolitan Teien Art Museum** has an outstanding Art Deco interior designed by French architect Henri Rapin.

It took 17yrs to complete construction of the **National Diet Building**, Japan's first permanent parliamentary building. It was finally completed in 1936.

for public building designs. Welcome exceptions to this rule were Shinichiro Okada's 1924 Kabukiza Theater, and his 1934 Corinthian-inspired Meiji Life Insurance Building, a successful blend of concrete and traditional Japanese architecture.

1945 to the present day

Most of Tokyo's corporate architecture is remarkable only for its indifference; it is as if some of the world's largest companies preferred to conceal their prosperity behind an anonymous facade. In opposition to this trend, Togo Murano's polished granite Industrial Bank of Japan (1974) stands out, and Kisho Kurokawa's 1984 Wacoal Kojimachi Building at least demands attention.

Stark utilitarianism, or dilettantist fancy masquerading as Post Modernism, are now regrettably the norm. However, Japan has one architect of truly international stature and originality: Kenzo Tange. The daringly curved roofline of tensile steel that hangs between concrete masts of his National Indoor Stadium in Yoyogi (part of the complex built for the 1964 Tokyo Olympics) combines both the graceful curve of the traditional Japanese temple roof with the boldness of new technology. His 40-story half-mirrored Akasaka Prince hotel, built in 1983, boldly restates in glass and aluminum the beauty of a Japanese folding screen. Tange's newest and most ambitious project, the 48-story Tokyo Metropolitan City Hall, is due for completion in 1991. Situated in the Shinjuku area, it will combine twin Gothic-style towers of granite and glass with latticed windows, as seen in traditional Japanese homes.

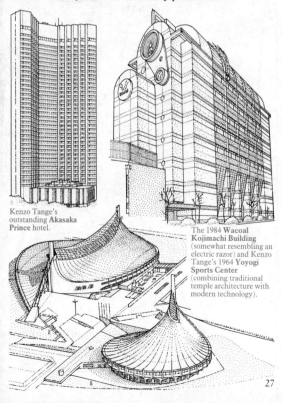

Kenzo Tange's outstanding **Akasaka Prince** hotel.

The 1984 **Wacoal Kojimachi Building** (somewhat resembling an electric razor) and Kenzo Tange's 1964 **Yoyogi Sports Center** (combining traditional temple architecture with modern technology).

27

Orientation map

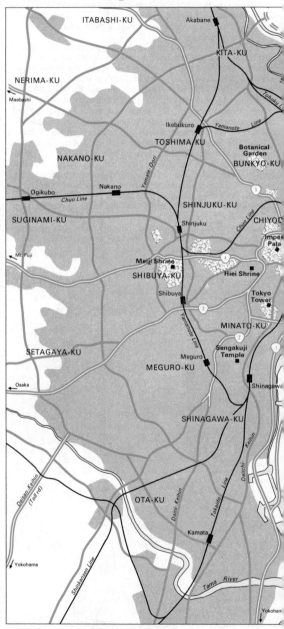

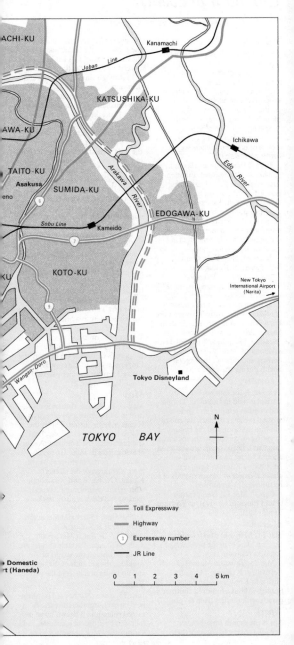

ACHI-KU

Kanamachi

Joban Line

KATSUSHIKA-KU

AWA-KU

Ichikawa

TAITO-KU

Asakusa

eno

⑥

SUMIDA-KU

Arakawa River

Edo River

EDOGAWA-KU

Sobu Line

Kameido

⑦

KU

KOTO-KU

New Tokyo
International Airport
(Narita) →

③

Wangan-Doro

Tokyo Disneyland

N

TOKYO   BAY

═══ Toll Expressway

━━━ Highway

③ Expressway number

━━━ JR Line

Domestic
rt (Haneda)

0   1   2   3   4   5 km

Calendar of events

See also *Public holidays* in *Basic information.*

January

Jan 1, *Ganjitsu* — New Year's Day (see Dec 31).

Jan 2, a ceremony called *ippan sanga* takes place in the grounds of the Imperial Palace. Although the grounds are normally closed, the public is allowed to enter through the main Nijubashi Gate, where the Emperor waves from behind bulletproof glass to the crowds of well-wishers. (For details see *Imperial Palace.*)

Jan 6, *Dezomeshiki* at Harumi Pier (*Chuo dori, 10am-noon*). Firemen dressed in Edo period costumes perform acrobatics on bamboo ladders. An unusual example of shogunal public relations: it was originally designed to impress the populace of fire-plagued Edo with the agility of their firefighters in confronting danger.

Jan 6-20, New Year's sumo tournament at Kokugikan.

Jan 8, *Dondo-yaki* festival at Torigoe Shrine (*Kuramaebashi avenue, Taito-ku, noon-3pm*). New Year decorations of pine and straw are taken to the Torigoe Shrine to be burned in a giant bonfire. Children beat the ground with bamboo stakes shouting, "Dondoya." Pounded rice cakes called *o-mochi* are cooked in the embers and eaten to bring good health during the year.

February

Feb 3 or 4, the famous *Setsubun* festival is held in Gokokuji Temple and in other temples and shrines around the city, to mark the end of the winter season and the beginning of spring (according to the old lunar calendar). Dried beans are scattered about to drive away the "evil spirits." At Asakusa Kannon Temple a classical dance of the seven gods of fortune is also performed.

Feb 15-Mar 15, *Ume Matsuri* (Plum Blossom Festival) at Yushima Tenjin Shrine.

March

Mar 18, *Kinryu no Mai* (Golden Dragon Dance) in the precincts of Asakusa Kannon Temple.

Mar 25, *Taimatsu Matsuri* (Torch Festival) at Kameido Tenmangu Shrine in Koto-ku, near Kameido JR Station. About a hundred children parade with torches from 6-7pm.

April

Apr is the month for *o-hanami* (viewing cherry blossoms); their

evanescent beauty symbolizes, for the Japanese, the impermanence of the material world. What better way to celebrate such fleeting splendor than through singing, dancing and drinking? "Cherry blossom parties," have long been the excuse for bacchanalian revelry under the trees. Ueno Park, the most popular spot, is the best place to see ordinarily straitlaced company employees (called *salariman*) getting involved in the uninhibited atmosphere: it could be called the "*salariman's* Woodstock." The shrine compound at Yasukuni offers a less distracting view of the cherry blossoms. There is also a magnificent display at Shinjuku Gyoen, where the prime minister has his own "cherry blossom viewing party" for invited guests.

Apr 8, *Hana-Matsuri* (Buddha's birthday festival) at Gokokuji Temple, which has become famous for this festival.

Apr 17, *Ueno Toshogu Taisai* at the Toshogu Shrine in Ueno Park, where traditional music, dance and ceremonies are performed in honor of the first Tokugawa shogun Ieyasu, enshrined there as a Shinto deity.

Apr 21-23, spring festival at Yasukuni Shrine.

Apr 29, *Tenno Tanjobi*, the Emperor's birthday. On this day the Emperor waves to the crowds allowed inside the inner palace grounds (as on Jan 2).

May

May 12-15, *Kanda Matsuri* festival, held in odd-numbered years, starts at Kanda Myojin Shrine. This is the Tokyo festival *par excellence*, held to commemorate the Tokugawa victory at Sekigahara in 1600. Up to 250 *o-mikoshi* (portable shrines) weave their way through the streets of Kanda, Otemachi and Nihonbashi, with geishas performing classical dances, and there is also a *shishimai* lion dance.

Mid-May, 15-day summer sumo tournament at Kokugikan.

May 17-18, *Sanja Matsuri* at Asakusa Shrine. Portable shrines are paraded through the streets of Asakusa, the grounds of the temple, and up to the precincts of the shrine.

June

June 15, *Sanno Matsuri* of Hie Shrine held on even-numbered years. A sacred palanquin is drawn by an ox, followed by scores of *o-mikoshi*, and shrine officials on horseback. The procession winds its way through the streets of Ginza and Kyobashi and through the Imperial Palace gates.

Second Sun in June, festival of Torigoe Shrine. This after-dark (7-9pm) procession includes what must be Tokyo's heaviest *o-mikoshi* portable shrine, its 4 tons borne by 200 chanting celebrants.

July

July 9-10, *Hozuki-Ichi* (Ground Cherry Fair) at Asakusa Kannon Temple.

July 13-16, *obon* takes place at Tokyo's ancestral homes. During Buddhist *obon* it is believed departed ancestors revisit their homes, and families return to welcome back the ancestral spirits. In Tokyo *obon* is held one month earlier than in the rest of Japan.

July 13-16, *Mitama* (Spirit of the Dead) festival at Yasukuni Shrine. During memorial rites for the war dead (who have been enshrined as deities), demonstrations are given of ancient Imperial Court music, dances and martial arts.

End July, *Edo no hana* (Flowers of Edo). Grand evening fireworks display on the Sumida River at Asakusa. Revival of 17thC ceremony to "open the river" by purging it of the evil spirits of cholera. *Edo no hana* is wordplay on the greatest scourge of Edo, which were its constant fires. Enormous crowds gather on two nearby bridges.

August

Aug 13-16, *obon* for all areas other than Tokyo. Tokyoites traveling for this occasion to and from their family homes frequently cause jams on the expressways, railroads, and at Haneda domestic airport. The end of *obon* is also the time for many local shrine festivals throughout Tokyo.

September

Sept 12-13, annual festival of Nogi Shrine. This shrine is dedicated to General Maresuke Nogi, who in 1905 captured Port Arthur from Tsarist Russia, after the loss of 60,000 of his own troops. In 1912 he fulfilled a ritual suicide pact with his wife.

Mid-Sept, 15-day autumn sumo tournament at Kokugikan.

Sept 21, *Nezugongen Matsuri*. On even-numbered years a portable shrine is carried around the neighborhood of Nezu Shrine and Shinto music and dance are performed.

Sept 25, *Ningyo-Kuyo*. On this day childless couples offer dolls to the Kannon goddess of mercy and pray for fertility, and at Kan'eiji

Kiyomizudo in Ueno Park (*between 2-3.30pm*) a mountain of dolls accumulated during the year are burned to the chanting of sutras.

October

Oct 1-20, Tokyo Festival. Includes "Miss Tokyo" contest, a parade of flower-decked floats, lantern procession and exhibitions.

Oct 12, *Oeshiki* festival at Ikegami Homonji Temple (*1-1-1, Ikegami, Ota-ku*). Colorful nighttime lantern procession toward the temple to commemorate the death in 1282 of the Buddhist priest Nichiren.

Mid- to end-Oct, *O-hanami kiku*. Throughout Tokyo there is viewing of chrysanthemums, many trained into doll-like shapes. The best shows can be seen at Yasukuni Shrine, Asakusa Kannon Temple, Hibiya Park, Korakuen and Meiji Shrine.

Oct 17-19, autumn festival of Yasukuni Shrine.

November

Nov 1-5, annual festival of Meiji Shrine. Demonstration of ancient martial arts.

Nov 15, *Shichigosan* (literally, "Seven-Five-Three"). Girls aged seven, boys aged five and boys and girls aged three are taken by their parents to Shinto shrines. Here, the parents give thanks for the safety of their growing children and to invoke future blessings. The festival dates from the old custom of putting up the hair of a girl at 3yrs old, giving a *hakama* (pleated skirt) to 5yr-old boys, and an *obi* (sash) to be worn by a girl from 7yrs onward. The Meiji, Hie and Kanda shrines are popular for this ceremony.

December

Dec 14, *Gishi-sai* festival at Sengakuji Temple, celebrating the loyalty of Lord Asano's vassals.

Dec 17-18, *Toshi-no-ichi* (Year-end Market) at Asakusa Kannon Temple.

Dec 29-30, Toshi-no-ichi of Torigoe Shrine.

Dec 31-Jan 1, *Joya no Kane* and *Ganjitsu* (New Year's Eve and New Year's Day). Japanese visit shrines and temples to pray for health, happiness and prosperity in the New Year. At midnight, Buddhist temple bells throughout Japan start tolling 108 times to clear away the 108 evil human passions (the public can strike the bell at Zojoji and Kan'eiji temples). Meiji Shrine draws crowds, who line up for hours to throw money into a huge collection box and buy *hamaya* (good-luck arrows). Tokyo trains run throughout the night on Dec 31.

When to go

Tokyo and the rest of Japan should be avoided at all costs during the extended New Year's festival. Although the eerie sensation of a ghost town is most acute during the official Jan 1-3 New Year's holiday, many businesses, stores and restaurants are closed for extended periods. Museums, landmarks, and even public parks are closed for a minimum of three days. Apart from hotels and the occasional store and coffee shop, only shrines and temples remain open, to receive worshipers. As a rule of thumb, Tokyo suffers its worst dearth of amusement and distraction from Dec 29-Jan 7 (disconcertingly, however, Dec 25 and 26 are considered normal working days).

Another black spot for visitors is the period from Apr 29-May 5. Japanese call this "Golden Week" because it has three national holidays (the Emperor's Birthday on Apr 29, Constitution Memorial Day on May 3 and Children's Day on May 5) and many businesses give employees a week's leave. Unlike New Year, services are relatively unaffected during "Golden Week," but hotels, trains and airlines are often solidly booked.

Tokyo has mild winters, and heavy snowfalls are rare. Air conditioning has now made Tokyo summers less a test of endurance than in the past, but although less oppressive than tropical climes such as Hong Kong, the heat and humidity from June-Sept still drive swarms of Tokyoites to swimming pools and beach resorts. The cooler, drier air of mountain resorts in Hakone, Nikko, Fuji's Five Lakes or Karuizawa offer especially welcome relief at this time.

Spring and autumn are the best periods in Tokyo. April is the month for cherry trees and *o-hanami* (cherry blossom viewing) parties are held; in autumn the climate is most temperate and invigorating, and Nikko's beauty excels itself in the changing hues of maple trees.

Tokyo's main *kabuki* theater, the *Kabukiza* in *Ginza*, has performances every month except in July and Aug. The main sumo tournaments at the Kokugikan are held in Jan, May and Sept. Tokyo shops and department stores have frequent "sales," especially after the New Year and at the end-of-season, but they never indulge in across-the-board price cutting as in the West.

Where to go

Tokyo is divided into 23 wards called *ku*, some so obscure as to be only vaguely guessed at by longtime residents near the center. In the three most central wards of Chiyoda, Chuo and Minato, their daytime population is six times greater than at night (this is known as the "doughnut phenomenon," as the people flocking out into the suburbs leave the center empty — like a doughnut ring).

Although the spiritual and geographical center of Tokyo is undoubtedly the *Imperial Palace* in Chiyoda-ku, the metropolis's many other attractions are sprinkled about with disarming irregularity. The JR Yamanote loop line serves as a useful sightseeing boundary — areas s of Shinagawa and w of Shibuya and *Shinjuku*, the last areas to be settled, are virtually barren of interest; yet in areas to the N and E, bold forays beyond the green circle are called for. Since Tokyo has the world's most efficient network of overhead and underground trains, in a maximum of

½hr you will usually be able to get to any destination within the city.

For general shopping Ginza/Yurakucho, Nihonbashi, Shibuya and Shinjuku offer the widest choice, especially in large department stores. But other areas have now become specialized in certain commodities or entertainments. For young fashion and designer boutiques, Harajuku, Omotesando and *Aoyama* are outstanding; Shinjuku is excellent for discount cameras; and *Akihabara* is renowned as an electronics mecca.

"Traditional" Tokyo lies in the old Shitamachi area to the E and N of the city, in *Asakusa*, Yanaka, Yushima, Nezu and Ningyocho; traces may also be found in the old heartland of Nihonbashi. The *Roppongi* district is dedicated to nightlife, and *Ueno Park* has probably the world's highest concentration of art galleries and museums.

Area planners

Central Tokyo

Imperial Palace (Map 9G9). This is the seat of the Emperor as well as being the spiritual and geographic focus, not only of Tokyo, but all Japan. Its first occupant was a provincial warrior in the 15thC. Later it became the castle of the Tokugawa shoguns, who ruled Japan until overthrown by imperial forces in 1867. Regular public access is only permitted to the shogun's old fortress in what is now the East Garden. The former N enclosure of the Palace (Kitanomaru) is now a park housing galleries, museums and the Budokan Hall. Most of the perimeter of the shogun's castle used to be lined with residences of *daimyo* nobility, but, swept aside by the Imperial Restoration, they have been supplanted by government and public buildings, hotels and office buildings.

Kasumigaseki and Nagatacho *(Maps 8H8 & 9H9).* This is the government district of Tokyo bordering the s perimeter of the Palace; Nagatacho is synonymous with the National Diet (Parliament) Building and offices of members of political parties; and Kasumigaseki is almost exclusively composed of government ministries.

Hibiya and Yurakucho *(Map 9H9).* Centuries ago Hibiya was an inlet of the sea where fishermen cast their nets. The land bordering the well-loved but slightly scruffy Hibiya Park is now phenomenally expensive, housing the Imperial hotel complex (see *Hotels*) and smart new office buildings. Yurakucho means "Quarter Where Pleasure Can Be Had," though with the demolition of the Nichigeki striptease theater, to make way for the massive Hankyu-Seibu department store's Mullion Building complex, its tenuous links with the past are fast being erased. (Some hardy survivors are the intimate *yakitori* stands (see *Restaurants*) still snuggled under the railroad bridges.)

Ginza and Shimbashi *(Maps 5J9 & 9I10).* Adjoining the E side of Yurakucho, Ginza had been suffering from a decline, due to the exit of its young admirers to more currently fashionable areas such as Harajuku and Shibuya. However, the new additions of the Seibu-Hankyu and French Printemps department stores in Yurakucho's Mullion Building seem to have reversed the exodus, and at peak times the streets are almost unnavigable for pedestrians (although thankfully on weekends cars are banned on the main shopping street). To the s, Ginza merges into Shimbashi, which blossomed with the arrival of the first train service in 1872. Many small businesses have their offices here, and the atmosphere is more Japanese than in Ginza, which had always been in the vanguard for absorbing Western culture. Geisha may still be seen at night in Shimbashi back streets bidding farewell to their suddenly impoverished customers.

Marunouchi and Otemachi (*Map 9G9*). This is the corporate and financial nexus of Japan, although the architectural standard of the formally laid out streets hardly does justice to the area's sterling services to capitalism.

Roppongi (*Map 4J7*). The center of Tokyo's nightlife, Roppongi caters to a wide range of tastes not satisfied by the more sophisticated scene in Ginza and Akasaka, or the less expensive haunts of Shinjuku and Shibuya. It boasts the Roppongi Square Building, which possibly holds the world record for the highest number of discotheques under one roof. Since its postwar rise Roppongi has always been the most international part of Tokyo, where one is most likely to encounter other *gaijin*, or foreigners. The steady rise in property prices and growing eclecticism of tastes has meant this "neon dazzle" has now spread out in all directions from the central Roppongi Crossing.

Shibuya and Harajuku (*Map 2*). Two private railroad lines bring in hordes of visitors from the densely populated dormitory suburbs of w Tokyo, but infrastructure alone does not account for its startling success. The character of Shibuya is a cross between Shinjuku's wildness, Harajuku's youth and Aoyama's trend-setting sophistication. Department stores on Koen-dori are smart and highly fashionable, yet its maze of record stores, bars, discos, cheap restaurants and "love hotels" still successfully cater to those on a low budget, especially students. Harajuku, the next stop N on the Yamanote line, is an area of contrasts. It clashingly embraces both the timeless beauty and anodyne dignity of the *Meiji Shrine* (w of the station), the carefully choreographed rebellion of the Sun afternoon dancers called the Bamboo Shoot Tribe and the crazed consumerism of pampered teenagers.

Omotesando, *Aoyama* and *Akasaka* (*Maps 7I5 & 8I7*). An invisible barrier separates the youngsters of Harajuku from the elegant sophistication that increases by the meter as you proceed up Omotesando-dori. By the time you arrive at the intersection at the top you will be in Aoyama, the most chic and well-dressed district in Tokyo, possibly due to the large number of designer boutiques in the neighborhood. Aoyama also has enough tasteful meeting places to make any young deb feel homesick. However, neighboring Akasaka is less stilted and self-conscious and more casual and vivacious in its elegance, partly due to its large daytime office population and the presence of a number of huge hotels nearby.

West Tokyo

Shinjuku (*Map 6*). Located two stops N of Harajuku on the JR Yamanote line, Shinjuku's reputation as part of the wild frontier harks back to its days as a new "post town" on the westbound highway, when in 1718 it was closed down due to rowdiness. Shinjuku's raucousness nowadays is confined to its entertainment/ sex district in Kabukicho; otherwise it is fast outgrowing its origins. Its railroad station is the most chaotically busy in the world (and the most difficult for foreigners to get around), and many chic boutiques have recently sprung up beside its huge department stores. Nishi, or West, Shinjuku, on the other side of the railroad tracks, is known as "Skyscraper City." Hitherto shunned for its characterless artificiality, w Shinjuku's star is now rapidly rising, thanks to the building there of Kenzo Tange's new City Hall.

East Tokyo

Nihonbashi and Ningyocho (*Map 10-11G11-12*). This was the center of business for merchant-townsmen in Edo (as Tokyo was known before the shoguns' fall in 1867), and Nihonbashi Bridge was the point from which all distances in Japan were measured. In a business sense, Nihonbashi remains the wholesale capital of Tokyo, and nowadays the imposing Mitsukoshi department store stands next to Mitsui Bank, the birthplace of today's huge Mitsui conglomerate. This is also where Will Adams, the man on whom the hero of the novel *Shogun* is based, had his house. Neighboring Ningyocho has escaped Nihonbashi's level of development, and still preserves many of the crafts and flavors of the old Shitamachi.

South Tokyo

Shinagawa, Takanawa, Meguro and Shiba (*Maps 2 & 3* and *4 & 5*). The importance of Shinagawa as the most significant "post town" on the old Tokaido (East Sea Rd.) has carried over to the present day with its role as hub of the JR railroad network. Apart from some fine hotels and a modern art gallery, its main appeal to tourists lies a little farther N, in Takanawa's *Sengakuji Temple*, inextricably linked with the saga of the 47 *ronin* buried there. Slightly to the w lies the unspoiled wilderness of the *Nature Study Garden* and the beautiful grounds of the *Tokyo Metropolitan Teien Art Museum*. Shiba, N of Takanawa, is noteworthy as the site of the *Zojoji Temple*; its imposing Sanmon gate is still extant.

North Tokyo

Ueno (*Map 15D11*). Ueno has two contrasting roles, as gateway for rural laborers from N Japan to the shangri-la prosperity of the metropolis, and as guardian of the nation's academic culture. Down-and-outs mingle with courting couples and art historians in *Ueno Park*, where most of the nation's major museums and art galleries are crammed. The park also has its prized giant pandas in the zoo, a boating lake, a temple and a pagoda, as well as a memorial to the historic battle that took place here in 1867 between forces loyal to the shogun and those of the emperor. For lovers of painting and architecture, the *Yokoyama Taikan Memorial Hall* is also worth a detour.

Asakusa (*Map 16C13*). Largely bypassed by the relentless postwar prosperity of other parts of Tokyo, Asakusa is now benefitting from a renaissance of interest in the culture and traditions of Edo, which it has carefully nurtured and preserved. During holidays and festivals huge crowds throng the approaches to its famous *Asakusa Kannon Temple*, but as ever, people tend to be more interested in its many tantalizing secular attractions.

Yanaka, Sendagi, Nezu and Yushima (*Map 15*). Large parts of the old temple town of Yanaka have escaped the bulldozer, and only now with the onset of "gentrification" are Tokyoites rediscovering the charms that made this a favorite haunt of artists, writers and academics earlier in the century. Among its many places of interest, the *Asakura Choso Museum* is outstanding. Neighboring Sendagi is similarly rich in temples and crafts shops; Nezu is noteworthy for its gorgeous *Nezu Shrine*; and farther s, Yushima is renowned for its *Yushima Tenjin Shrine* dedicated to the God of Learning.

35

Walks in Tokyo

Tokyo is truly a city of contrasts, and its character can best be appreciated by a stroll through some of its most individual and fascinating areas.

Walk 1/Imperial Palace, East Garden and around the Palace Walls

Allow half a day. Maps 8 & 9. JR: Tokyo; subway: Otemachi.

In the heart of Tokyo is a sight at once more noble and inspiring, solemn and impenetrable, than any you would find in a more grandiose capital. Rueful developers, gazing at the verdant lung of the Imperial Palace girded by its massive walls and deep moats in the center of the land-famished city, are wont to call it "the world's most valuable real estate." Despite its importance as Tokyo's birthplace (see *Introduction*), the main reason that these historic fortifications have been maintained is the sanctity of their current occupant: the Emperor. For the past 120yrs the Imperial Palace has been the geographical focus of Japan's spiritual energy, emanating from the world's longest reigning monarchy, a quasi-divine symbol of the unified Japanese state.

Permission to visit restricted areas of the palace is difficult to obtain. However, on two days of the year, well-wishers are allowed through the Nijubashi Gate, to the front of the **Sei Den** (State Hall), which is the main structure of the new palace: at the New Year ceremony called *ippan sanga* (*Jan 2 9.30am-3pm*), when the Imperial Family appears on the balcony, and on the Emperor's birthday (*Apr 29 8.30-11am*), when the Emperor waves to crowds from the Sei Den veranda. (See also *Calendar of events* in *Planning*.) Details are usually announced in newspapers nearer the time of these events.

Although wide tracts have been donated to the public (for example, **Kitanomaru Park**), the only part of the palace proper that is open on a regular basis is the **East Garden** (⊡ *open 9am-4pm (last entry 3pm); closed Mon, Fri (except hols), Dec 25-Jan 3 and on special state occasions*). In the historic and geographical sense this is where Tokyo began, and is, therefore, the logical starting point for an introduction to the city. Otemachi and Tokyo stations are both convenient points to start the tour.

Enter through **Otemon**, or Ote Gate, formerly the main entrance to the shogun's castle. Otemon (like the Hirakawa, Sakurada and Kikyo gates of the palace) is a surviving *masugata* (measuring vessel) double-doored gate. A small front portal (Koraimon, or Korean gate) opens into a narrow, walled courtyard, where invaders could only enter with a small number of troops to attack the much larger and well-fortified main gate (destroyed in the 1945 air raids, but rebuilt in 1967 according to the original plan). Thus locked in, the invaders could be fired on from the surrounding walls. Of special interest, in the Otemon courtyard, is an original roof tile depicting the mythical dolphin that was supposed to ward off fires.

After entering through the gate, collect a plastic admission token from the guard, which you must return on leaving, at any of three public gates. Walk up the drive, past police, hospital and administrative buildings, and a "rest house" on the right that sells soft drinks, maps and souvenirs. At the top are two sturdy walls that once supported the Ote Gejo (Dismount Gate) and its keep, where most of the *daimyo* alighted from their litters and left their attendants. The gate and its keep have gone, but two guardhouses remain. On the right-hand side is **Doshin-bansho** guardhouse built soon after 1863, and on the left is the long **Hyakunin-bansho** (Hundred-Men guardhouse) where four platoons, each with 100 men drawn from the four blood houses of the Tokugawa, would stand guard in rotation.

Turn right into the spacious **Ni-no-Maru garden**, which was originally laid out in 1630 by Enshu Kobori (an accomplished landscape gardener, tea-master, soldier and politician) on the shogun's orders. The public opening of the entire East Garden did not take place until 1968, by which time the garden had been completely changed. The **Ni-no-Maru**, or Second Fortress, used to be the shoguns' retirement residence after they handed power over to their successors. In the far E corner of the Ni-no-Maru stands a Japanese-style ornamental garden with pond, stone lantern, waterfall and bridge. On its far side is the **Suwa tea-ceremony house**, dating back to the early 19thC, which used to stand in the palace's **Fukiage Garden** (this is also where the Emperor and Empress currently have their residence). In the NW corner of Ni-no-Maru, there are 30 different kinds of tree each donated by one of Japan's prefectures.

The garden is dominated by giant slabs of volcanic rock that slant upward from the Moat of Swans to the **Hon Maru**, or Main Fortress. They were quarried in the Izu Peninsula, 100km (62 miles) distant, and when transported to Edo each one of the largest rocks needed a boat to itself, with 3,000 such boats being used in all. On arrival they were dragged by ox cart and teams of men to the construction site and heaved into position on primitive sleds. Most of the large rocks were jammed together with small stones in between, but some fitted perfectly together, as one can see standing at the top of the slope (on the right of the wall), leading up to the Hon Maru main citadel. The incline is called Shiomizaka, or Tide-Viewing Slope, because when Ieyasu Tokugawa arrived here in 1590, nearby Hibiya was still an inlet of the sea.

Retrace the path along the Moat of Swans and the Hyakunin-bansho and walk up past the site of the **Ote Naka** (Inner) Gate, and another guardhouse (*o-bansho*). The **Shoinmon** main gate to the shogun's inner citadel once stood where the road twists to the right and opens onto the Hon Maru. Inside the **Hon Maru Rest House**, photographs taken immediately after the fall of the Tokugawa shogunate in 1868 are on display on the walls in front of you, on the right. They show the gate you have just walked through to have been a very imposing structure with two tall guard towers on either side. Recent photographs of the same structures have been placed next to the old ones, and this presents a striking contrast. One photograph shows the overgrown dilapidated state the shogun's castle was in after a series of fires just before he was overthrown, and the other shows the present scene of immaculately tended gardens.

In the S corner, the **Fujimi Tower**, one of three out of 21 original *yagura* left standing, offers a rare reminder of how Hon Maru once appeared. Remodeled in 1659, it was the most important keep in the castle after the 1657 "Long Sleeves Fire" destroyed the main donjon. In the far side of Hon Maru is another survivor, the **Fujimi Tamon Arsenal** (one of two still extant).

It is hard to imagine that these neat lawns were once the site of an elaborate complex of shogunal buildings. In the S, nearest to the Fujimi Tower, stood the halls where affairs of state and audiences with the shogun were conducted, including the O-hiroma, or Grand Hall, where once every 4yrs the head of the Dutch trading mission on Dejima in Nagasaki came to pay obeisance; there are also the halls where *daimyo* would present themselves to the shogun twice every month. The center of today's lawn is where the shogun's own quarters once stood. Situated farthest from Fujimi Tower and nearest to the base of the old main keep were the inner chambers accommodating the shogun's wife and concubines.

The castle donjon, of which only the stone base remains, was rebuilt three times. It was first constructed in 1607 by Shogun Hidetada Tokugawa and rebuilt for the last time in 1640. It was considered a great spectacle, with its five floors, black walls, gold-lacquered roofs, which gleamed in the sun, and gorgeously decorated interiors. For a final brief 17yrs it soared 51m (167ft) over the sapling city, until it too was engulfed by the great conflagration of 1657, which reduced the Hon Maru, Ni-no-Maru and San-no-Maru (Third Fortress) to ashes. Though intended to be rebuilt within 2yrs, it was thought better not to reconstruct such a symbol of military power in time of peace. All that remained was the massive stone foundation, still visible today. However, the view of Kitanomaru Park and the Budokan Hall from this more modest pedestal is still worth the effort of climbing to the top.

Take the path to your right, behind the incongruous and hideous **Toka Music Hall** (built in the shape of the imperial chrysanthemum petal for the current Empress's 60th birthday in 1963), and the **Imperial Music Academy**, where annual performances of ancient *gagaku* court music are held for the Emperor's birthday (*apply in writing to the Imperial Household Agency for an invitation*); on the right-hand side is the grim concrete building housing the imperial archives. Proceed down the slope running w, called Bairin-zaka, or Plum Grove Slope, after the hundreds of plum trees planted here by Dokan Ota in 1478.

Follow the sign to Hirakawamon gate, and return your plastic token. **Hirakawamon** is thought to have been the main gate of San-no-Maru and was also a side exit used by women of the shogun's inner chambers. Before crossing the little wooden bridge, notice the slits where the stone walls join the plaster, which were used for firing arrows and bullets at invaders. There is also a small portal next to the main gate, known as the **Fujomon**, or Unclean Gate, as it was used for the exit of criminals and corpses.

The walk around the walls may, from this point, be broken at any of the following subway stations circling the Palace: Takebashi, Hanzomon, Sakuradamon and Hibiya.

If you wish to continue, walk along by the moat past Takebashi Subway Station passing, on your right, the Tokyo office of the Osaka-based *Mainichi*, Japan's third largest newspaper, and then cross Takebashi (Bamboo Bridge) into Kitanomaru, the north court, or fortress, of the old castle. During the Edo period this part of the castle was occupied by the mansions of Tokugawa relatives and high officials, but after the 1868 revolution it was appropriated for use by the new government. Here in Takebashi the barracks of the old Imperial Guard once stood. Up the hill on your right is the main building of the *National Museum of Modern Art*, and farther up on your left is the third of the entrances to the East Garden: Kita Hanebashi (North Drawbridge). You are now standing immediately behind the site of the Hon Maru keep and Inner Chambers — hence the dramatic depth of the moat and steepness of the walls.

Leave the walls of Hon Maru and turn to the right, past the **Inuimon** (Northwest Gate), the gate most often used by members of the Imperial Family. To the left side is the splendid *Crafts Gallery* (an annex to the National Museum of Modern Art), a listed Meiji-era building that once functioned as the

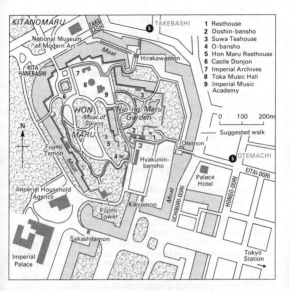

KITANOMARU
TAKEBASHI
National Museum of Modern Art
Moat
Hirakawamon
KITA HANEBASHI
HON MARU
Moat of Swans
Nio-no-Maru Garden
Fujimi Tamon
Hyakunin-bansho
Otemon
Imperial Household Agency
Kikyomon
Fujimi Tower
Palace Hotel
Sakashitamon
Imperial Palace
Tokyo Station
UCHIBORI-DORI
HONGO-DORI
EITAI-DORI
OTEMACHI

1 Resthouse
2 Doshin-bansho
3 Suwa Teahouse
4 O-bansho
5 Hon Maru Resthouse
6 Castle Donjon
7 Imperial Archives
8 Toka Music Hall
9 Imperial Music Academy

0   100   200m

— Suggested walk

Administrative Headquarters of the Imperial Guard.

A stroll around Kitanomaru Park behind the Crafts Gallery can be a welcome respite from Tokyo traffic — the main path through the park passes the **Japan Science Museum** and the **Budokan Hall**, a huge octagonal-shaped indoor arena opened in 1964 to host martial arts tournaments for the Tokyo Olympics, but nowadays more famous as a place for pop concerts and mammoth rallies. At the head of the park is the **Tayasumon** gate, which leads to the outer precincts of the *Yasukuni Shrine*.

Back on the main avenue, cross the overpass in front of the Crafts Gallery and walk along the embankment that traverses Chidorigafuchi (Plover Depths), a natural stretch of water that once resembled the wings of a plover in flight and was incorporated into the system of moats surrounding Edo Castle. The **Chidorigafuchi Water Park**, on the w flank of Kitanomaru, was lined with cherry trees in 1953 and is one of the most popular spots in Tokyo for springtime *o-hanami* (cherry-blossom viewing).

After crossing the moats, turn left along the main boulevard, passing the walled compound of the British Embassy, one of Tokyo's oldest foreign missions. Behind the embassy is an area called Bancho where the six *bangumi*, or regiments of *hatamoto* (warrior-retainers of the shogun), used to live. There are still six *bancho* (literally; "guard block") divisions to this area, but this has long since become an upper-class residential district of Tokyo. The **Diamond** hotel (see *Hotels*) offers a relatively affordable place to rest and enjoy a meal, in a predominantly chic, affluent area.

Farther along is a major intersection opposite **Hanzomon** gate (named after Hattori Hanzo, leader of the black-clad *ninja* samurai-spies who are skilled in making themselves "invisible") and to your right is the jarringly futuristic **Wacoal Kojimachi Building**. Next you will come to the National Theater, an austere testament to Japanese skill with concrete, built to resemble the Todaiji Treasure House in Nara (compare the earlier *Meiji Treasure Museum*, also in concrete *azekura* style). The theater is

39

a showcase for such traditional Japanese music, dance and drama as *bunraku*, *gagaku*, and *kabuki*; it also claims the distinction of once having its roof used as a parade ground for novelist Yukio Mishima's private army. Next door is Shinichi Okada's bleak monument to justice, the Supreme Court building finished in 1974. Whatever the intent, its solid windowless walls send out shivers of authoritarianism.

Proceed along the palace perimeter, with the *National Diet Building* visible through the trees to the right, past Kenzo Tange's grim fortress — the National Police Headquarters — opposite Sakuradamon Station. From here, pass through the historic **Sakurada** (Cherry Tree Field) Gate. It was here in 1860 that Regent Naosuke Ii was slain, together with eight of his guards, by samurai serving the Mito branch of the Tokugawa family. This was because Ii had signed the "unequal treaties" with the West and had punished opponents of the shogunate in a last desperate effort to maintain control of the country.

Sakuradamon opens onto a large concourse officially known as the Outer Garden of the Imperial Palace and was made a gift to the nation in 1889. (Before Meiji times, the area had housed the shoguns' loyal vassals and state counselors. Later, government buildings were cleared to make the park.) During World War II, the view up to your left of the two bridges and fortifications came to symbolize the lofty imperial ideal for which Japanese were sent into battle. Families came here to take photographs of their sons going off to war, and huge patriotic parades were held on this spot (the largest took place on Nov 10 1940 to commemorate the mythic founding of the imperial house 2,600yrs before). Passengers on streetcars, which used to run alongside the moat, would rise to their feet and bow in the direction of the invisible palace. After Emperor Hirohito made an unprecedented radio speech announcing Japan's surrender, fanatical Japanese officers chose this concourse to commit ritual *seppuku* (disembowelment), rather than accept the disgrace of defeat.

Viewed from the wide graveled space in front of Nijubashi Bridge, it is easy to see how the scene has captivated and inspired generations of Japanese: the first of the bridges is mirrored in a perfect oval in the waters of the moat, the white Fushimi Tower rises serenely and majestically from its ramparts, and the palace itself remains tantalizingly out of sight. The tower is one of only three left standing and was built in the first half of the 17thC to protect the sw corner of **Nishi-no-Maru** (East Fortress), the second most important citadel of Edo Castle after Hon Maru. The gate on the far side of the first bridge, **Seimon** (Main Gate), is the one opened to the public twice a year, on Jan 2 and Apr 29.

A short walk along the moat takes you to Sakashitamon (Gate at the Bottom of the Slope), used by officials of the Imperial Household Agency and **Kikyomon** (Bellflower Gate) used most often by tradesmen. Follow the right-angled turn in the moat to the busy Uchibori-dori and the third of the castle's three extant towers, **Tatsumi** (Southeast) tower. This spot offers an impressive view of Fujimi Tower rising behind Kikyomon from the walls of Hon Maru. Nearby is Otemon, point of departure for the palace walk, as well as being the nearest exit for the **Palace** hotel (see *Hotels*), and an ideal site for a well-deserved rest.

Walk 2/Shibuya, Harajuku and Omotesando
Allow half to full day (Sun best day). Maps 2&3 and 6&7.
JR/subway: Shibuya.

Tokyo has a way of compartmentalizing its distractions; not by

shogunal order, as in Edo, or by latter-day administrative
guidance, but organically, through human taste and fashion, and
other unfathomable processes. Shibuya, where this walk begins,
means Valley of *Shibui*, or astringent good taste, which illustrates
how much Tokyo has progressed from its origins. A nexus of
railroad lines drawing multitudes from the densely populated w
suburbs that have settled this century, Shibuya fits somewhere
between the robustness of *Shinjuku*, the teenage trendiness of
Harajuku and the upscale chic of *Aoyama*. Daytime crowds are
drawn to its abundant and sophisticated department stores,
theaters, music theaters, record stores and cafés, and at night
swarms of students and young office workers descend on its cheap
discotheques and *nomiya* (Japanese-style bars). Adjoining Shibuya
is Harajuku, an area dedicated to Japan's postwar pampered
teenagers and the instantaneous gratification of all their carefree
consumer desires. Continue up Omotesando-dori and you reach
the s tip of Aoyama, which is a yuppy area, equally fashion
conscious but living at a more elegant and expensive pace.

Start the walk at the small plaza in front of Shibuya Station
(altogether five overground and subway lines converge here at
Japan's third busiest rail station).

In the center of the plaza is a statue of a dog called Hachiko,
reputed to have met his master, a professor at Tokyo University, at
the station every evening after his day's work, and who continued
coming to meet him for 7yrs after his master's death. When the
dog died in 1935, he made the front page of all the major
newspapers. A national symbol of single-minded devotion and
fidelity, Hachiko's bronze statue in turn developed into Tokyo's
most famous meeting point. (The real dog was stuffed and forms
part of the collection of the *National Science Museum*.)

E of the plaza is a towering monument to more recent Japanese
values: the "109 Fashion Community" teenage paradise, of nearly
100 boutiques and a rooftop video studio.

Proceed N up Koen-dori (Park Street), once lined with cheap
"love hotels" but now transformed into a fashionable shopping
street for young urbanites. On the left side is the first and most
conventional of a string of Seibu department stores, Japan's largest
and most trend-setting chain. Opposite is **Young Marui**, a
successful attempt by the Marui group, which specializes in credit
card installment purchases, to tap Japan's affluent and free-
spending youth market. Turn left at the major intersection here,
and continue up what can be called "Seibu land." In the basement
of the Tokyo Yamate United Church of Christ (sandwiched next to
Seed, a new wave-type Seibu "concept" store aimed at fashion-
conscious young professionals) is **Jean-Jean** theater, still managing
to be avant-garde even after two decades.

Opposite Jean-Jean is **Soho's Loft**, a relatively inexpensive
café-bar popular with the young crowd, and one block farther
down is the sprawling **Shibuya Parco** shopping complex of music
and video stores, fashion boutiques and restaurants (all franchised
by Seibu). Divided into three parts, the older "Part One" houses
the Seibu Theater, which hosts modern drama performances.

One block up, on the opposite side, is the *Tobacco and Salt
Museum*, a unique legacy of the now disbanded state salt and
tobacco monopoly. From the intersection at the top of Koen-dori
the luxurious headquarters of Japan's state broadcasting network,
NHK (similar to Britain's BBC), can be seen on the right, and on
the left, looking like an enormous beached seashell encased in
concrete with a snail beside it, is the **Yoyogi Sports Center**, built
for the 1964 Tokyo Olympic Games. Designed by Japan's

foremost contemporary architect Kenzo Tange, it still ranks as Japan's most striking modern building (see *Architecture* in *Culture, history and background*) and is well worth a short detour. Cross the road and walk up the Sports Center slope, passing the basketball court (which resembles a snail in shape) and following the walkway that encircles the Indoor Stadium.

On any Sun, given decent weather, you will be subjected to ear-splitting decibels from Tokyo's most unorthodox tourist attraction. The length of road that runs from Harajuku (on your right) along the s perimeter of Yoyogi Park is car-free on Sun and is given over to Japanese youth. The original dancers in the late 1970s were called Takenoku-zoku or Bamboo-Shoot Tribe, after the bright Asian-style costumes made by a boutique called Takenoku, but their androgynous antics, strictly marshaled by a leader blowing a whistle, have now largely been superseded by the James Dean look and greased back rock'n'rollers. The latest additions are the teenage heavy metal bands (who make up in decibels what they lack in talent), and roller-skate dancers. On the fringes, nearest the park, avant-garde performers perform traditional drumming and dance. Many of the youngsters (often outnumbered by photographers and cultural anthropologists) are rejects from mainstream Japanese society. However, note the ironic display of group conformity — boys dance with boys, girls

with girls, and everything is tightly choreographed.

The opposite side of the road is lined with stalls selling Japanese and Western snacks, and farther on, behind a thicket, is **Yoyogi Park** (*open 5am-5pm*). The park began as a Japanese army drilling ground, was later requisitioned by the US Occupation Forces for barracks known as "Washington Heights," and then turned into the Athletes' Village for the 1964 Olympics. Appropriately for a place of such hybrid pedigree, Yoyogi Park now attracts many exhibitionist Tokyoites, and a few saxophonists or trumpeters can usually be heard playing in the far bushes (practicing is nigh impossible in cheek-to-cheek Japanese housing).

Just s of the lovely Harajuku JR Station (one of the oldest station buildings in Tokyo) is the bridge and entrance to the *Meiji Shrine*, well worth an extensive detour for some welcome quiet and contemplation; or you may proceed into the heart of teenage Tokyo by crossing the street in front of Harajuku Station and following the broad Omotesando-dori on the left side (on Sun the avenue is also closed to traffic).

Just before the major intersection with Meiji-dori, turn left at the sign to *Ota Memorial Museum of Art* to see Tokyo's finest museum of *ukiyo-e* woodblock prints and sample some Japanese desserts in its basement café.

In front of the Ota Museum is the rear entrance to **La Foret**, a quintessentially "Harajuku" fashion building, containing various moderately priced boutiques and designer stands. To the left of La Foret, on a small street running at right angles to Meiji-dori, is the vortex of the teenage jungle, but instead cross here and continue up Omotesando-dori, where you will find the district becoming more chic by the meter. On the right side of the street is **Café de Rope**, Tokyo's attempt at a Parisian street café (after all, this area is nicknamed the Champs Elysees), where the beverages are less important than the opportunity for people-watching. Farther up on the same side is the ultramodern **Vivre 21** building, a must for the fashion-conscious, with its ground-level **Café B Haus** where

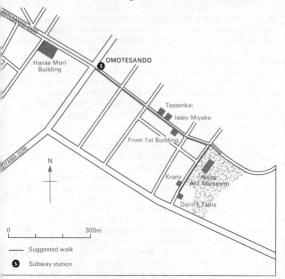

```
              OMOTESANDO  Ⓢ
Hanae Mori
Building

                          Tessenkai

                          Issey Miyake

                    From 1st Building

                          Kranz
                                Nezu
                                Art Museum

                          Daini's Table

    N

0              300m

——— Suggested walk

Ⓢ  Subway station
```

you can watch the world go by. However, the highly unusual, all-white **Key West** café-bar, just down the road, is a more interesting place to stop for refreshment. Two doors along is the Hanae Mori Building, dedicated to the work of the *doyenne* of Tokyo fashion designers. There is an expensive underground antique market in its basement.

At the top (Omotesando Crossing) continue straight down the extension of Omotesando-dori, one of Tokyo's most fashionable, elegant and quiet streets. On the left side you will soon come to the modern (1983) concrete exterior disguise of the **Tessenkai Noh Theater**. Next door is the first of Issey Miyake's three boutiques in this street, stocking his "Plantation" line. On the opposite side stands an interesting 1978 building in striking marine blue and white tiles (the headquarters of the Yoku Moku confectionery company), with a charming café overlooking the street. In the summer, refreshments are served under the cherry tree in the outside courtyard, which is a favorite shooting location for commercial photographers. The 1975 red brick building called **From 1st**, on the same side, houses several high-fashion boutiques such as Rei Kawakubo's Comme des Garçons and Issey Miyake.

If you walk to the end of the street, on the opposite right-hand corner, you will come to the grim outside wall and pink shuttered buildings that conceal the garden and treasures of the *Nezu Art Museum* from casual passers-by. It is well worth a visit.

From the corner of the Nezu Museum turn left. On the right side is a typically chic sign advertising **Bar-Tabac Kranz**, Tokyo's most distinctive and attractive brasserie. It was once the study-library of Shigenobu Okuma (Japan's prime minister in both 1898 and 1914-15), and the interior has been converted in a sparing and tasteful style. It has a billiard room upstairs. After a relaxing drink, **Daini's Table** (see *Restaurants*), across the street, offers a suitably polished reward for the day's exertions.

Walk 3/Asakusa
Allow 3-5hrs. Map 16. Subway: Asakusa.

Many mourn the lost glory of this northern suburb, yet the huge crowds that flock here in ever increasing numbers on weekends and public holidays attest to the enduring appeal of its traditions.

The *Asakusa Kannon Temple* (also known as Sensoji), has always provided the moral lodestar for the crowds, and yet, as so often in Japan, the surrounding secular distractions tend to obscure its religious significance (see also *Asakusa Shrine*). The popularity of the *Asakusa* area is rooted in the censorious puritanism of the Edo shogunate, which in 1657 banished the "Yoshiwara licensed quarter" in Ningyocho to the paddies N of here, and the *kabuki* troupes to Asakusa in 1841. Asakusa was an ideal resting place on a land journey from the center of Edo to the Yoshiwara, and it developed into a thriving pleasure center by the time the exiled *kabuki* troupes took up residence. In its heyday Asakusa blossomed into an "Everyman's Tokyo," and in 1920 prompted novelist Jun'ichiro Tanazaki to enthuse at its "innumerable classes of visitor and types of entertainment, and its constant and peerless richness preserved even as it furiously changes in nature and in its ingredients." The "Yoshiwara licensed quarter" was destroyed by fire in 1911 and never recovered. However, imported amusements had already begun to supplant it, and thanks to the citizens' obsession with novelty (still present today) they were enthusiastically received. They included Tokyo's first skyscraper, the "Twelve Stories" (Junikai), built here by a Briton in 1890 and destroyed by the 1923 earthquake; the first movie theaters in Japan; opera, cabaret and music halls; and the first Western bar. Although connected to *Ueno* in 1927 by Tokyo's first subway (now known as the Ginza line), Asakusa chose to ignore other rail links and paid for its error by subsequent neglect. Asakusa's loss has been the visitor's gain, for here more than anywhere else in Tokyo the richness, variety and "feel" of the old commoners' culture has been preserved.

Being one with the crowd has always been part of Asakusa's intrinsic appeal, and on weekends, national holidays and festivals, the main street, Nakamise-dori, and the precincts of Asakusa Kannon are submerged by an ocean of people. The walk begins at **Kaminarimon**, or Thunder Gate (see Asakusa Kannon), and should proceed at a languid pace (if possible) along Nakamise-dori, past the "Inside Shops" that from ancient times have lined the temple approach. About a half dozen or so of the hundred shops are run by families that have been in business since Edo times; nowadays, however, the majority of wares on sale have degenerated into modern kitsch and cheap souvenirs. At the first major intersection (Nakamise and Dembo'in-dori), turn right and then take the second back street on your left (Kannon-dori). On the left side you will see a small shop called **Fujiya**, famous for its inexpensive *tenugui* (literally meaning hand-wiping cloth), large kerchiefs once used in Edo. Of the original designs in the store, the one of Gozen Tamate, a heroine of *bunraku* puppet drama, is particularly prized. A few doors farther up is a unique cosmetics store, **Hyakusuke**, with traditional cosmetics and accessories on display. Two noted restaurants are in the vicinity: farther down Kannon-dori, on the left side, is **Tatsumiya**, serving traditional Japanese cuisine in an old country-style building overflowing with antiques and bric-a-brac (note the shop making *sembei* rice crackers on the corner of Kannon and Dembo'in-dori); on the left side of the main road, Umamichi-dori, running parallel and to the w of Kannon Metro-dori, the small and inconspicuous **Bentenyama Miyako** serves traditional Edo *sushi*.

Return to Nakamise-dori, bear right, and you will come to Kimuraya, in the block of shops closest to the inner gate of the temple, which was founded in 1868 and specializes in *Ningyo-yaki* molded sweets. Here, you can visit the Asakusa Kannon Temple and Asakusa Shrine, and can apply for permission to visit *Dembo'in Garden* at the temple office.

Retrace your steps along Nakamise-dori to the intersection with Dembo'in-dori and veer to the right. A few meters along on the left side is **Yonoya**, founded in 1673 and moved here at the turn of this century. It specializes in traditional wooden combs used in old-fashioned, elaborate hair styles. Street stalls selling eye glass frames, cheap clothing and bric-a-brac line the street. Farther down on the left is **Daikokuya**, a popular *tempura* restaurant. On the right you will soon see the entrance to the Dembo'in Garden, which is well worth a visit. Directly opposite is the beginning of "Orange-dori" (it derives its name from being painted a lurid orange), with **Asakusa Public Hall** on the left-hand corner and, on the other side of the street, the famous **Nakasei** *tempura* restaurant (its entrance is at the back of a small courtyard).

Proceed along Dembo'in-dori to the intersection with a main street, lined with movie theaters and entertainment houses. Known as **Rokku**, this area was where the famous "Twelve Stories" once stood, presiding over a cornucopia of disreputable bars, juggling and acrobatic acts, cabarets, and above all movie theaters (the first in Japan called Denkikan, or Electric Hall, opened here in 1903). Today's tawdry movie billboards, and even

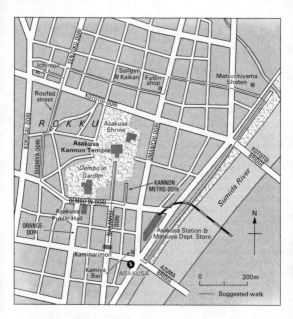

that hardy survivor, the **France-Za** striptease theater, are seedy and poignant leftovers of the Rokku's lost vigor.

From Rokku you may head back to the subway station, pausing to browse through the shopping malls on the way. For the more sturdy of limb wishing to explore N Asakusa, turn right heading N up the main street of Rokku, through a roofed shopping street, and at the first major intersection head straight along Senzoku-dori. A short detour along the first back street on the left leads to **Ichimon**, an Edo-style wooden building on the left side, immediately recognizable by the huge barrel over the entrance. Ichimon's specialty is sake, of which its cellar boasts more than 30 varieties, available for sampling in a delightful rustic setting. Return to Senzoku-dori, cross to the opposite side and take the first right turn from the junction of Senzoku-dori with Kototoi-dori. On the left of the second small intersection stands a graceful house with a willow tree and stone lantern in front, selling *kitsuba* (sweet bean cakes). Proceed straight along this road, noting the many sleek *machi'ai* (literally, "assignation places") where geisha are summoned to serve food and provide entertainment at expensive dinner parties. Sleepy during daytime, this district comes alive at night, when the streets are lined with the black limousines of influential politicians and businessmen, and the occasional geisha may be seen being brought to a *machi'ai* in one of the few rickshaws still used for this purpose. You will soon come to a 2-story modern building (decorated above with a strong lattice design), standing on the left corner of the intersection. This is the **Sangyo Kaikan** where reservations for geisha are made, and where they may often be seen coming and going. A large *machi'ai* compound opposite was once used by one of the three *kabuki* theaters that set up in this area after 1841.

Proceed straight on at Sangyo Kaikan until you reach a pedestrian crossing (on the left corner is a *futon* shop). Turn left here, and at the first set of traffic lights turn right. On the fourth corner from the intersection (on the right side) you will see a stone monument marking the site of the *kabuki* theater, **Ichimuraza**. At the end of this otherwise nondescript street you will reach another intersection with a major road; cross over and you will see a white temple marker. Straight ahead is the **Honryu'in Temple** (better known as Matsuchiyama Shoten) on a small wooded hill on your right. Founded in the 17thC, the temple often figures in Edo-era *ukiyo-e* prints, including one by Hiroshige, as this was where passengers on ferryboats plying the Sumida River would disembark for the "Yoshiwara licensed quarter." The temple is dedicated to a god of Indian origin called (in Japanese) Kangiten, associated with marital harmony and prosperity. Kangiten's symbols are two pronged *daikon* (giant radishes) arranged like crossed legs in conjugal embrace, with a purse underneath for prosperity. The symbols can be seen everywhere in the gables and beams of the main temple building, and even the water basins are shaped like money bags. Along the E side of the temple precincts stretches a surviving section of Edo-period tile and plaster wall.

Leaving the temple, take the pleasant riverside promenade to the right to return to Asakusa Station. The cherry trees lining this small park make it a favorite for *o-hanami* revelries during the Apr cherry blossom period. When you reach Matsuya department store, visit the **Kamiya Bar** on the opposite corner. The first Western bar in Japan, Kamiya is equally famous for its house cocktail, Denki-Buran or Electric Brandy, a potent mix of vermouth, Curaçao, gin and wine added to a brandy base. Authors Jun'ichiro Tanizaki and Kafu Nagai were among its famous patrons. To enter, buy a ticket at the counter (prices are displayed with models in the entrance window), then enjoy one of the more curious sights to be seen on a Tokyo summer evening — Japanese gulping down Denki-Buran, with huge steins of beer as chasers.

Walk 4/Ningyocho
Allow 1½-2hrs. Map 11. Subway: Ningyocho.

Fires, earthquakes, bombs, demolition and the relentless march of progress have destroyed most of old Tokyo, its customs and traditions. Ningyocho, a former entertainment district, escaped being bombed during World War II and contains a host of venerable stores and restaurants that offer the same services to nostalgic Tokyoites as those enjoyed by their grandparents. Its unspoiled attractions are conveniently concentrated on or near the main street, and Ningyocho offers a compact and intriguing insight into the pleasures and tastes of a vanishing lifestyle.

Leave the subway station at the clearly marked (EL) exit, and start your walk at Ningyocho Crossing, proceeding down the left-hand side of the road (the Bank of Tokyo on the opposite side of the main street will help you get your bearings). You will come to a side street, where two doors along there is a rare example of a 3-story wooden house, once common in Tokyo; thanks to a government decree, no more are to be built. With typical Japanese indifference to the culturally incongruous, there is a vintage (1926) *sukiyaki* restaurant called **Hiyama** (see *Restaurants*) competing for customers with a garish *pachinko* (Japanese pinball) parlor next door. (The 1st floor of Hiyama is a meat store and the restaurant entrance is upstairs to the left.)

Of the string of small shops on the next block, **Kyosen-do** is remarkable. One of the few *sensu* (fan) shops in Tokyo, it was founded in Kyoto in 1833 by a Buddhist monk who was taught the art of making traditional ceremonial fans by temple elders. On the sidewalk outside Kyosen-do, a copper plaque commemorates the founding in 1617 of the "Yoshiwara licensed quarter" in Ningyocho, where it remained for 40yrs. **Itakura-ya** (two doors before the next subway entrance, of the Hibiya line) is the first of many old shops selling the local specialty *ningyo-yaki* (animal-shaped spongecakes).

Turn left at the intersection with Amazake-dori (named after a former purveyor of *amai*, or sweet sake) and follow the aroma of burning tea to the store on the corner of the first alley. **Morino-en** has been selling *hojicha* (toasted Japanese tea) and Chinese oolong from the same premises since 1915. Carry on until you come to the corner of the next alleyway, where you will find **Iwai-shoten**, which since 1863 has been a workshop for *tsuzura* (traditional lacquered bamboo trunks), made to order and decorated with the customer's family crest. **Bachi-ei** (established in 1893), only three houses down, specializes in *samisen*, the three-stringed Japanese musical instrument, and *samisen bachi*, the spatula-shaped pick used to play it. The popularity of the **Yanagi-ya**, just opposite, is self-evident from the lines that form there every day (and have been doing so since the early part of the century). The store's sole specialty is their delicious *tai-yaki*, a baking hot "fish" of pastry stuffed with bean jam, handmade with amazing alacrity.

Continuing along Amazake-dori you will pass many more stores and restaurants of interest (including **Ajikura**, two blocks down from Bach-ei on the corner of a side street, which specializes in fresh octopus) as well as some intriguing alleys, which are well worth a detour.

Near the far end of Amazake-dori, on the left, is the *Kurita Museum*, a large, modern building with maroon imitation-brick tiles, which, despite its unfortunate exterior, houses a treasure of Imari and Nabeshima pottery. **Meiji-za**, on the opposite side of the intersection at the end of Amazake-dori, was originally a *kabuki* theater in 1893 and the scene of a real-life tragedy in 1945 when thousands who had sought refuge there from an air raid were incinerated. Nowadays Meiji-za is more likely to host pop concerts.

Proceed back down Amazake-dori, turning left into the main street once again. Continue down to **Ichikawa-toki** (founded in 1878), which is a large-fronted china store (a showroom is located down an adjacent side alley) stocking everything from tiny chopstick rests to the most expensive *Kiyomizu* ware vases. **Kotobuki-do** (established in 1883), on the opposite corner, inspired a popular Japanese television series and is a famous vendor of *wagashi* (Japanese candy, served with tea). Almost too exquisite to eat, the tiny handmade *higashi* (dry, brittle) candies make excellent presents in beautifully wrapped boxes. If you notice what appears to be a grilled *aiyu* fish on a bamboo tray in the front window, it is in fact a stunning example of Kotobuki-do's confectionery skills.

Farther on, past another famous cake store, **Zeitaku Sembei**, and across the next main intersection, you will come to **Suitengu**. Expectant mothers visit this famous Shinto shrine to pray for safe delivery of their babies. If you cross the road and walk back down the main street you will come to **Hatsune** (directly opposite the Ichikawa-toki china store), auspiciously founded in 1868, in the first year of Emperor Meiji's rule; it still serves the same traditional Japanese desserts as it did then.

Look left at the intersection with Amazake-dori and you can't miss a large billboard displaying a chicken, hanging above **Tagosaku**, a Japanese pub with its front festooned with traditional red lanterns. Directly opposite is **Tamahide** (see *Restaurants*), a famous restaurant founded by the "game-cutter" to the shogun in the 18thC. The nearby **Keiseiken** is an agreeable place to have a coffee. Return by subway (there is an entrance next door), or continue on to Ningyocho Crossing, passing another venerable cake store, **Hanami-Sembei**, close to the Bank of Tokyo, behind which you will find a temple dedicated to Kannon (Buddhist Goddess of Mercy) tucked away.

Walk 5/Yanaka, Sendagi and Nezu
Allow 5hrs. Map 15. JR: Nippori.

Yanaka is an old temple town, a vestige of the Tokugawa shoguns' policy of relocating temples on Edo's periphery after the "Long Sleeves Fire" of 1657, and the Yanaka-Sendagi district still has Tokyo's highest concentration of temples to have survived the ravages of earthquake, fire and World War II. Following the 1868 Meiji Revolution the area was much favored by professors, writers and artists, who were drawn to its scenic woodlands, clear streams and proximity to the new Tokyo University in Hongo, as well as the Tokyo Academy of Fine Arts (now Tokyo University of Arts) in Ueno. Today the district's old shopping streets, restaurants, temples and clapboard houses delight connoisseurs for their feel of rapidly vanishing Shitamachi life.

Take the JR Yamanote or Keihin Tohoku line to Nippori, exit at the platform end nearest Nishi Nippori Station, and turn left at the wicket. Immediately in front of the station ascend the staircase leading up to the Yanaka cemetery. Follow the stone paved path, which winds through Buddhist tombstones (and past a garish orange "love hotel" brazenly advertising itself nearby), turning left at the first fork in the path skirting the cemetery wall. You will soon reach a concrete road, with the entrance to **Tennoji Temple** on the left. It was founded in the 14thC on the route that 13thC Buddhist firebrand Nichiren used to take on his way to and from Kamakura (see *Excursions*). The strident priests of Tennoji later fell into disfavor with the shogunate, and in 1699 the temple was put under the control of the nearby *Kan'eiji Temple* (the Tendai sect temple patronized by the Tokugawas). The large bronze statue of Buddha inside the temple courtyard was cast a little earlier, in 1690. Tennoji used to be one of Edo's busiest temples, and one of only three places authorized to hold lotteries, a tremendously popular Edo pastime that drove expectant crowds into such wild excitement that it was eventually banned in the mid-19thC. Most of Tennoji's buildings were destroyed, along with Kan'eiji Temple, in the fighting between *Shogitai* (loyalists of the shogun) and imperial forces in the 1868 revolution.

Leaving the temple, cross the road and proceed along the main cemetery avenue, which is lined with cherry trees. The mood today is of pious serenity and bears little resemblance to the activity along this avenue in the days of Edo, when, like the Naka Mise approach to *Asakusa Kannon Temple*, it was lined with many shops, as well as teahouses where the sensual desires of male temple worshipers, including priests, were accommodated. Osen Kasamori, a woman of astonishing beauty who worked at one of the teahouses, rocketed to fame in the 18thC after one of her customers, the *ukiyo-e* pioneer and master Haronobu, made her the subject of many of his woodblock prints.

You will soon come to a police box on the left, but just N of it (in a fenced-off square) are the foundation stones of Tennoji's 5-story pagoda, all that remains after a pair of lovers burned it down in a 1957 suicide pact. Farther down the cherry-tree avenue are some interesting wooden buildings selling flowers to cemetery visitors. But instead turn right at the intersection by the police box, and proceed to the end of the street, where you will turn right again. On the left side of this narrow street look out for a new antique store (part of the slow process of "gentrification" overtaking the neighborhood) and, on the right, a store selling tortoiseshell jewelry and eye glass frames. (Along a narrow path to your left you will also see an Edo-era wall topped with old roof tiles.) Continue on until you come to the *Asakura Choso Museum*, a 3-story black concrete building with statues outside. This is one of Tokyo's most fascinating and beautiful buildings and worth a visit.

At the front entrance to the museum, turn right and walk to the crossing by Yanaka's main street, which deserves a diversionary stroll to see its many old shops and temples. Note the wooden gate of the temple directly opposite the side street leading to the museum. The bullet holes in the gate were caused by the violence in 1868 when *Shogitai* took refuge in the temple.

Walk down the steps at the end of Yanaka's main street heading toward the shopping area fancifully known to locals as Yanaka Ginza. At the bottom of the steps turn right. Six doors down on the same side is the store belonging to Suigetsu Buseki, who fashions beautiful, intricate baskets and vases for *ikebana* (flower arranging), from only the choicest bamboo. Prince Takamatsu (late brother of Emperor Hirohito) and US Ambassador Mike Mansfield have bought examples of his art, which may be purchased far cheaper here than in department stores.

Return to the foot of the stairs and continue until just before you reach a left fork, where you will see a tiny children's park, the former site of Tenshin Okakura's residence. The *doyen* of artistic circles during the Meiji era, Okakura was largely responsible for re-establishing Japan's artistic tradition and incorporating new Western concepts, by rejecting the Edo insistence on line drawing. The hexagonal monument opposite the entrance contains a bust of Okakura by sculptor Denchu Hiragushi.

At the intersection at the end of the street turn right. A short distance from the corner is the entrance to **Dai'enji Temple**. Facing the main temple hall (which is an unusual building with two stairways, porches and doors and lovely dragon carvings suspended from its eaves) you will notice the small **Kasamori Shrine**, with two statues of foxes and a statue of a woman in the middle. The tall stone statue to the right of the shrine is of *ukiyo-e* master Harunobu, and the memorial stone to the left is that of the shrine's namesake, Harunobu's model, the enticing Osen Kasamori, encountered earlier in the walk.

Turn right on leaving the temple. At the corner, by the next set of traffic lights, is a well-known noodle restaurant, **Oshimaya**, serving hot *jigoku* (hell) and cold *gokuraku* (paradise) noodles. A few doors down on the same side is the beautiful wooden **Kikumi** *senbei* store (selling *senbei*, or rice crackers), in business since 1875. A short distance farther down, on a corner, is the alluring **Bunhichi** store, selling beautiful (but very expensive) doll miniatures of *bunraku* puppets.

Your attention may already have been drawn to another store farther up on the opposite side, with large Edo-style store signs hanging above its door. **Isetatsu**, founded in 1858, specializes in colorfully printed, traditional *chiyogami* paper, which incorporates designs from kimonos worn by nobles, samurai and *kabuki* actors. Gift-hunters will appreciate the paper dolls and masks inside.

You may terminate the walk here at Sedagi Station or continue by walking uphill from Isetatsu for the last stretch towards Nezu.

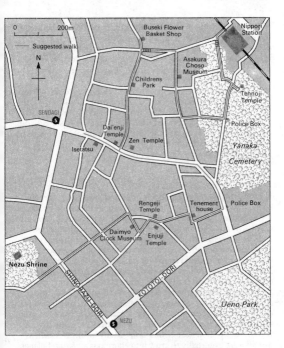

After passing Dai'enji, you will soon pass, on your left, a
modern Zen temple where Japanese political leader Yasuhiro
Nakasone practices *zazen* meditation. You will come to a set of
traffic lights at the top of the hill; then, around the corner on the
right side, is Makino Brothers & Co., a large white modern
concrete building. Makino makes and sells copies of ivory *netsuke*
and ladies' accessories. Continue along the same side and head
straight at the next traffic lights. When you reach a police box on
the left side, turn right to follow a street running diagonally
opposite that is lined with temples. At the end of the street, where
it veers sharply to the right, you will see by the corner an
old-fashioned wooden tenement house designed for four families.
Turn right at the corner of the house and then immediately left.
A short walk down this narrow street will take you past a
tombstone cutter and a garage workshop, on the left. Continue to
the end of the street, turn right, and you will see two interesting
temples. **Rengeji Temple**, on the right with a pretty Edo-era red
wooden gate, was well known in Edo for its efficacy in exorcising
worms. The mid-17thC **Enjuji Temple** opposite is related to a
priest of the Nichiren sect famous for his strong legs, and the
temple was renowned for its healing powers for leg ailments.
Grateful Edo worshipers who had been "cured" donated huge
straw sandals to Enjuji in appreciation, and these are hung from
the transoms of the prayer hall.

From Enjuji, turn left and left again, and continue until another
street joins it from the right. Here is one side of the *Daimyo Clock
Museum* (you will recognize it by the convex mirror for motorists
on the wall, at the corner). The museum entrance gate is just off to
the left on a side street.

51

Leaving the museum, turn right and then left when you rejoin the side street, and then left again at the first junction. Proceed down the slope, and at the intersection go straight ahead. The main street you have now reached is Shinobazu-dori, which, if you follow it far enough to the left, will take you to the w side of *Shinobazu Pond* in *Ueno*.

At the major junction cross the street and proceed directly up a very unpromising-looking, narrow street with a fruit store at the bottom, on the left-hand corner where it joins Shinobazu-dori. On the left side you will soon come to the entrance of *Nezu Shrine*, one of Tokyo's most beautiful historical buildings. Now head back to Shinobazu-dori and turn right. A few minutes' walk away is Nezu Subway Station (Chiyoda line).

Walk 6/Nihonbashi
*Allow 1½-2hrs. Maps **10**&**11**. Subway: Nihonbashi.*

Nihonbashi (literally, The Bridge of Japan) was the geographic and commercial center of the nation in the Edo era and cradle of the merchant-commoners culture that blossomed in *kabuki* and *ukiyo-e*. When Shogun Ieyasu Tokugawa had the bridge built in 1603 he decreed it should be the starting point for the five great roads leading out of the city, and even today all Japanese road distances are measured from Nihonbashi. For three centuries Nihonbashi was home to the city's great fish market, which only moved to Tsukiji after the devastation of the 1923 Great Kanto Earthquake. To supply the needs of the shogun's court, and of the *daimyo* and samurai classes, merchants from the more developed and sophisticated centers of w Japan (particularly from Ise, around the coast from Nagoya) and Omi (on the banks of Lake Biwa near Kyoto) set up shop near Nihonbashi. Many businesses such as Mitsui were eventually to grow into enormous *zaibatsu* (business conglomerates). Nihonbashi was the natural site for Japan's first national bank, and both the Bank of Japan and the Tokyo Stock Exchange are still situated nearby. Although gray office buildings now predominate, there are still enough reminders of the past to make an interesting short walk.

Take the exit marked A1 from Nihonbashi Station. Immediately to your right you will see the skyscraper head office of Yasuda Trust & Banking on the corner of a major interchange. The office buildings facing you on the opposite side are part of the Yaesu district, derived from Yayosu, itself a Japanese corruption of Jan Joosten, a fellow officer of Will Adams (see below) on the Dutch vessel shipwrecked off Kyushu in 1600. Joosten's house was actually situated near a section of the castle moat called Babasaki, but the name Yaesu carried over when the district was later "moved" here. Cross the street ahead and turn right, walking over a bridge underneath an expressway overpass, and then turn left. Cross the street again in front of another bridge, and pass to the other side of the next main street on the right.

The splendid Neoclassical building to your left is the former Main Hall of the Bank of Japan, built in 1896, and was the site of the old gold mint. One of the few surviving Meiji-era Western buildings in Tokyo, the **Bank of Japan Main Hall** is the work of Kingo Tatsuno, *doyen* of late 19thC and early 20thC architects in Japan, and also responsible for the 1914 Tokyo Station. Pass along the front courtyard of the Bank of Japan, and proceed straight at the next intersection.

The grand Neoclassical building on your left side, with its long row of huge fluted columns topped with ornate capitals, is the **Mitsui** main building (1902), and the decorative fantasy on the

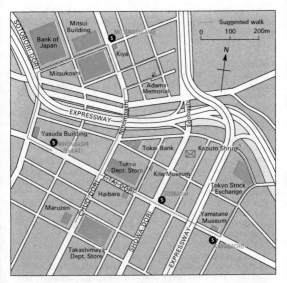

right is the main store (1914) of **Mitsukoshi** (note the bronze lions guarding its main entrance and the ornate bronze lanterns above). Both these buildings are the work of Tamisuke Yokogawa, one of Tatsuno's students.

The Mitsukoshi store is the descendant of an enormously successful Edo dry goods store that once stood nearby, called Echigoya. It was opened in 1673 by a merchant from Ise called Takatoshi Hachirobei Mitsui, whose winning business strategy was to list his prices (rather than charge arbitrarily as most other such stores did) and deal in cash instead of the customary practice of charging customers twice a year. The fortune made from Echigoya established the foundation for the present-day gigantic Mitsui business conglomerate, of which Mitsukoshi is a member firm.

Cross the main street to the **Kiya** cutlery store (in business since 1792) on the opposite corner. Next door is a French-style boulangerie restaurant (with a bakery on the 1st floor and a restaurant above) called **Nagafuji**. Proceed along the main street running opposite the front of Mitsukoshi, and turn left. The eel restaurant, **Isesada**, immediately to your left, is a legacy of the era of Ise merchants. Proceed past the first intersection on this street and at the next intersection turn right. Next, turn into the second small street on the right; a few meters along on the same side (in a tiny alcove with a low wooden fence in front) is a stone memorial to Will Adams, on whom the hero of the bestselling novel *Shogun* is based. After being shipwrecked in 1600 Adams was employed by Ieyasu Tokugawa as a diplomatic advisor and teacher of mathematics and geometry, and to build a British-style sailing ship, the *Shogun*. His Japanese name, Anjin Miura, derives from the Miura peninsula where he was rewarded by Tokugawa with his own fief, and "Anjin" is Japanese for pilot, which was his profession. The stone memorial is on the site of Adams's residence, where he lived until his death in 1620.

Proceed along the side street as far as the main road. There is a

53

pink stone-faced building on the left corner, called **Yagicho**, which has been selling dried bonito fish flakes in Nihonbashi since 1737. It is an interesting reminder of the days when this area was the site of the city's great fish market.

Next, turn left and you will approach Nihonbashi Bridge. Looking up, you will see a large plaque on the side of the expressway with the characters written for Nihonbashi, in the handwriting of the last shogun, Yoshinobu. To the left, the bronze statue of the sea goddess seated in a chair by a pine tree is a monument to the old fish market, scenes of which are depicted in bronze reliefs at the base. Cross the bridge (rebuilt in 1911) and you will see the wonderfully ornate bronze needles with Chinese dragons guarding either side, which have shamefully been crowded out by the overpass directly overhead; their lanterns illuminate little else but the steel sides of the overpass bridges. The police box on the left corner of the bridge was once the site where decapitated heads of criminals along with survivors from unsuccessful love suicides were exhibited for public scorn and as a warning to others. The monument on the opposite side marks the site of the old official bulletin board. In the early 18thC, when the 47 samurai were sentenced to death (see *Sengakuji Temple*), the announcement was posted here; however, infuriated citizens quickly tore it down.

On the left, past the police box, you will see the ultramodern, jaggedly geometric headquarters of the **Tokai Bank**, looking very much like an up-ended book from one direction. (Cross over this street, and the popular 3-story Chinese restaurant **Shodoten** can be found on the right of a small street, with a store selling decorative Japanese fans on its corner.) If you proceed straight across the next major intersection you will come to the main store of **Takashimaya** on the left, with the large **Maruzen** bookstore opposite. The **Tokyu** department store on the left corner of the intersection is the modern incarnation of the Shiragiya dry goods store, founded in 1662 by one of the Omi merchants who were allocated this side of the bridge by the shogunate. The **Tameiken** Western-style restaurant (with the **Kite Museum** on the 5th floor of the same building) is on the right of the alley that runs along the left side of the Tokyu department store. Opposite Tokyu on the main road is **Haibara**, a traditional Japanese paper shop, immediately recognizable as the only "old" building on the block.

Leaving Haibara, turn right and cross the main street, going under the expressway overpass and crossing to the left side of the street. Proceed as far as the Yamatane Securities Building by the Kayabacho subway entrance, and the *Yamatane Museum* is on the 9th floor.

Turn left outside the Yamatane Building, then left again, proceeding as far as the **Tokyo Stock Exchange** on the left side. The surrounding area is known as **Kabutocho**, a name now synonymous with the Exchange itself. The name comes from the nearby **Kabuto Shrine** (literally meaning War Helmet) nearby. Turn into the first side street on the left of the Exchange. The tiny shrine is on the right at the far end, dwarfed by the expressways shooting overhead. In the 11thC it is said a warrior paused here by a swirling torrent with his army to ask the assistance of the River God in passing. His prayer was answered, and returning from the campaign the warrior took off his helmet and buried it here as an offering. The shrine built on this spot became a popular place of worship for the latter-day "samurai" of the business world, seeking divine aid in their corporate battles! From here retrace your steps to Kayabacho Station.

Sights and places of interest

Thanks to a tax system that punishes inherited wealth, Tokyo has been endowed with an enormous number of museums. One of its grandest is the **Tokyo National Museum**, which has one of the world's finest collections of Asian art. However, some of the best collections are those gathered by former *daimyo* nobility, or business magnates, often with highly-specialized exhibits, such as *ukiyo-e* prints, or tea-ceremony ware. The houses and gardens of the museums only occasionally equal the interest of the exhibits inside, although display standards and organization are rarely adequate, and sporadic or nonexistent English labeling can be aggravating. Most of the museums and parks are closed on Mon (check individual entries). Precincts of temples and shrines are generally open 24hrs a day (entrance to the main prayer halls or inner courtyards usually being on a dawn-to-dusk basis). Other sights not mentioned here will be found under *Walks* in *Planning*.

Sights classified by type

Districts
Akasaka
Akihabara
Aoyama
Asakusa
Ginza
Roppongi
Shinjuku
Ueno

Parks and gardens
Dembo'in Garden
Hama Detached Palace Garden
Kiyosumi Garden
Koishikawa Botanical Garden
Koishikawa Korakuen
Meiji Shrine Outer Garden (Meiji Olympic Park)
Nature Study Garden
Rikugien Garden
Shinjuku Gyoen
Shinobazu Pond and Bentendo
Ueno Park

Temples
Asakusa Kannon Temple (Sensoji)
Gokokuji Temple
Jigendo (Ryo Daishi)
Kan'eiji Kiyomizudo Temple
Kan'eiji Temple
Sengakuji Temple
Zojoji Temple

Shrines
Asakusa Shrine (Sanja-sama)
Hie Shrine (Sanno-sama)
Kanda Myojin Shrine
Meiji Shrine and Inner Garden
Nezu Shrine
Toshogu Shrine
Yasukuni Shrine
Yushima Tenjin Shrine

Museums of art
Asakura Choso Museum
Bridgestone Museum of Art
Eisei Bunko Foundation
Goto Art Museum
Hara Art Museum
Hatakeyama Museum
Idemitsu Art Museum

National Museum of Modern Art
National Museum of Western Art
Nezu Art Museum
Okura Museum
Ota Memorial Museum of Art
Riccar Art Museum
Seiji Togo Art Museum
Suntory Museum of Art
Tokyo Metropolitan Art Museum
Tokyo Metropolitan Teien Art Museum
Tokyo National Museum
Yamatane Museum

Museums of history and culture
Bunka Fashion Museum
Crafts Gallery
Daimyo Clock Museum
Japan Folk Crafts Museum (Nihon Mingeikan)
Kurita Museum
Meiji Shrine Treasure Museum
Meiji University Museums
Parliamentary Museum and Gardens
Shitamachi Museum
Waseda University Tsubouchi Memorial Museum
Yasukuni Shrine Museum
Yokoyama Taikan Memorial Hall

Museums of Science and Technology
Communications Museum
National Science Museum
Science and Technology Museum
Tobacco and Salt Museum
Transport Museum

Historic buildings and landmarks
Akasaka Detached Palace (Geihinkan)
Imperial Palace
Dai-ichi Life Insurance Building
Kan'eiji Pagoda
National Diet Building
Tokyo Tower

Other sights
Kabukiza Theater
Nogi's House
Tsukiji Wholesale Fish Market
Ueno Zoo

Akasaka
Map 8/7.

In Tokyo's entertainment cornucopia, Akasaka stands somewhere between the exorbitant, expense-account hostess trade found in *Ginza*/Shimbashi, and the youth fantasy factory that is *Roppongi*. Toward the end of the 19thC Akasaka was noted for its geisha houses, which catered to the new breed of journalists, businessmen, and above all politicians and bureaucrats from the government area rising nearby in Nagatacho and Kasumigaseki. The inheritors of the "teahouse" tradition can still be seen in Akasaka's exclusive and forbiddingly expensive *ryotei* restaurants, recognizable by their high walls, and the sleek black limousines that are parked outside (and the occasional geisha shuffling past). Akasaka's night-time population is drawn from the thousands of smartly-dressed, fashion-conscious, socially-aspiring "OLs" (Office Ladies) and *salariman* from the many business headquarters here), as well as the TV crowd from the Tokyo Broadcasting (TBS) building, and a large number of tourists from the area's huge hotels. The combination is enlivening, but definitely respectable. Restaurants, cafés, pubs and nightspots cater to a wide range of tastes and budgets.

Akasaka Detached Palace *(Geihinkan)*
2-1-1, Moto Akasaka, Minato-ku ☎478-1111. Map 7H6.
Closed to the public. JR/subway: Yotsuya.

A Japanese version of Buckingham Palace or Versailles, this palace was built with the intention of showing that Japan could match the civilization, enlightenment and grandiose pomp of the West. Originally a converted residence of one of the great families related to the Tokugawa shoguns, the Akasaka Detached Palace became the home of Emperor Meiji from 1873-88 while the *Imperial Palace* was being rebuilt following fire damage. The present neo-Baroque palace dates from 1909, and became the residence of the present Emperor Hirohito while he was Crown Prince. Today the palace building serves as a state guesthouse for visiting prelates, royalty and heads of state, and was chosen as the venue for both the 1980 and 1986 Tokyo Summits of Western world leaders. In the grounds of the Palace are the residences of Crown Prince Akihito, and of Emperor Hirohito's brothers, Prince Mikasa and the late Prince Chichibu.

Akihabara
Map 15E11.

This is truly the world's electronics mecca, with hundreds of stores, ranging from tiny stalls selling cables, memory chips and assorted gadgets, to giant discount department stores with each floor dedicated to a different electronic product. Competition is intense, and the heavily discounted prices of items are usually open to negotiation. The best way to get a bargain is to visit several stores, compare prices, and then start haggling.

Aoyama
Map 7I5.

By common consent this is the most elegant and sophisticated of central Tokyo's districts, as well as one of the most expensive. Its focal point is Aoyama-dori, stretching from Shibuya to *Akasaka*. The Wacoal "Spiral Building" by architect Fumihiko Maki on Aoyama-dori (near the intersection with Omotesando-dori) is worth a look inside to see its large, semicircular atrium, enfolded by a spiral path that winds around its perimeter and up to the 2nd

floor. From here walk in the direction of Akasaka to the
intersection with Aoyama Bell Commons on the corner, and turn
left into Killer-dori (which was named by fashion designer Junko
Koshino for its notoriously high number of traffic accidents). The
sycamore-lined street is the main thoroughfare for Tokyo's
"in-crowd," and is lined with boutiques all potentially injurious to
one's pocket. Turn left at the first major intersection of Killer-dori
with Meiji-dori and head toward Harajuku, passing more inviting
boutiques, restaurants, bars and coffee shops, on the way.

Asakura Choso Museum ★
*7-18-10, Yanaka, Taito-ku ☎821-4549. Map 15B10 ▨ in
sculpture gallery ✿ ✗ ◁ Open Sat, Sun, Tues-Thurs
9.30am-4.30pm. Closed Mon, Fri. JR: Nippori.*
The interior of this museum is of exceptional Japanese beauty and
equally delightful Western fancy, although it is belied by its
bizarre, ugly black facade. The progenitor of this eccentric cultural
mélange was Fumio Asakura (1833-1964), a sculptor in the
Rodin-inspired "Western style" of realism and naturalism, who
lived and worked here from 1908 until his death. Many of his
prodigious works are on display inside his former atelier, which is
a curious tower built between 1928 and 1931, with a Western-style
roof garden and good views over Yanaka. The atelier forms one
side of an inner courtyard area and carp pond, filled with rocks
carefully chosen by the sculptor to reveal their intrinsic beauty.
The courtyard is surrounded on its other three sides by Asakura's
house, itself a model of timeless Japanese beauty and elegance.
Visitors are allowed to enter the *tatami*-matted rooms overlooking
the courtyard, after removing slippers provided at the entrance.
Note the traditional iron kettle (in one of the 1st-floor rooms)
suspended on a *jizai-kagi* hook from the ceiling over an *irori*
charcoal fire that is recessed in the floor, and upstairs details such
as the *kakemono* hanging scroll in the *tokonoma* (alcove), and an
exquisite inlaid lacquer table.

Asakusa
Map 16C13.
Still retaining the old Shitamachi spirit, this popular entertainment
quarter surrounding the *Asakusa Kannon Temple* is well
worth a visit. For a full tour see *Walk 3* in *Planning*.

Asakusa Kannon Temple *(Sensoji)* ★
*2-3-1, Asakusa, Taito-ku ☎842-0181. Map 16C13 ▣ ◁ Open
24hrs. Subway: Asakusa.*
No one is really sure why Asakusa Kannon, also called Sensoji, has
such a hold on the affections of Tokyoites. The most obvious
reason is the immense appeal of the Buddhist deity worshiped
here — the Bodhisattva Kannon, whose compassion for human
suffering is symbolically equivalent to the role of the Virgin Mary
in Catholicism. Another reason might be the temple's extreme age:
founded in the 7thC, it is one of the most ancient in the Tokyo
area. An equally compelling explanation is simply the Japanese
love of crowds — a popularity that is self-fulfilling.
    Legend has it that the temple was founded in 628 by two
fishermen who found a statue of Kannon in the nearby Sumida
River (see *Asakusa Shrine*). Some credence was lent to this story
when reconstruction work, following the 1945 air raids, unearthed
artifacts from the 7th-8thC. The Kannon-do main hall had already
been rebuilt four times before World War II — in the 9thC, 10thC
and 12thC, and again in 1651. This wooden Kannon-do and the

5-story pagoda (both "National Treasures") were burned down in a 1945 air raid, but have since been faithfully reconstructed. The present Kannon-do is a 1958 reinforced concrete copy.

The statue of Kannon, which survived the air raid, having been buried deep in the ground beforehand, is never revealed and is kept locked inside the gold-plated inner shrine beyond the altar. The huge foyer has many historic donations made by visitors and pilgrims. The three huge red lanterns hanging from the ceiling were given by the geisha of *Akasaka*, *Asakusa* and Yanagibashi (the great lantern outside the main hall is from the Shimbashi geisha). The ceiling is decorated with two paintings by leading contemporary Japanese artists: a dragon by Ryushi Kawabata, and a celestial beauty by Domoto Insho. Edo-period *ema* votive paintings (see *Yushima Tenjin Shrine*), hanging high on the ill-lit walls, were fortunately removed before the 1945 air raids.

The 1973 replica of the Edo-period pagoda contains relics of "Buddha's bones," donated to the temple. On the right and slightly behind the Kannon-do is Asakusa Shrine, inseparably linked to the founding of Asakusa Kannon. The Hozomon temple gate is a 1964 reinforced concrete reconstruction of the one lost in World War II, and contains a series of 14thC Chinese Buddhist sutras. The two outer lanterns suspended from Hozomon are donations from the tradesmen of the *Tsukiji Fish Market*; the middle one is from the traders of Kobunacho near Nihonbashi. The two giant straw sandals hung on the back of the gate were given by a village in rural Yamagata, in N Japan. To the far right of Hozomon is Bentenyama, or Benten Hill, an elevated ground that was once an ancient burial mound and has a statue dedicated to the goddess Benten standing beside it. Next to the statue is the famous **bell**, one of the nine in Edo that used to sound the hours of the day ("Through clouds of blossom/Would that be Ueno's bell/Or Asakusa's?" mused Bassho in a famous poem). Nowadays the bell is rung at 6am every morning and on New Year's Eve.

The Nakamise or "Inside Shops" that form the gaudy and commercial approach to Asakusa Kannon are so-called because they stand inside the temple precincts, although it should be remembered that the tradition of selling souvenirs and snacks here is almost as ancient as the temple itself. There are also many famous old shops here (see *Walks* in *Planning*).

Kaminarimon (Thunder God Gate), at the entrance to the Nakamise, was rebuilt in 1960, 95yrs after it had been destroyed by fire. Viewed from the front, the statue in the left niche is of Raijin (God of Thunder) and his colleague to the right is Fujin (God of Wind). In the rear part of the gate are two statues of dragon gods presented to the temple in 1978.

Ceremonies and festivals are held in the temple during most months of the year. The most popular attractions are the *Setsubun* ceremony (Feb 3); the *Kinryu-no-mai* (Golden Dragon Dance) on Mar 18 and Oct 18; the *Sanja* festival of Asakusa Shrine on May 17 and 18; the *Shirasagi-no-mai* (White Crane Dance) on Nov 3; and the year-end *Hagoita-ichi* market between Dec 17 and 18 when stalls sell *hagoita* battledores elaborately decorated with portraits of famous figures from *kabuki*. For some of these festivals see *Calendar of events* in *Planning*.

Asakusa Shrine *(Sanja-sama)*★

2-3-1, Asakusa, Taito-ku ☎844-1575. Map **16**C13 ☺ ➡ Open 9am-4.30pm. Subway: Asakusa.

The popular name of this shrine is Sanja-sama, meaning shrine of the three [guardians]. It is with typical Japanese disregard for

religious distinction that the two Hamanari brothers and their
feudal lord Haji no Nakamoto (whose reputed recovery of the
Buddhist image from the Sumida River led to the founding of
Asakusa Kannon Temple) are venerated in this Shinto shrine in
the temple's NE corner. Its construction was commissioned in 1649
by Iemitsu — the third Tokugawa shogun (who later ordered that
his grandfather Ieyasu be worshiped here also) — and is built in
the *gongen* style favored by the Tokugawas. The main structure
remains unchanged since the 17thC despite a major overhaul in the
Meiji era. The Sanja festival is held here every May.

Bridgestone Museum of Art

1-10-1, Kyobashi, Chuo-ku ☎563-0241. Map 10H10 ▨ ☀
*Open 10am-5.30pm (last entry 5pm). Closed Mon, 1wk in
summer, Dec 26-Jan 4. JR: Tokyo; subway: Kyobashi.*
A fine collection of more than 1,000 items of mainly Western art
have been donated by Shojiro Ishibashi (founder of the
Bridgestone tire company) to this museum, as well as a number of
subsequent purchases. Rodin, Moore and Giacometti sculptures
line the corridor, and the first room contains an incongruous
assortment of ancient Egyptian, Greek, Roman and medieval
French sculpture and pottery. The core collection consists of
French Impressionist masters; there are also a few works by
Picasso, Dufy, Rouault, de Chirico, Braque and Modigliani, and a
large selection of European and Japanese prints (shown in
rotation). One room is filled with Meiji-era Japanese paintings of a
highly derivative Impressionist style.

Bunka Fashion Museum

*Bunka Gakuen Endo Kinenkan, 3rd and 4th floor, 3-22-1,
Yoyogi, Shibuya-ku ☎375-3265. Map 6F-G3* ▨ ☀ ═ ▣
*Open Mon-Fri 10am-4.30pm (last entry 4pm), Sat 10am-
3pm (last entry 2.30pm). Closed Sun, hols, June 23. JR:
Shinjuku (s exit).*
Dedicated followers of fashion who make the trek to the concrete
wastelands bordering E Shinjuku, where the Bunka Gakuen
campus is located, will find it rewarding. The collection includes a
wide variety of textiles, costumes and kimonos worn by Japanese
royalty and nobility; *Noh* and *kyogen* costumes; furniture and
accessories; and Japanese, Indian, Taiwanese, Indonesian and
Persian folk wear.

Communications Museum

2-3-1, Otemachi, Chiyoda-ku ☎244-6831. Map 9G10 ▨ ♿
☀ *in TV section on 2nd floor* ═ *lunch only* ▣ ☀ ═ *Open
9am-4.30pm (last entry 4pm). Closed Mon, Dec 29-Jan 3.
Subway: Otemachi.*
This museum will mainly appeal to philatelists, as it probably has
the world's largest stamp collection (with over 200,000 Japanese
and foreign stamps), but it can also serve as an educational
playground for children on rainy days. The building itself is
somewhat gloomy and utilitarian, and the 2nd-floor modern
communications section is "low-tech" in comparison with Tokyo's
two science museums. But there are compensations: the 3rd floor
has a comprehensive display following the history of Japan's post
and telecom systems; in addition to the mammoth stamp collection
on this floor, adults will also be intrigued by the primitive
telephones, and children are allowed to play with working models.
English language labels and explanations are virtually nonexistent,
but a color brochure, in English, is available at the entrance.

Crafts Gallery★
1, Kitanomaru Koen, Chiyoda-ku ☎211-7781. Map 8F8 🚇
inc. admission to Tokyo National Museum of Modern Art.
Extra fee for special exhibitions 🎫 ♿ Open 10am-5pm (last
entry 4.30pm). Closed Mon (or Tues if Mon is public hol),
Dec 28-Jan 4. Subway: Takebashi.

The Crafts Gallery (Kogeikan) has been housed in this imposing,
red brick Gothic building since 1977. It was erected in 1910 as the
headquarters of the now defunct Imperial Guard and is situated
just 5mins away from the main hall of the *National Museum of
Modern Art*. Only the 2nd story displays exhibits; hence during
special exhibitions the normal displays are removed to gain space,
and an extra admission fee is charged. The museum treats its
"crafts" as "art" masterpieces, well-displayed in glass cases in
hushed rooms with subdued lighting (in contrast to the philosophy
of the private *Japan Folk Crafts Museum*). However, the
exhibits of kimono, pottery, ceramics, lacquer, metal and bamboo
ware are particularly beautiful, especially Shoji Hamada's iron-
glaze bowl, Kazuo Yagi's black pottery *Ring*, Rokubei Kiyomizu
VI's *Flower Vase* and Imaemon Imaizumi XII's traditional-style
Nabeshima ware — so perhaps the mood of reverence is not
inappropriate.

Dai-ichi Life Insurance Building
1-13-1, Yurakucho, Chiyoda-ku ☎216-1211. Map 9H9 🅿 X
🖥 ♿ Open 10am-4pm. Closed Sun, 2nd and 3rd Sat each
mth, Dec 31-Jan 3.

This grim stone fortress (a product of the militaristic 1930s) was
designed by the same architect responsible for the similarly leaden
Honkan (Main Hall) at the *Tokyo National Museum*. Its most
interesting occupant was General Douglas MacArthur, Supreme
Commander for Allied Powers, who set up his General
Headquarters here from 1945-51, during the postwar occupation
of Japan. From its windows the blue-eyed "shogun" could look
across the front concourse to the *Imperial Palace*, where the
defeated Emperor resided. MacArthur's study has now been
reoccupied by the chairman of the Dai-ichi Life Insurance
company, and his waiting room is used as a VIP reception — but it
is usually possible to visit his private office (☎*public relations
section one day ahead*). A brief guide in English is available.

Daimyo Clock Museum
2-1-27, Yanaka, Taito-ku ☎821-6913. Map 15C10 🚇 🎫
Open 10am-4pm. Closed Mon, July-Sept, Dec 25-Jan 15.
Subway: Nezu.

This museum houses some 50 clocks (out of a collection of about
200) owned by Kamiguchi Guro, a fashionable tailor in prewar
Tokyo. They are on display in a small annex of the Kamiguchi
home, in a residential district of Yanaka. Before the introduction
of the Gregorian calendar in 1872, the Japanese adhered to the
Chinese lunar calendar, when the time of day was dependent upon
the length of daylight and darkness. Daytime and night-time were
each equally divided into six periods called *toki* and named after
the animals of the traditional Chinese zodiac. Hence the time
between *toki* varied in length by day and night and according to the
different seasons. In midsummer, for example, the period between
the morning "dragon" *toki* and the "snake" *toki* lasted 2hrs
38mins, while the time between the midnight "rat" *toki* and "ox"
toki was only 1hr 21mins.

The first mechanical clocks were imported from Europe toward the end of the Muromachi era and subsequently were greatly modified to enable them to measure the Japanese *toki*. Such clocks were necessarily complicated and expensive, and were normally owned only by *daimyo* (feudal lords). The *daimyo* clocks at the museum are mostly of the large "pyramid" type, although few primitive "portable sundials" (an early type of watch) are also displayed. Unfortunately none of the labels or explanations at the Daimyo Clock Museum are in English. (*The National Science Museum* in *Ueno* also has a famous clock collection.)

Dembo'in Garden ★
2-3-1, Asakusa, Taito-ku ☎*842-0181. Map 16C13* 🅾 ♿ ⇐
Open 9am-3pm. Subway: Asakusa.
This serene refuge, a contemplative tonic to the noisy and plebeian distractions of Nakamise-dori and the constant crowds milling around *Asakusa Kannon Temple*, belongs to the temple and contains the chief abbot's residence.

Intimidating "Keep Out" notices help preserve its fragile tranquility from the multitudes, but arranging a visit to its 17thC garden is simple, only requiring prior signature of a book kept at the temple office (the first entrance, at the foot of the Asakusa Kannon pagoda on the left). After being given a ticket, double back down Nakamise-dori past the front entrance of Dembo'in, which is closed, and turn right at its corner. Proceed along Dembo'in-dori (skirting the side of Dembo'in) and enter by the gate on the right opposite **Asakusa Public Hall**. Give the ticket in and follow the red arrow into the garden.

A bronze bell, cast in 1387 and one of the oldest in Tokyo, stands near the entrance. Several of the wooden buildings, including a guest hall and the abbot's living quarters, date back to 1777. The garden is believed to have been designed by Enshu Kobori (1579-1647), a tea-ceremony master and noted landscape gardener who also laid out a garden for the shogun in Edo Castle. The shape of the large pond, which contains many carp and turtles, is that of the character for *shin* (heart, or mind). The presence of the Asakusa View hotel slightly spoils the outlook from the visitors' hall side of the pond, but the beautiful view from the far side — that of the temple pagoda rising majestically from the trees — more than compensates.

Eisei Bunko Foundation
1-1-1, Mejirodai, Bunkyo-ku ☎*941-0850. Map 12D5* �︎ �︎
inside, except with prior permission ⇐ *Open 10am-4pm. Closed 1st, 3rd and 5th Sat each mth, Sun, hols, Dec 20-Jan 12. JR: Mejiro.*
Situated in a leafy suburb of Mejiro, the museum is reached by bus or taxi from Mejiro Station. The art collection here was started in the 14thC by the Hosokawa *daimyo* of Higo (the present-day Kumamoto prefecture in southern Kyushu island). Today their ancestors estimate the inherited art hoard consists of a staggering 112,000 items, but until Kumamoto University completes its analysis the exact number will not be known. Some are designated "National Treasures," such as a rare Chinese bronze mirror from the Warring States period (5th-3rdC BC) and the 12thC Japanese saddle of inlaid lacquered wood. Other priceless works include handwritings from famous figures in Japanese history such as Nobunaga Oda and Ieyasu Tokugawa; signed letters from other historic figures such as Napoleon and Beethoven; a large store of Japanese paintings from artists such as Sesshu (1420-1506) and Taikan Yokoyama (1868-1958); beautiful old *Noh* drama costumes

61

and masks; samurai armor; metalwork; ceramics from ancient China to modern Japan; and Chinese statuary and furniture. Unfortunately only a tiny sample is on display during the three annual exhibitions held here (each lasting 4mths) at the Foundation museum. Two slight criticisms are that labeling is only in Japanese, and there is a lot of space that could be put to better use inside this converted old (1936) Hosokawa office building.

Ginza
Map 9.

For more than 90yrs Ginza has been synonymous with sophistication, luxury and smartness, for the Japanese. The origins of this mystique, encompassing more than the sum of its elegant stores, cafés and restaurants, lie in its history. Ginza was the first place in Japan wholeheartedly to import the trappings of Western "civilization and enlightenment"; it became a showcase for new ideas and modern affluence.

The land was originally a swamp until it was filled in by Shogun Ieyasu Tokugawa, who, having decided to unify the nation's coinage in 1598, set up a silver mint here in 1612, from which its name originates: *Gin*, meaning silver, and *za*, meaning mint. The mint closed in the 1790s after a serious corruption scandal involving the silver mint master, but it reopened in 1800 at a new site in Nihonbashi. The old Ginza, however, retained its name.

Overshadowed by prosperous Nihonbashi, Ginza remained a relative backwater of artisans and craftsmen during the Edo period. However, 4yrs after the Meiji Restoration of 1868, a great fire almost completely razed Ginza, and the governor of Tokyo was persuaded to embark on a daring innovation: instead of wood, Ginza was rebuilt in brick, with wide Western-style avenues lined with trees and arcades, and Japan saw its first paved roads and brick-built sidewalks. The opening of the first rail service between Yokohama and nearby Shimbashi, in 1872, also fortuitously made the new Ginza the gateway to the city.

In 1874 gaslights replaced Ginza's old wax-candle lanterns and created a sensation, but otherwise the new "Ginza Bricktown" was a disaster. All the sturdy willow trees withered and died. The buildings were badly ventilated and prone to damp and consequently many were left uninhabited. Only drastic government measures succeeded in getting most of the houses occupied, by 1881, when the first horse-drawn tram lines were laid down in the main street, on the run from Shimbashi to *Asakusa* (until electricity supplanted the horses in 1903).

Ginza's most famous monument, the **Hattori Clock Tower** still stands where it was erected in 1894, on top of the expensive **Wako** department store (see *Shopping*) on the corner of Ginza 4-chome crossing. (The phrase "meet me under the Hattori clock" has since become "meet me under the Wako clock." Wako is the postwar name for Hattori, the family that began the Seiko watch company and still owns the department store.) Many stores of the Meiji era remain in Ginza. **Kimuraya** bakery, next door to Wako, opened in Ginza in 1874 and counted the Emperor Meiji as one of its customers, especially for its delicious bean-curd bread, still sold in vast quantities to appreciative Tokyoites. On the opposite side of the intersection, next to the corner San-Ai building, stands **Kyukyodo**, the official purveyors of incense to the Imperial Family. They followed the emperor to Tokyo after more than 200yrs' business in Kyoto. In 1893 Kokichi Mikimoto succeeded in culturing his first pearl, and the **Mikimoto** store three buildings up from Wako is almost as old.

The proliferation of chic stores and cafés for which Ginza is renowned had, by 1911, already given rise to the phrase *Gin-bura* (strolling aimlessly through Ginza). A more recent rage is *depato meguri*, or department store cruising, through the **Matsuya, Mitsukoshi, Matsuzakaya, Hankyu** and **Seibu** emporia (see *Shopping*), which all have branches in Ginza and Yurakucho.

Ginza was also the birthplace of the first cafés and beer halls in Japan, and in the Meiji era both were exotic novelties and frequented by socially daring and occasionally licentious young men and women. Now highly respectable centers of people-watching, the oldest cafés in Ginza are **Fugetsudo** (farther up from Mikimoto), the **Shiseido Parlor** and **Senbikiya** (both farther down from Kyukyodo in the direction of Shimbashi). The **Ebisu Beer Hall** first opened in 1899, and the **Lion Beer Hall** on the SE corner of the Ginza Street intersection between 6- and 7-chome) still retains its original 1934 interior (see *Nightlife*).

Gokokuji Temple ★
5-40-1, Otsuka, Bunkyo-ku ☎941-0764. Map 13C6 ⚏ ⚐ ⚑
Main hall open 6am-5pm, temple precincts open 24hrs.
Subway: Gokokuji.

Gokokuji is little visited, despite the fact that it is one of the best preserved temples of the early Edo era. Its chief attractions are the graceful, sweeping roof of its original 1697 main hall and the classical lay-out of its precincts. Enter by the main gate (which has two fierce and sinewy Buddhist deities situated alarmingly close to a subway exit and main road) and ascend the steep flight of steps, passing under a raised 2-story treasure-repository gate leading to the courtyard. The beautiful main hall immediately catches the imagination, but to the left (next to the pagoda) is the Gekkoden visitors hall that was moved here from Otsu city and is a classic example of traditional Japanese domestic architecture. The temple was founded at the behest of the mother of the 5th Tokugawa shogun Tsunayoshi. Since 1873 the burial place for the Imperial Family has been situated here, on Toshimagaoka Hill, at the back of the temple.

Goto Art Museum ★
3-9-25, Kaminoge, Setagaya-ku ☎703-0661 ⚏ ⚑ ⚐ ⚑
Open 9.30am-4.30pm (last entry 4pm). Subway: Kaminoge.
Closed Mon, year end, New Year.

Like the *Nezu Art Museum* in *Aoyama* district the superb collection in this museum owes its existence to the tasteful hoarding of the late railroad baron Keita Goto (founder of the huge Tokyu rail and subway network). The best time to visit here is undoubtedly the first week of May, being the only time the fragile and priceless segments of the 12thC *Genji Monogatari Emaki* (Tale of Genji Scroll) are on view. On a day-to-day basis the gallery can only accommodate one-tenth of the huge collection at one time. Included in this collection are Chinese and Japanese paintings, calligraphy, sutras, ceramics, Chinese mirrors and jades, Japanese tea-ceremony, lacquer and archeological objects and Korean ceramics. Notable paintings are the *Pine Tree under Snow* and screens of the *Flowers of the Four Seasons* by Kenzan Ogata (1663-1743) and an illustration for the *Ise Monogatari* by his elder brother Korin (1658-1716); part of a famous scroll by Koetsu (1558-1637); and two decorated poems by Sotatsu with his design of *A Thousand Cranes*. There are also some famous Sung-dynasty (960-1280) Chinese paintings, a number of rare Han (206BC-AD221) and T'ang (618-907) mirrors, Sung and early Ming (1368-1644) porcelains and an extensive collection of old Japanese tea bowls, caddies, kettles and spoons. Exhibitions are changed approximately every 2 months and are usually on a theme, such as tea-ceremony ware, ancient bronze mirrors, etc. It can be very relaxing to stroll in the deliberately unkempt garden with Buddhist statuary and stupas, in unexpected places. (A small admission charge is payable for those visiting the museum as well.)

Hama Detached Palace Garden ★

Hamarikyu Teien, Chuo-ku ☎541-0200. Map 10J10 🚠 ♿ 🏪 🍴 ◁≋ Open Tues-Sun 9am-4.45pm (last entry 4pm). Closed Mon, Dec 29-Jan 3. JR (E exit), subway: Shimbashi.

Tokugawa shoguns were the original owners of the palace that once stood here, which eventually passed into the hands of the Imperial Family (in 1871). It was used as the residence for US President Ulysses S. Grant when he visited Japan in 1879, and later for imperial receptions and parties, and after the end of World War II it was donated to the city. The highlight of the 25ha (62-acre) garden is its serpentine tidal pond spanned by three bridges, each one shaded by wisteria trellises and leading to an islet. There is a beach here, bordered by elegant pine trees, at the mouth of the estuary, where the Sumida River empties into Tokyo Bay. In spring, cherry trees in blossom add to its charm.

Hara Art Museum ★

4-7-25, Kitashinagawa, Shinagawa-ku ☎445-0651. Map 4N7 🍴 🏪 Open Tues-Sun 11am-4.30pm. Closed Mon. JR: Shinagawa.

The Hara Museum is firmly established on the international contemporary art circuit, despite being hidden down a quiet residential backwater in Shinagawa. In 1979 Toshio Hara decided to turn his family's residence, a 1937 Bauhaus concrete curiosity surrounded by 0.6ha (1½-acre) grounds, into an alternative to the stifling conformity of Japanese government and corporate-funded museums, which, as he himself said, "tended to favor the most academic of contemporary Japanese artists who still practice styles of painting openly derived from European Impressionists and Post-Impressionists." Since then the Hara Museum has annually hosted three to four major exhibitions of postwar US and European art, drawing such avant-garde celebrities as Christo Javacheff (of the "wrapped walkways"). Every spring the museum hosts a "Hara Annual" of ten or more up-and-coming Japanese artists. A permanent collection of some 300 items include works by internationally known artists such as Rothko, Andre, Calder, Pollock, Le Witt, Rauschenberg and Dubuffet, and just as many Japanese and Korean artists (who perhaps deserve equal recognition). Jean-Pierre Raynaud's tiled room at the top of the museum is intriguing; equally striking is Nobuo Sekine's outdoor steel-and-granite sculpture. The museum's garden is delightful, there is a pleasant patio coffee shop, and reading material is provided in both English and Japanese.

Hatakeyama Museum ★

2-20-12, Shiroganedai, Minato-ku ☎447-5787. Map 4N6 🍴 🈵 no parking Sat, Sun ◁≋ Open Jan 8-Mar 15, Apr 1-June 15, July 1-Sept 15 10am-5pm (last entry 4.30pm), Oct 1-Dec 14 10am-4.30pm (last entry 4pm). Closed Mon. Subway: Takanawadai.

This is one of Tokyo's most select and rewarding museums; it lies largely hidden behind the garden of the **Hannyaen** *ryotei* restaurant, in a residential district close to Takanawadai Station. The restaurant occupies the wooden, tiled house and garden that used to belong to the late industrialist, Issei Hatakeyama, founder of the museum collection (which is now housed in a modern concrete building). The wooded hill on which the restaurant and museum now stand was once the Edo retreat of Shigehiro Shimazu, lord of Satsuma (present-day Kagoshima prefecture in southern Kyushu island), as well as the famously beautiful garden which visitors can walk round.

The 1,500-item collection (of which about one-tenth is on view at any one time) is of the highest quality: beautiful Japanese paintings by Korin Ogata, Sesshu, Sotatsu, Koetsu and Kensan; a particularly fine collection of Momoyama-Edo period tea-ceremony ware and Korean Yi dynasty (1392-1910) bowls; Muromachi Japanese pottery and Heian and Kamakura period lacquerware; Southern Sung (1127-1280) Chinese paintings, T'ang (618-907); and Sung- and Ming-dynasty (1368-1644) ceramics. Japanese *Noh* robes from the Edo period are strikingly beautiful.

The decor is hushed, subdued, *shibui*, and conducive to quiet contemplation, and in one corner water drips from a bamboo spout in a minature Japanese rock garden. There are four different seasonal exhibitions a year (Jan 8-Mar 15, Apr 1-June 15, July 1-Sept 15, Oct 1-Dec 14). Labels and catalogs are in English and Japanese.

Hie Shrine *(Sanno-sama)*

2-10-5, Nagata-cho, Chiyoda-ku ☎581-2471. Map 8H7 ▢ ↩
◁ Main hall open 6am-5pm, temple precincts open 24hrs.
Subways: Akasakamitsuke, Kokkaigijidomae.

The history of the first Hie Shrine began with the foundation of a Buddhist temple on Mt. Hiei, NE of Kyoto, to protect the new capital from evil spirits entering from this direction. The temple displaced the mountain's own Shinto deity, so it was necessary to build a nearby shrine to appease the god. Thus the Hie Taisha shrine was constructed for the worship of the *Sanno Gongen* (mountain-king avatar) who was called *Oyamakuni-no-kami*. The Mt. Hiei temple became the headquarters of the powerful Buddhist Tendai sect, and many subordinate Hie shrines were built as guardian deities for Tendai temples (there are now some 3,400 Hie shrines throughout Japan).

This Tokyo Hie Shrine (Sanno-sama) originated in 1478, when Dokan Ota built Edo Castle. At this time, he erected a Hie (*or Sanno*) shrine to Mt. Hiei's *Oyamakuni-no-kami* inside the castle grounds for protection. In 1607 Shogun Ieyasu Tokugawa decided to move the shrine outside the grounds to Kojimachi, where 50yrs later it was burned down in the great Edo fire of 1657. Shogun Ietsuna Tokugawa rebuilt the shrine in 1659 at its present location. The vermilion-lacquered buildings were in the richly decorated style favored by the Tokugawas and were ranked as "National Treasures," but were destroyed in the 1945 firebombings of Tokyo.

The present shrine was reconstructed in 1967 and continues in its role of protecting the *Imperial Palace* (the original Edo Castle). The biennial Sanno Festival (see *Calendar of events* in *Planning*), although smaller than in Edo times, still one of Tokyo's greatest, and the festival participants retain the honor of entering into the Imperial Palace (just as in earlier days they used to enter the castle and the festival would pass under the gaze of the shogun). Although the main entrance to the shrine is from the Nagatacho side by the **Capitol Tokyu** (see *Hotels*), a more attractive route is via the long flight of steps lined with red *torii* arches from Sotobori-dori avenue in the *Akasaka* district.

The **Shrine Museum** (🕮 *open Mon-Thurs 10am-4pm, closed Fri*) has an important collection of 31 swords, mainly donated by the Tokugawa family; one of these is designated a "National Treasure" and 14 others "Important Cultural Properties." Nowadays the shrine has a thriving trade from wedding ceremonies, aided by its proximity to the Capitol Tokyu hotel where banquets are often held.

Idemitsu Art Museum ★
9th floor, Kokusai Building, 3-1-1, Marunouchi, Chiyoda-ku
☎*213-3111. Map 9H9* 🖼 🏯 *except with prior permission* 🅿
◁ *Open 10am-5pm. Closed Mon, Dec 21-Jan 10 while changing exhibitions. JR: Yurakucho; subway: Hibiya.*

This excellent museum is worth a visit if only for its stunning view over the *Imperial Palace* from its strategic location, on the 9th floor of the building that also houses the Imperial Theater. Based on acquisitions by Sazo Idemitsu, founder and chairman of the Idemitsu oil company, the museum has the largest number of ink paintings and calligraphy by the Zen monk Sengai (1750-1837) in the world (a selection, showing his wild humor and deep humanity, are almost always on view), and probably the largest collection of Chinese ceramics (from the Neolithic period to the 18thC) in Japan. The Korean ceramic collection is scant, but Japanese ware includes famous pieces by Ninsei Nonomura (1574-1660) and Kenzan Ogata (1663-1743), plus many examples of Old Seto, Nabeshima, Imari, Kutani, Karatsu and Kakiemon ware. A selection of the museum's best ceramics is usually displayed in the central main room. An illustrated time chart of ceramics, showing parallel developments in China, Korea and Japan, with photographs from the museum's own collection, is usefully displayed on the far wall. The gallery owns a 12thC series of three handscrolls illustrating an imperial court intrigue of 866, which has been designated a "National Treasure"; another handscroll of the Kamakura era; several superb 16th and 17thC screens illustrating the *Tale of Genji* and scenes from Edo and Kyoto; and many early genre paintings. There are also distinguished groups of 17th-19thC *ukiyo-e* woodblock prints), Japanese calligraphy and choice pieces of Japanese and Chinese lacquer. Standards of lighting and display are excellent. Typical of the thoughtful labeling (which is both in English and Japanese), enlargements are also displayed of the seals from ancient Chinese bronzes, showing early pictograms which formed the root of modern Chinese writing characters.

One unique feature of the Idemitsu Museum is its permanent gallery of potsherds collected from old kiln sites in Japan, China, Korea, Thailand, Iran and Egypt. (The large windows in this gallery overlook the Imperial Palace.) A coffee/tea shop is in the next room.

Special exhibitions at the Idemitsu Museum usually last for 2 months.

Imperial Palace
Chiyoda, Chiyoda-ku. Maps 8G8 & 9G9.

Built on the site of the former Edo Castle, and home to the Emperor, the Imperial Palace can be called the heart of Tokyo. The palace itself is not open to the public, but a full tour around part of the extensive grounds is described in *Walk 1* in *Planning*.

Japan Folk Crafts Museum *(Nihon Mingeikan)* ★
4-3-33, Komaba, Meguro-ku ☎467-4527. Map 2K2 ■ ♿ ✍
➤ ◄€ Open 10am-5pm. Closed Mon, Dec 22-Jan 3, all Feb.
Subway: Komabatodaimae.

Mingei, or folk art, is a term now universally known by the Japanese, thanks to the proselytizing founder of the folk art movement in Japan, the late Soetsu Yanagi, who also began this museum to exhibit his own prodigious collection. Yanagi, with enthusiastic support from Japanese master potter Shoji Hamada and British potter Bernard Leach, taught appreciation of the intrinsic beauty of craft objects designed for daily use. To reconcile the contradiction of having such objects displayed in the unnatural surroundings of a museum, the Mingeikan wisely opted to show them in as "natural" a Japanese setting as possible. Thus, they are exhibited in the replica of a farmhouse from Tochigi prefecture, N of Tokyo, with wooden floorboards, paper windows, bare beams and white plaster walls (in contrast to the government's *Crafts Gallery* in Kitanomaru, which places such exhibits in spotlighted glass cases).

The museum now has at least 10,000 items, of which only one-tenth are shown at any one time, in exhibitions that are rotated four times a year. On the 1st floor, in the rooms on the left of the main entrance, are carvings and textiles (including a large selection from Okinawa); on the right, pottery and Western silk crafts can be found. Contemporary folk art by leading lights such as potter Kanjiro Kawai and textile designer Keisuke Serizawa, as well as furniture and Korean folk crafts, are exhibited upstairs. There is a new annex behind the building hosting special exhibitions, and the building situated across the street, housing the museum office, is an original farmhouse gate that was moved here from Tochigi prefecture.

Jigendo *(Ryo Daishi)*
14-5, Ueno-koen, Taito-ku ☎821-4050. Map 15C10 ▣ Open 24hrs. JR: Ueno (Ueno-koen exit).

This is one of the most attractive buildings of the *Kan'eiji Temple* complex, which escaped both the torching of 1868 and wartime bombing. The popular name of this early 18thC temple hall (situated on the left of the *Tokyo National Museum*) is Ryo Daishi, meaning "Two Great Masters." The first master was the original abbot of Kan'eiji, called Tenkai, and the second was a 10thC priest, Ryogen, who was revered by the abbot.

Kabukiza Theater ★
4-12-5, Ginza, Chuo-ku ☎541-3131. Map 9I10 ✍ ═ 🖪
Monthly performances except during most of Aug and Dec.
Subway: Higashi-Ginza.

The first theater constructed on this site in 1889 proved to be a turning point for *kabuki* drama, marking its transition from a strictly plebeian diversion in the Edo era, deemed immoral by the censorious shogunate (and as a result of an edict of 1842 confined to distant *Asakusa*), to its current status of *haute culture* in the center of modern Tokyo. The present Kabukiza is a 1950 reconstruction of Shin'ichiro Okada's famous example of eclectic "Japanese revivalism," originally built in 1924 but badly damaged during World War II. Its florid Momoyama-style facade, inspired by castle architecture of the 16thC, stands out in the architectural desert of E Ginza. This is unquestionably the best place to see *kabuki*, which is an absolute *must* during a stay in Tokyo (see *Kabuki* in *Nightlife*).

Kanda Myojin Shrine
2-16-2, Soto Kanda, Chiyoda-ku ☎255-8871. Map 15E10 ◻
◓ ◁ Main hall open 9am-4pm, shrine open 24hrs.
JR/subway: Ochanomizu.

Kanda Myojin is said to have been founded in AD730, originally to venerate an orthodox Shinto deity, Okuninushi no Mikoto. It later became associated with the rebel general Taira no Masakado who led a revolt against the Kyoto Emperor Suzaku in 935. When captured and beheaded in 940, legend has it that his head fell off and landed at the former site of the shrine (in present-day Kanda Surugadai). Masakado became a symbol of rebelliousness against established authority for the townspeople of Edo, themselves firmly subjugated by the Tokugawa shogunate.

In 1616, when Ieyasu Tokugawa died, the shrine was moved to its present position to reward loyal retainers from his province of Surugu (present-day Shizuoka prefecture) with land of their own; hence the name Surugadai. The shogunate, needing to placate the feelings of Edo townsmen, diplomatically made Kanda Myojin a guardian shrine of Edo; and its great festival, which celebrated Ieyasu Tokugawa's victory in 1600 at the Battle of Sekigahara, was allowed the same honor as the Sanno festival (see *Calendar of events* in *Planning*) — that is, to pass through Edo Castle, under the eyes of the shogun and his ladies. The Emperor Meiji worshiped here not long after arriving in 1868, perhaps to win the affections of the people of Edo. This prompted court officials to demand that the spirit of the 10thC rebel Masakado be moved to another place; but he was finally restored to the main hall in 1934.

The shrine was destroyed in the conflagration following the Great Kanto Earthquake in 1923, and rebuilt in 1934 using new materials such as reinforced concrete. The vermilion-painted main hall, main gate and other buildings are faithful reproductions of the flamboyant style of architecture popular with the Tokugawas. Although not as bustling as it used to be, the courtyard remains a very attractive place, with cherry trees, statues of guardian dogs and a water-spurting dragon.

Kan'eiji Kiyomizudo Temple★
1, Ueno-koen, Taito-ku ☎821-4749. Map 15C11 ◻ ◁ Open 7am-5pm. JR/subway: Ueno.

This temple was built in 1631 on the orders of Kan'eiji's Abbot Tenkai to house the image of the Thousand-Armed Kannon (the Buddhist goddess of mercy) sent by the abbot of Kyoto's famous Kiyomizudera. Then in 1698 it was moved forward on the hill to give it a vantage point over *Shinobazu Pond* (landscaped by Abbot Tenkai to resemble Lake Biwa near Kyoto). This small gem of a temple survived both the fire of 1868, which followed the battle between imperial and shogunal forces, and wartime bombing. In fact, today it still looks much the same as it did three centuries ago. On the left of the hall is an altar to Kannon surrounded by dolls given by parents whose prayers for the goddess to give them children have been granted (the accumulated pile of dolls are ceremonially burned every year) (see *Calendar of events* in *Planning*). Above the hall's entrance is a fascinating contemporary painting of the fierce battle of 1868 from which the temple of Kan'eiji Kiyomizudo miraculously escaped unharmed.

Kan'eiji Pagoda★
For details see Ueno Zoo.

To reach this 5-story pagoda of the *Kan'eiji Temple*, tantalizingly visible through the stone lanterns and trees leading up to the

Toshogu Shrine, you have to pay an entrance fee to *Ueno Zoo*. The 1639 pagoda, a government-listed art treasure, stands in regal solitude behind the deer enclosure, its square moat plied by indifferent geese.

Kan'eiji Temple
1-14-11, Ueno Sakuragi, Taito-ku ☎*821-1259. Map 15B10* ⊡
Open all year 24hrs. JR: Uguisuidani.

To capture the illustrious past of this great Tokugawa temple, which once covered Ueno Hill, requires plenty of imagination, as most of its former 119ha (294-acre) sacred precincts now host such secular distractions as a park, zoo and museums. Kan'eiji was originally built here in the 17thC to protect Edo, the shogun's new capital, from the evil spirits believed to come from the NE (such belief in Chinese geomancy also explains why Nara has Todaiji and Kyoto the great Enryakuji Temple to guard their NE approaches). It was also intended to serve as a family temple for the Tokugawa shoguns (as was *Zojoji Temple* in the s of the city). Surrounding the great hall (roughly where the park fountain now stands in front of the *Tokyo National Museum*, itself once the Kan'eiji abbot's residence) were 36 subsidiary temples. Nearly all these were destroyed in the fierce battle of Ueno Hill in 1868 between imperial and shogunal forces. Survivors of this battle were *Kan'eiji Pagoda, Jigendo, Toshogu Shrine* and *Kan'eiji Kiyomizudo Temple*.

The present Kan'eiji (main hall dating from 1638) was moved in 1875 from Kita'in Temple in the Saitama prefecture (where Abbot Tenkai was once a priest) to its new site (a subsidiary temple behind the Tokyo National Museum). Beside the temple are Kan'eiji's three cemeteries, which once contained the mausolea of six Tokugawa shoguns (out of 15) who were buried here. Except for two gates and washbasins, the mausolea were destroyed in the 1945 air raids. In the first cemetery (note the masonry lying on the ground bearing the 3-leafed Tokugawa crest) is the **mausoleum gate** leading to the burial place of the 5th shogun Tsunayoshi (1680-1709). The gate is a fine example of the showy Chinese style favored by the Tokugawas. In the second cemetery, which is best viewed from the side of the road, skirting the back of the National Museum, is a similar but smaller gate leading to his predecessor Ietsuna (1651-80).

Kiyosumi Garden
3, Kiyosumi, Koto-ku ☎*641-5892. Map 11G-H13* 🔳 ⑤ ◁€
Open Tues-Sun 9am-4.30pm. Closed Mon, Dec 29-Jan 6.
Subway: Monzen-nakacho.

One of Tokyo's best landscaped "strolling" gardens awaits those prepared to take a 15min walk through charmless urban blight from Monzen-nakacho Station on the E side of the Sumida River. In 1721 *daimyo* Kuze Yamatonokami built his Edo mansion here, but the garden you see today owes its existence to the plutocratic Baron Yataro Iwasaki, founder of the giant Mitsubishi empire, who bought the estate in 1878 to build a suburban villa. Water was drawn from the Sumida River to fill the central lake, and the abundant and skillfully placed rocks, which form the garden's most distinctive feature, were transported on Mitsubishi boats from all over Japan. Most of the villa was destroyed in the 1923 Great Kanto Earthquake, and the next year Iwasaki donated what was left to the city. The 5ha (12-acre) garden is immaculately maintained, and a stroll along its gravel paths and stepping stones, taking a rest inside a lakeside arbor, is most agreeable.

Koishikawa Botanical Garden
3-7-1, Hakusan, Bunkyo-ku ☎814-0138. Map 13C7 ⊠ tickets sold at convenience store opposite entrance ⥆ Open 9am-4.30pm (last entry 4pm). Closed Mon, Dec 28-Jan 3. Subway: Hakusan.

Originally the grounds of the Koishikawa Detached Palace, this old garden has intriguing medical associations. It was laid out by the 2nd Tokugawa shogun, Hidetada (1605-23), and it later became the Tokugawa's chief "pharmacy" when Tsunayoshi (1680-1709) had the shogunal herb garden moved to the N side of the palace in 1684, from its former site in Azabu, s Edo. In a rare show of shogunal concern for the plight of the poor, the austere Yoshimune Tokugawa (1716-45) decreed that a paupers' hospital should be established in one half of the garden (in 1723) to take advantage of the herbs' curative properties.

The hospital water-well and a small fenced-in herb garden are now all that remains of its role in Edo medicine, except for one other curious link with the past. In a far corner stands the city's oldest educational building, the first medical school of Tokyo's university. This gem of early-Meiji architecture, with pink and white walls, dormer windows and a comical little tower on top, now stands sadly empty and disused beside a small Japanese garden and carp pond.

As well as the botanical gardens, Tokyo University's science faculty maintains a botanical lecture hall and collection of specimens in a curiously attractive, early-Modernist building with a glass-fronted tower, near the entrance. The garden has more than 6,000 different plants including some 300yr-old trees. The most important are labeled in Japanese with their botanical names in Latin; no English information is provided, but a stroll around the garden's grounds can still be a delightful experience, especially during the plum- (*Feb-Mar*) and cherry- (*Mar-Apr*) blossom viewing seasons.

Koishikawa Korakuen★
1-6-6, Koraku, Bunkyo-ku ☎811-3015. Map 14D8 ⊠ ⥆ Open 9am-5pm (last entry 2.30pm). Closed Dec 29-Jan 3. JR: Iidabashi; subway: Korakuen.

To most Tokyoites Korakuen signifies an enormous pleasure complex, including a huge baseball stadium, an amusement park, swimming pool, movie theater, skating rink and bowling alley. Such instantaneous gratification of pleasure, however, was not what Korakuen's 17thC founders had in mind, as Korakuen means "Garden of Pleasure Last," derived from a Confucian saying that "a gentleman should be the first to worry about the world's troubles and the last to enjoy its pleasures."

Only 6ha (16 acres) of beautiful garden, the oldest in Tokyo, remains of the original 26ha (63 acres) encroached upon by today's citadel of hedonism. The garden was first laid out in 1629 as part of the Edo palace of Yorifusa Tokugawa, the first Lord of Mito, founder of one of the three most honored branches (*Gosanke*) of the Tokugawas. The work was completed by his son Mitsukuni, a keen Confucianist, with the help of Zhu Shunsui (1600-82), a scholar who fled China in 1644 after the fall of the Ming dynasty.

After the Meiji Restoration, the garden was reduced in size by a quarter, and what remained became an army arsenal. On a visit here in 1906 Lord Redesdale lamented that, "the sounds of courtly music and solemn dances are replaced by clank of steel, the blast of furnaces, and the endless din of giant forges." A plan to donate it to the city was aborted in 1923 due to extensive damage by the

Great Kanto Earthquake, but was eventually fulfilled in 1936.

The main E entrance, close to the baseball stadium, is now closed. Visitors enter and leave by the W gate nearest to Iidabashi; the China-Japan Association has appropriately sited its office opposite this entrance, guarded by two stone lions. There is a well-marked route leading the visitor on an edifying stroll — pilgrimage, even — past miniature views imitating noted Japanese and Chinese scenic spots, contrived by the Lord of Mito and his Chinese Confucian protégé.

Each view has its own identifying signpost in Japanese (the few in English are now peeling, but a color guide in English and Japanese can be purchased at the entrance).

The winding path takes you past a 100yr-old drooping cherry tree, then a bamboo-carpeted knoll loosely representing the steep slopes of Mt. Lushan (in China's Jiangxi Province), and finally over a miniature earthen bridge copied from one in Kyoto, where you can admire a Lilliputian version of the famous dike on Lake Hsi Hsu (West Lake) in China's Chekiang Province. If you stop to admire the lake on one of the terraces by the edge of the cliff, you will see the site of a former model of Kyoto's Kiyomizu Temple, which was destroyed in the 1923 earthquake.

Proceeding over an enchanting red bridge (modeled on Kyoto's Tsuten-Kyo) the next stop will be the Tokujin-Do, built in 1630 to house Mitsukuni's two statues (now missing) of Confucian paragons of brotherly love. On past further allusive stepping stones, bridges, apricot and plum groves, wisteria trellises and a dwarf-sized rice paddy, you will come to a charming sake house from the rural environs of Edo (rebuilt in 1959 after destruction in the 1945 firebombing). It is called Kuhachi-ya, or Nine-Eight-House derived from the worthy maxim that it is better to drink nine or eight than ten parts (or *jubun*, which also means enough). The small pond in the E corner of the garden near the disused main entrance was once the inner garden of Mitsukuni, with its own Chinese gate designed by Zhu (this was also destroyed in 1945). His adjoining "study" is now part of the brooding sports complex on the other side of the fence.

The path leading back to the W gate traverses the shore of the main lake, designed by the 3rd Tokugawa shogun Iemitsu, as well as the back of Toyota Motor's new Tokyo branch office. In the middle is a miniature Horaijima, the mythical island of immortality in the East China Sea, occupied here by a flock of herons and a small temple dedicated to the Indian goddess of good fortune, Benten (this has a double allusion to Chikubu Island on Lake Biwa (see *Shinobazu Pond*). Thus, the visitor's illusory odyssey is completed and it will come as no surprise to learn that the government has solemnly declared the garden to be an "Outstanding Scenic Place of Historical Importance."

Kurita Museum

2-17-9, Nihonbashi Hama-cho, Chuo-ku ☎666-6246. Map 11G12 ■ ✍ Open 10am-5pm. Closed Jan 1-3. Subway: Ningyocho.

Ceramics are capable of inspiring intense emotions among devotees, and collector Hideo Kurita is no exception. His distinctive maroon-brick modern tower on Ningyocho's Amazake Street, which houses part of his priceless collection, is for him a, "castle constructed with my love, attachment and burning passion." Kurita's specialties are the gorgeous overglaze-enameled **Imari**, **Nabeshima** and **Kakiemon-de** porcelain wares produced in the Edo period. Most of the collection is housed in a separate museum in the city of Ashikaga (in Tottori prefecture in western Japan), but the Tokyo branch has high standards of display for its choice treasures, with its opulent, boardroom-style rooms. An expensive catalog (eccentrically covered with a photograph of the building's maroon-tile brick) has good-quality color reproductions with ecstatic comments from Kurita.

Meiji Shrine and Inner Garden ★

1-1, Kamizono-cho, Shibuya-ku ☎379-5511. Map 6H3 ◙ ▩ for Iris Garden ⇌ ▣ ◣ ◁ Shrine and Inner Garden open sunrise-sunset; Iris Garden open Mar 1-Nov 3 9am-4.30pm, rest of year 9am-4pm. JR: Harajuku, Yoyogi; subway: Meijijingumae.

The Emperor Meiji's reign from 1867-1912 coincided with Japan's most tumultuous changes. The threat of domination by Western imperialist powers, symbolized by the intrusion of US Commodore Matthew Perry's "Black Ships" into Edo Bay in 1853, sparked a nationalist revolution that finally led to the collapse of the Tokugawa shogunate (who had held real power in Japan for more than 2½ centuries). One year after ascending the throne in Kyoto, Emperor Meiji relocated to Edo, following the defeat of Tokugawa diehards at the battle of Ueno Hill, and renamed the city Tokyo (Eastern Capital). By this act, but also through rejecting traditional court etiquette in favor of Western models, promulgating Japan's first constitution, opening its first parliament and a host of other measures, Meiji symbolized the opening of Japan, as it sought frantically to catch up with the West.

Meiji was buried in Fushimi, s of Kyoto, but in 1920 a shrine was constructed here, in memory both of him and of his consort, the Empress Shoken (died 1914). Until Japan's defeat in 1945, the Meiji Shrine was run by the State and, like the *Yasukuni Shrine*, was used by the military to foster a cult of national imperialism. Now stripped of these nefarious associations, it can be appreciated as one of the most magical and beautiful spots in Tokyo. Tranquil and cool even in summer, its dense forest, glinting brooks and ponds seem to radiate ethereal calm, soothing the visitor in the frenzied midst of the great city.

The shrine is meant to be approached by the wide avenue of Omotesando (Outer Approach Road) and across the shrine bridge just s of Harajuku Station. Pass under the front *torii* arch, made of *hinoki* (Japanese cypress), and follow the wide gravel walk toward the shrine, passing on your left a small, fenced-off fir tree that is an offshoot of the ancient "Tree of Ages" that lent its name to the Yoyogi district, in which the shrine stands (its parent tree was destroyed when a US B-29 fell on it during World War II). Walk farther down, turn left through another wooden *torii* (one of the largest in Japan), and on the left side of the path is the main entrance to the shrine's **Iris Garden**. This part of the shrine was formerly an imperial garden, frequented by Emperor Meiji and his consort for its famous irises (of which there are over 100 varieties), as well as its water lilies in the nearby South Pond (both of these are in bloom June-July).

The shrine itself, with its large courtyard surrounded by simple wooden gates, a hall and long cloister, appears after another bend in the path. Suspended from the eaves are square lanterns bearing the imperial chrysanthemum crest. The front eaves of the Honden inner sanctuary's copper-tiled roof flows outward to provide shelter to the worshipers — a type of Shinto shrine architecture called *nagare* (flowing) that originated in the 8thC. It may seem incredible, but the dignified simplicity and timeless beauty of the scene in front of you dates from reconstruction finished in 1958, after the shrine buildings were destroyed in a 1945 air raid.

At any time of the year Meiji Shrine is liable to be crowded with pilgrims and sightseers, but on four occasions during the year, the shrine is especially crowded. The shrine is the most popular in Tokyo for *hatsumode* (first visit) during the New Year festival (*Jan 1-3*), attracting millions of visitors. On New Year's Eve trains run throughout the night and a platform of Harajuku JR Station facing Meiji Shrine (normally closed) is opened to accommodate the rush. On the National Holiday for Constitution Memorial Day (*May 3*) there are performances of *bugaku* ancient court music and dancing, on a stage in front of the sanctuary. The same festivities can be seen on the first day of the Meiji Shrine Autumn Festival (*Nov 1*), culminating with Emperor Meiji's birthday (*Nov 3*). The shrine is also packed with children decked out in their best clothes for the Shichigosan (7-5-3) Festival (see *Calendar of events* in *Planning*).

After visiting the shrine itself, most visitors double back to the s entrance by Harajuku, but the best part of the magnificent 72ha (178-acre) grounds of the Inner Garden lies behind the shrine buildings near the interesting *Meiji Treasure Museum* and ought not to be be missed (see also *Meiji Shrine Outer Garden*).

Meiji Shrine Outer Garden *(Meiji Olympic Park)*

Kasumigaoka, Shinjuku-ku ☎401-0312. Map 7H5 ▣ ▨ for Meiji Picture Gallery ▤ ▣ ➤ Open 24hrs. Meiji Memorial Picture Gallery open 9am-4.30pm; closed Dec 31. JR: Sendagaya and Shinanomachi.

The funeral ceremony of Emperor Meiji took place here in 1912, but not until 1925, following 10yrs' work, were the grounds completely laid. This 47ha (116-acre) recreation area was one of the three major venues of the 1964 Olympics (together with **Yoyogi Sports Center** and **Komazawa Olympic Park**) and now contains the large **National Stadium**, a gymnasium, indoor swimming pool, rugby ground, concert hall and two baseball stadia. The bombastic **Meiji Memorial Gallery**, built near the site of the 1912 funeral ceremony, contains approximately 80 hagiographic paintings depicting events in the life of Emperor Meiji. On its w side is the **Meiji Memorial Hall**, where elder statesmen discussed the first constitution of Japan, drafted by Prince Hirobumi Ito in the presence of Emperor Meiji. The hall is now rented out for weddings and other functions.

Meiji Shrine Treasure Museum ★

1-1, Kamizono-cho, Yoyogi, Shibuya-ku ☎379-5511. Map 6H3 ▨ ▧ ▤ ◁ Open 9am-4pm. Closed 3rd Fri in every mth. JR: Yoyogi, Harajuku; subway: Meijingumae.

This museum, housing the memorabilia of Emperor Meiji and Empress Shoken, stands largely forgotten in a lush meadow, 10mins' walk through a brooding forest from the *Meiji Shrine* and its hordes of visitors, who usually double back and return straight to Harajuku. Built in 1921, the museum was one of the first concrete buildings in Japan, and was created in the style of the 8thC Shosoin reliquary hall of Emperor Shomu in Nara. The gloomy, wood-paneled interior houses some of the royal couple's kimonos, books and furniture (including an unusually comprehensive set of the Emperor's shaving brushes). There are also contemporary *ukiyo-e* prints, portraits and photographs (the long-chinned, egg-faced Empress was certainly no beauty). One of the high points is the imperial carriage, used by the Emperor for the promulgation of Japan's first constitution.

Meiji University Museums
Meiji Daigaku Kaikan, 1-1, Surugadai, Kanda, Chiyoda-ku. Map 14E9 ▣ ໕ ໖ except with prior permission ⊟ ▣ Opening hours various and complex (☎relevant museum for details). JR: Ochanomizu; subway: Shinochanomizu.
This large, modern university building, distinctively finished in pink stone, houses three museums. The **Archeological Museum** (*4th floor* ☎*296-4432*) has a representative display from the collection of more than 10,000 ancient artifacts excavated and restored by Meiji University's Archeological Institute. Pride of place is given to some stone tools from the preceramic-age (40,000-10,000BC) site at Iwajuku, in Gunma prefecture; when excavated in 1949 they were the earliest traces known of human culture in the Japanese archipelago. Most spectacular are the large *haniwa* terra-cotta cylinders and figurines from the earliest *kofun* (tumuli or burial mounds built between AD200-550) in the Kanto plain around Tokyo. The displays are generally excellent, with maps and photographs of Japanese archeological sites, and, usefully, labels are provided in both English and Japanese.

The **Commodities Museum** on the 3rd floor (☎*296-4433*), is run by the university's Commercial Science Department. Traditional industrial crafts from every region in Japan, as well as a few choice examples from Europe, are displayed here.

The 4th floor **Criminal Museum** (☎*296-4431*) was primarily designed for the serious academic study of historical Japanese legal documents, but the main attraction is its gruesome collection of antique instruments for the arrest, torture and punishment of criminals. Labels are only in Japanese, but exhibits such as a guillotine, manacles, crucifix and an iron coffin lined with sharp spikes need little explanation.

National Diet Building
1-7-1, Nagata-cho, Chiyoda-ku ☎581-5111. Map 8H8 ▣ ໕ ໖ ⅄ Open 8am-5pm (last entry 4pm). House of Councillors (Upper House) closed Sat pm, Sun. Opening hrs also dependent on current Diet business. All visits by foreign visitors must be prearranged through their own embassies in Tokyo. Subway: Kokkaigijidomae.
Japan has a century-old tradition of constitutional government, although Western-style parliamentary democracy is a more novel experience handed down by the postwar US Occupation. Japan's first constitution was established in 1889 (21yrs after the downfall of the shogunate) and made the Cabinet and Army and Navy ministers responsible solely to the emperor, and only 450,000 of the population of 40 million were allowed to vote for the largely powerless Imperial Diet. Universal adult male suffrage was only established in 1925, and it was not until after Japan's defeat in 1945 that women were given the vote. The US-drafted new constitution of 1946 finally relegated the emperor to a mere symbol of state, and granted the Diet, or Parliament, sole law-making power.

The National Diet Building, one suspects, partly owes its dungeon-like solidity to a conscious bid for permanence. Two of its three wooden-built predecessors in Uchisaiwaicho, opposite the Hibiya Public Hall, burned down with alarming alacrity. The building of its current, massive edifice was begun in 1920 during a brief flowering of party government, but by the time it was finished in 1936 Japan had already been hijacked by the military. Before it had even opened, the Diet was occupied for three days by army mutineers during a failed coup d'état.

Proceedings inside the **House of Representatives** tend to be very sedate, as may be appreciated from live Japanese TV coverage, which sometimes manages to capture a cabinet minister dozing during a debate.

National Museum of Modern Art

3, Kitanomaru Koen, Chiyoda-ku ☎214-2561. Map 9F-G9 ☒ inc. admission to Crafts Gallery. Extra fee for special exhibitions ☒ 🖾 ➡ ◄ Open Tues-Thurs, Sat-Sun 10am-4.30pm, Fri 10am-7.30pm. Closed Mon, Dec 27-Jan 5. Subway: Takebashi.

Frequent exhibitions of Japanese and Western modern art and design, from paintings of Picasso and Bacon to post-modern architecture and the Taisho-era school of realism, are held on the first two floors of this modern museum in Kitanomaru Park. The permanent exhibition on the 3rd and 4th floors is rotated from over 3,000 works of mainly post-Meiji Japanese works of art in the museum's collection, including such famous 20thC Japanese painters as Tsuguharu Fujita and Taikan Yokoyama; the collection anomalously includes a few Western works by artists such as Henri "Le Douanier" Rousseau. The collection strikingly shows how closely post-Meiji Japanese artists followed the mainstreams of European art, and the tensions caused by attempting to accommodate it within the Japanese tradition. There are some paintings that illustrate how many artists were swept away by the tide of militarism in the 1930s and 40s, even those of Fujita's stature (for example, he painted the awful *Battle of Haluha riverside, Nomonhan*).

Just 5mins' walk away is the *Crafts Gallery*, which is an annex of the museum.

National Museum of Western Art

7-7, Ueno-koen, Taito-ku ☎822-0111. Map 15C11 ☒ ᠔ ➡ Open 9am-4.30pm (last entry 4pm). Closed Mon, Dec 29-Jan 5. JR: Ueno (Ueno-koen exit).

Although the museum has recently broadened its collection through purchases and donations, the claim to represent "Western Art" remains overly ambitious; "Rodin sculpture and French Impressionist painting" would be a more accurate description. Although the Japanese are perhaps the world's greatest admirers of both Rodin and French Impressionism, their predominance in the museum is largely due to the tastes of the late shipping magnate Kojiro Matsutaka. The bulk of his collection was finally returned to Japan after World War II, having been sequestered by the French government.

The museum has 56 sculptures by Rodin, the third largest collection in the world. Seven are displayed outside in the front courtyard, including the *Gates of Hell* (with engraved dedication to Matsukata, who paid for the casting), *The Thinker* and *The Burghers of Calais*. Here they unsuccessfully vie for attention with the clashing modern concrete architecture created by Le Corbusier, who was responsible for the undistinguished main museum building. The rest of the Rodin collection, plus a few pieces by Bourdelle, is crammed into a small space flanked by stairs immediately behind the entrance.

The focal points of the paintings, on the floor above, are 19thC French works by Monet, Gauguin and Courbet, who are particularly well represented. In Kunio Maekawa's new wing (which often hosts special exhibitions, usually charging an inflated entrance fee) the emphasis has been placed on starting to fill out gaps in the history of European art with paintings by masters such as Rubens, Goya, Murillo, El Greco and Tintoretto, prints and drawings by artists such as Dürer, Rembrandt and Delacroix, and more modern works by Picasso, Miró, Pollock and Arp.

National Science Museum ★

7-20, Ueno-koen, Taito-ku ☎822-0111. Map 15C11 ◫ & ☜ only with flash ☕ ✸ Open Tues-Sun 9am-4.30pm (last entry 4pm). Closed Mon, Dec 28-Jan 4. JR: Ueno (Ueno-koen exit).

The five halls of this huge complex have everything from dinosaur bones to computers and space rockets. Although more orthodox in its approach than the Science Foundation's *Science and Technology Museum* in Kitanomaru Park, this state museum nevertheless combines instruction with "hands-on" experiments for children, and has a number of items to interest adults. One irritating drawback is that labels and explanations in English are often perfunctory, or sometimes nonexistent. However, there is a well-illustrated and detailed guide written in English, available at the museum shop in the basement (near the entrance).

The old-fashioned main hall, which appears aircraft-shaped when seen from above, contains fossils, dinosaur bones, models and some worthy explanations of Darwinian evolution on the 1st and 2nd floors. It is worth visiting the 3rd floor, where in the section on astronomy there are some gorgeous antique Japanese telescopes. Proceeding to the **Natural History Building** you will find, on the 5th floor, an interesting section on the "Origin and Development of the Japanese People," with explanations in English thoughtfully provided, and also the mummified heads of three nobles of the Fujiwara family. The **Science and Technology Building** has excellent scale models and explanations (some in English) of traditional Japanese architecture, as well as ancient and modern techniques for making pottery, porcelain, glass, metals, textiles, salt, Japanese paper (*washi*) and lacquer (*urushi*).

The star attractions of the **Air and Space Building** are authentic airplanes (on the 1st floor), including a famous World War II Zero fighter retrieved from the sea near New Guinea in 1972, and the oldest existing airplane made in Japan, a Maurice-Farman biplane, and a rocket and launcher tower over the building from the courtyard outside.

The **Science and Engineering Building** opposite is worth a visit to see the rare antiques in its collection. On the 2nd floor there is a calculating machine made in 1642 by French philosopher/mathematician Blaise Pascal, and on the 3rd floor, a magnificent collection of elaborate Edo-period (1615-1868) Japanese clocks, which measure time by the ancient and complicated Japanese system of "temporal hours" (see explanation for the *Daimyo Clock Museum* in the nearby district of Yanaka). The 1st floor and courtyard outside are a "Look, Think, Try" area, which can be fun for children of primary-school age.

Nature Study Garden ★

5-21-5, Shiroganedai, Minato-ku ☎441-7176. Map 3M5 ◫ ☜ 兼 ✸ ◁€ Open Sept-Apr 9am-4.30pm (last entry 3pm), May-Aug 9am-5pm (last entry 4pm). Closed Mon, Dec 28-Jan 4, day after public hol. JR: Meguro (E exit).

This 200ha (494-acre), carefully nurtured, primeval wilderness is like a green lung in the heart of the city. "The Garden of the Institute for Nature Study of the National Science Museum" (to give it its proper title) has a more serious purpose, however. It is the only place in Tokyo to have preserved original features and vegetation of the Musashino plain. The garden is perfect for aimless wanderings along the meandering gravel paths, but instead of lawns, herbaceous borders or picturesque bridges visitors are met by swamps, stagnant ponds, ancient trees and unregimented wild flowers. In medieval times the Shirogane Choka clan had a manor here, fortified with earthworks that are still visible today. In 1664 it became a residence of the powerful Takamatsu Matsudaira family, and then suffered the indignity of being used as a gunpowder store for both the Army and Navy from 1872 until it was handed over to the Imperial Household in 1918. A palace was then erected on three corner acres (now the directly adjacent *Tokyo Metropolitan Teien Art Museum*). The rest was left untouched, and became a public park in 1949, until it was presented to the *National Science Museum* in 1962 as a living showcase of natural history.

Nezu Art Museum ★

6-5-36, Minami Aoyama, Minato-ku ☎400-2536. Map 3J5 📧 📨 📨 *Open 9.30am-4.30pm. Closed Mon, day after public hol, year end and New Year. Subway: Omotesando.*

The Nezu is one of Tokyo's premier private museums, with over 7,000 Oriental antiquities, including many masterpieces, but it suffers from having only one gallery for display, inside a poorly lit 1955 reinforced concrete warehouse-like structure. Although one may occasionally squint at the surroundings, the superb quality of the collection donated by the founder of Tobu Railways, the late Kaichiro Nezu, is worth the discomfort. The collection includes two of Japan's most famous paintings: the 13thC *Nachi Waterfall* based on the concept of *suijaku* (the unity of Shinto and Buddhism), and a masterpiece by Korin Ogata (1658-1716) in the form of a pair of six-fold screens with irises stenciled on gold. Chinese paintings from the Southern Sung period (1127-1280) include Ma Lin's *Setting Sun* and Mu Qi's *Evening Glow over the Fishing Village* and *Bamboo and Sparrows*. One part of the main hall is devoted to a permanent display of Chinese bronzes from the (Shang second millennium BC) and Chou (1027-256BC) dynasties as well as ceramics and Buddhist images.

Apart from a distinguished collection of Japanese tea-ceremony ware, including a group of Korean Yi-dynasty (1392-1910) bowls, the Nezu boasts several pieces of pottery made by Kenzan Ogata (1663-1743) and painted by his elder brother Korin (1658-1716),and the artist Soshin (1683-1755). Rare embroidered textiles of the Asuka period, Nara brocades and Edo-period costumes add a fascinating dimension. Somewhere in the copious storeroom there is also an unusual collection of elaborate Ch'ing-dynasty (1644-1912) Chinese clocks, which may eventually surface for exhibition.

After the rigors of the gallery, a walk in the Nezu Museum's beautiful garden (*free admission*) is the perfect cure, where teahouses, stone lanterns and a stupa seem to grow out of the leafy vegetation.

Nezu Shrine ★

1-28-9, Nezu, Bunkyo-ku ☎821-4817. Map 14C9 🔲 📨 📨 *Shrine open 5.30am-6pm, precincts open 24hrs. Subways: Nezu and Sendagi.*

The Nezu Shrine is similar in style and construction to Ueno's *Toshogu Shrine*, and is certainly of equal importance and beauty. It was completed in 1706 for the Lord of Kofu, who had a mansion slightly N of the shrine in Sendagi, and was the appointed successor as shogun to his uncle, Tsunayoshi. On Tsunayoshi's death in 1709, the Lord of Kofu, Ienobu, became the 6th shogun, and his new tutelary shrine was fittingly magnificent. After being damaged in World War II, original plans and materials were used to rebuild the shrine. The main gate, forecourt lanterns and fence, shrine hall and courtyard gate are all as originally seen in 1706.

During the Edo period, Nezu belonged equally to both Shinto and Buddhist priests, but the Buddhist influence was pervasive. The main 2-story gate with its two protective deities is reminiscent of the Kaminarimon "Thunder Gate" of *Asakusa Kannon Temple*; and the forecourt lanterns and eaves of the courtyard front gate and prayer hall are all decorated with swastika religious symbols. The red-lacquer front courtyard gate is known as the Karamon, or Chinese Gate (see also Toshogu Shrine), and has richly decorated joists in gilt, green, black, orange and blue. The ends of the horizontal beams supporting the prayer hall's porch roof are fantastic Chinese-inspired carvings of tapirs and lions. Look at the brackets behind, and their gorgeously colored carvings of chrysanthemums and peonies. As visitors are blocked from walking around the outside they miss a similar effusion of color and fantasy that could otherwise be viewed on the wall of the rear sanctuary hall.

Nogi's House

8-11-32, Akasaka, Minato-ku ☎402-4151. Map 7/6 ◘ ⚑ Open 9am-4pm. Closed Dec 29-Jan 3. Subway: Nogizaka.

It is a rare honor indeed to have one's name linked both to a shrine and a district of Tokyo, but General Maresuke Nogi's (1849-1912) services to Japan were regarded as exceptional. Nogi participated in all the wars during Emperor Meiji's reign, and distinguished himself by twice capturing Port Arthur — during the war against China in 1894-95 and the war against Russia in 1904-5. (The latter "victory" led to the death of 20,000 Japanese troops, including two of Nogi's own sons.) Later, Nogi was appointed headmaster of the old "Peers" School, an elite institution for the former nobility. In 1908 Nogi received young Prince Hirohito into his care, and for 4yrs he endeavoured to tutor the future emperor in the virtues of *Bushido*, or way of the samurai.

After narrowly escaping ignominious defeat at the bloody 1905 siege of Port Arthur, Nogi reportedly asked Emperor Meiji for permission to commit ritual suicide, but was told, "Not when I am alive." On the day of Emperor Meiji's state funeral in Tokyo, the vow was fulfilled in front of an autographed picture of the late Emperor. On this fateful day, Nogi's wife first slit her own throat with a dagger, followed by her husband who committed *seppuku* (ritual disembowelment).

In the grounds of his house there is now a **shrine** to Nogi (another shrine and a mausoleum are to be found in Kyoto — see *Excursions*), and the surrounding area is called Nogizaka, meaning Nogi Slope. The shrine itself need not detain you, but the modest clapboard house where this bizarre suicide pact was performed is of macabre interest. Visitors are allowed to proceed along an elevated walkway that surrounds part of the house, although little can be seen through the dusty windows apart from a few old pictures and photographs. In the courtyard to the left of the entrance gate are the stables where Nogi kept the white horse given to him by Stoessel, the Russian general he defeated at Port Arthur.

On the second Sun of every month a flea market is held in front of the shrine, next to exit 1 of Nogizaka Subway Station.

Okura Museum

2-10-3, Toranomon, Minato-ku ☎583-0781. Map 5J8 ■ &
*☎☰ 里 ⌒ Open 10am-4pm (last entry 3.45pm). Closed
Mon, year end, New Year and while changing displays.
Subways: Kamiyacho, Toranomon.*

It is strange how few purposeful businessmen and well-heeled
guests ever notice this "Chinoiserie" folly, with its sweeping
gabled roof, pillars, verandas and large guardian bronzes,
marooned esthetically and physically in one corner of the **Okura**
hotel's large front courtyard (see *Hotels*). The original museum on
this site was the first private museum in Japan, opened in 1917 to
house the prodigious collection of the late industrial magnate
Kihachiro Okura, founder of the **Imperial** (see *Hotels*). His late
son Kishichiro subsequently started the Okura hotel. Six years
after it opened, the building and many items of the collection were
destroyed in the Great Kanto Earthquake. The present 1928
gallery is the work of Chuta Ito, who also designed the curious
Indian-style Tsukiji Honganji Temple.

The current highly eclectic collection of Japanese and Chinese
paintings, bronzes, calligraphy, ceramics, masks, swords, lacquer,
costumes and books, as well as the occasional Korean and Indian
work, is rotated for exhibition about three times a year.
Sculptures, however, are always on display in the darkish 1st-story
room; old-fashioned lighting sometimes makes viewing difficult,
but the venerable attendants are usually willing to lend you a
flashlight.

Paintings are generally upstairs, in marginally better display
conditions. The collection includes the beautifully composed and
richly decorated pair of screens, called *Floating Fans*, attributed to
Sotatsu; a unique 12thC Fujiwara wooden sculpture of a Buddhist
deity (designated a "National Treasure") in the lotus position, on
top of an elephant (carved from the artist's imagination — the
animal looks more like a bull); and an Edo-period hexagonal plate
by the famous potter and painter Kenzan Ogata and decorated by
his illustrious brother, the artist Korin Ogata. There are, in
addition, a superb Kamakura-era (1185-1333) lacquered *tebako*
(cosmetics) box and some exquisite Edo *Noh* theatrical costumes
on display.

The front veranda and small back garden sport a quixotic variety
of mostly Buddhist statuary.

Ota Memorial Museum of Art ★

1-10-10, Jingumae, Shibuya-ku ☎403-0880. Map 6I4 ■ ☎
*里 ◁€ Open 10.30am-5.30pm (last entry 5pm). Closed Mon,
every month from 25-end, Dec 1-Jan 3. JR: Harajuku;
subway: Meijijingumae.*

Tucked away on a side street behind Harajuku's **La Foret**
boutique building (see *Shopping*), with its blaring pop music and
fashion-conscious young clientele, stands this oasis of quiet and
good taste, its *shibui* modern Japanese exterior beckoning, to
soothe the excited nerves. The purpose of the museum is to show
part of the staggering bequest of 12,000 *ukiyo-e* prints collected by
the late Seizo Ota, former chairman of the Toho Mutual Life
Insurance Co. Although the small size of the gallery limits the
number of prints that can be shown at one time (they have to be
shown in rotation), the standards of display and lighting are
excellent, and the prints themselves are meticulously kept in prime
condition.

In the basement there is a restful, elegant coffee/tea shop serving
traditional Japanese desserts.

Parliamentary Museum and Gardens

1-1-1, Nagata-cho, Chiyoda-ku ☎581-1651. Map 8/8 🔲 ⬤ ⟲
📷 ⬤ ◁ Parliamentary Museum open Tues-Sat 9.30am-
4.30pm (last entry 3.30pm). Closed Sun, Mon, Dec 27-Jan 3,
last day of each mth. Gardens open 9am-5pm. Closed Dec
27-Jan 3. Subways: Kokkaigijidomae and Nagatacho.

Situated opposite the *National Diet Building*, this 1970 museum
stands inside a small garden, where an Edo *daimyo* residence once
stood, and which later became the headquarters of the US Chief of
Staff. The 1st floor chronicles the history of constitutional
government in Japan, with working models of the Lower House of
the Diet and the British Parliament (with most exhibits labeled in
English); special exhibitions are held on the 2nd floor. The
museum entrance forms part of an earlier (1960) memorial hall to
the late Yukio Ozaki (1858-1954), who holds a world record for
having been member of the House of Representatives from its
opening in 1890 almost until his death.

Beside the museum and the Ozaki Hall is a small Western-style
garden that contains an 1891 folly in the style of a miniature
Roman temple, designed by British architect Josiah Conder and
his pupils; nearby is a stone from where all altitudes in Japan are
measured. There is also a s garden, across the road, designed in
Japanese style.

Riccar Art Museum

6-2-3, Ginza, Chuo-ku ☎571-3254. Map 9/9 🔳 🔳 Open
11am-5.30pm. Closed Mon, year end, New Year. JR:
Yurakucho.

A large collection of over 5,000 *ukiyo-e* woodblock prints, some of
them by famous masters, are rotated for viewing in a cramped
gallery on top of the Riccar company building. To see *ukiyo-e* in
more attractive surroundings, visit the *Ota Memorial Museum
of Art* in the Harajuku district.

Rikugien Garden★

6-16-3, Hon Komagome, Bunkyo-ku ☎941-2222. Map 13A8
🔲 ⬤ 📷 ◁ Open 9am-4.30pm (last entry 4pm). Closed Mon,
Dec 29-Jan 3. JR: Komagome.

One of Tokyo's most beautiful and historical gardens, Rikugien
was laid at the beginning of the 18thC by Lord Yoshiyasu
Yanagisawa (1658-1714), chamberlain to the 5th Tokugawa
shogun, Tsunayoshi. Both the shogun (who was believed to have
been a frequent visitor to the garden) and his chamberlain shared a
taste for literature and poetry, and Rikugien derives its name from
the Rikugi (Six Definitions) of classical Chinese poetry. Each of
the garden's many scenic spots bears some literary connection, and
is accompanied by an explanatory noticeboard (but only in
Japanese). This garden is in the same walk-around style (with
artificial hill and fountain) as that of the **New Otani** (see *Hotels*).
The chief delight of this 8.6ha (21-acre) garden lies not in its
literary associations but in its carefully contrived beauty. The
Rikugien was subsequently bought by Baron Yataro Iwasaki,
founder of the huge Mitsubishi conglomerate, who in 1934
donated it to the city.

Roppongi

Map 4.

The name Roppongi, meaning Six Trees, was once the area where
six feudal lords with arboreal names such as Takagi (tall trees) and
Ichiryu (one willow) had their mansions. Later it became a

barracks and training area for the Imperial Army. After World War II the Occupation forces took it over. The US Army influence, and the proximity of many foreign embassies, are probably the main reason for Roppongi's famous international flavor. The pink-and-white-striped **Almond** coffee shop, for example, one of Tokyo's most congested meeting places on the Roppongi Crossing, dates back to the immediate postwar influence of the GI.

Roppongi by day is dull and drab, its skeletal daytime population composed of red-eyed night owls, storekeepers, commercial artists and fashion designers (Issey Miyake, among others, has a studio a short walk down the hill from the Almond). Apart from lunching at one of its fine restaurants, Roppongi's biggest daytime attractions are the futuristic **Axis** and **Wave** buildings, the latter being Japan's largest audiovisual store, with an art movie theater in the basement.

Roppongi is transformed by the first neon flare at dusk. On weekends the subway station disgorges multitudes of extravagantly dressed youngsters on their way to pubs, clubs and discos — or for those less well-off, merely a peacock parade down Roppongi's main street. The activity and bright lights are concentrated in a strip demarcated to the N by the Defense Agency's headquarters (a survivor from Roppongi's military past), and, heading toward *Tokyo Tower* to the s, by the Soviet Embassy (where police often cordon off the street to cars, to prevent Japanese Rightist loudspeaker trucks from getting too near).

Lately the Roppongi "in crowd," have been moving away from the area, complaining that out-of-towners have been invading their territory. They now frequent new discos, restaurants and clubs in Harajuku and most recently in the old warehouse district of Shibaura (copied from New York and London). As Tokyo's mainstream nightlife capital, however, Roppongi will continue to defy its critics.

Science and Technology Museum

2-1, Kitanomaru Koen, Chiyoda-ku ☎212-8471. *Map 8F8* ⬛
⬧ *with prior notice* 🎟 ⇄ ⚊ *Open 9.30am-4pm. Closed Dec 29-Jan 3. Subway: Takebashi.*

Not surprisingly, children account for most of the 800,000 visitors per year to the Japan Science Foundation's museum in Kitanomaru Park, but there is also a lot here to interest the more inquisitive adult. The avowedly educational content (much of it in Japanese) of the "theme rooms" — ranging from space and nuclear energy to earthquakes and agriculture — is lightened with lifesize satellites, computers and functioning robots, as well as video shows and a 360° "image show." A computer-controlled "Edison robot," which narrates the history of electricity, is one of the children's favorites.

Seiji Togo Art Museum

42nd floor, Yasuda Kasai Building, 1-26-1, Nishi-Shinjuku, Shinjuku-ku ☎349-3081. *Map 6F3* ⬛ ⬧ 🎟 ⚊ ◁€ *Open 9.30am-4.30pm (last entry 4pm). Closed Sat, Sun, Dec 27-Jan 4, hols and while changing exhibitions. JR (w exit), subway: Shinjuku.*

One of Vincent van Gogh's famed series of *Sunflowers* may normally be seen here, in the supremely alien setting of the Yasuda Fire and Marine Insurance company's art gallery. The company rocketed to international prominence in 1987 for paying a record $40 million (£24.75 million) for the painting at Christie's in

London. Apart from *Sunflowers*, two recently acquired Renoirs and a sculpture by Rodin, the gallery offers little else to interest the visitor. The late Japanese painter Seiji Togo, whose donations form the core of the exhibits, was sponsored as a student by the company. His later work, characterized by technically accomplished, commercial kitsch was used for corporate advertising, belying the promise of his earlier Fauvist period. The work of other Japanese painters, also patronized by Yasuda, are similarly uninspiring. However, the gallery does boast superb panoramic views of the city.

Sengakuji Temple★

2-11-1, Takanawa, Minato-ku ☎441-5560. Map *4M7* 🔲 🔲 *for museum only. Cemetery open Oct-Apr 7am-6pm, May-Sept 7am-5pm; museum 9am-4.30pm. Subway: Sengakuji.*
The 47 samurai buried in this temple's cemetery are the subject of one of the most famous stories in Japan, a standard feature in the repertoire of *kabuki* theater. The samurai served Lord Naganori Asano, *daimyo* of Ako Castle on the present w border of Hyogo prefecture. In Apr 1701 at Edo Castle Asano became involved in a fight in which he slightly wounded Lord Yoshinaka Kira, who was responsible for shogunal protocol; Asano believed Kira had deliberately kept him ignorant of the finer points of etiquette. The act of drawing a sword in the shogunal castle was a serious offense, and Asano was immediately deprived of his domain and ordered to commit *seppuku* (ritual suicide by disembowelment); he was buried in his family temple, here at Sengakuji. (Kira was not even reprimanded, although he later lost his office.) After Asano's death his samurai retainers were reduced to *ronin* (literally, "wave men," tossed by the waves of fortune), but they vowed to avenge their master's death. In 1703 the 47 *ronin* attacked and killed Kira at his Edo residence on the E bank of the Sumida River, and brought his severed head to Sengakuji to present to their master's grave. Having surrendered to the authorities, they were allowed the honor of also committing *seppuku* in atonement for their crimes, and buried next to their lord.

On the right, after the temple entrance, is a statue of Yoshio Oishi, leader of the *ronin* and Asano's chief retainer. Pass through the venerable-looking main gate (1836), and turn left to get to the **cemetery**. On the right-hand side on the way up you will see the well where the retainers washed the severed head of Lord Kira before presenting it to their master's grave.

The gate you will pass through was once the rear entrance to the Asano residence in Edo. The first grave on the right is that of Asano's wife, and slightly beyond this is the grave of Lord Asano himself. At the top of a small flight of steps are the tombs of the 47 *ronin*, forever enveloped in a haze of incense, and blackened by its smoke, from the countless Japanese who have come here to pay tribute to the unswerving loyalty of the feudal vassals. The gravestone of the youngest, 15yr-old Yoshikane Oishi, is in the far left-hand corner; that of his father Yoshio Oishi, the chief retainer to Asano and leader of the vendetta, is in the far right-hand corner.

On the right-hand side of the front courtyard of the temple is an old reliquary **museum** of the 47 *ronin* (*purchase a ticket at the small office in front of the museum*). An air of neglect hangs over the musty glass cases containing paintings, rows of cracked wooden images of the *ronin*, their faded and moth-eaten samurai costumes, and various paraphernalia such as personal teacups. Regrettably none of the labels are in English.

Shinjuku
Map 6.

Shinjuku means new lodgings, and despite the fact that it is now 200yrs old the name still fits. Shinjuku remains the most raffish area in Tokyo — it is a frontier boom town full of unbridled energy and brash self-confidence.

Once merely a "post town" catering to the physical and sensual needs of travelers, situated on a minor highway running w of Tokyo, Shinjuku's explosive growth began here in 1885 with the building of a railroad station. Now Shinjuku Station is the busiest in the world, handling more than 1.3 million commuters each day.

The w side of the JR rail line used to be a city water reservoir until the first skyscraper, the **Keio Plaza** (see *Hotels*), was built in 1971. Known as "Skyscraper City" for its forest of sleek, modern hotel and office buildings and its Manhattan-style skyline, Nishi (West) Shinjuku's foreign and artificial appearance makes many Japanese feel ill at ease. Attitudes may change, however, after the 1991 opening of Kenzo Tange's new 48-story "Gothic" City Hall (slightly w of the Keio Plaza).

As the crowds attest, the E side of the rail line is more congenial to the Japanese temperament, in its unplanned, organic mix of high-fashion stores, student hangouts, and vibrant, often seedy back streets.

The successor to this disreputable "new lodgings" tradition is Kabukicho, which is Tokyo's premier "entertainment" or red-light district. It is named after a *kabuki* theater, which in fact was never built, and there are now some 16 discos, 20 game centers, 3,000 restaurants, innumerable "soapland" massage parlors, no-panty bars and other x-rated establishments, all squeezed into Kabukicho's 300sq.m (359sq.yds). Kabukicho walks a fine line between earthy vitality and downright sleaze, and in 1985 the authorities intervened to keep the area from slipping too far into decadence. Although nearly all the sex parlors are owned or controlled by *yakuza* (gangsters), foreign visitors have little to fear by walking down its streets at night.

The area behind Kabukicho, toward Shin-Okubo JR Station, caters to couples with its "love hotels" that rent rooms by the hour; and Shinjuku 2-chome area is the largest gay-bar district in Tokyo.

Diversity is the clue to Shinjuku's success, with the baser amusement areas coexisting cheek-by-jowl with thriving shopping, fashion and culture venues. A whole literary and artistic subculture is centered around the huge **Kinokuniya** bookstore, Kinokuniya Hall (which is in the same building), and **Suehirotei**, a nearby theater for traditional *rakugo* comic monologues (only performed in Japanese). Shinjuku's mammoth department stores, camera discount stores, smart boutiques and elegant coffee shops add the greatest ballast to the low life of Kabukicho, and the **Takano** building near the station, a fruit store that has blossomed into high-fashion, offers the greatest contrast.

Shinjuku Gyoen ★
Naito-cho, Shinjuku-ku ☎350-0151. Map 6G4 🔄 ♿ ▣ 🚗 ⇜ Open 9am-4pm. Closed Mon, Dec 29-Jan 3. Subway: Shinjukugyoenmae.

In the land-starved metropolis that is Tokyo, green space of any kind is a treasured commodity. Tokyoites especially value Shinjuku Gyoen (Shinjuku Imperial Park) not only for its expanse of greenery (all 85 oxygen-replenishing hectares (210 acres) of it), but also for its varied beauty. The broad lawns to the N, with the Shinjuku skyscrapers looming over, are perfect for uninhibited lounging or play and are reminiscent of New York parks; by the N wall there is a large greenhouse containing exotic plants. To the E is a formal French garden, laid out at the turn of this century, and to the W and S the park becomes more "Japanese" with serpentine ponds, meandering paths, bridges, islands and pavilions. Shinjuku Gyoen is famous for its cherry blossoms in spring (the prime minister hosts a huge *o-hanami* party here; see *Calendar of events* in *Planning*) and for its autumnal chrysanthemums.

Shinobazu Pond and Bentendo
Map 15D10.

The Shinobazu (or Without Patience) Pond next to Ueno Hill reminded *Kan'eji Temple*'s Abbot Tenkai of Lake Biwa near Kyoto, and to complete this resemblance he built an island in the middle of the pond, with a small temple dedicated to the *biwa* (lute) played by the goddess Benten, after whom Lake Biwa is named. In 1670, a causeway to connect the island to the shore was built, and during the Edo period the embankments were lined with teahouses where lovers could watch the famous lotus plants in the pond. From 1884-93 the pond was circled by a racecourse as entertainment for the Meiji elite. During World War II the pond was turned into a paddy field and in 1945 Benten's hall was burned down in an air raid; it has since been replaced with an acceptable copy. Shinobazu Pond is now divided into three parts: the N segment belongs to *Ueno Zoo* and is used as a sanctuary for cormorants; the W is used as a boating lake; and the S retains its famous lotus lilies.

Shitamachi Museum ★
2-1, Ueno-koen, Taito-ku ☎823-7451/61. Map 15D10 ▨ ୧ ▧ on 2nd floor, allowed with prior permission on 1st floor ✱ Open Tues-Sun 9.30am-4.30pm. Closed Mon, Dec 29-Jan 3. JR: Ueno (Shinobazu exit); subway: Ueno, Ueno-Hirokoji and Yushima.

What little remained of the old Shitamachi (literally, lowtown or downtown) area, where ordinary folk of Edo lived and worked, after the twin devastations of the 1923 earthquake and the 1945 bombing, has been steadily eroded by postwar development. In the 1960s enough Tokyoites were concerned about their vanishing popular heritage to persuade the local Taito ward, in which *Ueno* and *Asakusa* are situated, to open this admirable museum on the banks of *Shinobazu Pond* to re-create typical Shitamachi scenes.

The 1st floor has a typical Meiji-era (1868-1912) merchant's house selling *hanao* cloth-straps used to fasten clogs and sandals. Worth noting is the *yojin-kago* bamboo basket suspended from the ceiling, in which families would carry away their valuables in the event of a fire (an extremely frequent occurrence due to the then largely wooden construction of Tokyo). An old-style *nagaya* back street tenement has also been reconstructed, showing the inside of a coppersmith's workshop and home, and the inside of a *dagashiya* (store selling cheap sweets). The emphasis is on realism and authenticity; details down to cooking utensils and towels are displayed. Upstairs is an old-fashioned schoolroom and a jumble of curios and nicknacks donated by residents of Taito-ku. Anything, it seems, can be exhibited here, as long as it is "old," including music hall guides, irons and toys. This is a community museum, which encourages children to clamber in and out of the houses and play with exhibits, and it is a natural favorite for Japanese schoolgroups. Foreigners are well catered to, however, with copious explanatory literature and guides in English.

Suntory Museum of Art ★

11th floor, Tokyo Suntory Building, 1-2-3, Moto Akasaka, Minato-ku ☎470-1073. Map 8H7 ▨ cheaper Sun, hols ⚐ ⚌ ▣ ⇚ Open Mon-Thurs 10am-5pm, Fri 10am-7pm. Closed Mon, Dec 22-Jan 5. Subway: Akasakamitsuke.

This is an elegant and sophisticated gallery in the center of the expensive *Akasaka* area. The gallery holds seven exhibitions a year, all well displayed, and also labeled in English. The first, from Jan-Feb, has representative pieces from the museum's own, all-Japanese, collection of more than 2,000 art objects; the other six exhibitions are combined with loan exhibits. Applied art such as lacquer, ceramics, costumes and tea kettles from the Muromachi-Edo period predominate, but there are also a number of paintings and prints. Highlights include a Kamakura 13thC gold lacquer *tebako* cosmetics box with mother-of-pearl inlay (listed as a "National Treasure"), flower screens by Korin, and scenes from *Tales of Ise* by 17thC master Sotatsu. There are excellent views from the 11th floor of the Suntory beer and whisky company building, of sights such as the *Akasaka Detached Palace* stretching towards the *Shinjuku* district, and the **Akasaka Prince** (see *Hotels*) to the *Imperial Palace*. For a small extra charge, tea and cake are available in a tea-ceremony room.

Tobacco and Salt Museum ★

1-16-8, Jinnan, Shibuya-ku ☎476-2041. Map 2J3 ▨ � ▣ ✳ Open 10am-6pm (last entry 5.30pm). Closed Mon, 2nd Tues in June, Dec 29-Jan 3. JR/subway: Shibuya.

This modern and carefully laid out museum is a unique relic of the recently dissolved state monopoly on salt and tobacco. It is unfortunate that explanatory materials are only written in Japanese; but the visual exhibits are nonetheless fascinating and really require little explanation. The exhibition on the 2nd floor traces the worldwide history of tobacco cultivation and smoking, including a comprehensive international collection of pipes and cigarette packs. The floor above is devoted to the history of tobacco in Japan, with lifesize models of Edo-period tobacco farmers, smoking implements and cigarette packs (airships were in vogue in the 1920s, but by the turn of the war these labels switched from English to Japanese and started showing fighter planes). On the 4th floor the history of salt is displayed: exhibits include pillars of rock salt and interesting scale models of Japanese salt farms. Special exhibitions are held on the top floor.

Tokyo Metropolitan Art Museum

8-36, Ueno-koen, Taito-ku ☎823-6921. Map 15C10 ▨ for special exhibitions ら ⚐ except with permission ⚌ Open 9am-5pm (last entry 4pm). Closed 3rd Mon every mth, Dec 29-Jan 3. JR: Ueno (Ueno-koen exit).

A welcome respite from the rather grim and somber regimentation of the other big *Ueno* museums, this attractive multilevel red brick building (which opened in 1975), is the work of Kunio Maekawa, who also designed the nearby **Metropolitan Festival Hall**, and the new annex of the *National Museum of Western Art*. The museum's own collection of some 2,600 modern Japanese works of art is shown twice a year in spring and autumn for 100 days each (*admission free*) in the **Museum Gallery**, which at other times charges a largish fee for viewing loan exhibitions of both contemporary Japanese and foreign art. A separate **Public Gallery** is rented out to organizations and individuals; the entrance fee for these exhibitions can also be expensive.

Tokyo Metropolitan Teien Art Museum ★

5-21-9, Shiroganedai, Minato-ku ☎*443-0201. Map 3M5* ▨
⊆ ☂ *inside museum only* ◁⊱ *Open 10am-6pm (last entry
5.30pm). Closed 2nd and 4th Wed each mth, day after public
hols, year end and New Year. JR: Meguro (ᴇ exit).*

One of the most idyllic corners of Tokyo, the chief attraction of
this recently opened (1983) art museum is not its variety of loan
exhibitions but the building's interior, and its extensive grounds.
It was formerly the palace of Emperor Hirohito's late uncle, Prince
Yasuhiko Asaka, commander-in-chief of the army during the
infamous Nanking Massacre of 1936. The interior of the 1933
main villa, designed by French architect Henri Rapin, is entirely
Art Deco, which was very popular in Europe during Prince
Asaka's stay in Paris from 1922-25. Especially noteworthy are
René Lalique's beautiful opaque glass doors in the vestibule and
the Art Deco mantelpieces and ceiling lights. Behind the villa is a
modern guesthouse for the Tokyo metropolitan government,
which is off limits, although visitors are free to wander around the
landscaped grounds, lounge on the lawn and admire the carp pond
in the Japanese garden. See also *Nature Study Garden*.

Tokyo National Museum ★

13-9, Ueno-koen, Taito-ku ☎*822-1111. Map 15C11* ▨
*admission to Horuji Treasure House included. Extra fee for
special exhibits* ☂ ⥋ ▣ ◁⊱ *Open 9am-4.30pm (last entry
4pm). Closed Mon, Dec 25-Jan 3. JR: Ueno (Ueno-koen
exit), Uguisuidani.*

The largest museum in Japan, with the most extensive collection of
Japanese art and archeology in the world and some of the finest
East Asian art, presents at first an architecturally disjointed scene.
On what was once the temple residence of the Abbot of *Kan'eji
Temple*, three separate museum wings of opposing styles and
periods compete for attention around a large courtyard.

The ornate beaux-arts style **Hyokeikan** wing to the left of the
main entrance houses Japanese archeological exhibits. It was
opened in 1909 to celebrate the marriage of the future Emperor
Taisho, and was designed by Tokuma Katayama, creator of the
similarly florid *Akasaka Detached Palace*.

Rooms 3-6 on the 2nd floor cover the Kofun period, when
powerful clan chiefs in w Japan were buried in huge tumuli
together with weapons, armor, farming implements, ornaments
and large, terra-cotta figurines called *haniwa* (rm 6). Among the
display of striking *haniwa* of humans, animals, houses and boats,
the most beautiful is generally thought to be the *Man in Keiko
Armor*, designated a "National Treasure." Turning again to the 1st
floor, rm 9 has an interesting collection of hunting and fishing
implements from the indigenous Ainu race, who once occupied
much of Honshu main island but were successively forced back by
the Yamato race into the northernmost island of Hokkaido (where
a few direct descendants now live miserably under government
"protection").

The central Honkan (Main Hall) dates back to 1938, and typifies
the heavy, monumental pan-Oriental style that was in vogue
during the militaristic 1930s (the equally grim *Dai-ichi Life
Insurance Building* in the Yurakucho area was designed by the
same architect). Its interior is gloomy, and although exhibits are
labeled in English, the only piece of explanatory material is a
turgid English-language museum guidebook. But the superb
quality of the exhibits redeem it.

The first room to the right of the main entrance is devoted to

Buddhist sculpture of astonishing beauty and craftsmanship from the Asuka, Nara and Heian periods. Next, pass through a small room of gilt bronze Buddhist statuettes to another room of sculpture, abruptly divided between some impressive works from the Kamakura period. Included in this collection is a famous carved image of the scheming warlord, Yoritomo Minamoto, who started the Kamakura shogunate; there are also modern, heavily Rodin-influenced sculptures of the Meiji and Taisho eras. A wooden statue of Erasmus, carved in Holland in 1568, is also exhibited on occasion. The statue was once the figurehead of the Dutch ship *Liefde* disabled off the Japanese coast in 1600 and piloted by Will Adams (who has become famous through the popular novel *Shogun*). Well-preserved suits of samurai armor are on display in rm 6, and a representative selection of graceful ceremonial and court costumes largely from the Edo to Taisho periods are displayed in rm 8. The last two rooms cover pottery and ceramics, arranged chronologically from the 5thC Kofun to the Edo period. They are also arranged by wares, from "rough" Sue stoneware to "polished" Imari and Nabeshima enameled porcelain, but all are of exquisite beauty.

Paintings on the 2nd floor (sometimes used for special exhibitions) begin chronologically with mainly Buddhist paintings of the Early Historic-Medieval periods (6th-16thC), such as the famous Heian-era *Fugen Bosatsu* (listed as a "National Treaure"). Also of interest is the Kamakura-period *Heiji Monogatari*, an illustrated handscroll of the Heiji Civil War (another "National Treasure"). The second, small corner room covers Muromachi-era *Kanga* or Chinese-style painting, mostly of the *suiboku* school of monochrome ink paintings, influenced by imported Sung- and Yuan-dynasty art.

Several masterpieces by Zen priest Toyo Sesshu (1420-1506), as well as Shubun and Gakuo, belong to the Muromachi collection. Bright, powerful paintings took over in the Momoyama period, as can be seen in rm 13, especially the magnificent *shohei-ga* (partition paintings) by the artists Eitoku and Tohaku, which used to decorate rich Buddhist temples and *daimyo* castles. The large Edo-era *ukiyo-e* woodblock print collection, in the next corner room (changed every month), covers every famous name from Moronobu to Sharaku, Hokusai and Hiroshige. Among the lacquerware masterpieces displayed in rms 15 and 16 are the Heian *Tebako* (cosmetic box) with mother-of-pearl inlay and the Edo *Maki-e* (gold lacquer) writing boxes by Koetsu and Korin.

To the right of the main hall is the **Toyokan** wing of antiquities from the rest of Asia. This modern (1968) split-level structure is relaxing to visit but suffers from inadequate explanations in English. After a 1st-floor introductory pot-pourri of Asian art, an Egyptian mummy and a few statues placed up the steps to the next level, there is a bewilderingly eclectic assortment of antiquities from all over w and se Asia compressed into rm 3. Chinese art, the nucleus of the collection, spreads from rms 4-8 and is of exceptional quality: Shang- (1523-1027BC) and Chou- (1027-256BC) dynasty jades and bronzes; the finest Sung-Yuan (AD960-1368) paintings, many classed as "National Treasures"; and masterpieces of ceramics, lacquerware and calligraphy. The small amount of Korean art (reflecting the unduly small acknowledgment that is accorded to Korea in Japan's artistic and cultural heritage) in rms 9-10 is of lesser interest.

Over the years the grounds of the Tokyo National Museum have become a resting place for examples of traditional Japanese architecture. To the left of the museum entrance, facing the street, is the former main gate of the Edo *yashiki* (official residence) of the Ikedas, the *daimyo* of Inaba (present-day Tottori prefecture), which moved here in 1954. Behind the Hyokeikan stands a small log house repository for Buddhist scriptures, and behind the Honkan are two resettled wooden Edo halls and three well-traveled Edo teahouses.

Horyuji Treasure House

A priceless collection of treasures are kept here, in what appears at first sight to be an ugly, concrete warehouse behind the Hyokeikan. The items in this collection, which were gifts to the Imperial Family and later given to the nation, came from Horyuji Temple in Nara (founded in the 7thC). Most of the 318 exhibits are from the 7th and 8thC and are designated "Important Cultural Properties"; 12 are "National Treasures." The windowless, institutional display settings on the upper floor are drab, but a few of the works still make a vivid impression: for example, the illustrated biographies of Prince Shotoku, who founded Horyuji (of which the first, painted in 1069, is faded and fragmented, though the second Kamakura-era painting is in much better condition). Also impressive is the large collection of grotesque masks from the now extinct *Gigaku* masked drama, a very popular art form in Nara 1,200yrs ago.

The Horyuji gallery is only open on Thurs. Even then, because of the fragile nature of the objects, it may be closed if the weather is too hot, humid, rainy or polluted. It is therefore advisable to check in advance.

Tokyo Tower

4-2-8, Shibakoen, Minato-ku ☎433-5111. Map 5J8 ▨ half price for disabled ⇄ ▣ ⚓ ⇐ ⇇ Open 9am-8pm. JR: Hamamatsucho; subway: Kamiyacho.

With the mushrooming of skyscrapers in Tokyo since the 1970s much of the novelty of Tokyo Tower's once stupendous height has been lost. It was modeled on Paris' Eiffel Tower, but at 333m (1,089ft) it is 30.5m (100ft) taller than the original. The Tokyo Tower was a huge hit when it began broadcasting to eastern Japan in 1958, and the views from the 250m-high (820ft) **crow's nest** are still breathtaking (but so is the price to reach it). The building downstairs (now a little scruffy) houses an aquarium and wax and science museums. In front of the tower is a statue dedicated to Ando Takeshi, the sculptor of that inexplicably popular monument, the Hachiko dog in front of Shibuya Station, as well as statues of two other famous Japanese dogs, who went to the South Pole.

Toshogu Shrine ★

9-88, Ueno-koen, Taito-ku ☎822-3455. Map 15C10 ⇄ ✿ inside shrine ⇐ Open 7am-5pm. JR/subway: Ueno.

This shrine was built in honor of the first shogun Ieyasu Tokugawa, whose title after deification was Sun God of the East. Despite its unpropitious location — sandwiched between the zoo and a restaurant, with a children's amusement park and food vendors outside its entrance — such jarring contemporary disregard is quickly forgotten once you begin to walk down its long tree-shaded avenue, lined with the remnants of over 200 stone lanterns (donated by *daimyo* eager to show their respect) and further fine bronze lanterns.

Toshogu, built in the early 17thC, is the only shrine in Tokyo listed as a "National Treasure," and, apart from Toshogu (the Tokugawa's mortuary shrine) at Nikko, it is the finest example of the richly carved, gorgeously colored shrine decoration favored by the Tokugawas.

A compulsory tour route, interrupted with crackly but informative broadcasts in Japanese, leads the visitor around the back of the shrine to the entrance on the far side. The **prayer hall** on the left (connected in the *gongen* style by a short corridor to the sanctuary) has doors and pillars covered in gold leaf, an elaborately carved ceiling and four paintings by Tan'yu Kano (1602-74), a famous artist of the early Edo period. The large tablet hanging between the paintings bears calligraphy by the Emperor Gomizuno-o (1596-1680).

The shrine's Chinese-style front gate, or **Karamon**, has openwork carvings of a pheasant, plum trees, pine and bamboo. The most famous parts of the gates are the *Nobori-ryu* and *Kudari-ryu* (ascending and descending dragons), said to be the work of a famous Edo sculptor Jingoro Hidari, or Jingoro "Lefty" (he was left-handed).

Transport Museum ★

1-25, Kanda Suda-cho, Chiyoda-ku ☎251-8481. Map 15E10 ▣ English tours may be arranged ▣ ☀ ➛ Open 9.30am-5pm (last entry 4.30pm). Closed Mon, Dec 29-Jan 3. JR: Akihabara, Ochanomizu, Kanda; subway: Awajicho, Kanda, Ogawamachi and Shin-Ochanomizu.

Japanese people of all ages, especially families, flock on weekends and holidays to this museum in a *déclassé* corner of Kanda district next to the railroad tracks. Little more than a dilapidated warehouse, the old (1936) building is crammed with things to see and do. Before World War II, it was solely a railroad museum, and trains are still very much to the fore, with an old steam engine and carriage incongruously parked in the forecourt, and the front ends of another steam engine and Shinkansen "bullet" train jutting out from the front wall.

The 1st floor is devoted to the history of the old Japanese National Railways (finally broken up and privatized in 1987) and is undoubtedly the most interesting exhibition. The very first train engine in Japan is displayed here. Built in 1871 by the Vulcan Foundry in Lancashire, England, it created great excitement and commotion when it ran on the new Tokyo-Yokohama line in 1872. In reality it looks remarkably like its rendering by contemporary *ukiyo-e* Japanese woodblock artists. Another early Japanese steam locomotive, together with one built in Germany (with its inner workings exposed), are housed in the main 1st-floor hall, and there are numerous "cut-away" engines and carriages, both antique and modern, which visitors are welcome to sit in or handle. Early carriages built for the Emperor Meiji in 1877 and the Emperor Taisho in 1916 are elegantly furnished in Victorian and Edwardian style, though they look impossibly tiny to the modern eye, more like toy trains. A large "panoramic" train set is invariably a crowd-puller, and many working models of trains and bridges, and real signaling equipment, which may be set in motion by visitors, offer similar enjoyment.

On the 2nd floor there is a display of model ships. Aero engines, propellers and model airplanes are displayed on the 3rd floor, with models of next-generation "magnetic levitation" trains tucked into one room. On this level too you can see, suspended from the roof of the main hall, a helicopter and a primitive biplane, which made the first flight in Japan in 1910. A cafeteria on the uppermost 4th floor can be missed. English labeling is patchy, but as most of the exhibits are self-explanatory this is hardly a problem.

Tsukiji Wholesale Fish Market
5-2, Tsukiji, Chuo-ku. Map 10J10. Subway: Tsukiji.
For 300yrs the old fish market at Nihonbashi was a major landmark and the focus of life in Edo. Although meat-eating has increased dramatically since the market was relocated here in 1935, the vast size and bustling prosperity of the Tsukiji market is testimony to the continuation of the Japanese love affair with fish. This is one of the world's largest fish markets, handling 90 percent of the fish consumed in Tokyo, and is well worth the bother of rising early to watch its lively morning auction. A huge variety of freshwater fish, long fish (e.g., swordfish), frozen fish from distant waters (mainly tuna), as well as oysters, shrimp, octopus and squid, are laid out in boxes for the wholesalers who, with notepads in hand and licenses strapped to their caps, come to inspect them. The auctions start at about 5am, with the wholesalers shouting to draw the auctioneer's attention and raising their fingers to indicate the price being bid. The best tuna, whose frozen carcasses often hail from the distant South Pacific, sell for thousands of dollars each. (Later the choicest portions will be carved into expensive slices, to be eaten raw as *sashimi* or *sushi*.) The wholesalers then transfer the fish to their own stalls within the market, and sell to restaurateurs and retailers (this lasts from approximately 7am-9am).

Ueno
Map 15C10.
For the past century, the most persistent image of Ueno district in the minds of most Tokyoites has been as a gateway to prosperity for impoverished farmers from the far N of Japan, who ever since the opening of Ueno Station in 1883 have sought work in Tokyo during the snowbound winter months. Such migratory labor has declined considerably with the general rise in living standards, but Ueno still retains a distinctly rustic and plebeian air. Apart from the seedy sex cinemas, a more interesting vestige of the past is to be found in the Ameya Yokocho shopping alley (generally known as Ameyoko) that runs along the JR railroad tracks from Ueno to Okachimachi. It started as a black market after Japan's defeat in World War II, and with more than 500 small shops and stalls, it still retains some of the same flavor.

Ueno's other associations are of a far more "elevated" character. Ueno Hill has, in its time, been the location of a vast Tokugawa temple complex; it was the site of a fierce battle in 1868; and it now boasts a park, a zoo and the highest concentration of historical monuments and highbrow cultural museums, art galleries and concert halls in Tokyo.

Ueno Park ★
3, Ikenohata, Ueno-koen, Taito-ku ☎827-7752. Map 15C10
⊡ ⴺ ⇌ ▣ ✳ ◁ Open 24hrs all year. JR/subway: Ueno.
Every spring the cherry blossoms burst into bloom, and suddenly uninhibited Tokyoites take over Ueno Park (Ueno Koen) from its perennial habitués: museum and gallery vultures, courting couples and winos. With huge crowds vying for prime space beneath the blossoms, each small plot is jealously guarded, although visitors are often invited to join in the drunken revelry to celebrate the blossoms' evanescent beauty, symbol of the Buddhist idea of the transience of the material world (at least, that's the excuse).

At other times of the year, Ueno Park can either be a pleasant place to stroll, an intensive illumination in Japanese and European art, or a course in historical detection.

Until the Meiji Restoration, the entire park area formed the precincts of *Kan'eiji Temple*, one of two family temples of the Tokugawa shoguns. Although the surrender in 1868 of the shogun's Edo Castle (now the *Imperial Palace*) to the forces of the emperor advancing from Kyoto had been settled peacefully, there were 2,000 diehard Tokugawa loyalists (known as *Shogitai*) who staged a last stand at Ueno Hill by the entrance to Kan'eiji. Outnumbered and outgunned, they were completely routed and decided to take Kan'eiji with them into oblivion. The victorious imperial forces completed the destruction, torching halls that still stood as reminders of the hated Tokugawas. Kan'eiji's former grandeur can only be glimpsed at today through the few buildings that have survived: *Kan'eiji Pagoda*, *Toshogu Shrine*, *Kan'eiji Kiyomizudo*, *Jigendo*, the rebuilt Benten temple at *Shinobazu Pond* and the Tokugawa mausolea gates in the Kan'eiji cemetery.

A gravestone marks the site of the funeral pyre of the vanquished *Shogitai*, and where some of their ashes were buried. The descendants of one of the surviving *Shogitai* still tend the grave, and there is now a small **museum** beside it (⊡ *open 10am-4pm, closed Thurs*). Although the writings are in Japanese, a contemporary *ukiyo-e* print behind glass on one wall graphically illustrates the battle of Ueno Hill. With typical Japanese pragmatism, a statue dedicated to one of the foes of the *Shogitai*, Takamori Saigo, stands close by. Saigo was rewarded by the emperor for his loyalty by being made commander of the imperial forces after the 1868 Restoration, but soon fell out with the new government for encouraging Westernization and leading a 7-mth-long rebellion from his home province of Satsuma (present-day Kagoshima prefecture in southern Kyushu). Defeated, he committed ritual *seppuku* suicide and became an instant hero. Rehabilitated in 1890 by the emperor, the bronze statue of Saigo and his dog nonetheless shows him in casual provincial clothes, rather than in his military dress, in deference to imperial sensitivity.

The first museum, as well as the zoo, opened in 1882 in the grounds of Kan'eiji, but since then the modern "culture invasion" has been unabated. Real history, however, lingers in the most unexpected places in Ueno Park, such as the 1666 **Toki no Kane** (Bell of Time), which is hidden in the bushes next to the **Seiyoken** (see *Restaurants*), and whose chimes were once the inspiration for poets such as Bassho.

Ueno Zoo

9-83, Ueno-koen, Taito-ku ☎*828-5171. Map 15C10* 🚇 ⑤ ▣
✴ ◁≋ *Open 9.30am-4.30pm (last entry 4pm). Closed Mon, Dec 29-Jan 3. Kan'eiji Pagoda closed to the public. JR: Ueno (Ueno-koen exit).*

This national zoo's main claim to fame are its giant pandas. They are kept in a glassed-in enclosure near the entrance, and are privileged, having their own security guard (to ensure the huge crowds do not get too excited) and being permitted to rest every Fri. Unfortunately the other 12,000 animals are less luxuriously confined in tiny cages, although this does not seem to deter the visitors, who on weekends and public holidays far outnumber the exhibits.

Among the zoo's oddities are the 17thC *Kan'eiji Pagoda* behind the deer enclosure, a tea-ceremony hut in which the Tokugawa shoguns are said to have been entertained, and a cormorant rookery at *Shinobazu Pond*.

Wasada University Tsubouchi Memorial Theater Museum

*Waseda Daigaku, 1-6-1, Nishi-Waseda, Shinjuku-ku ☎203-4141. Map **12D5** ◻ ⅀ ✗ English tours may be arranged. Open Mon-Fri 9am-4pm, Sat 9am-2pm. Closed Sun, hols, Oct 21, Aug 1-3rd Mon in Sept, Dec 29-Jan 7. Subway: Waseda.*

On display here is an impressive collection of props, stage models, costumes, musical instruments, prints and memorabilia covering the whole range of Japanese dramatic arts, from primitive magic dance to Heian-era (794-1185) court music and dancing, *Noh* drama, *bunraku* puppet theater, *kabuki* and modern Variety. The museum also has many fine *ukiyo-e* woodblock prints (especially of *kabuki*) and showrooms reserved for the development of drama in the West and in other Asian countries. A serious drawback is that none of the labeling is in English, although a free English pamphlet outlining the various forms of Japanese drama is available on request.

The 3-story museum building, inside the campus of Waseda University, was built in 1928 to celebrate the 70th birthday of "The Father of Japanese Theater," Dr Shoyo Tsubouchi (1859-1935), and his completed translation, that year, of all the works of Shakespeare. Loosely modeled on London's 16thC Fortune Theater — with a mock Tudor facade — the building has an outdoor replica of the Fortune's stage in its portico, where performances of Shakespeare are held during April.

Yamatane Museum

*7-12, Kabuto-cho, Nihonbashi, Chuo-ku ☎669-7643. Map **10H11** ▩ ⅀ Open 10.30am-5pm. Closed Mon, Dec 26-Jan 3. Subway: Kayabacho.*

This museum specializes in modern Japanese paintings of the Meiji (1868-1911) and post-Meiji periods. Most of the 1,500 paintings now owned by the museum were from the collection of the late Taneji Yamazaki, chairman of Yamatane Securities. Yamazaki appears to have had a developed *penchant* for Japanese kitsch, the kind of paintings favored by interior decorators to match carpets and wallpaper. The top two museum floors of the Yamatane building in the Kabutocho (stock exchange) district are tastefully designed; the only jarring note is the paintings.

Yasukuni Shrine ★

*3-1-1, Kudankita, Chiyoda-ku ☎261-8326. Map **8F7** ◻ ▱ ⅍ Main hall open 9.30am-4.30pm, shrine open 24hrs. Subway: Kudanshita.*

When Yasuhiro Nakasone made an official visit here, in 1985, as Japan's prime minister, he unleashed a torrent of protest from China as well as his own domestic adversaries. One reason they objected was that "war criminals" (such as Hideki Tojo, executed by the Allies in 1948) are among the 2.5 million *kami*, or spirits, of Japanese who died in battle that are worshiped at Yasukuni. Yet the Japanese government secretly ordered their enshrinement here.

However, the controversy surrounding Yasukuni runs deeper than just the issue of "war criminals." Built in 1869, Yasukuni developed, in the 1930s and in the suicidal war that followed, into a potent tool of militarism. Native Shintoism was then the state religion, and Yasukuni was directly administered by the Japanese Army. A whole generation were then indoctrinated into believing that if they died for the Emperor and Japan they would achieve equality and glory in the afterlife, among the spirits of warriors enshrined at Yasukuni (similar to the Viking belief in Valhalla).

The shrine is best approached from the direction of Kudan Slope and Kudanshita Station. An enormous steel *torii* (built to replace the original arch melted down in 1943 for the war effort) stands at the entrance to an avenue leading to the shrine, lined with stone lanterns, cherry and ginkgo trees. Halfway down the avenue is a bronze statue of Masujiro Omura, the first Mnister of War after the Meiji Restoration. In 1868 he crushed the resistance by loyalists of Tokugawa shoguns to the might of the imperial forces; he was assassinated one year later. After another colossal bronze *torii* (1887), you arrive at the imposing main gate, its doors embossed with the imperial crest of the 16-petalled chrysanthemum. The inner sanctuary of the shrine was built in 1869 and is in the primitive *shinmei* style of the ancient shrines at Ise.

Noh drama performances and sumo contests are held in the shrine for 3-day periods starting on Apr 21, July 14 and Oct 17. Early Apr is an especially delightful time at Yasukuni, when cherry blossoms and a flock of doves take over its courtyard, and the shrine's dark associations, best symbolized by the grim mementoes housed in the museum on the right, can be forgotten.

Yasukuni Shrine Museum ★

3-1-1, Kudankita, Chiyoda-ku ☎261-8326. Map 8F7 🖼 ㄴ ☆ inside ➴ ⇜ Open Mar-Oct 9am-5pm (last entry 4.30pm), Nov-Feb 9am-4.30pm (last entry 4pm). Closed Dec 28-31. Subway: Kudanshita.

Nowhere is the pervasive ambiguity of the *Yasukuni Shrine* better exemplified than this military museum, situated on the right side of the shrine's courtyard. The front of the museum is a veritable arsenal, with exhibits such as Japanese cannons, a naval gun, a tank and a "human torpedo" (lent by the US Army Museum in Hawaii). The most recent (and controversial) addition is a steam locomotive, "the first to pass the junction" on the Thai-Burma "Death Railway" built by the Japanese army with Allied POW slave labor. The locomotive is now dedicated to the numerous casualties sustained during the railroad's construction and in prayer "for the repose of their souls and for eternal world peace."

A visit to the inside of the museum is a similarly thought-provoking experience (although none of the exhibits are labeled in English). Grouped around a central hall are rooms filled with memorabilia (photographs, letters, uniforms and scale models) of certain heroes and units from the 1868 Meiji Restoration, the Sino-Japanese (1894-95) and Russo-Japanese (1904-5) wars, as well as World War II. The walls to the rear of the main hall have stirring paintings of *kamikaze* attacks on US ships. The centerpiece of the main hall is a Mitsubishi Zero fighter plane, surrounded by a variety of machine guns and a model of the great Japanese battleship *Yamato*. The floor above has two rooms filled with suits of samurai armor, saddles and some early weaponry. There is another room that is used for special exhibitions relating to the Yasukuni Shrine.

Yokoyama Taikan Memorial Hall ★

1-4-24, Ikenohata, Taito-ku ☎821-1017. Map 14D9 🖼 𝄪 ⚌ 🅿 ➴ ⇜ Open 10am-4pm. Closed Mon-Wed, Dec 15-Jan 15. Subway: Yushima.

On the w side of *Shinobazu Pond* stands the house of one of Japan's most famous artists, Taikan Yokoyama (to use the

Western name order), the giant of the *nihonga* Japanese painting movement. While Yokoyama dwelt on traditional themes (such as endless views of Mt. Fuji) and similar styles, his originality lay in adopting Western shadings and the bold use of color, as well as an emphasis on light and de-emphasis of line, which resulted in softly blurred contours in his paintings. Although critical response was almost entirely negative, his pioneering work paved the way for further innovation and experiment by modern painters. With the exception of a 9yr break after World War II, Yokoyama spent most of his adult life here on the western bank of Shinobazu Pond, from 1909 (when he was 41yrs old) to his death in 1958. The present house, which was rebuilt in 1954, opened as a memorial hall on the death of his wife in 1976. Under the enthusiastic direction of his grandson, three rooms on the 1st floor and his 2nd-floor studio have been carefully laid out with displays of his paintings and sketches, as well as photographs, ink and painting equipment. In the alcove of a 1st-floor room facing the beautiful Japanese garden is a Heian-period wooden statue of the Buddhist god Fudo. Though unfortunately none of the labels are in English, the traditional, tasteful Japanese architecture and interiors make the house well worth a visit.

Yushima Tenjin Shrine★

3-30-1, Yushima, Bunkyo-ku ☎836-0753. Map 15D10 ⊙ ⊲⋲ Open 24hrs. Subways: Yushima and Uenohirokoji.

Tenjin, meaning heavenly god, was the posthumous name given to the 9thC poet and statesman Sugawara no Michizane. It was believed that his death in exile caused the ancient capital of Kyoto to be stricken with calamities. To appease his angry spirit, a shrine was built, and Michizane became deified as the patron god of arts and scholarship.

Believed to have been founded in 1355, and later restored by Dokan Ota in 1478, Yushima Tenjin (one of the shrines dedicated to the god of learning) was burned down in the so-called "Long Sleeves Fire" of 1657. The fire started when monks at the nearby **Honmyhoji Temple** tried to burn a long-sleeved kimono they believed had brought death to three girls, staying at the temple, who had worn it. Strong winds whisked up the burning fabric and spread the fire. In the next 200yrs the shrine was burned down four more times, the last time in 1863 (reconstruction finished in 1885). The present building is appropriately situated on a slope halfway between the two large universities: Tokyo, slightly to the N of the shrine, in Hongo, and Meiji, s of the shrine, in Ochanomizu.

Thousands of students visit the shrine every year to appeal to Tenjin's compassion to help them through the "exam hell" to enter a good school or university, or later find a good job. Their prayers are inscribed on small wooden tablets called *ema*, or picture horses, hung outside the front of the main hall. (The reference to horses derives from when they were the most highly prized offering to be made to the gods; but since common people could not afford horses they offered pictures of them instead.) The *ema* today occasionally have some roman letters, such as IBM or NTT, showing the student's wish to enter one of these prestigious companies.

The shrine is famous for its plum trees (traditionally associated with scholarship) and during the annual *Ume Matsuri* (plum festival) the courtyard is often thronged with visitors. However, the many "love hotels" that today stand near the shrine's precincts would be less likely to meet with Tenjin's approval.

Zojoji Temple

4-7-35, Shibakoen, Minato-ku ☎432-1431. Map 5K8 ▣
▣ open 11.30am-1.30pm ▬ ⇚ Main hall open 9am-5pm,
precincts open 24hrs. Subway: Onarimon.

As with *Kan'eiji*, the other great family temple of the Tokugawa
shoguns, visitors to Zojoji will find it hard to imagine the awesome
power, size and majesty which this temple once held. Founded in
1393 in what is now Tokyo's Kojimachi district, the *Amidist*, or
Pure-Land sect, temple was visited by Ieyasu Tokugawa in 1590,
on the way to his triumphal entry to the future capital. Tokugawa
also practiced Amidism, and according to legend he immediately
struck up a firm friendship with the head priest and, in 1598,
rewarded the temple with a huge tract of land in Shiba. On its 66ha
(164-acre) precincts here in Shiba, there once stood 48 subsidiary
temples and 100 priests' seminaries and dormitories. Apart from
the temple's gates very little remains of its former grandeur.

The main hall was destroyed in 1873 by arsonists, who were
fanatics protesting against the temple's mixture of "foreign"
Buddhism and "pure" Japanese Shinto. It was rebuilt, burned
down again on April Fool's Day 1909 by a cold beggar making a
fire, and then razed, yet again, by wartime bombing. Fortunately
the beautiful, 2-story **Sanmon** main temple gate survived. Viewed
from the main road it is immediately recognizable, with its aged
red lacquer and sweeping gray-tiled roof. Sanmon means triple
gate, and each of its three portals represents three stages in the
passage to nirvana, or Buddhist salvation. Built in 1605 by Ieyasu
Tokugawa, the Sanmon is Tokyo's oldest wooden structure and is
an "Important Cultural Property."

The late 17thC Black Gate (lacquered black) stands immediately
to the left of the Sanmon and is connected by a restored section of
the original earth and tile wall. Farther s is the main gate to the
former mortuary shrine of the second shogun, Hidetada
Tokugawa, recognizable by its two fierce protective deities (now
guarding the front parking lot to the Shiba Park golf club).

To the N of the Sanmon stands an equally forlorn and neglected
former gate built in 1717 for the 7th shogun, Ietsuga Tokugawa,
now guarding the huge front parking lot to the **Tokyo Prince** (see
Hotels). Just around the corner stands Onarimon, the gate once
used by shoguns visiting the temple.

Behind the Black Gate stands a hexagonal sutra repository, built
in 1605 under Ieyasu Tokugawa's patronage, which contains over
18,000 volumes of ancient Buddhist sutras engraved in wood. Also
of interest, in the temple courtyard, is a gigantic temple bell, made
in 1673, the first to be cast in Edo. Weighing 15,000kg (33,000lb)
and standing 3.3m (11ft) high, it is one of the largest in Japan, and
its muffled boom is said to reach across Tokyo Bay to Kisarazu in
Chiba prefecture. The temple's main hall was rebuilt in 1974 from
reinforced concrete, and the Ankoku-den Hall on the right, built
in 1952, contains the revered *Black Image of Amida*, a wooden
image that has turned black through centuries' exposure to incense
smoke; it was worshiped by the Minamoto clan and later by Ieyasu
Tokugawa, and today is shown to the public only three times a
year.

The most poignant reminder of the ill fortunes that befell the
Tokugawas after the Meiji Restoration is tucked away behind the
Ankoku-den. Next to the fine 1712 gate, designated an "Important
Cultural Property" but now serving no purpose, are crammed the
removed tombs of no less than six Tokugawa shoguns and three
shoguns' wives on a patch of land smaller than the average
Japanese front garden.

Where to stay

One of the great myths said to turn visitors off Tokyo is that its hotels are phenomenally expensive. While some, though admittedly among the world's best, do charge a small fortune, prices at the majority of Tokyo's hotels compare favorably with their counterparts in New York. Indeed, until recent upheavals in exchange rates, it was generally cheaper to stay in Tokyo than in New York.

With few exceptions, most Tokyo hotels lie on or within the central circumference of the JR Yamanote line (picturesque Shitamachi areas, such as Asakusa being farther out, suffer a conspicuous dearth). Close proximity to the Imperial Palace is still a good indication of prestige, yet even here there are wide differences in price and standards between cheaper hotels on the residential w side and the luxurious **Imperial** and **Palace** hotels on the E and N (closer to the Marunouchi and Otemachi business centers). Akasaka benefits from its central location and image as a high-class entertainment area; the nearby **Okura** and **Capitol Tokyu** hotels occupying an exclusive fringe (more sedate at night). Until the discreet arrival of the **Seiyo** on its northern border, Ginza had more middle and economy range hotels catering to those lured by its bright lights. Two of the largest concentrations of hotels (of every classification), are found in relatively far-flung Shinagawa and Shinjuku (the latter's western sector still known by locals as "Skyscraper City"). However, don't be bound by local convention, as many of the worthiest choices are in the least likely locations. There is certainly plenty of contrast, ranging from the swinging modernism of Roppongi's **Prince** hotel to the cultured conservatism of the **Hilltop** near Ochanomizu.

Budget travelers would do well to consider one of the numerous business hotels (especially in the Tokyo Station area), primarily intended for company men but used often by other, thrifty visitors. Though quality and value vary considerably, and none offers room service, all of them have a bar and a restaurant. Bedrooms are generally boxlike but well equipped.

So squeezed is the city for space that a hotel garden or a good view is a scarce asset. But excellent service and meticulous housekeeping are to be found in all price categories. Bear in mind, however, that in some hotels room service ceases abruptly as early as 11pm. 24hr room service is increasingly rare, its absence being especially marked in those very hotels, such as the Imperial and **Okura**, where it is most demanded.

Tokyo's range of accommodations, from the restrained, quietly elegant to the latest high-tech fantasies, will appeal to young and old alike. And despite the number of dull, over-priced hotels, discerning travelers will find a surprising number of genuine bargains, many of them possessed of considerable charm.

Tipping is neither required nor expected, as service charges and government tax (both 10 percent) are added automatically to the bill.

Ryokan

A stay in a *ryokan* (Japanese inn) is recommended for first-hand experience of traditional Japanese lifestyle. Guests sleep on *futon* mattresses laid out on *tatami* straw mats (no shoes are to be worn inside the room) and bathe in *o-furo* (see below). In *onsen* (spas), *ryokan* usually have their own hot spring water in a separate room or in an open-air rock pool in the grounds. Chambermaids will provide towels, *yukata* (light cotton wrap-around robes, worn in the summer and after a bath) and sandals or *geta* (traditional thronged wooden clogs). In winter a *tanzen* gown is also worn over the *yukata*. The better class of *ryokan* will serve evening meals and Japanese breakfast in your room, but check to see if this price is included. Cheaper *ryokan* will only serve breakfast in the dining room. For information on expensive, higher-class *ryokans*, contact the **Kokusai Kanko Ryokan Renmei** (*Kokusai Kanko Kaikan, 1-8-3, Marunouchi, Chiyoda-ku* ☎*231-5310*). For economical *ryokans*, contact the **Japanese Inn Group** (*c/o Sawanoya Ryokan, 2-3-11, Yanaka, Taito-ku* ☎*822-2251*).

Minshuku

These family inns are a cheaper alternative to the *ryokan* and one step above youth hostels. They normally offer a minimum of service (and spoken English), communal *o-furo*, for which you need to bring your own towels, and Japanese-style toilets. *Minshuku* accommodations can range from charming old farmhouses to modern, utilitarian cubicles. For further information and to make reservations contact the **Japan Minshuku Center** (*1st Basement, Kotsu Kaikan Building, 2-10-1, Yurakucho, Chiyoda-ku* ☎*216-6556*).

O-furo

An *o-furo*, or Japanese bath is most likely to be encountered in a *ryokan* or *minshuku*. A chambermaid will first heat the water in the bath tub (which traditionally is made of wood with a lid placed on top when not in use). Then instead of getting into the bath, you soap, wash and rinse yourself (using a small bucket and/or shower) while standing *outside* the tub; the water and soap suds drain through a hole in the floor. Next you get into the hot bath and relax. The clean hot water in the tub may be used by more than one person, so do not remove the plug.

Onsen

The idea of "taking the waters" at a mineral spa has a slightly archaic ring in the West; not so in Japan, where the tradition still thrives. *Onsen* (spas) tend to be located in scenic and mountainous spots, which lends them a romantic air for the Japanese. Two famous *onsen* areas in the Tokyo vicinity are Hakone and the Izu peninsula. *Ryokan*, as well as Western-style hotels in *onsen* areas, usually have their own source of hot spring water. A similar procedure to *o-furo* is followed — firstly you wash and rinse yourself, then climb into the hot spring-water bath. It is especially invigorating to alternate this with a bath of icy-cold water.

Hotels classified by area

Akasaka, Nagatacho and Toranomon	**Hibiya**
Akasaka Prince ▥	Imperial ▥
ANA Hotel Tokyo ▥	**Iidabashi**
Capitol Tokyu ▥	Edmont ▮▢
New Otani Hotel and Tower ▥	Grand Palace ▮▢
Okura ▥	**Ochanomizu**
Aoyama	Hilltop ▮▢
President ▢	**Palace North Side**
Ginza and Shimbashi	Palace ▥
Ginza Dai-ichi ▮▢	**Palace West Side**
Ginza International ▢	Diamond ▮▢
Ginza Nikko ▮▢	Fairmont ▮▢
Ginza Tokyu ▮▢	Kayu Kaikan ▮▢
Mitsui Urban ▢	**Roppongi**
Seiyo ▥	Ibis ▢
Shimbashi Dai-ichi ▮▢	Roppongi Prince ▮▢
	Shiba and Toranomon

Hotels

Akasaka Prince

*1-2, Kioi-cho, Chiyoda-ku, Tokyo
102* ☎*234-1111* IDD ☎*2324028*
℞*262-5163. Map 8H7* ▮▮▮ *721 rms*
🚗 ⊒ AE ⏀ CD VISA *Subway:
Akasakamitsuke.*

*Location: Opposite Akasakamitsuke
Subway Station, across the street from
New Otani hotel.* Designed by the
renowned architect Kenzo Tange,
the new (1963) Akasaka Prince is one
of Tokyo's most outstanding postwar
buildings. The tower, shaped with a
multitude of vertical folds like a
Japanese fan or *origami*, casts a
shimmering reflection over
Akasaka. Tange is also responsible
for its interior design, yet the
lobby — cold and square marble
columns and all-glass frontage — is
oddly disappointing. But the rooms
are highly unusual, with large
windows (each one seen as a "fold"
from outside) offering excellent
views. Room furnishings are modern
and tasteful, with large corner sofas
under the windows, silver parachute-
style bedcovers and white laminated
furniture. The charming and elegant
annex (somewhat dwarfed by
Tange's ultramodern tower) is a
rather incongruous delight. It was
formerly the old hotel and once the
villa of an exiled Yi-dynasty prince of
Korea. The entrance is that of a
Bavarian hunting lodge, but the
furnishings inside are French Empire
style. The 1st floor houses an
intimate bar and "private rooms,"
and the original chandeliered rooms
upstairs house, in authentic
surroundings, the fine **Trianon**,
certainly the most aristocratic French
restaurant in Tokyo.
🍴 ◁€ ☗ 🏌

ANA Hotel Tokyo

*1-12-33, Akasaka, Minato-ku,
Tokyo 107* ☎*505-1111* IDD
☎*34858* ℞ *505-1155. Map 8I7* ▮▮▮▮
900 rms 🚗 ⊒ AE ⏀ CD VISA
Subway: Kokkaigijidomae.

*Location: In the Ark Hills office/
residential complex.* The Japanese are
ardent devotees of novelty and
fashion, and the huge new Ark Hills
complex in central *Akasaka* has yet
to lose its glow of excitement. All
Nippon Airways (ANA) obviously
wanted to create an atmosphere of
international luxury in their new
hotel as part of the new complex; but
though it may match the image of
urban sophistication expected by
Japanese coming in from the
countryside, it would hardly
overwhelm the foreign traveler.
Features of the airport-like lobby are
cream marble, an artificial waterfall
with a model Venetian gondola at the
bottom, and an escalator that
disconcertingly runs to one side. The
rooms are well furnished with
matching colors; there's pink marble
in the bathrooms, and ingenious
showers that can emit concentrated
jets of water, suitable for massage.
Executives benefit from an extra
lounge and late check-out, for a small
extra charge.
🚹 ◁€ ≋ *(summer)* ☗ ☛ *(men
only)* 🏌

Capitol Tokyu

*2-10-3, Nagatacho, Chiyoda-ku,
Tokyo 100* ☎*581-4511* IDD
☎*2223605* ℞ *581-5822. Map 8I7*
▮▮▮ *479 rms* 🚗 ⊒ AE CB ⏀ CD
VISA *Subway: Kokkaigijidomae.*
*Location: Behind Hie Shrine, near the
National Diet Building and prime
minister's residence.* Here is a tranquil
oasis in the heart of central Tokyo's
government district, with a deserved
reputation for fine cuisine:
compelling reasons why Tokyu
Corp. was so eager to take over
occupancy of this hotel in 1984 from
its former tenant, the **Tokyo Hilton**.
Tokyu has retained all the previous
outstanding features (expect possibly
the Chinese chef, who moved to
Shinjuku with the Hilton).
Overlooking a serene Japanese pond
and garden, the excellent Japanese
teppanyaki, *sushi* and *tempura*
restaurant and the lobby bar are
favorite meeting places for
politicians, government officials and
hangers-on; and the culinary
pleasures of the **Keyaki** French-style
grill are renowned. Many of the
rooms overlook the famous *Hie
Shrine.* 24hr room service.
⊡ 🚹 ☗ ◁€ ≋ *(summer)* ☗ ☛

Century Hyatt
2-7-2, Nishi-Shinjuku, Shinjuku-ku, Tokyo 160 ☎349-0111 ⅢDD
☎29411 ® 344-5575. Map 6G2 ⅧⅢ
800 rms ← ⇌ AE CB ⓞ ⒸⒹ VISA
JR/subway: Shinjuku.

Location: W Shinjuku ("Skyscraper City"). A squat, pink brick exterior, stark geometric design and physical resemblance to the next-door office building provide scant preparation for what awaits you inside. The resplendent lobby of mosaic, the marble floor and three enormous bell-shaped chandeliers hanging from the roof of an 8-story-high atrium have Japanese visitors exclaiming their delight as they ascend in a glass-fronted elevator. The bedrooms are not as luxurious as the nearby Hilton, but the floor-level windows are convenient for city-gazing. 24hr room service is restricted in choice, but the Century Hyatt boasts some excellent-value restaurants: **Hugo's Grill** in particular, and **Le Chenonceaux** for reasonably priced *haute cuisine*.
◁€ ⇌ ♟ 🍴 🍽

Diamond♥
25, Ichiban-cho, Chiyoda-ku, Tokyo 102 ☎263-2211
☎2322764 ® 263-2222. Map 8G7
▢ *471 rms* ← ⇌ AE ⓞ ⒸⒹ VISA
Subway: Hanzomon.

Location: Behind the British Embassy, next to Hanzomon Station. Visitors will find this hotel very good value because of its prime location. In Edo times, the Bancho area, bordering the Chidorigafuchi moat, was where the shogun's retainers were given very spartan accommodations. Nowadays Bancho and nearby Kojimachi are high-class residential and embassy districts, with a number of excellent French restaurants catering to those with educated palates and expense accounts. The facilities are reminiscent of an earlier simplicity. Tokyoites appreciate the wide variety of modestly priced food in this hotel's seven restaurants, which include Japanese, Chinese, Korean and Western food.
🍴 🍽

Edmont
3-10-8, Iidabashi, Chiyoda-ku, Tokyo 102 ☎237-1111 ⅢDD
☎2324510 ® 234-4371. Map 14E8
ⅧⅢ *450 rms* ← ⇌ AE ⓞ ⒸⒹ VISA
JR/subway: Iidabashi.

Location: 5mins' walk from Iidabashi Station. A startlingly smart new (1985) hotel in a nondescript back street of N Tokyo. A large vacant lot owned by Japanese Railways (JR),

co-partners in the hotel with the Seibu group, was the reason for such an inauspicious site. But the Edmont's pride is its beautiful lobby, where the soft lighting enhances the warm colors of the pinewood and stone-effect walls. Bright, medium-sized double rooms have useful extras such as push-button telephones. The lounge and coffee shop are comfortable, but the French restaurant is impossibly cramped.
🍴 🍽

Fairmont♥
2-1-17, Kudan Minami, Chiyoda-ku, Tokyo 102 ☎262-1151 ⅢDD
☎2322883 ® 264-2476 Map 8F8
▢ *240 rms* ← ⇌ AE ⓞ ⒸⒹ VISA
Subway: Kudanshita.

Location: Near the Nippon Budokan and Yasukuni Shrine. The chief merit of the Fairmont is its superb location: in a quiet, leafy corner of central Tokyo on the edge of the Chidorigafuchi outer moat of the *Imperial Palace*, it overlooks Kitanomaru Park and the enormous sloping roof of the Budokan Hall. Rooms are spacious and have good views, but are sparsely furnished. There is one Western-style dining room, and a Japanese restaurant offering a limited choice of fairly plain food. Room service could improve.
😐 ◁€ ⇌ *(summer)* 🍴 🍽

Ginza Dai-ichi♥
8-13-1, Ginza, Chuo-ku, Tokyo 104 ☎542-5311 ⓦ 2523714
®542-3030. Map 10/10 ⅧⅢ *800 rms* ← ⇌ AE ⓞ ⒸⒹ VISA JR/subway: Shimbashi.

Location: 5-10mins' walk from Shimbashi Station, behind the Tenkuni restaurant. Moderate prices, efficient hotel services and its *Ginza* location (even if a little off the main shopping streets) make the Ginza Dai-ichi popular with both Japanese and foreign visitors. Rooms are tolerable if you ignore the garish furnishings. Bars and restaurants are merely serviceable, so eating out may be preferred. The room service menu, available until 4am, serves *sushi* and Western dishes. Not a bad choice for cost-conscious travelers needing to stay in Ginza.
🍴 ♟ *(men only)* 🍽

Ginza International (Ginza Kokusai)
8-7-13, Ginza, Chuo-ku, Tokyo 104 ☎574-1121. Map 9/9 ▢ *92 rms* ← ⇌ AE CB ⓞ ⒸⒹ VISA
JR/subway: Shimbashi.

Location: Near Shimbashi Station. Its

gaudy, neon-lit street entrance hardly invites, and the somewhat worn interior isn't to everyone's taste. Worth considering, though: some twin rooms are more spacious than other comparable business hotels in the area. There are some middling restaurants, and bars that are occasionally boisterous. No room service.

♈

Ginza Nikko

8-4-21, Ginza, Chuo-ku, Tokyo 104 ☎*571-4911* |□□| ☎ *2522812* ℗ *571-8379. Map 9/9* |□| *112 rms* ═ |AE| |◐| |CD| |VISA| *Subway: Shimbashi.*

Location: 5mins' walk from Shimbashi Station. One of the Japan Air Lines Nikko chain, the Ginza Nikko is situated on the main Shimbashi thoroughfare, close to the lively *Ginza* district. It claims to be more than a business hotel, but falls really within the same bracket; very modest comfort and space, but reasonable price. No room service.

♈ ♨

Ginza Tokyu

5-15-9, Ginza, Chuo-ku, Tokyo 104 ☎*541-2411* |□□| ☎ *2522601* ℗ *541-6622. Map 9/10* |□□□| *449 rms* ⊝ ═ |AE| |CB| |◐| |CD| |VISA| *Subway: Higashi Ginza.*

Location: Near Nissan Motors head office, Kabukiza Theater and Higashi-Ginza Subway Station. Until the new Seiyo stole the limelight, this was the most luxurious of a small number of good hotels in the prized *Ginza* area, recommended for hedonists who feel they must be near the center of shopping and the many bars in the area. Rooms compare favorably in size and restrained decor with their more expensive equivalents in the **Imperial**. *Shoji* sliding paper windows are an added touch, though baths are Lilliputian. The hotel has a decent selection of restaurants, a good bar, and although room service expires at 3am the hotel coffee shop is open 24hrs. A rooftop beer garden can be fun in summer.

♈ ☞ *(men only)* ♨

Grand Palace

1-1-1, Iidabashi, Chiyoda-ku, Tokyo 102 ☎*264-1111* ☎*2322981* ℗ *230-4985. Map 14E8* |□□□| *500 rms* ═ ═ |AE| |◐| |CD| |VISA| *Subway: Kudanshita.*

Location: Between Iidabashi and Kudanshita stations. The Grand Palace's chief claim to fame is that it was here in 1973 that South Korea's leading dissident, Kim dae Jung, was kidnaped by his government's agents, provoking an international crisis. One can only assume that in those days the Grand was in better condition — and that tastes in decor perhaps were different. But the Chinese restaurant in the basement has a sound reputation, thanks to its Hong Kong chef.

♈ ♨

Hilltop (Yama-no-ue)♣

1-1, Surugadai, Kanda, Chiyoda-ku, Tokyo 101 ☎*293-2311* ☎*2226712* ℗ *233-4567. Map 14E9* |□| *75 rms* ═ |AE| |◐| |CD| |VISA| *JR/subway: Ochanomizu.*

Location: At the top of Kanda Surugadai Hill, 5mins' walk from Ochanomizu JR Station. The novelist Yukio Mishima used to stay at the Hilltop before his tragic suicide in 1971, and since then its charms have been a well-guarded secret of Tokyo's high society. The Hilltop is clubby and very small, the management seem to have an obsession with guests' health, and there are excellent restaurants and moderate room-rates. The Chinese restaurant, has a Peking chef, while the impressive French restaurant's *maitre d'hôtel* fittingly was the chef at the Japanese embassy in Paris. There is another French restaurant in the annex opposite, a steak house fronting a small garden where outside dining is encouraged in clement weather, and close by is an elegant coffee shop. Farther down is a cozy wine cellar, and a snug, counter-only paneled bar, efficiently tended until 2am (an Englishman's delight). A combination of oxygen and negative ions are thoughtfully pumped into guests' rooms to clear the fumes of overindulgence. To avoid disappointment reservations should be made well in advance, as demand for the hotel's 75 rooms can be phenomenal.

♐ ◁€ ♈ ♨

Ibis

7-4-14, Roppongi, Minato-ku, Tokyo 106 ☎*403-4411. Map 4J6* |□| *200 rms* ═ |AE| |◐| |CD| |VISA| *Subway: Roppongi.*

Location: Close to Roppongi Crossing and Roppongi Subway Station. This is a basic, no-frills business hotel housed in a modern building, on the main street running down from Roppongi Crossing to the Defense Agency. It offers reasonably clean rooms and a convenient location for dedicated sampling of Roppongi's nightlife.

♈

Imperial (Teikoku)

1-1-1, Uchisaiwaicho, Chiyoda-ku, Tokyo 100 ☎504-1111 IDD
⑩ 2222346 *(reservations 2222367)* ⑫ 581-9146 *(reservations 504-1258).* ˙Map 9/9 ▩▩▩ 1,140 rms ⇦ ⊡⊟ AE CB ⑩ ⑥ ⑥
VISA *Subways: Uchisaiwaicho and Hibiya.*

Location: On the E side of Hibiya Park. Tokyo's most central hotel remains a legend, though perhaps now overrated. Building of the first Imperial was completed in 1890, and the hotel today still owes its world fame to its illustrious and daring Frank Lloyd Wright design. The hotel opened in 1923, the year of the Great Kanto Earthquake, which it survived intact. In 1967 it was torn down in an act of unparalleled cultural barbarism. The present hotel and new tower annex would hardly win architectural prizes, but have managed to retain pride of place in Tokyo society. While the **Okura** is discreet about its opulence, the Imperial tends to flaunt its sybaritism. Throngs of extroverts and voyeurs lend the lobby the air of a carpeted Grand Central Station, but a traditional Japanese wedding and banquet at the Imperial still remains *de rigueur* for the socially aspiring. The hotel occupies some of Tokyo's prize real estate, a point noticeably reflected in the modest size of the bedrooms, although good views of the city can be obtained from the tower annex. The cuisine is excellent, though unavailable after 1am. The shopping arcade offers the most concentrated selection of luxury items in the city. Part of the Aztec-inspired stone, tile and brickwork from Wright's former creation is preserved in the **Old Imperial Bar**, the perfect place for wistful nostalgia over a drink.
௬ ⊲⊱ ⇌ ⍭ ⇦ ⛬

Kayu Kaikan

8-1, Sanban-cho, Chiyoda-ku, Tokyo 102 ☎230-1111
⑩ 2323318 ⑫ 230-2529. Map 8F7
▢ 127 rms ⇦ ⊡⊟ AE ⑩ ⑥ VISA
Subway: Hanzomon.

Location: Between Yasukuni Shrine and the British Embassy. This hotel is under the same management as the **Okura**: traces of miniaturized grandeur and good taste show themselves in the elegant lobby and Japanese restaurant. Otherwise the Kayu Kaikan cannot match its big brother's reputation, and is less well located. Rooms are spacious and simply furnished. No room service.
⌂ ⍭ ⛬

Keihin ♣

4-10-20, Takanawa, Minato-ku, Tokyo 108 ☎449-5711 ⑫ 441-7230. Map 4M7 ▢ 52 rms ⊟ AE
⑥ ⑩ VISA ⑥ *JR: Takanawadai; subway: Shinagawa.*

Location: Opposite W exit of Shinagawa JR Station, on the main Dai-ichi Keihin road. One of Tokyo's oldest, if least known, "hostelries," the Keihin was strategically sited, having been built in 1871, 2yrs before the opening of the Shinagawa Station. Dwarfed by the enormous **Pacific** and **Seibu** hotels, you could easily miss the Keihin nowadays, as its street frontage is largely given over to moneyspinning restaurants. Although not overly luxurious inside, there are a few comfortable, old-style rooms redolent of English inns — or what 19thC Japanese eager to emulate the West imagined them to be like.
⍭

Keio Plaza

2-2-1, Nishi-Shinjuku, Shinjuku-ku, Tokyo 160 ☎344-0111 IDD
⑩ 26874 ⑫ 344-0247. Map 6G3 ▩▩▩
1,485 rms ⇦ ⊟ AE CB ⑩ ⑥ VISA
JR/subway: Shinjuku.

Location: W Shinjuku ("Skyscraper City"). The Keio Plaza is part of the Intercontinental Hotel chain), with its 47 floors, is still the tallest hotel in Japan, but with the addition of the new **Hilton** and **Century Hyatt** nearby it can hardly be called the most glamorous or luxurious in *Shinjuku.* However, the rooftop lounge offers suitably stunning views over the metropolis.
௬ ⇌ ⍭ ⇦ ⛬

Marunouchi

1-6-3, Marunouchi, Chiyoda-ku, Tokyo 100 ☎215-2151
⑩ 2224655 ⑫ 215-8036. Map
9G10 ▩▩▩ 194 rms ⊟ AE CB ⑩
⑩ VISA *Subways: Tokyo and Otemachi.*

Location: In the Otemachi business area, near Tokyo Station. A recent refurbishment of the 1st floor has done little to dispel the pervading gloom of this centrally-located "old faithful." But the restaurants are good, and a brightly-lit café-bar cheers the atmosphere considerably.
⍭ ⛬

Mitsui Urban

8-6-15, Ginza, Chuo-ku, Tokyo 104 ☎572-4131 ⑩ 2522949
⑫572-4254. Map 9I9 ▢ 263 rms
⇦ ⊟ AE ⑩ ⑩ VISA *JR/subway: Shimbashi.*

Location: Close to Shimbashi Station.

Hotels

This garishly orange business hotel on the edge of the Shimbashi business district (noted for its high concentration of bars) is further distinguished by a grotesque metal tree with a clock planted in its foliage situated on the street corner. Bedrooms are small but affordable, with well-matched color schemes. A good Japanese restaurant can be found in the basement, and generally the hotel is clean and sprightly. No room service.
Ψ

Miyako Hotel Tokyo
1-1-50, Shirogane-dai, Minato-ku, Tokyo 108 ☎ *447-3111* IDD
📞*2423111* 🖷 *447-3133. Map 4M7*
▥ *500 rms* ➡ ⊒ AE CB ⓓ ⓓ
VISA *JR: Meguro, Gotanda and Shinagawa.*
Location: 5mins' taxi ride from Meguro, Shinagawa or Gotanda JR stations, off Meguro-dori Ave. This Tokyo sister of the famous Miyako Hotel in Kyoto suffers from relatively poor public transportation links, a disadvantage for the harried businessman, but a boon for those who benefit from cheaper room-rates than they would find in comparable hotels elsewhere in the city. The bedrooms at this hotel are quite spacious, simply but tastefully decorated in subdued colors, but room service terminates at a provincial 11.30pm. There is a pleasant, comfortable bar and good Japanese and Chinese restaurants, but the otherwise fine French grill room is marred by an "electone" (electronic organ/synthesizer) player who ought to be disconnected. There are only short paths in the Japanese garden, which frustratingly lead to dead ends.
▨ ♿ ♨ ◅ ≋ Ψ ➳ ♨ ☗

New Otani Hotel and Tower
4-1, Kioi-cho, Chiyoda-ku, Tokyo 102 ☎ *265-1111* IDD 📞 *24719*
🖷*221-2619. Map 8H7* ▥ *2,057 rms* ➡ ⊒ AE CB ⓓ ⓓ VISA *JR: Yotsuya; subway: Akasakamitsuke.*
Location: Opposite Akasakamitsuke Subway Station. Posterity is indebted to the late Yonetaro Otani (however pure his intentions) for retaining one of Tokyo's most beautiful gardens when developing the bloated Otani hotel complex. It has a 4ha (10-acre) Japanese "strolling" garden, in the *Kaiyu shiki chikusan sensui teien*, or walk-around style, with artificial hill and miniature lake, similar to the *Rikugien Garden* in N Tokyo. The hotel's garden belonged to the huge

estate given by Shogun Ieyasu Tokugawa to one of his top generals, Kiyomasa Kato, more than 370yrs ago. Sandwiched nowadays between a busy expressway and the massive hotel and tower annex, the garden remains a soothing delight, with grassy knolls, trees and a waterfall, concealing intimate restaurants and a tea-ceremony room. It is equally impressive viewed through large glass windows from the lobby lounge. The hotel itself is the largest in Japan and rather inhuman in scale, but offers a wide choice of restaurants, of which the Polynesian-style **Trader Vic's** and the re-creation of Paris' famous **La Tour d'Argent** are the most notable. Room interiors are unexceptional and tend to be cramped, but have good views, the best being from the tower annex.
♿ ♨ ◅ ≋ *(summer)* Ψ ➳ ♨
♨ ☗

New Takanawa Prince (Shin Takanawa Prince)♨
3-13-1, Takanawa, Minato-ku, Tokyo 108 ☎*442-1111* IDD
📞*2427418* 🖷 *444-1234. Map 4N7*
▥ *1,000 rms* ➡ ⊒ AE ⓓ ⓓ VISA
JR: Shinagawa; subway: Takanawadai.
Location: On a gentle hill near Shinagawa JR Station, off main arterial road. The glaring white exterior of this new sister of the **Takanawa Prince** is deceptively tasteless. Marble walls and floors mirror brilliant ceiling lights in the impressive lobby, its restful lounge overlooking a verdant, leafy garden and skillfully soothing waterfall. Fancy wrought-iron rails marking off room entrances, and sliding windows opening onto tiny balconies, are further unusual features. Bedrooms contain light chestnut furniture, and pastel carpets and decorations. The classically conceived Japanese tea-ceremony room on the lobby roof exudes *shibumi*. For scale and grandeur, no other Japanese hotel can match the enormous adjoining domed conference/banqueting hall, which is reached via a stunning spiral entrance promenade encircling a cascading fountain.
♨ ◅ ≋ *(summer)* Ψ ☗

Okura
2-10-4, Toranomon, Minato-ku, Tokyo 100 ☎*582-0111* IDD
📞*22790* 🖷 *582-3707. Map 8I8* ▥
910 rms ➡ ⊒ AE CB ⓓ ⓓ VISA
JR: Shimbashi; subways: Toranomon and Kamiyacho.
Location: Next to the US Embassy. A

physical association with the massive US Embassy next door has doubtless contributed to the aura of power, prestige and opulence that can be felt here, but like most venerated "institutions" the Okura defies ready analysis. The main building is eccentrically perched on top of a hill, so that the entrance is actually the 5th floor, leading into a lobby of unsurpassed *shibumi* and good taste. The Okura is thought to have been modeled on an imperial palace in Kyoto, the lounge chairs appear artfully placed on the brown carpet, resembling rocks in a Zen garden or lotuses growing from a muddy pond, and require some deportment when sitting. Hotel staff are stiff, correct and intimidating, the men wearing morning suits or old fashioned bell-caps, the women clad in traditional kimonos. Tokyo gastronomes occasionally compare the Okura's *haute cuisine* with that of the **Imperial**, though visitors who can afford to dine at the Okura may treat the question as academic. Habitués of the **Orchard Bar** insist it is the best in Tokyo; certainly it is the best-stocked and tended. The **Starlight Lounge** has regrettably become a misnomer since tall office buildings have blocked out most of the view (and hence the night sky), but the nightly jazz players and singers, although similarly dated, are still of the highest quality. Unfortunately complacency crept in: bedrooms stand badly in need of refurbishment, though little can be done about the indifferent views.

♨ ≋ ☿ ☞ ☖ ♨

Palace
1-1-1, Marunouchi, Chiyoda-ku, Tokyo 100 ☎ 211-5211 ⅠⅮⅮ
☏ 2222580 ☏ 211-6987. Map *9G9*
▥ 404 rms ⇌ ⇌ ⒜Ⓔ ⒞Ⓑ ⓓ ⓓ
ⓥⓘⓢⓐ JR: Tokyo; subway: Otemachi.
Location: Bordering the moat and Imperial Palace outer garden. The Palace can boast the best views of any central Tokyo hotel, from a superb vantage point very close to the *Imperial Palace* grounds. It is, however, oddly lacking in either the *shibumi* of the **Okura** or the strident opulence of the **Imperial** hotel. The bedrooms are moderately sized and reasonably furnished, with some useful accessories such as two telephones (in double rooms), a Japanese tea set and specially adapted "massage head" shower in the bathroom — although window-gazing is the most obvious attraction. The Palace has some excellent

restaurants, but with staid, uninspiring decor.
▱ ☿ ☿ ☖

President ♣
2-2-3, Minami Aoyama, Minato-ku, Tokyo 107 ☎ 497-0111 ⅠⅮⅮ
☏ 25575 ☏ 401-4816. Map *7/6* ▢
212 rms ⇌ ⇌ ⒜Ⓔ ⓓ ⓓ ⓥⓘⓢⓐ
Subway: Aoyama 1-chome.
Location: Next to Honda Motors head office, opposite Aoyama 1-chome Subway Station. The only hotel in fashionable *Aoyama*, with unfashionably moderate room-rates and two good-value (Japanese and Western) restaurants. The carpeted lobby is remarkable for its hideous, lifelike pottery sheepdog gazing with fawning eyes at a vacant imitation-leather chair. Other kitsch hotel fixtures are mercifully more subdued. Most rooms have good views over the verdant Aoyama Cemetery and central Tokyo's skyline; all are well furnished and have useful extras such as hairdryers, bilingual TVs and complimentary tea sets. Bathrooms are molded marvels of economy.
☿ ☖

Roppongi Prince ♣
3-2-7, Roppongi, Minato-ku, Tokyo 106 ☎ 587-1111 ⅠⅮⅮ
☏ 2427231 ☏ 587-0770. Map *4J7*
▢ 221 rms ⇌ ⒜Ⓔ ⓓ ⓓ ⓥⓘⓢⓐ
Subway: Roppongi.
Location: Between Tameike and Iikura main roads, directly behind IBM Japan. Another highly original new (1984) hotel of the Prince chain, hidden behind two modern IBM office buildings in a wedge of land between two major thoroughfares. The hotel, situated (if only marginally) in an area of fashionable nightlife, has been designed to appeal to the stylish young Japanese who frequent the *Roppongi* district. It has windows all along one side, with corridors overlooking a hollow core in the 4-sided tower down to an illuminated ameba-shaped pool at the bottom. On one side the pool is encased in plexiglass, allowing spectators in the curving terrace to get a view from below water level, similar to looking into a human aquarium. Moderately priced rooms are decorated in black, silver, white and gray; "high-tech minimalism" prevails. Two 1st-floor *teppanyaki* steak houses are awkwardly squashed in to fit the architecture, and another restaurant resembles a nightclub. The other bars and restaurants are excitingly distinctive.
☿ ☖

Hotels

Seiyo
1-11-2, Ginza, Chuo-ku, Tokyo 104 ☎ 535-1111 ⅢⅮ ☎ 2523118 ℻ 535-1110. Map ⅢⅮ ☎ *80 rms* 🚗 ⛽ AE ⓓ CB VISA *Subways: Ginza and Kyobashi.*

Location: On Ginza's main street. For years, Seiji Tsutsumi (head of the sprawling Seibu department store chain) had dreamed of creating a small, residential-style, ultra-exclusive hostelry in Tokyo, to match the levels of service given at Claridge's in London or New York's Mayfair Regent. Within a few months of Seiyo's opening in 1987, celebrities such as Elizabeth Taylor, Citibank's John Reed, an occasional Rothschild and the president of Sotheby's had already been drawn to this oasis of quiet European elegance on this bustling main street in the *Ginza* district. The phenomenal cost of staying here is certainly reflected in its standards. Guests without reservations are not allowed. The Seiyo only has 80 rooms and suites and staff far outnumber the guests, each of whom is assigned a personal secretary. Their services, ranging from handling dinner reservations to organizing interpreters, are available from the moment guests check in (at the reception lounge — no ordinary lobby here) to when they check out. Each of the spacious rooms and suites is individually designed (the bedroom in the most magnificent suite was modeled on Catherine Deneuve's own bedroom). Room telephones have buttons to call one's personal secretary or the concierge; sheets are made of Egyptian cotton, and guests can choose from seven different pillows; each room has separate humidity as well as air conditioning controls, and a private safe; TV sets come with VCRs, and the hotel has an extensive library of 200 video titles. The huge bathrooms, finished in white marble, have gold-plated taps and plugs, and separate glassed-in showers (some with steam-bath attachments). When Prime Minister Yasuhiro Nakasone dined here, he was among the first to marvel at the very extensive wine list (150 different Bordeaux and 97 Burgundies) in the **Pastorale** French restaurant on the 2nd floor. A branch of **Kitcho**, the famous *kaiseki* restaurant, and a northern Italian restaurant, with elegant lavender decor, are in the basement, together with a daringly designed, neon-lit coffee shop, which might be mistaken for a set from a Stanley Kubrick film.
🏨 🍽 🍴

Shiba Park
1-5-10, Shibakoen, Minato-ku, Tokyo 105 ☎ 433-4141 ☎ 2422917 ℻ 433-6327. Map *5J9* Ⅲ *400 rms* 🚗 ⛽ AE ⓓ CB VISA *Subway: Shibakoen.*

Location: Near Shibakoen (Shiba Park) and Tokyo Tower. Aggressive marketing probably accounts for the unusual predominance of foreign guests (especially Australians and New Zealanders) at this bustling hotel. Restaurant fare is aimed at *gaijin* (foreign) taste and is a poor substitute for Tokyo's culinary delights, which you can so easily find nearby. Rooms are decorated in clashing colors, and service is impersonal; but overall this is slightly above the usual business hotel standard.
🍽 🏨

Shibuya Tobu
3-1, Udagawa-cho, Shibuya-ku, Tokyo 150 ☎ 476-0111 ☎ 2425585 ℻ 476-0903. Map *2J3* Ⅲ *200 rms* 🚗 ⛽ AE ⓓ CB VISA *JR/subway: Shibuya.*

Location: At the top of Shibuya's Koen-dori Ave., near NHK broadcasting center and the Olympic stadium. A business hotel strategically poised on Shibuya's prime strolling-and-shopping street, close to Meiji and Yoyogi parks and to Harajuku (a teenage fashion paradise). It has a better-than-average choice of restaurants, but bedrooms are typically plain.
🍽 🏨

Shimbashi Dai-ichi
1-2-6, Shimbashi, Minato-ku, Tokyo 105 ☎ 501-4411 ☎ 2227262 ℻ 595-2634. Map *9J9* Ⅲ *1,106 rms* 🚗 ⛽ AE ⓓ CB VISA *JR/subway: Shimbashi.*

Location: Opposite Shimbashi JR Station. Brusque and businesslike, but with acceptable bar and restaurants, the chief attraction of this hotel is its close proximity to Shimbashi Station (for a quick getaway), and, like its sister hotel, the **Ginza Dai-ichi**, it is a cost-effective compromise for Ginza *aficionados*.
🍽 🏨

Shinagawa Prince 🏨
4-10-30, Takanawa, Minato-ku, Tokyo 108 ☎ 440-1111 ☎ 2425178 ℻ 441-7092. Map *4N7* ▢ *1,273 rms* 🚗 ⛽ AE ⓓ CB VISA *JR: Shinagawa; subway: Takanawadai.*

Location: Near Shinagawa JR Station, on Dai-ichi Keihin main road.

The hotel is part of a large sports/ leisure complex catering to exercise-starved young Tokyoites. The check-in lines at the reception areas set the tone of zippy functionalism. Annoyingly, hotel guests have only restricted access to the gym, bowling alley, tennis courts, skating rink and summer swimming pool, and also have to pay. Rooms are modern, bright and functional, suiting the sporty young image, and are surprisingly unboxlike and comfortable, considering the moderate room-rates. There is a 24hr coffee house, bar, three restaurants and a variety of shops. A business service room, fully-equipped with word processors, photocopier, fax and telex machines, is available. No room service.

⇒ *(summer)* ⍫ ♨ ♨ ♨

Shinjuku Prince♥
*1-30-1, Kabuki-cho, Shinjuku-ku,
Tokyo 160* ☎*205-1111* ⅢⅮⅮ
Ⓟ*2324733* Ⓧ *205-1952. Map 6F3*
☐ *571 rms* ⛵ ⊒ AE ⊕ ⓒ VISA
JR/subway: Shinjuku.

Location: Bordering Shinjuku's Kabukicho entertainment area. A respectable hotel on the borders of Kabukicho, an insalubrious, even disreputable, but always exciting part of town, Tokyo's equivalent of London's Soho. Neon lights offering a full course of pleasures form an interesting view from room windows, and there is a panoramic city view from the 25th-floor bar-lounge. Bedrooms are compact, but the rates are moderate considering the hotel's central location. With its affordable restaurants, 24hr room service and efficient staff, the Shinjuku Prince can be considered very good value.

⇐ ⍫

Takanawa Prince
*3-13-1, Takanawa, Minato-ku,
Tokyo 108* ☎*447-1111*
Ⓟ*2423232* Ⓧ *446-0849. Map 4N7*
ⅢⅢⅠ *413 rms* ⛵ ⊒ AE ⊕ ⓒ VISA
JR: Shinagawa; subway: Takanawadai.

Location: On a gentle hill near Shinagawa JR Station, off main arterial road. After the end of World War II the US Occupation forces confiscated the lands, properties and titles of all but the closest members of the Imperial Family. Seibu Tetsudo (Seibu Railways) was one of those corporations astute enough to seize upon the spoils of defeat; its Prince hotel chain was founded on lands that formerly belonged to dispossessed princes. Staff at the Takanawa Prince (1953) and its

ultramodern (1982) sister hotel next door still refer to Tsuneyoshi Takeda, the land's original owner (and cousin of Emperor Hirohito) as Prince Takeda, now resigned to living in a small commoner's house in the grounds that he formerly owned. His old house, a European-style Meiji-era villa, is now an annex to the main hotel and used for wedding receptions and banquets, as is the Neoclassical red brick **Prince Kaikan** banqueting hall, once residence to another family branch jointly owned by the Takanawa and New Takanawa hotels. The dazzling **New Takanawa Prince** nearby has made the dark gray "old" hotel look forbiddingly somber. Although the lobby has become increasingly shabby, well-used luxury still pervades the fine lounges and restaurants, and costly, colorful Japanese weddings provide a roaring business. Recently renovated rooms are simply but elegantly decorated, and generally offer good views. The extensive Japanese garden, the hotel's best asset, is a delightful place in which to stroll. Behind the pond, brimming with carp, are a Japanese teahouse, shady arbors and even a Buddhist temple, its own gate and belfry leading to a sanctum containing a statue of Kannon carved in the Kamakura period (moved here in 1954). Guests have use of three summer swimming pools, two in the grounds of the Takanawa Prince and one in the **New Takanawa Prince**. *Sukiyaki, shabu-shabu* and *teppanyaki* restaurants are located behind the annex; Chinese and *shippoku* (Nagasaki cuisine) restaurants are located in the two traditional-style buildings by the main entrance drive.

▭ ⛵ ⇐ ⇒ *(summer)* ⍫ ♨

Takanawa Tobu
*4-7-6, Takanawa, Minato-ku,
Tokyo 108* ☎*447-0111
(reservations 445-4521)*
Ⓟ*2425252* Ⓧ *447-0111. Map 4N7*
☐ *198 rms* ⛵ ⊒ AE ⊕ ⓒ VISA
JR: Shinagawa; subway: Takanawadai.

Location: Near Shinagawa JR Station. This spartan, dormitory-style concrete hotel is in complete contrast to the **New Takanawa Prince's** hedonistic showpiece directly opposite. Though it resembles the kind of dormitory accommodations provided by companies for their Japanese factory workers, it may well appeal to thrifty travelers.

⛵ ⇐ ⇒ *(summer)* ⍫ ♨

105

Hotels

Tokyo Hilton
6-6-2, Nishi-Shinjuku, Shinjuku-ku, Tokyo 160 ☎344-5111 IDD
ⓣ2324515 ⓕ 342-6094. *Map 6G2*
IIIII *841 rms* 🚗 ⟺ AE CB ⓪
VISA *JR/subway: Shinjuku.*
Location: w *Shinjuku ("Skyscraper City").* The Hilton has put a brave face on its forced move from the nerve center of Nagatacho to the concrete wasteland of w Shinjuku, known as "Skyscraper City," but whatever praises are sung about its new location, the Hilton is still not only on the wrong side of the city but also the wrong side of all the fun in Shinjuku. To draw the crowds it now provides a far more impressive range of facilities than it did in its former premises (now the **Capitol Tokyu**). These include a swimming pool, tennis courts, gym, massage and sauna facilities and a battery of executive services — though a garden view would have been welcome. One fortunate inheritance is the fine cuisine, in particular the excellent **Dynasty** Chinese restaurant. A younger clientele now fills the luxurious, Oriental-style lobby lounge, and the Nagatacho politicians of the old days are hardly missed. Rooms are spacious and well furnished, with *shoji* sliding windows, room-temperature control, a well-stocked bar and an extra telephone in each bathroom. 24hr room service.
& ⟺⟺ ≋ 🍴 🚗 ⟋⟍ ♨ ⚐ 👙

Tokyo Kanko
4-10-8, Takanawa, Minato-ku, Tokyo 108 ☎443-1211
(reservations 447-5881)
ⓣ2422804 ⓕ 443-1221. *Map 4N7*
☐ *150 rms* 🚗 ⟺ AE ⓪ VISA
JR: Shinagawa; subway: Takanawadai.
Location: On a hill near Shinagawa JR Station, off the main Dai-ichi Keihin arterial road. A slightly down-at-heels business hotel. In exchange for cheap room-rates, guests can expect clean sheets and small bedrooms.

Tokyo Prince
3-3-1, Shiba-koen, Minato-ku, Tokyo 105 ☎432-1111
ⓣ2422488 ⓕ 434-5551. *Map 5J8*
IIIII *480 rms* 🚗 ⟺ AE ⓪ ⓪ VISA
JR: Hamamatsucho; subway: Onarimon.
Location: In Shibakoen (Shiba Park) by Zojoji Temple, near the Tokyo Tower. Built on the site of the Tokugawa shoguns' mausolea next to the once mighty *Zojoji Temple*, the Tokyo Prince now has a faded look.

Japanese politicians are still attracted by its massive banqueting halls and enormous parking lot, which are ideal for fund-raising parties, but otherwise it appeals mainly to those impressed by its past luxuries.
🖼 & 🚲 ≋ *(summer)* 🍴 👙

Tokyo Station
1-9-1, Marunouchi, Chiyoda-ku, Tokyo 100 ☎231-2511 ⓕ 231-3513. *Map 9H10* **IIIII** *63 rms* 🚗 ⟺ AE ⓪ ⓪ VISA *JR/subway: Tokyo.*
Location: Tokyo Station building. The hotel occupies most of the ornate red brick Tokyo Station building, one of the city's most distinctive landmarks. Completed in 1915, the interior structure has changed very little, making a night's stay a nostalgic experience. All the rooms are spacious, with high ceilings and comfortable chairs and sofas, the better class having good-quality furnishings and modern bathrooms. Window views, however, would only be appreciated by train spotters. The dining room, a curiosity like much of the hotel, is at the top of one of the two corner towers, its elegant atmosphere sporadically broken by the rattle of express trains, which occasionally drown the strains of classical music. No room service.
🍴 👙

Yaesu Fujiya
2-9-1, Yaesu, Chuo-ku, Tokyo 100 ☎273-2111 ⓣ 2223801 ⓕ 273-2180. *Map 9G10* ☐ *377 rms* 🚗 ⟺ AE ⓪ ⓪ VISA *JR: Yurakucho; subway: Ginza-itchome.*
Location: Between Ginza-itchome and Kyobashi subway stations. A large, modern business hotel with a superior marbled entrance lobby and some good restaurants, including Japanese and French, but only small bedrooms. No room service.
🍴 👙

Yaesu-Ryumeikan 🏠
1-3-22, Yaesu, Chuo-ku, Tokyo 103 ☎271-0971. *Map 9H10* ☐ *32 rms* ⟺ ⓪ VISA *Subway: Nihonbashi; JR/subway: Tokyo.*
Location: Near the N *exit (Yaesu side) of Tokyo Station, next to the Aeroflot office on main road.* A Japanese-style *ryokan* inn in the heart of the city. The best place to experience a *ryokan* is probably not in Tokyo but in the more peaceful and natural surroundings of the country. However, the Yaesu-Ryumeikan at least offers the chance to sleep in a *futon* on *tatami* mats, and has excellent Western and country-style Japanese food.

Where to eat

Tokyoites probably eat out more often than city dwellers of any other nation, which has given rise to an astonishing range of restaurants to suit every conceivable taste and budget. At the last count there were 52,000 eating places in metropolitan Tokyo, nearly twice as many as there are in New York. One reason for this glut is that Tokyo is plagued by a shortage of living space, which makes home entertaining impossible for the majority of people. (The typical Tokyo restaurant is also very small: only 12 seats.) However, the most important reason is the Japanese love of food, amply demonstrated by their native culinary genius.

When it comes to food, absolute freshness is the basic prerequisite for the fastidious Japanese. Housewives shop every day for fresh vegetables, fish or meat; deepfreezes are virtually unheard of in the kitchen, and pantries are almost devoid of cans. As you would expect, this concern carries over into restaurants as well.

Japanese cuisine aims at satisfying far more than mere hunger. At its most sublime, it is inextricably linked with esthetics, religion, tradition and history. A Japanese gourmet might say that although Chinese food concentrates solely on flavors, and the French are masters of artificial disguise and presentation, only Japanese cuisine adheres closely to natural tastes as well as paying equal attention to the beauty of service.

Cha kaiseki
Cha kaiseki evolved in the 16thC as a means of taking the edge off hunger for participants in the tea ceremony, but still adhering to a spirit of frugal but refined estheticism. The name derives from the warm stones (*seki*) that Buddhist monks placed in the pockets (*kai*) of their robes during long meditation, to alleviate hunger. A *kaiseki* meal can still best be described as a highly formalized communion with nature. Some restaurants serve as many as 12 courses (often tiny bite-sized morsels), each meticulously chosen and regularly varied to be evocative of seasonal change. Equal care is taken that the vessels complement the exquisitely prepared food, satisfying the eye as much as the palate.

Ryotei
The finest and most exclusive *kaiseki* restaurants are called *ryotei*, where business executives and politicians entertain or conclude important deals. The best clue to the existence of a *ryotei* is the number of black limousines lined up outside, or the scurry of geisha into what is usually a small, dark and hidden entrance. The discreetness of *ryotei* exemplify a major difference in attitude to European or American diners, who partly pay high prices to wallow in social celebrity. In Japan one pays an equivalent price to withdraw from society altogether, into the privacy of a small *zashiki* room, laid with bare *tatami* mats. The discriminating eye will soon pick out a beautiful flower arrangement or *sumi-e* (ink painting) in the *tokonoma* (alcove), and nearby there is certain to be the burble of a stream in a Japanese garden. These pleasures, and the miniature works of culinary perfection laid before you, are designed to be savored in a mood of tranquil contemplation rather than social exuberance.

To become a patron at a high-class *ryotei* requires an introduction, as well as an expense account befitting a director of Honda or Sony. However, there are many *kaiseki* establishments that are less expensive and more accessible, and also other Japanese restaurants who display a similarly refined esthetic approach in their decor.

Restaurants

Sushi

Sushi needs no introduction, except perhaps the revelation in taste that will come from eating the genuine article in Tokyo. The cheapest and most filling *sushi* meal is usually a set course, but connoisseurs prefer to sit at the counter and order individually. Some favorites are: *uni* (dark yellow sea urchin eggs); *ikura* (red salmon roe); *o-toro* (the finest grade of tuna, pink in color and cut from the belly of the fish); *maguro* (plain red tuna taken from the back and with much less fat); *take* (octopus); *ikka* (squid); *ebi* (shrimp); *temaki*, which is a cone of rolled seaweed with rice and another ingredient — such as *nigi toro maki* (with chopped scallions and *toro*) or *uni maki* (served with *uni*). Also served at *sushiya* restaurants are *sashimi* (slices of raw fish eaten with a dip of soy sauce into which some *wasabi*, or Japanese horseradish mustard is mixed).

Teppanyaki

If you don't like the idea of eating raw fish, try one of the restaurants specializing in prime Kobe sirloin, the finest, and probably most expensive, in the world. *Teppanyaki* restaurants slowly grill the expertly cut beef (as well as chicken, seafood, pork and vegetables) on table-top metal hotplates. Some restaurants still use traditional hot stones (*ishi-yaki*) for extra tenderness.

Sukiyaki and shabu-shabu

Prepared at one's table, *sukiyaki* consists of thin slices of beef cooked together with vegetables in an iron pan containing a thick, slightly sweet soy-based broth. You will be given a bowl with a beaten egg for dipping the cooked beef in. Sometimes chicken is substituted, to make a cheaper meal. The name *shabu-shabu* derives from the sound the meat makes when swished around the boiling bouillon broth, which is clear and only lightly seasoned. In *shabu-shabu* dishes, the dip will be either *ponzu* (juice pressed from bitter oranges) or *gomadare* (with a base of ground sesame seeds and *miso*). At the end of the meal the waitress seasons the broth and adds noodles to make a tasty soup.

Nabemono

In winter a popular and filling meal is *nabemono* (literally, things in a pot), a sort of Japanese bouillabaisse. An artfully arranged platter of leeks, Chinese cabbage, mushrooms, *tofu* (soybean curd), firm white meat — fish or chicken — is brought to the table and boiled inside the thick-walled earthenware *nabe* (pot), a typical feature of the Japanese farmhouse. As each morsel is ready, the waitress takes it out with long chopsticks and places it on your plate. At the end of the meal the broth is often used to cook either *zosui* (rice porridge) or *udon*, a type of noodle (see below). A cheaper and simpler version, originally eaten by sumo wrestlers in training, is *chanko-nabe*. Such restaurants are often decorated inside with sumo fan paraphernalia.

Tempura and kushiage

Tempura is equally beloved by both Japanese people and foreigners. Some say the technique of deep-frying battered fresh seafood, fish and vegetables was introduced by Portuguese missionaries in the 16thC, others that it originated in China. The *tempura* is usually dipped in a bowl of *tentsuya* sauce (made from fish-based stock, *mirin* — sweet sake — and soy sauce) with grated radish and ginger added to taste. Some restaurants offer an alternative dip of freshly ground sea salt, or simply wedges of lemon. Cheaper, and highly filling, is *tonkatsu*: a pork cutlet, dipped in *tempura* batter then covered with breadcrumbs, deep fried, and served with a heap of crisp, freshly shredded raw cabbage. It is also eaten with lashings of a Japanese-style

Worcestershire sauce, which is either *amakuchi* (slightly sweet) or *karakuchi* (slightly hot) — both pots will be found on the table.

Less well known are *kushiage* restaurants, where fish, meat or vegetables are skewered, battered, covered with breadcrumbs and deep fried.

Yakitori

On his way home from the office the Tokyo *salariman* will often stop at a *yakitori* near the railroad station. Large volumes of drink (usually beer) are an essential accompaniment to skewers of chicken (*tori*) basted in sweet soy sauce and grilled (*yaki*) over charcoal. Typical orders are for *sasami yakitori* (chicken breast), *shiitake yaki* (Japanese mushrooms), *piiman toriyaki* (chicken and green peppers) and *ginnan yaki* (ginkgo nuts). There are a great many earthy *yakitori*, recognizable by their red lanterns hanging outside, around the JR railroad line in Yurakucho, as well as more "refined" versions in Roppongi.

Robatayaki

Almost as simple are *robatayaki* restaurants, where fish, seafood and vegetables are grilled over an open fire, similar to the traditional *robata* set in the middle of an old Japanese *tatami*-matted living room. *Robatayaki* are some of the noisiest and most picturesque of Japanese restaurants, with a rustic atmosphere to match the style of cooking. They serve a wide range of Japanese food, much of it is conveniently displayed around the counter, so diners can easily point out what they want. Drink — usually sake or beer — plays more than a supporting role in the festivity.

Japanese noodles

Japanese noodles, which bear no relation to pasta, are taken very seriously by Tokyoites. The coarse and unrefined appearance of handmade (*te-uchi*) buckwheat noodles (*soba*) appealed to the ascetic tastes of Buddhists, who helped disseminate the taste until there were more *soba* restaurants than any other in Edo. In summer connoisseurs head for long-established stores to slurp cold *soba*, piled on a bamboo lattice inside a lacquer box (*zary*) and briefly dipped in a small bowl of delicious sauce into which some grated horseradish and thinly sliced leeks have been added. At the end of ht meal the waitresses present apitcher of *soba-yu* (the hot water used for boiling the *soba*) for mixing with the sauce to make a soup, which is drunk from the from the same bowl.

Cha soba, also popular in the summer months, is green-colored, due to the addition of powdered green tea. For a more filling meal, ask for *tenzaru*, which is shrimp and vegetable *tempura* served with plain *zaru soba*. Hot *udon soba* come in a fish stock soup with diced leeks: ask for *tempura soba*, served with *tempura* shrimp, or *tsukimi soba* served with an egg on top (said to make it look like a "moon").

Udon are thick, white wheat noodles served in similar soup combinations as *soba*. Among the combinations you can try are *tempura udon*, or *sansai udon* (served with mountain vegetables). *Ramen*, thin Chinese noodles served in bowls of hot soup, are one of Tokyo's cheapest and most filling standbys. Although patronizing a *ramen-ya* is considered slightly *déclassé*, Japanese of every standing are prone to sudden cravings — often late at night —for a bowl of *cha shiu'mei* (barbecued pork in *ramen* soup), often with a serving of *gyoza* (crescent-shaped pork dumplings dipped in soy, vinegar and chili sauce).

Unagi

Freshwater eels, or *unagi*, may be unattractive in their natural appearance, but no gourmet would ever turn up his nose at the delicious eel fillet served at a Tokyo *unagi-ya* restaurant. These delicacies are basted with sweet soy-based sauce, grilled over a bed of hot charcoal, steamed, rinsed, basted and grilled again to a consistency of rich, tender pâté. Japanese men still believe eating *unagi* improves virility, and in fact they are so rich in calories and vitamins it is little wonder that Japanese of either sex flock to *unagi-ya* during the stamina-draining hot summers. Ask for *unaju*, eel fillet on a bed of rice inside a lacquer box; *kabayaki*, eel fillet by itself; or the *unagi teishoku* full set course. The *unagi* are often ranked into *nami* (regular), *jo* (choice) and *tokujo* (special) qualities. Be sure to sprinkle some ground, tangy *sansho* (Japanese pepper) on top of the eel. *Dojo* (loach), a plump little fish (that looks like sardine when cooked) is a cheaper delicacy.

Specialty restaurants

Some restaurants are licensed to sell a poisonous pufferfish delicacy called *fugu* that can cause death if not prepared in capable hands. Others cater to delicious matchings of *tofu*, or *shojin ryori* (Buddhist temple food), and some even go to the length of exploring the gastronomic possiblities of the mountain potato. In Shinjuku there is a restaurant called **Toshigiya**, which has a "beastly" reputation for its venison, wild boar and bear meat.

International restaurants

The majority of foreign restaurants in Tokyo are Korean and Chinese (being the only two sizeable ethnic minorities); but French, Italian, German and Indian also abound. You can also find Vietnamese, Thai, Indonesian, Cambodian, Mexican, Greek, Spanish, African, Pakistani, Lebanese, Swiss, Brazilian, Russian, Hungarian and Czech restaurants competing for the jaded gastronome's attention.

However, *aficionados* may balk at the transformation many familiar ethnic dishes have undergone to suit the mythical "Japanese taste." For example, the amount of natural spices used in Tokyo's typical Korean barbecue restaurants (called *yaki-niku* by Japanese) has been heavily reduced, and many dishes served in cheap Chinese restaurants have been similarly sanitized by adding too much monosodium glutamate (invented by the Japanese company Ajinomoto). The resulting blandness is probably all too familiar.

Happily there are many flourishing havens of culinary authenticity. Tokyo can undoubtedly boast some of the finest French cuisine anywhere E of Lyons or Paris. Many were started by French pioneers, employ French chefs, or are run by Japanese who have learnt their craft in famous French establishments. Unfortunately, prices, even without wine, tend to be unnecessarily steep. The best Italian and Indian restaurants in Tokyo may be ranked next in quality, but don't take size and interior splendor as reliable guides to what comes out of the kitchen.

The following selection omits (with one exception) some of the truly excellent restaurants in Tokyo hotels, as most tend to be more expensive than their equivalents outside. (Before leaving the hotel, be sure to check the location of the restaurant to which you are heading — see *Japanese addresses* in *Basic information*.

Dining customs

Gratuities are never expected in Japanese restaurants, except in the most exclusive *ryotei*, and any tip will either be handed back or cause acute embarrassment. In most cases 20 percent, for service and government tax, is added to bills above a certain level.

Some brazen confidence (but not bravado) is required to enter many smaller restaurants where English menus may not be available, and where the staff are likely to be terrified of foreigners' painful inability to express what they want. However, with a little prior research you should get by — although pointing often works wonders, and many restaurants have wax duplicates of dishes in the window.

Service is generally excellent, particularly in better-class restaurants, where the waiters display a courtesy, deportment and efficiency that will leave many Westerners weeping in nostalgia.

The Japanese abhor public fuss or confrontation, and should any lapse in standard occur, a polite word usually suffices to set things right. Few Japanese diners would send a dish back to the kitchen; they would rather pay the bill and tacitly express their displeasure by not returning.

Etiquette

It is accepted practice for pieces of solid food in a soup to be eaten with chopsticks, and the liquid drunk directly from the bowl. Japanese consider it correct to slurp their noodles noisily, as the air sucked in helps in cooling. Sauces are generally intended for dipping, not soaking, which would destroy the food's flavor, and are almost never added to rice (one exception is the rice porridge made in a *nabe* at the end of a meal). However, do not rest your chopsticks vertically in the rice, or pass food from chopstick to chopstick — both are associated with death and are considered very bad manners.

O-nomimono (drinks)

The habit of drinking tea (*o-cha*) throughout the day remains so pervasive that in most Japanese restaurants you will be given a pot or bowl without being asked. Contrary to the international opinion that Japanese always drink green tea, the most popular is in fact cheap *bancha*, brown-colored tea made from the tougher leaves and stems. *Hojicha* (toasted *bancha*) is also common in everyday restaurants and has a distinctive smoky flavor. In summer you may also get the chance to drink chilled *mugicha*, which is made from barley. *Sencha* is green tea, the type usually served to guests, and available in a prodigious range of subtly graded qualities. *Matcha* is the original powdered green variety used in the tea ceremony, now often served after being whisked in a beautiful bowl, to complete an elaborate *kaiseki* meal. *Matcha* is thick and bitter — decidedly an acquired taste.

O-sake is the Japanese word for any alcoholic drink, although in restaurants, and *nomiya* drinking places, it often refers to the fermented Japanese rice wine (more properly *Nihon shu*, or Japanese sake) with which sake is exclusively associated abroad. Mentioned in the earliest chronicles, this national drink is served on all important occasions, and remains integral to Shinto ceremonies as a ritual libation to the gods. Japanese couples seal their nuptial vows by sharing a sake cup; sumo wrestlers drink it at their moment of triumph; sake is offered at dedications of new buildings; and no traditional party would be complete without breaking open a sake cask. To bring good luck at New Year, family members share cups of *toso*, a mixture of sake, *mirin* (sweet seasoned sake) and medicinal herbs.

Sake goes well with every Japanese dish, and is often used as an ingredient in cooking. There are over 2,500 sake brewers in Japan, and endless disputes as to which is the best label, with many Japanese swearing fidelity to their local brew. For tax purposes, sake is ranked into *ikkyu* (first-) or *nikyu* (second-class); but the most important, and sometimes unrelated, consideration is purity. The best sake is always *junmaishu*, containing only fermented rice, yeast and water. *Junmaishu* is sometimes classed as *nikyu* for tax purposes. *Honjozoshu* sake may contain up to 25 percent industrial alcohol, and *Sanbaizoshu* (the rotgut sold in cans at railroad stations) may be laced with up to 75 percent industrial alcohol and brewer's sugar. Of the more common *amakuchi* (sweet varieties) of sake *Goshun, Kikunoshiro* or *Toyonoaki* can be recommended; for *karakuchi* (dry) sake try *Kusudama* or *Hitorimusume*.

Sake is best drunk warmed, *not* piping hot, from a *tokkuri* (ceramic flask). In cheap restaurants a small glass bottle may be substituted. At parties, you may be given cold sake inside a *masu* (square wooden cup), with a sprinkling of salt on one side for drinking tequila-style.

Japan's only distilled liqor is *shochu*, made from rice, sweet potato or millet. When undiluted it has a powerful kick, and was once frowned upon as a proletarian drink (like gin in 18th-19thC England). Recently, however, there has been a *shochu* cocktail boom, especially among the young. Popular *shochu* mixes are lemon high (with lemonade), oolong high (with oolong Chinese tea), *goma-jochu* (with sesame) and *kuri-jochu* (with chestnut). *Umeshu* is made by steeping *ume* (green Japanese plums) in *shochu* and sugar for at least 1yr, and is often served at the start of a *kaiseki* meal.

Beer has long since overtaken *Nihon shu* as the most popular drink to accompany a meal. Similar in taste and quality to German "blond" beer, it is always served chilled. Ask for *nama biru* when you want draft. *Ko bin* is a small bottle, *chu bin* is medium-sized and *dai bin* is large-sized. Yebisu is often rated the best brand, though many brewers are now turning out malt beers.

Wine consumption progresses by leaps and bounds in Tokyo, but it is still rare to find wine served with Japanese cuisine in any but the more fashionable or international restaurants. Japan's climate, especially the heavy summer rainfalls, is not conducive to good wine as the grapes tend to be large and watery, with a low alcohol content. One suspects Japanese wine, such as Suntory's infamous Chateau Mercian owes its popularity only to an iniquitous tax structure that makes imported bottled wine far more expensive than mixing native produce with dehydrated grape musk and bulk wine imported from Spain, Eastern Europe and South America. You may well find that a bottle of decent French wine in a Tokyo restaurant will cost more than the meal.

The Japanese have a passion for whisky, usually drunk with water and called *mizu-wari*. Having been protected by tax barriers from the real thing, many Tokyoites now claim that local Suntory or Nikka whiskies are just as good as Scotch. However, the only Japanese ingredients are the neutral spirits used in the blend, and the "whisky" base is imported in bulk carriers from Scotland. No such qualification is required for Tokyo's excellent tap water!

Restaurants classified by area

Nagasaka Sarashina ☐ Jap
  (soba)
Nodaiwa �‖☐ Jap (unagi/dojo)
Daikanyama
Daikon-ya ‖‖‖ Jap (kaiseki)
Ginza
Dai-ni Manmaru Zushi ‖☐ Jap
  (sushi/sashimi)
Maxim's de Paris ‖‖‖ Fr
Sabatini di Firenze ‖‖‖ It
Ten-ichi ‖‖‖ Jap (tempura)
Hakusan
Goemon ‖☐ Jap (tofu)
Jingumae
Isen ☐ Jap (tonkatsu)
La Patata ‖☐ It
Kojimachi
Tambaya ☐ Jap (unagi/dojo)
Meguro
Tonki ☐ Jap (tonkatsu)
Nihonbashi
Sunaba ☐ Jap (soba)
Ningyocho
Hiyama ‖‖‖ Jap (shab/suki/tepp)
Tamahide ‖‖‖ Jap
  (shab/suki/tepp)
Roppongi
AD Colliseum ‖☐ Viet
Bengawan Solo ‖☐ Indon
Brasserie Bernard ‖☐ Fr
Chisen ‖☐ Jap (kushiage)
Fukuzushi ‖☐ Jap
  (sushi/sashimi)
Ile de France ‖‖‖ Fr
Kamakura ‖☐ Jap (yakitori)
Kisso ‖‖‖ Jap (kaiseki)

Metropole ‖‖‖ Ch
Minokichi ‖‖☐ Jap (kyo-ryori)
Moti ‖☐ Ind
Mr Stamp's Wine Garden ‖‖☐
  intnl
Nanban-tei ‖☐ Jap (yakitori)
Seryna ‖‖‖ Jap (shab/suki/tepp)
Spago ‖‖☐ Am
Stockholm ‖‖☐ Scand
Takamura ‖‖‖ Jap (kaiseki)
Toricho ‖☐ Jap (yakitori)
Shibuya
Chotoku ‖☐ Jap (udon)
Ishikawa ‖‖☐ Jap (nabemono)
Tsukiji
Sushiiwa ‖☐ Jap (sushi/sashimi)
Tamura ‖‖‖ Jap (kaiseki)
Ueno
Honke Ponta ‖☐ Jap (tonkatsu)
Santomo ‖‖‖ Jap (fugu)
Seiyokan ‖‖‖ Fr

Key to types of cuisine

Am American
Ch Chinese
Fr French
Ind Indian
Indon Indonesian
intnl international
It Italian
Jap Japanese *
Kor Korean
Scand Scandinavian
Viet Vietnamese
*shab/suki/tepp shabu-shabu,
  sukiyaki, teppanyaki

AD Colliseum

*Ark Towers West, 1st floor, 1-3-
40, Roppongi, Minato-ku ☎505-
4545. Map 4/J7 ‖☐ ☐ ▼ AE ⊕
⊡ VISA Last orders Mon-Sat
1.30am, Sun, hols 11.30pm.
Subway: Roppongi.*
The gleaming Ark Hills complex
consists of swank residential towers,
a "financial center," concert hall and
expensive hotel, and has rapidly
become a stronghold of well-heeled,
style-conscious Shinjin rui, the new
breed of Japanese yuppy. AD
Colliseum made its entrance here in
1986 and immediately established
itself as one of the most fashionable,
if not gastronomically satisfying,
restaurants in Tokyo. The London
textile partnership Timney and
Fowler designed the striking interior
that cleverly combines the "new
wave" obsession for dynamically
contrasting black with ancient
Roman motifs (such as emperors'
busts, Classical statuary and vases).
The menu is similar to the
Vietnamese-French *nouvelle cuisine*
dispensed at the Vifian brothers' **Tan
Dinh** restaurant in Paris, but here
they have added more seafood-based
dishes in deference to Japanese taste.

Portions are predictably minuscule
but reasonably priced and include
such exotic encounters as
chrysanthemum leaf salad with spicy
yogurt dressing, or ark-shell soup
with Japanese radish vermicelli
(although some aren't as delectable as
they sound). The choice of drinks is
cosmopolitan, although a bottle of
decent wine will probably cost more
than the food. Monochrome-
costumed staff (ranging from baggy
peasant trousers and Khmer Rouge
black shirts to wing collar and bow
tie) help set the tone, and can either
be seen as reflecting fashionable
fancy, ethnic eclecticism or culinary
confusion, depending on individual
taste.

Bengawan Solo ♣

*7-18-13, Roppongi, Minato-ku
☎408-5698. Map 4/J7 ☐ ☐ AE
⊕ ⊡ VISA Last orders 9.45pm.
Closed year end and New Year.
Subway: Roppongi.*
It seems unusual, but this modestly
priced Indonesian restaurant is very
popular with Japanese wedding
parties. Their jollification is not
diminished in the least by the dusty
potted palms, faded batik pictures,

battered national banners of Indonesia and Japan and Balian statue of a maiden in an immodest pose. The rest of humanity comes here merely to eat well and cheaply on dishes such as spicy shrimp and crisp fried chicken, delicious *gado-gado* (Indonesian salad with peanut dressing and shrimp crackers). In addition to importing Indonesian condiments and gaudy shirts, Bengawan Solo also runs a travel agency, so after licking your fingers (perfectly acceptable here) and paying the bill, you could buy a ticket to Bali.

Bistro de la Cité♨
4-2-10, Nishi-Azabu, Minato-ku ☎406-5475. Map *4/J7* ▥ AE ⓪ *Last orders 10pm. Closed Mon. Subway: Roppongi.*

Its unprising position (tucked away on one of Nishi-Azabu's more prosaic small shopping streets) perhaps explains why this jewel of provincial French gastronomy has yet to win the same renown as competitors in nearby Roppongi. First-time visitors inevitably suffer the *trompe l'oeil* bewilderment of Alice following the White Rabbit. A dark narrow passageway opens into a snug room fitted in rich dark wood that seems so authentically French it takes a while to notice that the waiters, in wing collars and white bows have Japanese faces. As well as excellent service the surroundings are attractive — tables are set with classic French silverware, and the French windows at the far end open onto a tiny garden. The small but select menu centers around delicious fish and seafood; but you can't go wrong with the generously portioned meat dishes either, with such delights as *canard rôti aux poivres verts avec marrons à l'orange*; and their set lunches offer one of the best deals in town. The Burgundy, Bordeaux and Loire wines from the cellar are expensive, but the much cheaper French house wine is gratifyingly potable. The Bistro is under the same management as **Aux Six Arbres** in Roppongi.

Botan♨
1-15, Kandasuda-chu, Chiyoda-ku ☎251-0577. Map *9F10* ▣ ▢ *Last orders 8pm. Closed Sun, hols, 2wks during Aug. Subway: Awajicho/Ogawamachi (A3 exit).*

As befits this Shitamachi neighborhood, which time seems to have passed by, the main sign of progress at Botan in the past century has been the introduction of electric

lights. Botan has no need of a menu, as there is only one dish: *tori sukiyaki*. The chickens that go into this dish come from the same free-ranges in Gumma and Saitama prefectures as when the restaurant was founded four generations ago. The waitresses in kimonos, who live on the premises, bring the glowing charcoal for the brazier, and the original sake (sweet Sakura Masamune) is still served. The waiting room is heated in the traditional way by old *hibachi* (charcoal brazier), and the rooms are all *zashiki* style, with tables as low as those at nearby **Yabu Soba**. Many of the customers are the grandchildren of neighborhood craftsmen and storekeepers, who first frequented Botan during the Meiji period. The Japanese name "Botan" comes from the "button" factory where the founder originally worked.

Brasserie Bernard♨
7th floor, Kajimaya Building, 7-14-3, Roppongi, Minato-ku ☎405-7877. Map *4/J7* ▥ ▢ ▿ ▭ AE ⓪ ⓒ vISA *Last orders midnight. Subway: Roppongi.*

Tokyo's celebrity chef André Bernard has catered to embassy parties, and French President François Mitterrand when he visited Tokyo in 1986. Although there is now a branch in the **Printemps Ginza** department store (see *Shopping*), his main restaurant remains in an oddly obscure roost on the 7th floor of the Kamimaya building just past the **Ibis** (see *Hotels*). You will know you have arrived safely by the babble of French tongues from habitués clustered around the bar. It is best visited in the evening for a candlelit dinner, when there is an *à la carte* as well as two set-price menus. Bernard (like his nearest rival chef Pachon at **Ile de France**) offers traditional *cuisine bourgeoise*. The question of which restaurant, for instance, serves better *aiguillette d'agneau* or *coquilles St. Jacques* often provides meat for postprandial dispute.

Chez Figaro
4-4-1, Nishi-Azabu, Minato-ku ☎400-8718. Map *4K6* ▥ ▢ AE ⓪ ⓒ vISA *Last orders 9.30pm. Closed Sun. Subway: Hiro.*

The novelty, for Tokyoites, of authentic French cuisine has been wearing thin since 1969 when owner and chef Takashi Iribe founded Chez Figaro (after extensive training in Cannes and at **Maxim's**). But it is the orthodox, traditional dishes that command a loyal following of French expatriates and no-nonsense Japanese diners, who appreciate "Chez Fig's" stolid, bourgeois self-assurance. The wrought-iron chandeliers, faded French travel posters and foreign banknotes plastered to the wood-paneled wall are nostalgic reminders of a less cosmopolitan, sophisticated age.

Chez Pierre ♣
1-23-10, Minami Aoyama, Minato-ku ☎*475-1400. Map 3J5* ▉▉▉ ⬜ 🍴 ⬅ AE ⓪ ⓒ VISA *Last orders 10pm. Closed every Mon in Aug. Subway: Nogizaka (w exit).*

Owner Pierre Prigent is a member of France's Academic Culinaire and humbly describes his new restaurant overlooking verdant Aoyama Cemetery as offering simple *cuisine familiale*. This doesn't do justice, however, to his rigid insistance on serving utterly authentic French provincial cuisine, an infectious devotion shared by every member of his young Japanese staff. Chez Pierre serves some of the finest *bouillabaisse* in Tokyo, and with typical fastidiousness has the Dover sole flown in from Paris. This is also one of the few French restaurants in the city to offer *filet de cheval*, as well as *grenouilles*, *confit de cailles* and *ris de veau*. Chez Pierre now has its own wine label (red Loires were a recent unusual addition to an impressive list), and the mouthwatering *gâteaux* are all made on the premises. The simple decor is warm, homey and typically French. Opposite a front counter (popular with single customers) is a small terrace, ostensibly for boulevard-watching, although diners invariably draw most of the stares from startled Japanese motorists.

Chinya ♣
1-3-4, Asakusa, Taito-ku ☎*841-0010. Map 16C13* ▉▉▉ ⬜ 🚗 ⓪ ⓒ *Last orders 9pm. Closed Wed. Subway: Asakusa.*

A famous *sukiyaki* and *shabu-shabu* restaurant of early Meiji provenance, with a prime location on the main street (on the left of the Kaminarimon gate of *Asakusa Kannon Temple*). The *sukiyaki teishoku* and *shabu-shabu teishoku* courses offer the best value, with *sashimi*, rice, *miso* soup, side dishes and dessert included. Western seating is available at a basement counter. The other floors are all *zashiki* rooms of varying elegance.

Chisen ♣
7-16-5, Roppongi, Minato-ku ☎*478-6241. Map 4J7* ▉▉▉ ⬜ AE ⓪ ⓒ VISA *Last orders 10pm. Closed Dec 30-Jan 4. Subway: Roppongi.*

Unsuccessfully vying for attention with the exterior of the nearby Turia disco, Chisen's unusual wooden entrance, reminiscent of temple architecture, beckons the more traditional into a tasteful and relaxing Japanese setting for simple *kushiage*. The "flexible" course, which includes side dishes and all the *kushiage* skewers one can eat, is the chief attraction. English menus are available.

Chotoku ♣
1-10-5, Shibuya, Shibuya-ku ☎*407-8891. Map 2J3* ▉▉▉ ⬜ AE ⓪ ⓒ VISA *Last orders 9.30pm. Closed last week of Aug. JR/subway: Shibuya.*

The aristocrat of plain *udon-ya*, Chotoku has Haydn and Beethoven slurp its thick handmade noodles, which have been prepared on the premises. A samurai mask and Japanese kites adorn the walls, and bordering one small *zashiki* area of split-bamboo mats are original Japanese paintings entitled *Lunchtime* and the *Seasons of Sanuki* (the birthplace in Shikoku island of Chotoku's famous noodles). The bulky menu, bound in embroidery and with English translations plus full-color photographs of every dish, includes a filling *chotoku nabe*; *tofu*; tempura; Japanese desserts; and 49 different *udon* dishes and courses, ranging from *kaiseki* to plain *zaru*.

Dai-ni Manmaru Zushi ♣
Marugen 53 Building, 7-6-14, Ginza, Chuo-ku ☎*572-0484. Map 9I10* ▉▉▉ ⬜ AE ⓪ ⓒ VISA *Last orders Mon-Fri 2am, Sat 10pm. Closed Sun, hols. JR/subway: Shimbashi; subway: Ginza.*

Cheap and delicious *sushi* and *sashimi* on one of the most exclusive shopping streets in Ginza. This possibility would seem laughable to many hardened Tokyoites, yet on six days a week the *itamae* — who cut the fish — load the single L-shaped counter with the freshest of delicacies at heart-quickening prices. With draft beer served at glacial temperatures in its modern, cool interior, this is the perfect Ginza shopping break in the sweltering summer heat. The larger Dai-Ichi Manmaru Zushi branch, a few doors down, offers the same food but in less intimate surroundings. English menus are also available.

Daikon-ya

Daikanyama Parkside Village, 1st Basement, 9-8, Sarugakucho, Shibuya-ku ☎496-6664. *Map 2J3* ▊▊▊ ⌂ AE ⓓ ⓒ VISA *Last orders lunch 1.30pm, dinner 9pm. Closed Sun. Private railroad: Daikanyama.*

Daikon-ya is the most elegant and refined *kaiseki* restaurant in Tokyo catering to the *nouvelle japonaise* boom, and discreetly hidden away in a *très chic* new residential satellite of western Tokyo. Popular with fashionable and affluent Japanese women, Daikon-ya is a feast for feminine eyes rather than ravenous stomachs. Adjustable table lamps pinpoint delicate wall paintings and corner flower arrangements stand next to artfully raised *tatami* platforms. Low tables and trays are vermilion-lacquered, and the chopstick rests are in the shape of tiny Japanese radishes (*daikon*), tying in with the name of the restaurant. Each of the ten *kaiseki* courses (changed every month) is exquisitely presented on miniature Japanese fans, kites, or *geta* wooden clogs.

Daini's Table

San Trope Minami Aoyama, Basement, 6-3-14, Minami Aoyama, Minato-ku ☎407-0363. *Map 4J6* ▊▊▊ ⌂ Ⓨ AE ⓓ ⓒ VISA *Last orders Mon-Sat 1.15am, Sun, hols 11.15pm. Closed Jan 1-4. Subway Omotesando.*

There could be no better site for experiencing Chinese *nouvelle cuisine* than in Aoyama, where the eminently chic Daini Okada (to whom we owe Tokyo's first Alsatian brasserie, and one of its most fashionable discos) finally chose to hang his name. Designer boutiques, a fine art museum and several antique shops can all be found nearby, and denizens of the area, dedicated to "total fashion" or "life-as-applied-art," compose much of the clientele. The decor is suitably "*nouveau chinois*" in black and green designer-lacquer effect, and the waiters appear to be auditioning as Issey Miyake models. For those used to gargantuan banquets at traditional Chinese restaurants, a meal at Daini's Table will inevitably seem like a succession of exquisite appetizers. Although far from filling, a few of the dishes — such as the shrimp in Chinese tea leaves — are flattering to the jaded palate. Others,

like Peking duck, fail to compensate in taste for their minute portions. The Chinese liqueur, made from fragrant olives, is deliciously addictive. To the uninitiated the Chinese wine may revive unpleasant memories of childhood cough medicine.

Fukuzushi

5-7-8, Roppongi, Minato-ku ☎402-4116. *Map 4J7* ▊▊▊ ⌂ Ⓨ AE ⓓ ⓒ VISA *Last orders Mon-Sat 11pm, Sun, hols 10pm. Subway: Roppongi.*

When "Roppongi seekers of the Beautiful Life" tire of eating Mongolian sausage pizza at **Spago**, they have only to duck downstairs for some delicious *sushi* without any grave loss in fashionable ambience. A former parking lot has been successfully transformed into an attractive gravel and bamboo Japanese entrance garden, but once past the door of Fukuzushi you leave esthetic traditions behind. On the right-hand side there is a modern cocktail lounge where you can sip an apéritif before going over to eat *sushi* at a dazzlingly bright counter, or at spotlit sleek black tables. The *sushi* and *sashimi* courses at Fukuzushi (fully described in English menus) are beautifully presented and, reassuringly, their taste is indisputably Japanese.

Goemon♣

1-1-26, Hon-komagome, Bunkyo-ku ☎811-2015. *Map 13C7* ▊ ⇜ *Last orders Tues-Sat 8pm, Sun, hols 6pm. Closed Mon. Subway: Hakusan.*

This is the most charming of Tokyo's eight or so restaurants specializing in *tofu*, the miraculous soybean curd so extolled by Western health-food addicts. A *pachinko* (pinball parlor) jangles, flashes and blares next door, but after entering the lantern-lit alley and walking down the moss-covered paving stones your senses will be suitably restored. In summer the sliding *shoji* screens are opened to reveal a small and attractive Japanese garden of tiny, closely trimmed shrubs, trees, fantastically shaped rocks and waterfalls. Like the *yudofu* temple restaurants in Kyoto (see *Excursions*), visitors can dine *al fresco* on broad wooden benches covered with red fabric. Several rustic teahouses are set in the upper reaches of the garden, and there are four appetizing set meals which vary with the season; in the winter they will be cooked on a brazier at your table in a *tatami* room.

Hasejin♣
3-3-15, Azabudai, Minato-ku
☎*582-7811. Map 4/J7* ▯▯▯ ⌨
[AE] ▯ ⌨ ⊙ *Last orders 9.30pm.*
Closed Jan 1-3. Subway:
Roppongi.

A long-time favorite among Japanese
beef fanciers willing to forego the
more esthetically luxuriant pleasures
of **Seryna** in favor of slightly cheaper
but equally delicious food. Founded
in the Horidome area of Nihonbashi,
where *sukiyaki* is said to have
originated, Hasejin is renowned for
its innovative and delicious beef
kaiseki courses, which include
sashimi and *tempura* dishes. Standard
shabu-shabu and *sukiyaki* may also be
ordered. Hasejin's *obasan* (old
women) waitresses may lack the
allure of Seryna's neophytes, but
their efficiency merits the steep 15
percent service charge. There is
Western-style seating on the 1st
floor, and private *zashiki* rooms on
the floor above.

Hiyama
2-5-1, Ningyocho, Nihonbashi,
Chuo-ku ☎*666-2901. Map 11G12*
▯▯▯ ⌨ ⊙ *Last orders 9pm.*
Closed Sun, hols. Subway:
Ningyocho.

Only the finest beef from Matsuzaka
heifers is served on the 2nd-floor
restaurant of this beautiful old
building. Seating is all in *zashiki*
rooms, and the menu is only in
Japanese. Ask for *shabu-shabu* or
sukiyaki special, *bata yaki* or *oil yaki*
(butter or oil-fried beef) courses.
Sashimi, fish, or more exotically beef,
is also offered à *la carte*.

Honke Ponta♣
3-23-2, Ueno, Taito-ku ☎*831-*
2351. Map 15D11 ▯▯ ⌨ *Last*
orders lunch 1.30pm, dinner
7.30pm. Closed Mon. JR:
Okachimachi; subway: Ueno-
hirokoji.

Situated in the Ueno district (where
the popular dish originated), this is
the oldest *tonkatsu* restaurant in
Tokyo. The second generation
family owners take pride in serving
the thickest and most tender pork in
their *tonkatsu*. Other delicious
specialties are tongue stew, sautéed
salmon, flounder or thinly sliced
abalone and shrimp cream
croquettes. Not only the original
decor has remained unchanged, old-
times assert that Honke Ponta is one
of the few places where the "tastes of
prewar Tokyo" are still preserved.
Its reputation soon spawned many
imitators, so the prefix "Honke," or
originator, was later added.

Ile de France♣
3-11-5, Roppongi, Minato-ku
☎*404-0384. Map 4/J7* ▯▯▯ ⌨ [AE]
⊙ ⊙ [VISA] *Last orders lunch*
2.30pm, dinner 10.30pm.
Subway: Roppongi.

It is difficult to decide which of its
many attractions brings the
lunchtime crowds of businessmen,
diplomats, journalists and
housewives — whether it is the
unadorned, quintessentially
provincial French atmosphere, the
cheap but delicious set courses,
mouthwatering desserts and cheeses,
superb duck specialties, or the
breezy affability of *maître d'hôtel*
Philippe or chef André Pachon. The
noisy French chatter from many of
the tables is perhaps one of its best
recommendations. Chef Pachon,
from Languedoc, takes pride in his
duck dishes, especially the *magret de
caneton grillée* and the *canard confit*,
but if a quick budget lunch of *biftek*
and *frites* is required, it may be
relished without the slightest
embarrassment.

Inakaya♣
3-12-7, Akasaka, Minato-ku
☎*586-3054. Map 8/7* ▯▯▯ [AE] ⊙
⊙ [VISA] *Last orders 10.30pm.*
Subway: Akasaka.

One of the most picturesque
restaurant interiors in Tokyo has
helped to make Inakaya a favorite
among foreigners. Dressed in *happi*
coats and with *tenugui* towels
wrapped around their foreheads, the
staff sit on raised platforms behind
counters loaded with fresh fish,
seafood and vegetables. Orders are
repeated with a chorus of shouts to
enhance the robust and hearty
atmosphere expected in *robatayaki*
and, after grilling, the staff hand
customers their dishes on long-
handled wooden paddles. A Japanese
kite hangs from the ceiling, and
Japanese umbrellas are used as wall
decoration. A sampling from
Inakaya's prodigious collection of
local sake will aid in overcoming any
reserve. There is another branch in
Roppongi.

Isen♣
4-8-5, Jingumae, Shibuya-ku
☎*470-0071. Map 6/4* ▯ ⌨ ⌨
Last orders 10pm. Subway:
Omotesando (A2 exit).

A simple Japanese lunch course here
costs less than a single cup of coffee
at a luxury Tokyo hotel, which is
enough recommendation for many of
the young clientele in this
fashionable back street area of small
boutiques, design studios and coffee

shops. Isen's main boast, however, is not of penny-pinching but of having one of the most unusual interiors in Tokyo. Enter the cedar-finished front counter area and you will come to a rear hall that was once a neighborhood *sento* (public bath). The twin entrances derive from the *sento*'s division into male and female sections, and the identical small Japanese gardens on either side were where bathers would cool off after a dip in the hot tub. The fans hanging from the lofty ceiling and the old wall clock, staff will lovingly recall, are original fixtures. The house specialty is *tonkatsu*, a glutton's delight, but there are other Japanese dishes such as *sashimi* and *tofu*, and there is also an English menu. The staff is friendly and helpful.

Ishikawa ✿

Q Mansion, 1st Basement, 1-6-10, Shibuya, Shibuya-ku ☎406-4488. *Map 3J4* ▯▯ ⒶⒺ ⊙ ⒸⒹ ⱱⁱˢᵃ *Last orders 9.30pm. Closed Sun. JR/subway: Shibuya.*

An unusual chain of restaurants dedicated to propagating *sekki ryori*, or stoneware cuisine, the esoteric culinary art once exclusively reserved for Korean and Chinese nobility. Each table is set with a large, hand-hewn plate of Korean stone (on a not-so-ancient gas ring). The house specialty is *nabe ryori*, a delicious, slowly stone-simmered stew of beef, fish, shrimp, fishy *gyoza* dumplings and vegetables, with a valedictory dish of noodles cooked in the broth. In summer the stoneware is also used to barbecue a feast of much the same constituents. With most of the activity occurring on the plate, the absence of other worthy visual distractions in the sleek Western-style surroundings may be overlooked. The wine is palatable Tokichi from Hokkaido, or there is a Chinese variety.

Kamakura ✿

4-10-11, Roppongi, Minato-ku ☎405-4377. *Map 4J7* ▯▯ ▭ ⒶⒺ ⊙ ⒸⒹ ⱱⁱˢᵃ *Last orders midnight. Closed 1st and 3rd Tues each month. Subway: Roppongi.*

A foreigner's favorite. The *yakitori* is simple but tasty, and easily ordered from English menus. Start with the cheapest *Kamakura* course, and supplement with individual dishes later. Visitors often find Kamakura's "rustic farmhouse" interior, Japanese music twanging in the background, and the blunt directness of its staff conducive to quaffing large quantities of draft beer.

Kisso

Axis Building, 1st Basement, 5-17-1, Roppongi, Minato-ku ☎582-4191. *Map 3J4* ▮▮▮ ▭ ⒶⒺ ⊙ ⒸⒹ ⱱⁱˢᵃ *Closed Sun. Subway: Roppongi.*

A favorite among modish Japanese women and eager-to-impress dandies, Kisso is the best known and most photographed exponent of *nouvelle japonaise* cuisine. Found in the basement of one of Roppongi's most ultramodern buildings, Kisso's interior is sleek, cool and high-tech, with Western-style seating. The ideal customer pecks at a succession of beautifully presented *kaiseki* morsels, with a glass or bottle of white wine (a daring innovation), ever alert for the welcome intrusion of fashion photographers. The food is delicious, and *kaiseki* courses are available for a lighter appetite. Bargain lunches are another surprise.

Komagata Dojo ✿

1-7-12, Komagata, Taito-ku ☎842-4001. *Map 16C13* ▯▯ ▭ ➡ ⊙ ⱱⁱˢᵃ *Last orders 9pm. Closed 3rd Tues every month. Subway: Asakusa.*

Founded in 1801, Komagata Dojo has twice been destroyed by an earthquake and once by American bombs dropped on Asakusa, yet apart from adopting electricity it has scarcely changed at all. The main floor is of split bamboo, on which cushions are spread, next to thick boards in place of tables. The menu is of matching minimalism, centering around the poor man's eel, the humble *dojo* (loach). The most popular dish is *dojo nabe*, in which about a dozen steamed *dojo* are brought to you in a *nabe* pan over a charcoal-fired brazier, together with a wooden pitcher of semisweet sauce and a box of sliced scallions and spices. *Dojo jiru* (soup), *Yanagawa* (a thin omelet of *dojo*), and *koi arai* (carp *sashimi*) are also available. For a full-course evening meal ask for *dojo teishoku*.

Kusa no Ya ✿

4-6-7, Azabu Juban, Minato-ku ☎455-8356. *Map 4K7* ▮▮▮ ▭ ⒸⒹ ⱱⁱˢᵃ *Last orders 1.30am. Closed Aug 10-13. Subway: Roppongi.*

One of Tokyo's few restaurants dispensing genuine Korean food, its branch in Azabu Juban is frequented by homesick diplomats from the Korean Embassy nearby. No concessions to Tokyo chicness in the minimalist decor, or to overprotected Japanese taste buds in the *yaki-niku* (barbecue), *reimen* (cold noodles with vegetables), or pungent meat soups. There is another branch in Akasaka.

La Granata ♣

TBS Kaikan Building, Basement, 5-3-6, Akasaka, Minato-ku ☎582-3241. Map 8/7 ▥▯□ AE ⊕ ⓒ VISA Last orders 9.30pm. Closed Dec 31-Jan 4. Subway: Akasaka.

When not entertaining at one of the hallowed shrines of expense-account European gastronomy, members of Tokyo's Italian community tend to relieve pangs of homesickness in the basement of Akasaka's TBS Kaikan. The Italian ambassador has given La Granata a plaque for propagating genuine Italian cuisine at prices everybody can afford (a 5-course *table d'hôte* for half the price of one *entrée* at a Tokyo temple of *haute cuisine*). In addition to pasta standards, La Granata excels in fish dishes, including such exotica as "Boiled Octopus in Pot" and "Charcoal Broiled Tuna." Kobe beef is done to perfection on an open grill. No Italian would claim its endearingly fake "Mediterranean" decor (mercifully bare of plastic vine trellises) substitutes for home, but the breezy informality and warmth are quite genuine.

La Patata ♣

2-9-11, Jingumae, Shibuya-ku ☎403-9664. Map 6/4 ▥□ AE ⊕ ⓒ VISA Last orders 10.30pm. Closed Mon. JR: Harajuku; subway: Meijijinumae.

Simple but elegant Italian home cooking in a cozy and intimate atmosphere. Japanese chef Koichi Tsuchiya cures his own ham and salts his own beef, and spends at least one month a year in Italy brushing up his skills. Fish dishes are delicious and vary each day according to what takes Tsuchiya's fancy at the Tsukiji market. A summer specialty is steamed eel in the chef's own *balsamico* jelly.

La Tour D'Argent

New Otani hotel, 4-1, Kioi-cho, Chiyoda-ku ☎239-3111. Map 8H7 ▥▯□ ¥ ⇔ AE ⊕ ⓒ VISA Last orders 9pm. Subway: Akasakamitsuke.

When in 1984, after four centuries' reign as the cathedral of French gastronomy (uniting in modern worship such diverse souls as Queen Elizabeth II, Jean Cocteau, Emperor Hirohito, Imelda Marcos and Mick Jagger), La Tour D'Argent finally

opened its first branch outside Paris in Tokyo's New Otani hotel, the event was deemed of sufficient magnitude to merit a long article in *Le Monde*. Since then Tokyo's La Tour D'Argent has set a standard to which any restaurant purveying *haute cuisine* outside France, let alone Japan, must be measured. Setting a respectful tone, a glass case in the corridor shows the original table settings of the Paris Tour D'Argent for a famous dinner in 1867 of the Russian Tsar, French Emperor and German Kaiser. None of these would feel out of place in the splendid French Empire interior re-created in Tokyo, more gorgeously opulent even than that in Paris. The finest dishes, both Japanese-inspired and classics copied from Paris, are the only examples in Tokyo of Western cuisine comparable in visual beauty to *kaiseki*. The wine cellar, with 30,000 carefully selected bottles in stock, must surely rank as the best in Asia.

Mamiana Soba ♣

3-5-6, Azabudai, Minato-ku ☎583-0545. Map 4J7 ▯□ ⇔ Last orders 7.45pm. Closed Sun, hols. Subways: Roppongi and Kamiyacho.

Passing Mamiana Soba's threshold, opposite Azabu Post Office in one of Tokyo's more cosmopolitan and sophisticated districts, is to enter another world of rustic Japanese tranquility and simplicity. Behind the gloomy and spartan front room is a hidden Japanese garden, with secluded *zashiki* rooms bordering one side. Try *tanuki* or *tori namban soba*, or for a simple meal in hot weather, *zaru soba* with *tempura*. A romanized menu is available. Three kinds of sake are offered, but *genshu* is the best.

Maxim's de Paris

Sony Building, 3rd Basement, 5-3-1, Ginza, Chuo-ku ☎572-3621. Map 9/10 ▥▯□ ¥ ⚊ AE ⊕ ⓒ VISA Last orders 9.30pm. Closed Sun, Dec 31-Jan 3. Subway: Ginza.

Maxim's opens onto an underground parking lot and a passage leading to the Ginza Subway Station, but bizarre contrasts otherwise vanish when you step inside its doors. In 1966, to construct an exact replica of Maxim's in the 3rd and 4th basements of his new Ginza building, co-founder of Sony Corporation Akio Morita recruited the best interior decorators in Japan. From Maxim's in Paris he brought five cooks, a *pâtissier*, a *maître d'*, a *sommelier*, four waiters and five musicians. Localization has since proceeded rapidly, but all the Tokyo staff are still required to spend at least 6mths' training in Paris. Enamoured of working for such a prestigious name, many of the Japanese waiters regrettably affect an intensely irritating superciliousness toward customers, who may be less impressed by some overpriced dishes of bistro-standard indifference. On occasion, however, the kitchen is capable of matching the sublime classics of its famous Parisian progenitor, and the quality of the wine cellar, with a choice of 10,000 bottles, is beyond reproach.

Metropole ♥
6-4-5, Roppongi, Minato-ku
☎405-4400. Map 4J7 ▦▮▮ ☐ 𝕐
▱ AE ◉ ⬡ VISA Last orders
10.30pm. Subway: Roppongi.

It's difficult to say which is more appealing about this new restaurant: the bizarre Western eclecticism of its bohemian interior or its expertly prepared Chinese cuisine. Once in Roppongi's Terebi Asahi-dori you will certainly have no problem locating the Metropole: even without the flags and potted ferns, the mock-Classical pillars with gilt capitals scream for attention on this hitherto nondescript street. The startling interior, by Nigel Coates of England, is a masterpiece of compression. Above a large marble fireplace hangs a gilt-framed mirror that might have last seen service as a prop in a Dracula movie, with two large and striking oil canvases by Adam Lowe on either side. Huge leather sofas, a graceful Regency side table with potpourri and a vase of beautifully arranged orchids and grasses, Grecian urns and Art Nouveau statuary provide added touches. Behind the bar a staircase leads up to a narrow gallery lined with two bookcases and more chairs for cocktails or apéritifs. The rear dining room, behind a draped curtain of faded crimson and gold tassels, is dark-blue *moderne*, with various busts and limbs and Classical statuary littered above the cornices. Although the Metropole advertises itself as serving "Shanghai Modern Cuisine," the menu draws from every Chinese region, and its only novelties for Tokyoites are generous portions and a clean, authentic taste, undosed by grease and undisguised by dreadful sauces supposedly needed to protect the tame Japanese palate. The 82 dishes listed (in English and Japanese) will satisfy a broad

spectrum of tastes, but the Kung Pao Shrimps with Pine Nuts and the delicious Hunan Style Crispy Chicken can both be unreservedly recommended. Even a dish as ubiquitous as "assorted sautéed vegetables" comes as a revelation for Tokyo — the three kinds of mushroom, water chestnut, tiny corn, Japanese radish, asparagus and ginkgo nuts are all perfectly crisp and retain their distinctive flavors sealed inside. The wine list is indifferent, and although typically stiff-necked, service tends to be sporadic on busy nights. You will hear few complaints among the satisfied buzz of conversation.

Minokichi ♥
Roi Building, 1st Basement, 5-5-1, Roppongi, Minato-ku ☎404-0767. Map 4J7 ▮▮▮ ☐ AE ◉ ⬡ VISA Last orders 10pm. Subway: Roppongi.

An old Kyoto restaurant founded in 1735, Minokichi has successfully traded on its reputation for fine *kyo-ryori* (Kyoto cuisine) by opening a nationwide chain of branches that also serve favorites such as *sukiyaki*, *shabu-shabu*, *unagi*, *tempura* and *sashimi*. Connoisseurs who relish the exclusive atmosphere of expensive *kaiseki* courses may find Minokichi a little touristy, but in Tokyo there is probably no better an introduction to some fine Japanese cuisine. Minokichi's dark, slatted windows (typical of Kyoto) stand out in the dreary basement of Roppongi's Roi Building, and one soon enters a world apart. Seating, except for a *zashiki* room for parties, is at Western-style tables, but the waitresses in kimonos are models of traditional courtesy. The *kyo-ryori* courses, a series of beautifully balanced and artfully displayed morsels, are excellent value. Diners are presented with a tiny glass of fresh blood from the *suppon* (snapping turtles) before they are turned into delicious soup — hardly a sign of accommodating to foreign tastes! In winter, try the *fugu* (blowfish delicacy).

Miyako ♥
2-1-16, Asakusa, Taito-ku ☎844-0034. Map 16C13 ▮☐ ☐ Last orders 8.45pm. Closed Mon, 4th Sun every month. Subway: Asakusa.

Established here in 1866, Miyako is famous among connoisseurs for still serving Edo-style *sushi*, and the owners hold equally reactionary views about modern interior decor. The easiest sample is to order either the 12-piece *"Bentenyama* course," 17-piece *"Miyako* course," or *chirashi zushi* (bowl of seafood on a bed of *sushi* rice). Freer spirits should aim for *anago* (conger eel), *tamago yaki* (egg), *ika* (squid) and *kohada* (shad gizzard).

Moti❤
3rd floor, Hama Building, 6-2-35, Roppongi, Minato-ku ☎479-1939. *Map 4J7* 💵 🖵 AE ⊙ ⓒⓄ 🆅🆂🅰 *Last orders 10pm. Subway: Roppongi.*

A straw poll among foreign residents would probably find Moti heading the list of favorite Tokyo restaurants. With increasing numbers of Japanese having heard the word, the resulting crowd at the door of the main Roppongi branch can be daunting. Have patience as the combination of quick service and customers who consume their meals with great gusto will assure you of a seat before long (although a shared table may prove inevitable). A lot of money was spent initially on interior decoration to evoke the "exotic" appeal of Kashmiri river barges, but Moti's phenomenal popularity rests squarely on its food, sustained by an insistence on never exploiting success by unreasonably increasing prices or compromising on quality. Novices are usually tempted first by the tandoori chicken barbecues, served with a large helping of *nan* bread, which you may see being baked behind the glassed kitchen by North Indian chefs. Moti's real glory, however, is its *Muglai* style of rich, creamy curries. Hot curry *aficionados* should try Chicken Multani: its deliciously rich and smooth sauce is unequaled, the management claims, by anything in India.

Mr Stamp's Wine Garden❤
Kyowa Building, 1st floor, 4-4-2, Roppongi, Minato-ku ☎479-1390. *Map 4J7* 💵 🖵 AE ⊙ ⓒⓄ 🆅🆂🅰 *Last orders 10.30pm. Closed Sun, hols. Subway: Roppongi.*

Being Roppongi, the "garden" in the title turns out to be redundant fiction (a small slice of inanimate piazza, with a few chairs scattered around for show), but the wine does exist in American Al Stamp's renowned cellar. The chief attraction is undoubtedly the moderately priced wine (for Tokyo), often of unusual and exciting provenance, especially when Stamp decides to host one of his regional fairs of European gastronomy. The normal menu is jet-set Western-ecumenical, strong on rather tasteless American-style

steaks and fashionable standbys such as *gravlax*, pâtés, Waldorf salad, caviar and cheeses. Expatriates easily warm to the cozy and informal atmosphere, which has a certain frisson of excitement for Japanese. The young staff occasionally manifests laid-back lapses in decorum when Al Stamp is not around to impose order.

Mugitoro❤
2-2-4, Kaminarimon, Taito-ku ☎842-1066. *Map 16C13* 💵 AE ⊙ ⓒⓄ 🆅🆂🅰 *Last orders 9pm. Subway: Asakusa.*

If a restaurant that specializes in grated wild potato (*tororo*) sounds too much of a challenge, rest assured that Mugitoro's refined culinary skills equal those of *kaiseki*. Founded in 1929, Mugitoro uses *yamaimo* (wild potatoes) from Akita prefecture in northern Honshu and serves it in beautifully presented courses with combinations of seaweed, tuna, sea bream, salmon roe and *tempura*, depending on the season. The *Mugitoro gozen* course is recommended. The traditional Japanese decor upstairs is especially elegant and the benches outside are for the lines that form on weekends and holidays.

Nagasaka Sarashina❤
1-8-7, Azabu Juban, Minato-ku ☎585-1676. *Map 4K7* 🖵 ⊙ ⓒⓄ *Last orders 7.30pm. Subway: Roppongi.*

Once a shogunal favorite, Nagasaka Sarashina still makes its *soba* by hand on the premises, served with a choice of either its renowned *amakuchi* (sweet) or *karakuchi* (slightly hot) sauces. Try either *seiro* (plain), *gomakiri* (ground sesame) or *chakiri soba* (green tea noodles) for a taste of history in delightful Japanese surroundings.

Nakasei
1-39-13, Asakusa, Taito-ku ☎841-7401. *Map 16C13* 💵 🖵 ⤶ *Last orders 7-7.30pm. Subway: Asakusa.*

Frequented by such connoisseurs of Edo tradition as the late novelist Nagai Kaifu (1879-1959), Nakasei still serves original Edo-style *tempura*: piping hot, with a crisp and crunchy layer of batter, served on tiny metal racks inside lacquer bowls. If you order the standard *teishoku* set (the best buy) you will not receive any *tempura* vegetables, which are a post-Edo innovation. Counter prices are much cheaper, but the old-fashioned *tatami* rooms at the rear overlook a pretty Japanese garden (ask for *zashiki*). Nakasei is at the end of a tiny alley directly opposite Asakusa Public Hall on Orange-dori.

Nanban-tei♨

4-5-6, Roppongi, Minato-ku
☎402-0606. Map 4J7 ▯▯▮ ▯ AE
◉ ◉ VISA *Last orders 11pm.*
Closed Dec 31-Jan 3. Subway:
Roppongi.

One of Tokyo's best-known *yakitori* restaurants, the mood at Nambantei is slightly more refined than at **Kamakura**, and some of the dishes are more delicately flavored. Try the house specialty, *namban-yaki* of beef dipped in hot *miso* and grilled, or the *asapura-maki* green asparagus wrapped in thinly sliced pork. Like Kamakura, there are also set dinner courses. Lunch menus are a bargain.

Nodaiwa♨

1-5-4, Higashi Azabu, Minato-ku
☎583-7852. Map 4K7 ▯ ▯ *Last*
orders 8pm. Closed Sun.
Subway: Kamiyacho.

In 1876 Nodaiwa was ranked one of the three best restaurants in the new Tokyo metropolis, and it has since maintained its pre-eminence among *unagi-ya*. The 5th-generation owner prides himself on serving eels fit for the *daimyo* lords who once made mansions in this area and patronized Nodaiwa in the late Edo period; only natural eels (not bred) are used to give the tenderness and sweetness demanded by connoisseurs, and they are basted in Nodaiwa's "secret sauce". A rich, warm patina of varnished dark wood dominates the interior, in the traditional *gasho zukuri* style of central Gifu prefecture. In the *zashiki* rooms one floor above are low tables, which have lacquer inlays of Japanese fans to complement the elegant lacquer trays and bowls in which simple meals are served. Patterned after a feudal castle keep or a *daimyo* storehouse, Nodaiwa's imposing building stands out on an otherwise prosaic busy main street s of Iikura Crossing.

Rakutei

6-8-1, Akasaka, Minato-ku ☎585-3743. Map 8I7 ▮▮▮ ▯ *Last orders*
9pm. Closed Mon. Subway:
Akasaka.

Lines at lunchtime disrupt the refined spell of this most discreet refuge for *tempura* connoisseurs, but at night strangers may feel like gatecrashers at a private tea ceremony. A bare pine counter forms the altarpiece of the very *shibui* interior, around which there are only 12 seats. Affluent Japanese supplicants dripping in chunky gold watches and jewelry vie for one another's attention and that of stony-faced *itamae* Ishikawa, who with his sister opened Rakutei after a long stint at the Hilltop hotel. There are only three items listed on the Japanese menu: *sashimi* and two *tempura* courses. Ishikawa reverentially manipulates his long chopsticks like a priest dispensing Holy Communion, and is credited with equal miracles of transubstantiation from such simple fare as battered shrimp, eel or squid, as well as more exotic fare such as the root of the lily. The porcelain, lacquer and pewter vessels are duly consonant with the exquisite taste to which Rakutei and its clientele constantly aspire.

Sabatini di Firenze♨

7th floor, Sony Building, 5-3-1,
Ginza, Chuo-ku ☎573-0013. Map
10/10 ▮▮▮ ▯ ▯ AE ◉ ◉ VISA
Last orders Mon-Sat 10.30pm,
Sun, hols 10pm. Closed Dec 31,
Jan 1, 2 days Feb, 3 days Aug.
Subway: Ginza.

Incongruity, accidental or discretionary, being so pervasive in Tokyo, it should come as no surprise by now to find one of the city's finest restaurants (a virtual duplicate of its renowned twin in Florence) on the 7th floor of the Sony Building. One could easily be in the City of Flowers — marble floors, fine paneling, Italian lighting, table settings and house crystal are all identical to those in Florence. The finest North Italian food in Tokyo does more than justice to the surroundings, from the classic *sformatino di spinacci* soufflé created at the Florence headquarters, to the delicious *cacciucco alla Livornese bouillabaisse*. The extensive wine list covers all regions of Italy.

Sabatini Roma

Suncrest Building, 1st Basement,
2-13-5, Kita Aoyama, Minato-ku
☎402-3812. Map 7/6 ▮▮▮ ▯ ◒
AE ◉ ◉ VISA Last orders 10pm.
Subway: Gaienmae.

With its wandering minstrels and smoky candles, coffered ceiling and gaily frescoed arches, Sabatini Roma appeals most to Japanese celebrants of special occasions who associate the surroundings with Latin passions and dramatic sunsets. The Sabatini brothers claim that the menu here is the same as their original restaurant in Rome. From antipasti to desserts, all is well prepared, competently served and tasty, although one wonders at the stratospheric cost of Roman authenticity. The house specialty is baked and charcoal-grilled fish, especially sea bass, delicious to Westerners but bland for spoiled Japanese palates. Next door, Sabatini's new pizzeria-grotto serves authentic pizza baked in a traditional Italian oven, and spaghetti at more affordable prices.

Santomo ♥

6-14-1, Ueno, Taito-ku ☎*831-3898. Map 15C11* ▮▮▮ ▭ *Last orders 9pm. Closed 2nd and 4th Sun each month. JR/subway: Ueno.*

Japanese fanatics of *fugu* occasionally ask the *itamae* to serve them a tiny part of the forbidden liver, containing deadly poison. Eat just a little, and it induces a tingling numbness; overindulge in this gourmet's Russian roulette and one is liable to share the fate of a famous *kabuki* actor who died after eating the liver. All restaurants serving *fugu* require a special government license and since most will never let you touch the liver, there is no danger attached to sampling this delicacy. During the *fugu* season from late Sept to Mar, Santomo offers an excellent 8-dish *fugu teishoku* course, which includes wafer-thin slices of *fugu sashimi* to be dipped in *ponzu* sauce and a *fugu nabe* casserole, all for a quarter of the price normally demanded at more high-class *fugu* restaurants. For the rest of the year Santomo's staple menu of "normal" fish is hard to distinguish from dozens of other restaurants in this entertainment district.

Seiyoken

4-58, Ueno-koen, Taito-ku ☎*821-2181. Map 15C11* ▮▮▮ ▭ ▭ ◁≔
AE ⊕ ⊙ VISA *Last orders 8pm. Closed Dec 31-Jan 3. JR: Ueno.*

Japan's first Western restaurant opened in the foreigner's settlement of Tsukiji in 1872; 4yrs later a branch was fittingly opened here in *Ueno Park*, the new showcase of Japan's opening to Western "civilization and enlightenment." Once impressing a steady stream of royalty, visiting dignitaries and gawking, gauche natives, Seiyoken's glory days have long since faded, but its old standards remain gratifyingly unchanged. Do not expect any surprises, as the French culinary classics enshrined in its extensive menu and its choice wines are testaments to another age. One change for the worse has been Seiyoken's "new" (1959) building: a squat, concrete eyesore, which includes a cheap family restaurant. Ignore it and head for the subdued French dining room, which commands an excellent view of *Shinobazu Pond*.

Seryna ♥

3-12-2, Roppongi, Minato-ku ☎*403-6211 Map 4J7* ▮▮▮ ▭ ⅄
▬ AE ⊕ VISA *Last orders 10.30pm. Subway: Roppongi.*

Whether for its successful aspiration to Western luxury or for the high standards of its service and food, Seryna has long been a preferred evening haunt of foreign visitors to Tokyo. Relieved of any of the pitfalls suspected to lurk in the more overtly "ethnic" establishments, the Western visitor to the main *Honkan* can sink into an atmosphere of recognizable plush and opulent comfort, with English menus and even instructions on how to use chopsticks, while there are enough native touches (cedar wood, a small Japanese garden encased in a smoked-glass pillar upstairs, young waitresses in kimonos much admired for their grace and beauty) to add that necessary exotic frisson. This is all a prelude to the best *shabu-shabu* course (*sashimi*, noodles and cooked seafood in addition to pot-boiled prime Kobe beef and vegetables), well-balanced, carefully presented and delicious: a culinary soft-landing to Japan. Seryna's success has spawned three equally appetizing offshoots in the same block. The basement **Mon Cher Ton Ton** serves *teppanyaki* steak and seafood at two huge circular counters in dimly lit, tastelessly overfurnished surroundings. **Saraebo**, on the 3rd floor, offers grilled (*yaki*) beef and Chinese seafood in a gaudy setting of unabashed Oriental kitsch. Next door to the main building, with a more restrained and tasteful interior, **Kani Seryna** specializes in *kani* (crab) *shabu-shabu*, Maine lobster and steamed fish. Also recommended is its Kobe steak, which is traditionally grilled on a heated stone (*Ishiyaki* steak).

Spago

5-7-8, Roppongi, Minato-ku ☎*423-4025. Map 4J7* ▮▮ ▭ ⅄
AE ⊕ ⊙ VISA *Last orders 10.30pm. Subway: Roppongi.*

The original Spago in Hollywood is a breezy and stylish repository of

Restaurants

Beverly Hills chic, where glitterati from the movie industry are given a reassuring welcome. Wolfgang Puck, the boyish-faced prime mover behind Spago, who affects a baseball cap in the kitchen, is credited with launching "California cuisine," which Ronald Reagan tried on unsuspecting world leaders when he made Puck chef for the Williamsburg Summit. Puck's subversive genius lies in the improbable juxtaposition of exotic ingredients, titillations and conversation pieces for fashionably jaded palates, which in the Roppongi Spago normally belong to bankers and stockbrokers. An appetizer might be salad with sautéed spicy shrimp and Pernod or sautéed foie gras with mango chutney and field greens. The pasta tastes extraordinary, and not only for being combined with the likes of "spicy duck mousse." Pizzas are topped with anything apart from what one would expect, such as duck or Mongolian lamb sausage, goat cheese, baby conch and scallops. *Entrées* are only slightly more conventional: grilled tuna with tomato and basil vinaigrette, or sliced duck breast with Mandarin pancakes. Spago's is also one of the best places to try Californian Cabernet Sauvignon wines. Girders, with dozens of track lights attached, buttress the big room like a designer aircraft hangar. Abstract color spasms writhe along one wall, and next to the entrance there is a tropical orgy of orchids exploding from a vase. Seating is on lawn chairs, and the tables are set with starched white linen. Background music chimes with the hip decor. A patio-terrace is especially quiet and cool, although the view of a moonlit Roppongi parking lot would never excite rhapsodies in L.A.

Stockholm♣
Sweden Center, Basement, 6-11-9, Roppongi, Minato-ku ☎ *403-9046. Map 4J7* ▥ ▯ ☐ ♉ ☎ ▦ ⏣ ▦ ▨ *Last orders 10pm. Subway: Roppongi.*

The smorgasbord in the basement brick vault of Roppongi's Sweden Center daily groans under the weight of such Scandinavian delicacies as meatballs on slices of smoked ham, herring filets in sour cream, or fresh shad roe in a huge earthenware crock. Limitless indulgence in the smorgasbord, washed down with aquavit, with sorties to the cheese and dessert table, and a final quaff of Swedish pear liqueur, will not appreciably lighten your wallet.

Sunaba♣
4-5-4, Nihonbashi Muromachi, Chuo-ku ☎ *241-4038. Map 10G11* ☐ ▯ *Last orders Mon-Fri 7.30pm, Sat 7pm. Closed Sun, hols. JR: Shin Nihonbashi; subway: Mitsukoshimae.*

After 400yrs of serving *soba*, Sunaba has no need to tout for custom. Lunchtime lines of office workers block the entrance to what is probably Tokyo's oldest restaurant. Pedigree is not overtly displayed, except in the deceptively expensive-looking exterior, reminiscent of a *ryotei*. Downstairs is bright and modern, although there is a raised *zashiki* area, in addition to Western-style seating, and a small Japanese garden behind plate glass. Menus have fulsome English accounts of each dish. Habitués would claim they are drawn by the "quality" of the soup, or the texture of the plain *zaru soba*, bolstered as often as not with some fried chicken, fried egg cake, or *tempura*. The private *zashiki* rooms upstairs are incredibly elegant anachronisms for such simple and inexpensive fare.

Sushiiwa♣
2-14-8, Tsukiji, Chuo-ku ☎ *541-0655. Map 10I11* ▥ ☐ ▦ ⏣ ▦ ▨ *Last orders 10pm. Closed 1st, 3rd and 5th Sun each month, hols. Subway: Tsukiji.*

Loyalists perpetually exchange verbal blows over which is Tokyo's best *sushi-ya*, but many depart Tsukiji's Sushiiwa committed to its banner. Situated next to the market, the freshness of the fish is assured; and the quality of the *sushi* and *sashimi* is guaranteed by some of the most expert *itamae* in the city. Choice *o-toro*, which envelop their beds of rice, melt deliciously in the mouth. The *uni* has to be loaded into its tiny buckets of *nori-* dried seaweed. You could either ask the *itamae* for his recommendation (*Osusume wa nan desu k a?*); or simply leave the seasonal choice up to him (*Shun no sakana o kudasai*). A modern branch, with counter and Western tables, is easily found on the opposite corner to the entrance of Tsukiji Honganji Temple. The older main shop, with just two counters, is a brief walk away on Harumi-dori.

Takamura♣
3-4-27, Roppongi, Minato-ku ☎ *585-6600. Map 4J7* ▥ ▨ ◁ ▦ ⏣ ▦ ▨ *Last orders 8pm. Closed Sun. Subway: Roppongi.*

Climbing the stone steps, lit by bamboo lanterns in the evening, you'll find the roar of Roppongi traffic is soon exchanged for a tranquil oasis of such exquisitely crafted rustic simplicity that you'll soon imagine being on a hill overlooking Kyoto rather than perched on top of a concealed Tokyo expressway. The *kaiseki* courses, which vary according to season, are another *trompe l'oeil* in Kyoto delicacy and refinement. Each of the beautiful *tatami* rooms has an *irori* sunken hearth — modeled on the traditional Japanese farmhouse — for grilling quail, sparrow or duck (except in Aug) on the iron flat of a plowshare (the probable origin of *teppanyaki* cuisine). Sake is served in tiny bamboo cups and from a bamboo pitcher. Although popular with foreigners, Takamura is far from being pretentious or a tourist trap. In fact, none of the staff speaks English! Only prior reservations are accepted, so ask someone in the hotel to handle negotiations and fix a menu.

Tamahide ♥

1-17-10, Ningyocho, Nihonbashi, Chuo-ku ☎668-7651. *Map 11G12* ▥ ▭ *Last orders 8.30pm. Closed Sun, hols. Subway: Ningyocho.*

One of Tokyo's most historic restaurants, Tamahide was founded in 1760 by the shogun's "game-cutter," who mastered a secret technique of cutting crane caught by falcons without letting a drop of blood appear in the shogunal presence. In the mid-Meiji his fifth descendant first invented the now ubiquitous Japanese dish called *oyako donburi*, or "filial bowl," in which rice is steeped in the soup from *sukiyaki* with a "parent-child" topping of chicken and egg. As well as *oyako don* (if ordered alone, served only at lunch until 1pm), the all-chicken menu at Tamahide offers more lavish fare such as *sukiyaki teishoku* with five different kinds of chicken *sukiyaki* and dessert.

Tambaya ♥

3-2, Kojimachi, Chiyoda-ku ☎261-2633. *Map 8G7* ▭ ▭ ➤ *Last orders 8pm. Closed Sun, hols. Subway: Kojimachi.*

The Japanese craving for *unagi* (eel) as a tonic during the stamina-draining hot summer months dates back at least to the 8thC, so perhaps Tambaya's claim to have been in business for at least 350yrs is rather modest. One of the shoguns in Edo Castle, his samurai who lived in the nearby *bancho* and more recently the

Imperial Household Agency have all sent their messengers to Tambaya to collect some *unagi*. The eels at Tambaya were bred in Shizuoka prefecture (they are nowadays imported from Taiwan), broiled, steamed to soften them up, dipped in a secret soy-based sauce and then grilled (in the Osaka-Kyoto area the eels are not steamed, and the sauce is less salty). Around the lunar calendar Day of the Ox in late July, prescribed as the day for eating *unagi*, the rush of custom and the lengthy preparations required can make a wait of 40mins commonplace. Although bamboo blinds and decorative paper windows persist, this is certainly not "Ye Olde Unagi-ya": the menu is bilingual with photographs of the dishes; seating is imitation leather; and the potted plants complement the linoleum floor. Other recent innovations include Eel *meunière provençale*, a "salad bar," Budweiser and "Hawaiian Music" played in the room at the back. The shogun spins in his tomb.

Tamura

2-12-11, Tsukiji, Chuo-ku ☎541-1611. *Map 10I11* ▥ ▭ AE ⊙ ⊙ VISA *Last orders lunch 1pm, dinner 8pm. Subway: Tsukiji.*

One of Tokyo's most famous *kaiseki* restaurants, now housed in a discreet 7-story building in Tsukiji, betrayed by the black limousines parked outside in the evening. The 1st floor has a spruce, modern room with Western-style tables and chairs overlooking a bamboo grove. *Zashiki* rooms are upstairs, and there is a large room for parties on the 2nd floor, with more private rooms on the 3rd and 4th floors. One *tatami* chamber on the 4th floor thoughtfully has backs on the seats, better "to entertain guests from overseas." Waitresses are "mature," extremely proper and occasionally forbidding.

Ten-ichi ♥

6-6-5, Ginza, Chuo-ku ☎571-1949. *Map 10I10* ▥ ▭ AE ⊙ ⊙ VISA *Last orders 9.30pm. Subway: Ginza.*

Isao Yabuki, who founded Ten-ichi in 1930, raised *tempura* from its humble street origins as a simple food of Shitamachi commoners to an internationally recognized, high-class Japanese cuisine worthy of being eaten in *zashiki* private rooms. Yabuki devised a method of eliminating the noxious smells of cooking oil used to deep-fry the

Restaurants

tempura, and now, in addition to a chain of restaurant outlets, Ten-ichi is privileged to have its own kitchen in the Akasaka State Guest House to make *tempura* for visiting foreign dignitaries. The tasteful Japanese interior includes a latticed ceiling of stripped bark, wood and plaster walls, paper windows and a small stream running through the stone floor. *Tempura* and *sashimi* are served à la carte, but the best value is the beautifully balanced *tempura table d'hôte* (small salad and raw beans, two courses of fresh, crisp and thinly battered *tempura*, *tsukemono* pickles, rice, *aka dashi miso* and clam soup, oolong and Japanese tea, and dessert), perhaps with a bottle of the white Burgundy that Yabuki found complements the taste of *tempura*. English menus are available.

Tokyo Joe's♣
Akasaka Eight-One Building, 1st Basement, 2-13-5, Nagatocho, Chiyoda-ku ☎508-0325. Map 9H8 ▥ ☐ ☑ AE ⊕ ⓒ Last orders 10.30pm. Subway: Akasakamitsuke.

After a bold Tokyo launch, the lines that now form in the basement of this modern office building, next to the charred shell of the old New Japan hotel, nearly equal those of its famous progenitor: Joe's Stone Crab restaurant in Miami. The Japanese families and couples who patiently wait their turn are drawn not just by the novelty of eating stone crabs from the Florida Keys, but lobsters, fresh conch *sashimi*, scallops and T-bone steaks served at affordable prices. Portions are American-sized, with onion and tomato cut in giant slabs that invariably elicit giggles when served. The nautical theme of the large dining hall (barrels, rigging, masts and bits of rope) adds to the jollity. The drinks list is surprisingly extensive, with 15 California wines, cheap spirits and beer.

Tonki♣
1-1-2, Shimo-meguro, Meguro-ku ☎491-9928. Map 3N4 ☐ ☐ ➠ ▥ Last orders 10.45pm. Closed Tues. JR: Meguro.

You will recognize Tonki through its plate-glass window by the glare from dozens of white lights hanging from the ceiling, and the crowd patiently lined up by the wall to receive their turn sitting at the counter. Tokyo's largest *tonkatsu* restaurant, Tonki feeds more than 800 every day. Place your order immediately for either *hire* (lean filet), or *rosu* (roast) *teishoku* set (which comes complete with rice,

miso soup and all the shredded cabbage you can eat), or *kushikatsu* (lean chunks of pork on a skewer). Tonki's pork is of a high quality and is dipped in batter three times to keep it crunchy. The portions are generous and the preparation renowned. Above all, Tonki is very cheap — which explains why you may have to wait as long as 30mins.

Toricho♣
Hosho Building, 1st floor, 7-14-1, Roppongi, Minato-ku ☎401-1827. Map 4J7 ▥ ☐ ☑ AE ⊕ ⓒ ▥ Last orders Mon-Sat 11pm, Sun, hols 10pm. Subway: Roppongi.

Black granite steps lead down through a stylishly discreet Japanese entrance to an equally smart but inexpensive *yakitori* counter in the basement of Roppongi's swinging Hosho Building. It is a refreshing complement to the blasts of disco beat, live fusion jazz and imitation Beatles music upstairs.

Yabu Soba♣
2-10, Awajicho, Kanda, Chiyoda-ku ☎251-0287. Map 9F10 ☐ ☐ ⫷ Last orders 7pm. Closed Mon. Subway: Awajicho/Ogawamachi (A3 exit).

The most famous *soba* restaurant in Tokyo, deserving a visit as much for its beautiful interior as for the renowned taste of its noodles. Founded in 1881, the name *Yabu* refers to a bamboo bush that once grew outside a predecessor in Hongo's Dangozaka. Rebuilt after the 1923 earthquake, the current restaurant has a charming *zashiki* area with tables as tall as an upright chopstick. Summer specialties are a bowl of *nameko soba* (cold *soba* noodles with tiny *nameko* mushrooms), *nori* (dried seaweed and shredded *daikon*) or plain *seiro soba* (served on a bamboo mat on a lacquer tray, often accompanied with *tentane*); a round *tempura* patty (the water used to boil the *soba* will be served in a teapot). Among the hot dishes *kamo namban* (*soba* with duck meat) and *anago namban* (*soba* with conger eel) are also delicious. By tradition, orders are not shouted to the kitchen but "sung" by a member of staff.

Yakko♣
Kaminarimon Dori, 1-10-2, Asakusa, Taito-ku ☎841-9886. Map 16C13 ☐ ☐ AE ⊕ ⓒ ▥ Last orders 9pm. Closed Tues. Subway: Asakusa.

On the far w side of Asakusa's main

Kaminarimon street, this 200yr-old *unagi-ya* is at once recognizable by its lovely old wooden frontage, with a view of a kitchen on the right, and on the left a tempting window array of *unagi* and *dojo* dishes. Tradition is maintained inside, with a raised *zashiki* area, and Western seating next to a small Japanese garden. The *unaju teishoku* complete course is good value, or just ask for the *kabayaki* filet. The more adventurous may try *Yanagawa*, a thin egg omelet of *dojo* and bean sprouts.

Yonekyu ♥
2-17-10, Asakusa, Taito-ku
☎*841-6416. Map 16C13* ▯ ▭
▭ *AE ▣ ▣ VISA Last orders*
9pm. Subway: Asakusa.
Situated on the left side of a covered street that continues N from Sushiya-dori, and festooned with a row of lanterns, this *sukiyaki* restaurant, once eulogized in verse by the Japanese poet Kotaro Takamura, owes its origin to a rice dealer from the western Shiga prefecture, who came to Tokyo in the early Meiji era with three cows and high hopes of the new craze for meat-eating. Yonekyu quickly prospered to its present size, but since then seems stuck in a time warp. Customers are still greeted at the door with a resonant bang on a huge drum, and the rustic interior appears little changed over the decades. The beef still comes from Shiga, and is cooked in a strong, soy sauce said to appeal to Edokko. Ask for the cheap *Shimofuri* course, or the more

expensive *Tokushimo*, which has leaner beef, for a filling *sukiyaki* dinner. Partitioned *zashiki* seating on the 1st floor offer more privacy than the long communal tables in a large upstairs *tatami* room.

Zakuro
Nihon Jidensha Kaikan, 1st Basement, 1-9-15, Akasaka, Minato-ku ☎*582-2661. Map 16C13* ▥ ▯ ▭ *AE ▣ ▣ VISA Last orders 10pm. Subway: Toranomon.*
This restaurant provides a luxurious and carefree *entrée* to Japanese cuisine, especially its more recent beef manifestations that are most immediately accessible to foreigners. Zakuro excels in *shabu-shabu*, serving what many would claim to be the best in town, with some banquet courses sufficiently huge to topple a Nero from his cushion. Menus are available in English; in addition to the house recommendation, they offer oil-fried or *teppanyaki* Kobe steak, fried chicken, charcoal-broiled fish, *sashimi*, *tempura* and even the common man's *yakitori*. Elegant surroundings are decidedly Japanese, the abundance of folk art and crafts perhaps overstated. The main culture shock is liable to be the bill, but Zakuro after all is opposite the US Embassy and in the heart of a business area. Reassuringly, many of the clientele are Japanese paying with their own money, drawn here only by its fine reputation. Zakuro is under the same management as **La Granata**.

Nightlife and the arts

Tokyo's boundless nightlife reflects not so much its vast population as the importance of personal relationships in Japanese society. Entertaining is an essential component of the business world, and the annual Japanese corporate expenditure on wining and dining exceeds the GNP (gross national product) of some small nations. Until recently it was expected that an employee's social life should center around the company: it is only the new breed of young Japanese who reject the idea that evenings are for cementing the office *esprit de corps*, often cited as an ingredient of Japan's business success. The prohibitive smallness of Japanese city dwellings and their often long distance from the center are two reasons why entertaining is rarely done at home. Equally, under the marital division of labor, "home" is supposed to be ruled by the wife.

In Japan's traditionally male-dominated society, sex and eroticism have played important roles in nightlife. Since women members of parliament pressed the government to outlaw prostitution in 1958, there have been no "licensed" quarters like the old Yoshiwara (now a seedy strip of cheap bars and "massage" parlors), but **pink bars** and **cabarets** abound, mostly run by *yakuza* (gangsters) and devoid of any cultural charm. The most notorious concentration is in Shinjuku's Kabukicho, where every heterosexual predilection is accommodated; a smaller cluster has formed near Shibuya's Dogenzaka.

In a different category, geisha are high-class entertainers, accomplished at singing, dancing and playing the *samisen*, and regarded as the ideal of Japanese femininity and grace.

Although still in evidence today in *Asakusa*, *Ginza*, Shimbashi and *Akasaka*, their costly services are mainly reserved for exclusive parties where important business or political deals are struck.

Except for a few well-defined areas, nightlife in Tokyo begins and ends relatively early. Neon starts to blaze around 6pm, when the first flood of *salariman* and "OL's" (Office Ladies) disgorge onto the streets. By midnight in the older entertainment areas such as Ginza or Shimbashi, most hostesses in kimonos have already escorted their middle-aged customers to waiting limousines, and lesser fry bolt to the station for the last train home. Nightowls who disavow the more risqué pleasures of Shinjuku should then head for *Roppongi*, which has more discos, all-night clubs and insomniacs than normal hardworking Japanese care to imagine.

Nocturnal caution is largely unwarranted, apart from ventures into x-rated zones, or certain "hostess" bars and clubs where the bill might be mistaken for Japan's trade surplus.

The English-language *Tokyo Journal*, a monthly magazine, carries a comprehensive listing of current and forthcoming plays, concerts and other entertainments. It is available at all English-language bookstore outlets.

Several Japanese agencies sell tickets for everything from *kabuki* to rock concerts and tennis matches. Every branch of Seibu department store (plus the Wave building in Roppongi) has a **Ticket Saison** counter, and Marui stores have their own **Marui Ticket Guide** booths. **Playguide** (*Playguide Building, 2-6-4, Ginza* ☎*561-8821*) and **PIA Station** (☎*237-9999*) are both big independent agencies with branches throughout Tokyo. Try also **Kyukyodo Ticket Service** (*5-7-4, Ginza* ☎*571-0401*), by the entrance of Tokyo Kyukyodo stationery store.

Bars, brasseries and nomiya

A deep impression is left on visitors observing the flushed faces, raucous laughter and not infrequent staggering stupor of respectably attired Japanese after an evening's imbibing. Intoxication carries little social stigma in Japan, not only because many Japanese get drunk more quickly than Caucasians, but because alcohol (*o-sake*) is such an important lubricant in a society still rigidly inhibited by daytime conventions.

Nomiya

Japanese like to eat while they are drinking, and in a traditional Japanese pub, or *nomiya* — recognizable in any neighborhood by its red lantern hanging outside — you will be expected to order some small dishes as well. **Chichibu Nishiki** (*2-13-4, Ginza, near Ginza Dai-ichi hotel* ☎*541-4777, closed Sun, hols, map 9I10*), the Tokyo outlet for a sake maker of the same name is in a beautiful old wooden townhouse complete with *shoji* paper screens, *tatami* mats and a Shinto altar in the back room. Popular with theatrical types from the nearby *Kabukiza*, **Ichimon** (*3-12-6, Asakusa* ☎*875-6800, closed Sun, hols, map 16C13*) boasts 30 different sakes (some quite rare) in its cellar; it also has a delightful farmhouse interior. A *mon* was the lowest form of currency in Edo, and you pay here for drink and food with *mon* wooden tablets bought at the entrance. Built into the wall are special warmers for the sake bottles. And **Zizake** (*1-15-8, Dogenzaka* ☎496-5790, *map 2K2*) offers more than 40 local varieties of sake and also has a special sampling course with food for beginners (called the Hon-jozo course). It is nearly always full, so book ahead.

Another well-known traditional Japanese pub may be found in the unlikely setting of Roppongi's premier disco building. At the entrance to **Gonin Byakusho**, or **Five Farmers** (*Roppongi Square Building, 4th floor, 3-10-3, Roppongi* ☎470-1675, *map 4J7*), you leave your shoes behind. The rural decor (you sit on *tatami* and tuck your feet into pits underneath low tables) is reminiscent of a farmhouse in Japan's northern snow country.

By walking alongside the JR line at Yurakucho toward the Imperial hotel, you can easily imagine it is still 1946. Conversation struggles against the overhead rumble of trains in a string of cheap *yakitori* bars (see *Restaurants*) tucked inside the railroad arches (they are as popular now, on hot summer nights, as they were 40yrs ago).

If you relish the boisterous company of students, there are several cheap *nomiya* chains, which dispense assembly-line traditional fare. **Tengu**, identifiable by its sign of a *tengu* (red mask with a long nose), is well known. There are a number of branches in Shinjuku and Shibuya. Try the one at **Shinjuku Daikyo Building** (*1-18-2, Nishi-Shinjuku* ☎342-2763, *map 6G3*).

Beer halls and beer gardens

Closely related to *nomiya*, in scale if not pedigree, are the cavernous beer halls, which suddenly became all the rage after the Meiji Revolution. Still going strong is the **Lion Beer Hall** (*7-9-20, Ginza* ☎571-2590, *map 9I9*), which retains its original 1934 wall mosaics by Eizo Sugawara. Despite its name, the **New Tokyo** (*New Tokyo Building, 2-2-3, Yurakucho* ☎572-5711, *map 9H9*) celebrated its 50th anniversary in 1987. 5mins' walk from Asakusa Station, across the Azumbashi Bridge, you will find the **Azumabashi Asahi Beer Hall** (*1-23-1, Azumabashi* ☎622-0530, *map 16D13*), a good place to feel the pulse of the commoners' Shitamachi.

In summer rooftop beer gardens can be fun if you are with a group, although the grass underfoot is likely to be plastic. The beer garden on top of the **Kudan Kaikan Hotel** (*1-6-5, Kudan-Minami* ☎261-5521, *open mid-May to late Aug, map 8F8*) and the **Tokyo Suntory Building** (*1-2-3, Moto-Akasaka* ☎470-1131, *open May-end Aug, map 6H6*) both offer exceptional views. The earthbound **Gajoen Green Beer Garden** (*1-8-1, Shimo-Meguro* ☎491-4111, *open June 1-Aug 31, map 3N5*) is possibly unique in the land-starved capital: a leisurely oasis reached after a long lamplit stroll over bridges and through a Japanese garden.

Bars and brasseries

The **Kamiya Bar** (*1-1, Asakusa* ☎841-5400, *open to 9pm, closed Tues, map 16C13*) on the corner near Asakusa Station (on the Ginza line), was established in 1880 by the founder of Japan's first brandy distillery, and claims to be the oldest Western bar in Tokyo. Home of the electrifying Denki Buran cocktail, and once frequented by famous writers such as Junichiro Tanizaki and Kafu Nagai, its style remains distinctly plebeian. Buy tickets for drinks and food at the counter by the door, when you enter.

Some of the most serious faces in Tokyo are to be found in a basement Ginza bar called **Lupin** (*5-5-11, Ginza* ☎571-0750, *closed Sun, hols, map 9I10*), situated in a side alley behind the Jun men's boutique. Opened in 1929, Lupin was once a favorite watering hole for novelists such as Kyoka Izumi and Osamu Dazai, who used the far end of the bar as a prop.

Finding Western-style bars still presents a challenge, and their habitués inevitably tend to be foreigners. Expatriate old-timers swear by the first-class **Orchid Bar** of the **Okura** (see *Hotels*), where the happy-hour coterie on weekends claims to be open to "anyone interesting." **Pub Cardinal** (*Sony Building, 1st Basement, 5-3, Ginza* ☎573-0011, *map 9I10*) has the feel of a plush London pub and is popular with young, often elegant Japanese "Office Ladies." Cut-price **Henry Africa's** (*Hanatsubaki Building, 2nd floor, 3-15-23, Roppongi* ☎403-9751, *map 4J7*) and the all-American **Hard Rock Café** (*5-4-20, Roppongi* ☎408-7018, *map 4J7*) contain a better-than-average mix of young Japanese and *gaijin*. **Hub Bar**, in the lobby of Haiyuza Cinema Ten (*4-9-2, Roppongi* ☎478-0393, *map 4J7*), serves some of the cheapest drinks in town to slightly arty youngsters. If the **Kasumi Club** (*Kasumi Building, 3-24-17, Nishi-Azabu* ☎405-1090, *map 4J6*) has the feel of a London pub, it's because most of its fixtures were bought in England and lovingly transplanted; the downstairs "stand bar" only lacks imported sawdust.

More resolutely expatriate-oriented, **Maggie's Revenge** (*Takano Building, 1st Basement, 3-8-12, Roppongi* ☎479-1096, *map 4J7*) has live folk music and a welcoming atmosphere that breeds among patrons fanatical devotion to the formidable Australian owner, Maggie. A faithful re-creation of a small *bierstube*, the regulars at **Ex** (*Roppongi Maisonette, 7-7-6, Roppongi* ☎408-5487, *map 4J7*) are almost exclusively German. The rugger-and-darts brigade haunt the British pub lookalike **Berni Inn** (*Daisan Goto Building, 2nd floor, 3-13-14, Roppongi* ☎405-4928, *map 4J7*). Decorated like a seedy bordello, the **Charleston** (*3-8-11, Roppongi* ☎402-0372) is suitably degenerate late at night. Many of its less desperate denizens have recently migrated to **Deja Vu** (*Tohgensha Building, 3-15-24, Roppongi* ☎403-8777, *map 4J7*), a cheap bar that livens up in summer when it opens onto the street.

More Japanese in taste and clientele, the craze for café-bar/brasseries has produced countless glassy, marbled and wood-paneled imitators, all vaguely French-inspired. Among the first, and more resilient, are the **Café La Boheme** group. It has branches in Harajuku (*Jingubashi Building, 2nd floor, 6-7-18, Jingumae* ☎ 409-2091, *map 6I4*) and Kasumicho (*Azabu Palace Building, 2nd floor, 2-25-18, Nishi-Azabu* ☎407-1363, *map 4J6*). There is also **Takagicho** (*Kaneko Building, 1st floor, 7-11-4, Minami Aoyama* ☎499-3377, *map 3J5*) and **Brasserie D** (*Ecsaine Plaza Aoyama, 2nd floor, 3-5-14, Kita-Aoyama* ☎470-0203, *map 7I5*), run by Daini Okada of **Daini's Table** (see *Restaurants*). The most interesting is undoubtedly **Kranz** (*6-1-19, Minami Aoyama* ☎499-4683, *map 3J5*), near the *Nezu Art Museum*. The building that now houses the café-bar and restaurant was once the library of Shigenobu Okuma (1838-1922), founder of Waseda University and twice Japan's prime minister. Downstairs the decor is tasteful but spare, and upstairs there is a rental billiards room and a room, complete with *chaise-longue*, for elegant parties.

Smart and stylish recent entrants are the two **Suntory Jigger** bars in Ginza and Roppongi, run by the Suntory beer/whisky giant. The Ginza basement **Jigger Bar** (*Sunny Building, 1st Basement, 3-4-15, Ginza* ☎564-2550, *map 9I10*) has the dark wood-paneled, dimly lit mystique of a London club, and is very popular with Japanese in their twenties and thirties. The Roppongi branch (*No. 3, Gotoh Building, 1st floor, 3-13-14, Roppongi* ☎404-2409, *map 4J7*) has an equally tasteful but lighter interior and good modern jazz piano music. Prices at both are reasonable.

Drink takes second place to decor in Roppongi's now ubiquitous "fashion" and "cocktail" bars, as you will soon discover at **Paradiso** (*3-13-12, Roppongi* ☎*478-4212, map 4J7*). Decorated in a très sleek potpourri of new wave, neo-Japonesque and Art Deco, Paradiso must be the only bar in Tokyo where the table charge is less expensive than at the bar, where young males linger to ogle at barmaids in tight, black-sequined dresses. At the trend-setting **Mint Bar** (*Casagrande Miwa Building, 1st Basement, 7-5-11, Roppongi* ☎*403-1537, map 4J7*) a designer-plate poise is required to settle on the stools, and the mint-glow interior, reminiscent of a beautiful bathroom, inhibits free conversation. It is managed by Isao Matsuyama, also owner of the **Ink Stick** next door. Still chic but less pretentious is Matsuyama's earlier **Red Shoes** (*Azabu Palace, 1st Basement, 2-25-18, Nishi-Azabu* ☎*499-4319, map 4J6*). Red predominates inside, and the bar has a much sought-after (but exaggerated) reputation for late-night decadence. Nearby the **3.2.8** bar, catering to younger fans of deafening New Wave music, has concrete floors, spray graffiti, cans of Budweiser and waiters who occasionally zoom around on roller skates.

Wine bars have yet to catch on as much as in the West, probably because of the high cost of imported wine and the still poor quality of Japanese imitations. **The Wine Bar** (*The Basement, Roppongi Forum Building, 5-16-52, Roppongi* ☎*584-5790, map 4J6*) has a good cellar but dispenses wine in a frivolous manner that might offend high-minded oenophiles. The Mediterranean-inspired wine grotto of the **Crescent Restaurant** in Shiba-koen or the excellent wine cellar of the **Hilltop** (see *Hotels*) in Surugadai are more respectful and orthodox. Also recommended is Mr Stamp's renowned Wine Garden in Roppongi (see *Restaurants*). **Wine Pub Tokachi** (*3-14, Shinjuku*, ☎*356-5946, map 6F4*), a cozy nook tucked into the E side of Shinjuku's **Isetan** department store (see *Shopping*) with its own entrance on Meiji-dori, serves cheap but palatable wine from Hokkaido's Tokachi district, accompanied by typical Hokkaido snacks such as smoked salmon.

No sampling of Tokyo "drinking wells" could be complete without a foray into Shinjuku's **Golden Gai**, a rabbit warren of 250 or so tiny establishments sandwiched between rowdy Kabukicho, the 2-chome homosexual quarter, the ward office and a police station. The haunt of artists, intellectuals, ex-student agitators, tragic existentialists and more than a few *yakuza*, Golden Gai is best visited with a knowledgeable Japanese companion. The intrepid explorer should first ask to be directed to either the **Ari**, **Gu**, **Nana** or **Paru** (Pearl) bars to begin experimenting. Golden Gai is currently threatened with redevelopment, but there is still enough time left for a few drinks.

Classical music

There are classical concerts almost every night in Tokyo, with performances either by Japanese soloists and ensembles, or visiting foreign musicians. Tokyo is well endowed with symphony orchestras, some of which are listed below.

Japan Philharmonic (☎*354-9011*)
New Japan Philharmonic (☎*501-5639*)
Tokyo Metropolitan Symphony (☎*822-0726*)
Tokyo Philharmonic (☎*591-6742*)
Yomiuri Nippon Symphony (☎*270-6191*)

Two of the best concert halls are **Bunka Kaikan** (*Tokyo Festival Hall, 5-45, Ueno-koen, Taito-ku* ☎*828-2111, map 15C11*) and the new, acoustically excellent **Suntory Hall** (*Ark Hills, 1-13, Akasaka, Minato-ku* ☎*505-1001, map 8I7*).

Discos

Admission to most Tokyo discos is undoubtedly expensive, but normally includes limitless drink and basic food, or an ample equivalent of "coupons" to be exchanged. Whimsical fashion dictates that many discos have notoriously short lifespans. Relative longevity is one prime consideration in the following selection. "Respectable" discos operate a simple dress code that bars entry to those in jeans and sneakers. Male "stags" without a female companion will also find it very hard to cross the threshold of some smarter discos.

Cipango

Nittaku Building, 3rd floor, 3-8-15, Roppongi, Minato-ku ☎*478-0039. Map 4/J7* ⚑ Ⓐ🄴 Ⓘ 🄳 Ⓥ🄸🅂🄰
Open Mon-Sun 5pm-midnight. Subway: Roppongi.
Cipango's claim to Oriental exotica rests on the odd Chinese fan and fake Thai statue, probably bought from the same supplier as the **Samba Club**. It attracts an energetic but totally unfashionable young crowd, including many girl couples. Anyone over 25yrs old would feel distinctly uncomfortable.

Cleo Palazzi

Shadai Building, 1st Basement, 3-18-2, Roppongi, Minato-ku ☎*586-8494. Map 4/J7* ⚑ *Open Mon-Sun 8pm-6am. Subway: Roppongi.*
A small club somewhat off the beaten Roppongi track, best visited late at night when the crowd veers toward more bacchanalian venues.

Club D

Villa Bianca, 1st Basement, 2-33-12, Jingumae, Shibuya-ku ☎*423-1471. Map 6/I4* Ⓐ🄴
Open Mon-Sun 7pm-4am. JR: Harajuku; subway: Meijijingumae.
Imaginative restaurateur Daini Okada transformed this onetime "underground" club with an unpronounceable name into one of Tokyo's most fashionable discos packed nearly every night with trendily attired Japanese and foreigners. The 1st Basement is a rather elegant lounge. Laser lights pierce the dungeon gloom of the dance floor and bar below with geometric splashes of color. The music veers to New Wave, with steps and gyrations known only to the chosen few.

Crazy Horse

3-18-12, Roppongi, Minato-ku ☎*582-6886. Map 4/J7* ⚑ ⇌ Ⓐ🄴 Ⓘ 🄳 Ⓥ🄸🅂🄰 *Open Mon-Sat 6pm-3am. Closed Sun. Subway: Roppongi.*

The chandeliers and tinted mirrors of this supper club match the tastes of its customers, who often arrive in black limousines and wear dark glasses. The Filipino band plays disco and oldies. 'Supper' officially stops at 9pm.

Lexington Queen

Daisan Goto Building, 1st Basement, 3-13-14, Roppongi, Minato-ku ☎*401-1661. Map 4/J7* ⚑ ⇌ Ⓐ🄴 Ⓘ 🄳 Ⓥ🄸🅂🄰 *Open Mon-Sun 6pm-midnight (closing time varies). Subway: Roppongi.*
Opened in 1980, the "Lex" reigned supreme over Tokyo's disco nightlife for about 2yrs and still manages to draw the biggest stars of music, movies and fashion. (Visits by the likes of Sylvester Stallone, Stevie Wonder and Rod Stewart are all dutifully recorded for posterity along one wall.) The ever-flamboyant Bill Hersey is the impresario, who ensures every visitor of note is photographed for his "Party Line" column in the local *Weekender*. The decor has become staid, but the dance music keeps up with fashion and the high proportion of foreign models, who get in free, supposedly enhance the glamor. The entrance fee includes a helping from the Lex's own *sushi* bar.

Rajah Court

Hotel Ibis, 4th floor, 7-14-4, Roppongi, Minato-ku ☎*479-5555. Map 4/J7* ⚑ Ⓐ🄴 Ⓘ 🄳 Ⓥ🄸🅂🄰
Open Mon-Sun 6pm-5am. Subway: Roppongi.
The Rajah Court is best distinguished by its incredibly cheap entrance fee, which includes food-and-drink tickets.

Samba Club

Roppongi Square Building, 5th floor, 3-10-3, Roppongi, Minato-ku ☎*470-6391. Map 4/J7* ⚑ ⇌ Ⓐ🄴 Ⓘ 🄳 Ⓥ🄸🅂🄰 *Open Mon-Sun 6pm-4am. Subway: Roppongi.*
An adult disco, where most of the male ravers come in suits and ties. The theme is supposed to be "Hot

African Passion," but apart from a moth-eaten stuffed black panther near the entrance and some strategically placed bronze statues of birds from the Dark Continent, the influence seems tenuous. The entrance fee is normally cheap, but drinks are not, especially if one wants to impress by buying a ludicrously priced "keep" bottle of spirits for return visits. There is a large, softly lit lounge area, which has such comfortable sofas that more than a few overworked executives have been known to fall fast asleep here. An old-fashioned balance is kept between upbeat disco/current hits and slow dances, and the decibels are never allowed to kill the possibility of conversation. The Samba Club also has a branch at the **Century Hyatt** (see *Hotels*).

Tsubaki Ball

Roppongi Square Building, 1st and 2nd basements, 3-10-3, Roppongi, Minato-ku ☎478-0087 Map 4J7 Ⴤ ☰ AE ⊕ ⊙ VISA Open Mon-Sun 6pm-midnight. Subway: Roppongi.

This place caters to graduates of its sister, **Tsubaki House**, in Shinjuku. The 1st Basement has a chic lounge area and the largest dance floor in Roppongi, one floor down, where there's ear-splitting New Wave music, which attracts fashion-conscious post-punkers.

Tsubaki House

Teatoru Building, 5th floor, 3-14-20, Shinjuku, Shinjuku-ku ☎354-3236. Map 6G4 Ⴤ AE ⊕ ⊙ VISA Open Mon-Sun 5-9.30pm. JR/ subway: Shinjuku; subway: Shinjukusanchome.

One of the pioneers of Tokyo disco, now catering to the more outrageous youth fringe. Although the decor is basic and it closes early, Tsubaki has "theme nights" offering ample fodder for social anthropologists.

Turia

7-13-7, Roppongi, Minato-ku ☎408-0105. Map 4J7 Ⴤ ☰ AE ⊕ ⊙ VISA Disco open Mon-Sun 6pm-midnight; bar and restaurant Mon-Sun 6pm-4am. Subway: Roppongi.

Having penetrated the gray skin of Turia, you will first encounter some gangling monsters' heads. The galleries and dance floor continue the theme of *Aliens*, *Mad Max* and *Star Wars*, and the restaurant, with sand on the floor and tarpaulins slung over the tables, is supposed to represent the surface of another planet. Strangely, most of the space travelers — supposedly picked from the line outside by a monitored video camera — are uniformly ordinary, at least compared to the motionless waitresses clad in ferocious leather thongs.

Jazz

One of the few American imports to have successfully pierced Japan's bamboo curtain and taken deep root, jazz flourished briefly in Tokyo during the 1920s and 1930s before being swept underground (as it was thought to be a dangerous form of Western decadence) in the tidal wave of militarism. Returning with the GIs in 1945, jazz has since grown and prospered into a cultural institution, with performers sometimes claiming they have more opportunity here than in the USA, as the Japanese fans treat jazz "with more respect." Outdoor jazz festivals in the Tokyo area regularly attract top musicians, and Tokyo itself has a number of clubs featuring live jazz in all its permutations – from Dixieland and mainstream to fusion, progressive and avant-garde. Japanese jazz fans are certainly loyal and dedicated, and the atmosphere in the Tokyo clubs borders on reverential.

Birdland

Roppongi Square Building, 2nd Basement, 3-10-3, Roppongi, Minato-ku ☎478-3456. Map 4J7 Ⴤ AE ⊕ ⊙ VISA Open Mon-Thurs, Sun 6pm-1.15am; Fri, Sat 6pm-2.30am. Subway: Roppongi.

A favorite of "mature" buffs of the 1940s and 1950s jazz standards. Cozy, warm brick interior.

Body and Soul

German Bakery Building, 3rd floor, 7-14-1, Roppongi, Minato-ku ☎408-2094. Map 4J7 Ⴤ AE Open Mon-Thur, Sat 7pm-2am; Fri 7pm-3am. Closed Sun. Subway: Roppongi.

Jazz standards of the 1940s and 1950s are the staple diet of this small but respected club in the Roppongi district.

Nightlife and the arts

Roppongi Pit Inn
Shimei Building, 1st Basement, 3-17-7, Roppongi, Minato-ku ☎585-1063. *Map 4J7* ⚑ *Open Mon-Fri 6.30-11pm, Sat, Sun 6.30pm-3am. Subway: Roppongi.*

The Roppongi branch of the famous **Shinjuku Pit Inn** inclines more toward live fusion jazz and occasionally rock. Regulars tend to be purists indifferent to the garagelike interior.

Satin Doll
Haizuka Building, 3rd floor, 4-9-2, Roppongi, Minato-ku ☎401-3080. *Map 4J7* ⚑ 🍴 AE ⊙ ⊙ VISA *Open Mon-Sat 5.30pm-1am, Sun, hols 5.30pm-midnight. Subway: Roppongi.*

An elegant jazz club with an ingredient usually missing at such establishments: good French food. The music menu runs from 1950s standards and jazz-blues female vocals to funky fusion.

Shinjuku Pit Inn
YK Building, 1st Basement, 3-16-4, Shinjuku, Shinjuku-ku ☎354-2024. *Map 6G4* ⚑ *Open Mon-Sun 11.30am-11pm. JR: Shinjuku; subway: Shinjukusan chome.*

The most famous and long-established live jazz house in Tokyo, drawing the cream of Japanese performers and many top-name foreign musicians. Like its Roppongi offshoot, the decor can best be described as minimalist; however, it's the music that counts.

Valentine
Roppongi Hosho Building, 4th floor, 7-14-1, Roppongi, Minato-ku ☎478-5068. *Map 4J7* ⚑ AE ⊙ ⊙ VISA *Open Mon-Sun 6pm-5am. Subway: Roppongi.*

Sundays are still reserved for female jazz vocalists, but on other nights the live music menu ranges from reggae and disco funk to fusion and trad (☎ *ahead to check performances*).

Karaoke bars

Singing before a room full of people may strike the average foreigner as masochistic humiliation, yet millions of normally restrained Japanese enjoy the experience tremendously. At *karaoke* bars young and old take turns at the microphone to blare out their favorite song against a background of recorded music. Song books are usually provided, but in some laser disc *karaoke* bars the words appear on the screen against suitable images (sometimes a celebrity mouthing the words, or perhaps a snow scene, or a moonlit beach). Staff are usually on hand to prod the shy or mask ineptitude with mellifluous accompaniment, but no one cares if the singing is appallingly off-key (as it usually is!). *Karaoke* bars (sometimes misleadingly called "Snack" or "Snaku" bars) are found in every neighborhood. The following are some upscale examples.

Lorelei
5-1-16, Ginza, Chuo-ku ☎571-5403. *Map 9I10* ⚑ VISA *Open Mon-Sat 5pm-2am. Closed Sun. Subway: Ginza.*

The decor and waitresses' uniforms are pure Bavarian, as is the enforced camaraderie. The songs, however, are mostly Japanese *enka* (traditional popular ballads).

Roaring 20'
Mizobuchi Building, 1st Basement, 3-13-6, Roppongi, Minato-ku ☎479-6220. *Map 4J7* ⚑ 🍴 AE ⊙ ⊙ VISA *Open Mon-Sun 6pm-5am. Subway: Roppongi.*

One could easily be forgiven for assuming this ultra-sleek marble and metallic interior bar belonged to the fashionable Roppongi cocktail set, but the mainly young clientele soon dissolve the frigid atmosphere with the help of high-tech *karaoke* equipment. Quite a few songs (mainly Beatles) are in English, and foreigners are strongly encouraged to try their hand at the microphone.

Saint Julian
Zex Bamu-kan, 4th floor, 3-9-5, Roppongi, Minato-ku ☎403-0817. *Map 4J7* ⚑ AE ⊙ ⊙ VISA *Open Mon-Sun 7pm-4am. Subway: Roppongi.*

Serious *karaoke*. Nightly amateur shows and coaching by a resident crooner.

Nightclubs and hostess bars

Horror stories about innocent foreigners falling prey to the outrageous prices of Ginza and Akasaka watering holes are now so numerous the following caveat may be unnecessary. For instance, the price of a few drinks and some titbits, in a well-appointed bar that resembles a living room, with an exquisite hostess whose golden smile and silken knee dissolve all cares, may well equal that of a one-way air ticket to Japan.

Hostesses are often a standard fixture at cabarets, although changing tastes have made them an endangered species (witness the closure in 1985 of the famed Mikado in Akasaka).

Foreigners are welcome at the following clubs, where the charges will not cause cardiac arrest.

Club Maiko
Aster Plaza Building, 7-7-6, Ginza, Chuo-ku ☎574-7745. *Map 9/10* ⬛ AE ⬤ ⬤ VISA *Open Mon-Sat 6pm-midnight. Closed Sun. Subway: Ginza.*
An accessible and relatively inexpensive way of receiving the prized ministrations of geisha. In a Japanese setting, geisha and *maiko* (apprentices) perform four dances a night, and they also wait on customers before and after shows.

Cordon Bleu
6-6-4, Akasaka, Minato-ku ☎582-7800. *Map 8/7* ⬛ ⬛ AE ⬤ ⬤ VISA *Open Mon-Sat 7pm-3am. Closed Sun. Subway: Akasaka.*
The name is a tongue-in-cheek reference to its French food, but the main "lure of Paris" of this mirrored nightspot is the thrice-nightly show of topless dancers.

Five Season
A-One Building, 6th floor, 5-16-4, Roppongi, Minato-ku ☎585-1415. *Map 4/7* ⬛ ⬛ AE ⬤ ⬤ VISA *Open Mon-Sat 7pm-2am. Closed Sun. Subway: Roppongi.*
This "Executive" club is a welcome aberration from the usual hostess bar. The small room (ten or more customers would induce claustrophobia) has all the comforts of hostess clubs (marshmallow sofas, soft lights, inlaid floors and glitzy ornaments) on a miniature scale. The *mamma-san* has a soft spot for foreigners, and her ravishing daughters (identical twins) have already learned the trick of getting uptight businessmen to unwind and start talking. A brilliantined, moustachioed crooner strums his guitar in the background, and ramrod stiff waiters keep the oil flowing. Best of all, the bill will never risk an encounter with the bailiffs.

New Latin Quarter
2-13-8, Nagatacho, Chiyoda-ku ☎581-1326. *Map 8H7* ⬛ ⬛ AE ⬤ ⬤ VISA *Open Mon-Sat 6.30pm-1.30am. Closed Sun. Subway: Akasakamitsuke.*
Reminiscent of the 1950s blend of seedy elegance and kitsch that marked the old Mikado, the velvet-draped circular room of the New Latin Quarter now hosts such inspiring performances as Californian swimsuit models and magic stunts. The long entrance porch runs next to the fire-gutted shell of the New Japan hotel. The tuxedoed touts nowadays seems a trifle desperate.

Pop, rock and country and western

The still vibrant tradition of *enka*, or Japanese popular songs (as heard with wildly unpredictable degrees of fidelity in *karaoke* bars) has many worthy practitioners. The market for Western pop music (albeit with Japanese lyrics) is, on the other hand, seemingly saturated with teeny-bopper "idols."

Heavy metal predominates in Japanese rock, with its veneer of machismo, ear-splitting decibels and wild stage antics barely concealing the insipid music. Although reggae is now gradually winning converts from a hardcore of Japanese disciples, it is still confined to one live outlet: the **Hot Co-Rocket**.

Country and western entered Japan with the GIs during the Occupation, and has since matured beyond being a fad, although it has yet to institutionally ripen like its American sibling, jazz.

Aspen Glow
GM Building, 6th floor, 2-28-2, Dogenzaka, Shibuya-ku ☎496-9709. Map 2K3 ♈ ⬤ Open Mon-Sat 5pm-2am. Closed Sun. JR/subway: Shibuya.
The "cowboy hat brigade" will immediately warm to this loving re-creation of an American country and western bar, in the center of Tokyo. Good foot stompin' to the electrified bands. Cheap cover charge and drinks.

Cavern Club
Roppongi Hosho Building, 3rd floor, 7-14-1, Roppongi, Minato-ku ☎405-5207. Map 4J7 ♈ AE ⬤ ⬤ VISA Open Mon-Sat 6pm-2.30am, Sun 6pm-midnight. Subway: Roppongi.
A shrine to the ever-replenishing hordes of Japanese Beatlemaniacs, where a now veteran and hilarious Japanese lookalike band nightly crank out the Lennon and McCartney favorites.

Cay
Wacoal Spiral Building, 1st Basement, 5-6-23, Minami-Aoyama, Minato-ku ☎498-5790. Map 6I5 ♈ ☰ AE ⬤ ⬤ VISA Open Mon-Sat 6.30pm-1am (last food order 11pm); closed Sun. Subway: Omotesando.
A restaurant/bar "event" house in the basement of one of Tokyo's most exciting new buildings, Cay hosts good modern music bands, off-beat cinema, *buyo* (traditional Japanese dance), modern ballet and anything else that takes the management's fancy.

Crocodile
New Sekiguchi Building, 1st Basement, 6-18-8, Jingumae, Shibuya-ku ☎499-5205. Map 6I4 ♈ ☰ Open Mon-Sun 6pm-6am. JR: Harajuku; subway: Meijijingumae.
The rock groups who play here tend to attract leathered Japanese zombies with dyed orange hair, dangling crucifixes, padlock chains and platform boots. The live samba, reggae, soul and blues concerts are regrettably less colorful.

Hot Co-Rocket
Daini Omasa Building, 1st Basement, 5-18-2, Roppongi, Minato-ku ☎583-9409. Map 4J7 ♈ AE ⬤ ⬤ VISA Open Mon-Sun 7pm-3am. Subway: Roppongi.
Watch the Japanese expressions of tingling horror as the musicians maniacally shake their dreadlocks and the club starts to throb to strange, hypnotic rhythms. Foreigners usually start the dancing, but it doesn't take long for even the most timid to abandon themselves to the reggae beat, and the Jamaican band clearly enjoys every minute of their liberating seduction. Caribbean cocktails complement the music and tropical plants. For "different" music and laid-back, un-Japanese spontaneity, Hot Co-Rocket is one of the best spots in the Roppongi district. Reggae is still not accepted in Japan as mainstream fashion, so the cover charge remains gratifyingly cheap.

Ink Stick
Casa Grande Miwa Building, 1st Basement, 7-5-11, Roppongi, Minato-ku ☎401-0429. Map 4J7 ♈ ☰ AE ⬤ VISA Open Mon-Thur, Sun 7pm-4am. Fri, Sat 7pm-5am. Subway: Roppongi.
The most chic "New Music" spot in town until it was upstaged by its own new satellite in far-flung Shibaura. Lofty ceilings, modern Oriental screens, glassed-in dining area, dance floor and a little stage for modern music performances. David Bowie partied here, and jazz guitarist Pat Meheney was inspired to give an impromptu rendition.

Ink Stick Shibaura Factory
2-2-20, Shibaura, Minato-ku ☎798-3921. Map 5L8 ♈ Open Mon-Sun 6-11.30pm. JR: Tamachi (Shibaura exit).
An inspired move by "His Hipness" Isao Matsuyama brought the Roppongi swingers to the declining Tokyo Bay dockland of Shibaura, E of Tamachi JR Station. A novelty for Tokyo, the Factory carefully retains the image of a warehouse with concrete floors and artfully applied silver foil over ventilator shafts. The excellent music/dance stage resembles a large boxing ring surrounded by aluminum scaffolding. Little comfort, except for an upstairs "members only" gallery/lounge, and the simplest of drinks, but exciting live New Wave/rock/R&B music, both Japanese and foreign. Usually some seasonal excuse is found for young disco parties, which engender lots of whooping and shouting.
(Matsuyama's **Tango** restaurant/bar opposite the Factory dispenses minuscule portions of fashion food at exorbitant prices. The trendy **Venice** restaurant nearby relies on the same formula. It pays to be square and eat in a different part of Tokyo.)

Kennedy House Ginza
*Koridogai Building, 1st
Basement, 7-108, Ginza, Chuo-ku*
☎572-8391. Map 9/10 ☗ ⓐ ⓒ
ⓒ ⓥⓘⓢⓐ *Open Mon-Sat 5.30-
11.30pm. Closed Sun. Subway:
Ginza.*

Office parties from the Ginza, clap
their hands and shout applause as
two Japanese women dressed as
schoolgirls, backed by undertaxed
musicians, belt out sugary pop songs.

Kennedy House Roppongi
*Shimojo Building, 2nd floor, 3-
14-8, Roppongi, Minato-ku*
☎423-0083. Map 4/7 ☗ ⓐ ⓒ
ⓒ ⓥⓘⓢⓐ *Open Mon-Sun 6.30pm-
midnight. Subway: Roppongi.*
Situated above the **Chimney House**
spareribs restaurant and owned by
the same company, Kennedy House
Roppongi has smartly attired
Japanese yuppies whooping it up to
the safe sounds of a Japanese house
band playing Californian surf music
and 1960s rock 'n' roll.

Kento's
*Fukuyama Building, 1st
Basement, 4-10-3, Roppongi,
Minato-ku* ☎401-5755. Map 4/7
☗ ⓐ ⓒ ⓒ ⓥⓘⓢⓐ *Open Mon-Sat
6pm-2.30am, Sun, hols 6pm-
midnight. Subway: Roppongi.*
Packed with young Japanese office
workers, many not born when the
nostalgic 1950s and early 1960s rock
'n' roll songs, played by the house
band, were first performed.

Live Inn
*Ekimae Kaikan, 8th floor, 1-3-1,
Dogenzaka, Shibuya-ku* ☎464-
8381. Map 3/4 ☗ *Open Mon-
Sun, times vary. JR/subway:
Shibuya.*

This place competes with **Crocodile**
for the attention of Shibuya foot-
stompers with a varied diet of rock,
R&B, blues, soul and funk. Decor is
suitably spartan.

Loft
*Daini Mizota Building, 1st
Basement, 7-5-10, Nishi-
Shinjuku, Shinjuku-ku* ☎365-
0698. Map 6/3 ☗ *Open Mon-
Sun 4.30pm-4am. JR/subway:
Shinjuku.*
A long-established rock venue, and
still one of the best places to hear new
groups. Heavy on the eardrums and
light on interior frills.

Pickford Live Hall
*Landic Building, 1st Basement,
4-11-13, Roppongi, Minato-ku*
☎423-1628. Map 4/7 ☗ ⓐ ⓒ
ⓥⓘⓢⓐ *Open Mon-Sat 5pm-5am.
Closed Sun. Subway: Roppongi.*
Three live bands perform every night
(American "funk," Japanese "comic"
and Filipino "schmaltz") in a large
room of gray and black modern
design. Cocktails, not beer, are the
drink; more inspiring than love-all at
the **Tennis Club** next door . . . .

Tennis Club
*Landic Building, 1st Basement,
4-11-13, Roppongi, Minato-ku*
☎478-0070 Map 4/7 ☗ ═ ⓐ
ⓐ ⓒ ⓥⓘⓢⓐ *Open Mon-Sun 5pm-
4am. Subway: Roppongi.*
Targetted at Japanese young people,
it is reputedly favored by students of
the prestigious Keio University who
are drawn by its odd marketing logo
of "corn/onion/potato and Scotch"
and the magic word "Tennis."
Otherwise an ordinary bar lounge,
with soft music performed by a live
band dressed in striped sailor suits.

Traditional performing arts
Many young Japanese confess, with some embarrassment, to never
having seen performances of their traditional arts except, perhaps,
on television. Devotees find this a hard truth to swallow, but the
obvious discordance between modern urban life and the feudal
mores of *kabuki* or *bunraku*, or the rarified aristocratic esthetics of
Noh drama (not to mention the archaic language incomprehensible
to modern Japanese) helps explain why Tokyo audiences are
increasingly elderly or academic.
Bunraku
Bunraku is a smaller version of *kabuki*, similar in look and staging,
but using hand-held puppets roughly one-third life size. Half of
the *kabuki* repertoire is drawn from *bunraku*, which had its origins
in simple storytelling with puppets, in shrines and temples as far
back as the 8thC. Each main puppet is controlled by three men:
the master puppeteer wearing formal kimono and operating the
head and right arm, and two assistants in black hoods, who work
the left arm and legs.

The **Bunraku National Theater** is in Osaka, but performances can also be seen in the small hall of Tokyo's National Theater (for address see below).

Gagaku and bugaku

Probably the oldest form of orchestral music in the world, much of the *gagaku* court music heard today is basically the same as 1,000yrs ago, and the accompanying *bugaku*, highly stylized court dances, are of nearly similar antiquity. The Imperial Court Orchestra is the most famous performing group and play twice or three times a year at the National Theater. Performances are also given inside the East Garden of the Imperial Palace to celebrate the Emperor's Birthday (advance applications by postcard should be made to the Imperial Household Agency).

Kabuki

The most accessible and popular form of classical Japanese theater for modern audiences, *kabuki* began as an erotic form of dance-drama and long remained associated with lewdness and prostitution. Nowadays regarded as an "elevated" art form, it draws on a repertoire of some 350 plays, many of which center around the conflict between *ninjo* (human feeling and emotion) and *giri* (social obligation). Although famous *kabuki* actors (women were banned from the stage in an early clean-up drive) no longer have the huge nationwide followings they enjoyed in the Edo and Meiji periods, during the high points of the performance you will still hear fans shouting the actor's family name in approval.

The two best places to see *kabuki* are at the *Kabukiza* or at the main hall of the **National Theater** (*4-1, Hayabusacho* ☎265-7411, *map 8H8*), which both offer earphone guides in English of the performance for a small rental fee plus refundable deposit.

Modern theater

Tokyo has a flourishing modern drama scene, but as you might expect, most of it is performed in the Japanese language. One theater worth a visit for its curiosity is the **Takarazuka** (*1-1-3, Yurakucho* ☎591-1711, *map 9H10*), a 500-strong all-girl troupe immensely popular with teenage girls and middle-aged housewives. The Takarazuka specializes in lavish musicals, with song, dance and chorus line. "Male" roles are all played by women — the inverse of *kabuki* — and stars receive fanatical adulation. Crowds of young girls regularly gather outside the Takarazuka (near the Imperial hotel) just for a glimpse of their female idol entering or leaving.

The **Albion-za** (*20-2, Ichibancho, Chiyoda-ku* ☎234-6871, *map 8G7*) English theater troupe have a loyal following among foreign residents for their comic satires of everyday life in Japan.

Noh and kyogen

The uninitiated are likely to find the chanting of ancient Japanese poetry, minimal acting and symbolic dance movements of *Noh* to be soporific, the sacred, trancelike atmosphere more religious ritual than drama. *Kyogen*, brief comic interludes that intersperse *Noh* performances, could not be more opposite in their wordliness and satire. The **National Noh Theater** is at 4-18-1, Sendagaya, Shibuya-ku ☎423-1331, map *6H4*. The following schools also have their own theaters in Tokyo.

Kanze Noh Theater (*1-16-4, Shoto, Shibuya-ku* ☎469-5241)
Hosho Noh Theater (*1-5-9, Hongo, Bunkyo-ku* ☎811-4843)
Yarai Noh Theater (*60 Yaraicho, Shinjuku-ku* ☎5268-7311)
Kita Noh Theater (*4-6-9, Kami-Osaki, Shinagawa-ku* ☎491-7773)
Tessenkai Noh Theater (*4-21-29, Minami Aoyama* ☎401-2285)
Ginza Noh Theater (*Ginza Nogakudo Building, 9th floor, 6-5-15, Ginza* ☎571-0197)

Shopping

One of the main reasons why Japanese products enjoy such a high reputation nowadays is because they are required to pass an extremely rigorous approval system at home. Japanese consumers are probably the most fastidious in the world concerning quality. Although goods sold at any reputable store in Tokyo may seem expensive, you are assured they will not split at the seams or break down with indecent haste.

High standards of service, now debased to folklore legend in the West, are still taken for granted in Tokyo. From the smallest family-run shop to a branch of a national chain store, every customer can normally expect to be accorded the same degree of respect, attention and politeness reserved in other countries for visiting oil sheiks and aristocracy.

The epitome of culture shock for visitors are Japanese department stores, which at their stupendous best can make famous stores such as Harrods appear distinctly understaffed, unimaginative, scruffy and down-at-the-heels. Not only does the Japanese equivalent boast of satisfying every possible consumer need from the cradle to the grave — from food, fashion, furniture, fine-art, round-trip air tickets, a wedding bouquet and honeymoon, or a new home — but they also provide entertainment and culture as well. Some of Tokyo's finest art exhibitions (often European "Old Masters" or Impressionist paintings) are held in department store galleries. **Seibu** and **Mitsukoshi** even have their own theaters. Helpful staff are always immaculately uniformed, and Japan is probably the only country where elevator girls in white lace gloves must bow to customers at a precise angle and announce each floor in a special "nightingale voice." Many stores have mouthwatering food halls in their basements, and a wide range of good restaurants and cafés on their top floors. The roof may house a tennis court, a beer garden, or a place to sell potted plants and bonsai trees.

Japanese women vie with their Italian and French counterparts as the most fashion and clothes-conscious in the world, and recently young Japanese men have started to equal their vanity. In the 1980s a "new wave" of Japanese designers, led by Issey Miyake, Rei Kawakubo, Yohji Yamamoto, Kenzo and Yamamoto Kansai, overran the traditional Parisian and Milanese houses and caught the imagination of the West. A new generation of designers is now emerging in Tokyo, hard on the heels of these established stars who each have their own showcase boutiques in the chic fashion capital of Aoyama. (The quasi-religious reverence such designers enjoy in Japan has given a few of their boutique staff the same irritating aloofness one encounters in the USA or Europe.)

Dedicated "fashion buildings" are one sign of the Japanese obsession with appearance; another is the extraordinarily catholic plethora of small clothes stores. If you have endless energy, and shoe leather, the best Tokyo reconnaissance (see *Walks* in *Planning*) starts in the large fashion emporia in Shibuya, and continues with a stroll through the pubescent jungle of Harajuku to the rarefied designer climes of Aoyama.

Ginza was in danger of losing the moneyed youth it had attracted, to newer centers in the w of the city, but after strenuous efforts it has reclaimed its undisputed title as Tokyo's main shopping area. Here you'll find not only large department stores, art galleries, famous jewelers and astronomically expensive, imported luxury stores (often Italian leather articles), but a wealth of long-established firms selling lengths of dazzling kimono silk, delicate paper products, beautiful porcelain — and lotus-jam buns (as eaten by the Emperor Meiji).

Certain other districts have taken on distinct commercial identities over the years. The Kanda Jimbocho area is a bibliophile's dream, where close to 100 secondhand bookstores are crammed eave to eave. Asakusabashi is the center of many old firms making *ningyo* (Japanese dolls); their stores are only a few minutes' walk in either direction of the railroad station. In general, the old Shitamachi area (including Asakusa, Ueno, Yanaka, Yushima, Nihonbashi, Kyobashi and Kanda) is where you will still find the highest concentration of antiques and "traditional" Japanese products. Shinjuku and Ikebukuro are noted for large discount camera stores. The average Tokyoite only goes to Akihabara to buy discount electrical goods, for which it is already famous outside Japan.

Credit cards are widely accepted, except by small, often family-run shops. For foreigners, finding the right clothing size has become much less of a problem thanks to the enlarged Japanese physique, but if you have large feet, long arms or "ample proportions," you may still have difficulty.

Tokyo department stores have sales on selected items during most of the year, but bargain hunters should avoid promotion periods in the days preceding Mother's Day (2nd Sun in May), Father's Day (3rd Sun in June), Children's Day (May 5), the *o-chugen* (late June-mid July) and *o-seibo* (end Nov-mid Dec) gift-giving seasons. Discounts of 30-50 percent are common during the summer (mid July-end Aug) and New Year (Jan 3-mid Feb) main sales.

Department stores open at 10am, and close between 6pm and 7pm. Most retailers also adhere to these times. However, designer boutiques open and close later and old-fashioned and family-run stores vary widely in their hours of business. Department stores are closed one day each week (the day varies with each store), and for the New Year holiday (Jan 1-2).

Antiques, curios and mingei

Connoisseur collectors of Oriental ceramics have long made their way to the Kyobashi-Nihonbashi area of old Tokyo. **Mayuyama** (*2-5-9, Kyobashi* ☎*561-5146, map 9H10*), the most famous name among Tokyo fine art dealers, specializes in ancient Chinese (the earliest pieces from the Shang dynasty, 1500-1100BC) and Japanese (Jomon, 3rdCBC) ware, discreetly displayed in museumlike surroundings on its first two floors. In the same class is **Kochukyo** (*3-8-5, Nihonbashi* ☎*271-1835, map 9F10*), situated behind the s entrance of the Takashimaya department store. It sells mainly ancient Chinese pottery and bronzes. You will find several smaller antique shops patronized by connoisseurs in the same area.

More eclectic are the antique and curio shops on Yushima's Kasuga-dori, farther up the hill, which skirt the Yushima Tenjin Shrine. The showpiece of the neighborhood is undoubtedly the costly but first-class **Ohno Art Shop** (*2-31-23, Yushima* ☎*811-4365, map 15D10*), noted for its collection of more than 100 decorated screens, as well as *netsuke*, bronzes, and ceramics from China, Korea and Japan. Nearby are several cheaper antique ceramic stores, as well as some intriguing curio-junk stores run by enthusiasts, which are good fun for browsing.

Scattered over the city are the following dealers of repute.
Harumi Antiques 9-6-14, Akasaka ☎403-1043. Map 8I7. Tansu, Hibachi and blue-and-white china.
Heisando 1-2-4, Shiba Koen ☎434-0588. Map 5K8. Noted for scrolls and screen paintings.

Japan Art Center Tokyo Green Heights, 1-22-10, Takadanobaba ☎200-5837. Map 12D4. Old Japanese furniture.

Kura 2-2-18, Shiba Daimon ☎434-1300. Map 5K9. Quality antiques, and modern Japanese prints, in an old geisha house.

Kurofune 7-7-4, Roppongi ☎479-1552. Map 4J7. Traditional Japanese furniture.

The Gallery 1-11-6, Akasaka ☎585-5019. Map 8I7. Situated opposite the Okura hotel, this store has a good but pricey collection of Japanese, Korean and Chinese antiques. It also specializes in furnishings and jewelry.

Oriental Bazaar 5-9-13, Jingumae ☎400-3933. Map 6I4. This slightly touristy store on Omotesando-dori has a good selection of reproduction Oriental exotica, plus some genuine old kimonos, Imari and blue-and-white porcelain and assorted antiques in the basement.

The indoor gallery-markets of London, Paris and New York have two well-known equivalents in Tokyo:

Tokyo Ochanomizu Antique Hall Kenkyusha Building, 1st Basement, 2-9, Kanda-Surugadai ☎295-7110. Map 15E10. Old kimonos, swords, screens, *tansu* chests, Imari ware, lacquer and folk art.

International Antique Market Hanae Mori Building, Basement, 3-6-1, Kita-Aoyama. Map 7I5. 35 shops selling everything from *tansu*, old kimonos, and *ukiyo-e*, to French clocks, Art Nouveau fixtures, cameos and assorted jewelry. You won't find any bargains here, but it's pleasant just browsing.

Mingei (folk crafts)

Crafts Center Plaza 246, 2nd floor, 3-1-1, Minami Aoyama ☎403-2460. Map 7I5. Devoted to the propagation of Japanese crafts, examples of which are available.

Ishizuka 1-5-20, Yaesu ☎275-2991. Map 10G11. Situated in the heart of the city with a good selection of crafts and a pleasant coffee shop upstairs.

Takumi 8-4-2, Ginza ☎571-2017. Map 10I10. Still acknowledged as the leading outlet for *mingei*, Takumi specializes in the famous Mashiko folk pottery.

Tsukamoto Tokyu Plaza 4th floor, 1-2-2, Dogenzaka ☎461-4410. Map 3K4. A small but good stock of Mashiko ware is on sale here, with prices slightly lower than at **Takumi**.

Books and records

A cartel of book importers and distributors operating in Tokyo ensures a price mark-up of around 50 percent on foreign books in their original currency. Foreign newspapers and magazines are also exorbitantly priced. As Japan is a nation of audiophiles, there is a predictably large selection of recorded music, mostly labeled in Japanese, although helpful staff are always ready to direct foreigners. Japanese disc pressings are of the highest standard. Despite Japan's near monopoly of video hardware, video tape and disc, new foreign movie releases still lag far behind the USA.

Imperial Hotel Book Shop
Imperial Hotel, 1st floor, 1-1-1, Uchisaiwaicho, Chiyoda-ku ☎503-8254. Map 9I9 (AE)
A surprisingly good choice of highbrow books about Japan, in English.

Jena
Chuo Ginza Building, 3rd floor, *5-6-1, Ginza, Chuo-ku* ☎571-2980. Map 10I10 (AE) (O) (CB) (VISA)
Jena (pronounced *Yena*) has an import bazaar on the 3rd floor, with books ranging indiscriminately from pulp fiction, romance and pornography to cookery and fine art. Imported magazines of every genre and taste are its specialty, as well as hobby and photography books.

Shopping

Kinokuniya
3-17-7, Shinjuku, Shinjuku-ku
☎ 354-0131. Map 6F4 AE ⓐ ⓒ
VISA

Kinokuniya had its heyday as the intellectual rendezvous of the Shinjuku counterculture in the 1960s and early 1970s, and a few vestiges still linger: one literary remnant is the still voluminous corpus on Marxism. The foreign department, on the 5th floor, is heavily patronized for its Japanese- and English-language teaching materials, but there is also an extensive range of other books, including French, German, Italian, Spanish and Russian. Kinokuniya Hall, on the 4th floor, caters to minority tastes such as silent film festivals and traditional *rakugo* (comic storytelling). There are boutiques on the 1st floor, and the basement passage branching off Shinjuku's underground walkway has many inexpensive restaurants. The elevators here are notoriously cramped and slow, so it is often easier to walk.

Maruzen
2-3-10, Nihonbashi, Chuo-ku
☎ 272-7211. Map 10G11 AE ⓐ
ⓒ VISA

Founded during the Meiji Restoration, in order to disseminate Western knowledge in Japan, Maruzen's main strength remains its academic books. The foreign section, which caters to most major European languages, is on the 2nd floor and has a contemplative atmosphere, where it is easy to lose track of time among the maze of shelves. Noted for new and old hardbacks, often unavailable elsewhere in Tokyo; there is also a voluminous section on Japan.

Nihon Gakki Ginza-ten
7-9-14, Ginza, Chuo-ku ☎ 572-3131. Map 10I10 AE ⓐ ⓒ VISA

This is the "shop window" for Yamaha's musical instrument and audio empire, founded in 1887 when Torakusa Yamaha's Nihon Gakki company started making organs. The basement has an enormous collection of mainly classical sheet music and music books. Records of every genre, concert tickets and audio equipment are on the 1st floor. The mezzanine level displays electronic keyboards and guitars. Yamaha classical pianos,

which have a major slice of the world market, are found on the 2nd floor. Wind, string and percussion instruments are on the 3rd floor, and topping it all on the 4th and 5th floors, is a 500-seat concert hall.

Sanseido
1-1, Kanda Jimbocho, Chiyoda-ku
☎ 233-3312/5. Map 14F9 ⓐ ⓒ
VISA

A landmark in the Kanda Jimbocho bibliophile's paradise, Sanseido has Japan's largest stock of current books and magazines, on seven floors. The foreign book corner on the 5th floor, however, is less comprehensive than at either **Maruzen** or **Kinokuniya**.

Wave
Wave Building, 6-2-21, Roppongi, Minato-ku ☎ 408-0111. Map 4J7
AE ⓐ ⓒ VISA

A perfect illustration of a Seibu department store. Chairman Seiji Tsutsumi's philosophy of "concept" retailing is to cater to the sophisticated new Japanese life-styles, and Wave is entirely devoted to audio and visual "software." The large street-level window is used as a showcase for "experimental" art (of extremely varied quality). The latest Japanese and international pop/rock/reggae/New Wave releases are on the 1st floor, next to a stylish café/bar. The four floors above stock video tapes and discs, compact discs and music cassettes, more than 20,000 records, sheet music, art books and magazines for audio and cinema fans. **Cine Vivant**, a small art movie theater in the basement, screens many foreign films, which are not shown elsewhere in Tokyo.

Yamano Music
4-5-6, Ginza, Chuo-ku ☎ 562-5051. Map 10I10 AE ⓐ ⓒ VISA

A blast of pop jingles and, outside, the raucous calls of staff hawking music discs or cassettes have made Yamano Music known to every Ginza shopper. Most of the action is on the 1st floor, where youngsters relish the noise and scrimmage for discs and tapes. The music is classified in Japanese, but sales staff can usually point bewildered foreigners to the right section. Musical instruments are upstairs. Like its competitor, Nihon Gakki, Yamano boasts concert halls on its 4th and 5th floors.

Cameras
Tokyo has the world's largest camera store, **Yodobashi Camera**, as well as a wide selection of discount camera stores, particularly in the Shinjuku and Ikebukuro districts.

BIC Camera
1-11-7, Higashi-Ikebukuro,
Toshima-ku ☎988-0002. Map
12B5 AE ⓘ VISA
This claims to be the cheapest
camera store in Japan, with a
standing offer to refund the
difference if you find a lower price
elsewhere for the same article. Also
sells video and audio equipment,
tapes, computers and contact
lenses.

Camera No Sakuraya
3-17-2, Shinjuku, Shinjuku-ku
☎354-3636. Map *6F4* AE ⓘ ⓘ
Cameras, watches, video games,

Clothing for men
Japanese men are becoming increasingly fashion-conscious and
Tokyo now has a wide selection of stores selling good-quality
designer menswear.

Boutique Barbiche
Daini Masago Building, 1st floor,
3-1-28, Jingumae, Shibuya-ku
☎404-8757. Map *6I4* AE ⓘ ⓘ
VISA
The top-quality men's label of
Yoshie Inaba's Bigi line. Yuppie-
type conservative sportswear,
strongly influenced by 1940s US
fashion.

Comme des Garçons Hommes
5-12-3, Minami Aoyama, Minato-
ku ☎498-0921. Map *7I5* AE ⓘ
ⓘ VISA
The men's line of Rei Kawakubo's
Comme des Garçons still emphasizes
the baggy style of jackets and
primary colors for which she is
noted.

Hamilton Shirt Boutique
3-2-5, Kita-Aoyama, Minato-ku
☎475-1971. Map *7I5* AE ⓘ ⓘ
VISA
Two floors of exquisite shirts. The
1st floor stocks only Issey Miyake
designs, and Hamilton's own brand
are found on the 3rd floor.
Fashionable pajamas are lodged in
between.

Hanae Mori Monsieur
Hanae Mori Building, 1st floor,
3-6-1, Kita-Aoyama, Minato-ku
☎400-6223. Map *7I5* AE ⓘ ⓘ
VISA
Elegant ties, attractive sweaters,
beautifully cut ready-to-wear suits
and jackets, and computer-aided
tailoring are all available here. Such
quality — and the high prices — are
what one would expect from Mme
Hanae.

Walkmans and electrical goods (at
20-60 percent discount) are arranged
on six floors. Special bargains in Feb,
and a good place at any time to check
prices against competitor **Yodobashi
Camera**.

Yodobashi Camera
1-11-1, Nishi-Shinjuku, Shinjuku-
ku ☎346-1010. Map *6G3* AE ⓘ
ⓘ VISA
Yodobashi Camera is the largest
camera store in the world, with more
than 30,000 items in stock (all with
20-50 percent discount). Also video
games, computers and word
processors, watches and
Walkmans.

Issey Miyake Men's
4-21-29, Minami Aoyama, 1st
floor, Minato-ku ☎423-1407.
Map *7I5* AE ⓘ ⓘ VISA
Issey Miyake shirts or jackets are one
of the few items of men's clothing
immediately identifiable without a
label: loose-fitting and comfortable to
wear, deceptively simple, yet always
stamped with some innovative design
twist. Unfortunately buying even one
of the plainest shirts normally
represents a considerable
investment. Wise hands wait for the
sale, either here or at one of the many
department store outlets.

Teijin Men's Shop
4-3-10, Ginza, Chuo-ku ☎561-
7519. Map *10I10* AE ⓘ ⓘ VISA
Head-to-toe outfitting for the vast
horde of Japanese preppies and
yuppies, with enough English brogue
shoes, old school ties, paisley
handkerchieves, polo sweaters,
tweed and Italian-cut jackets to grace
several country estates or stock
exchanges. Seen collectively, the
effect is hilarious; individually,
however, the clothes are well made
and in good taste. Inevitably one
pays dearly to join either club.

Y's
5-3-6, Minami Aoyama, Minato-
ku ☎409-6006. Map *7I5* AE ⓘ
ⓘ VISA
A pleasant break from the drab
austerity still characterizing his
women's line, Yamamoto is now
producing jackets and trousers that
are sporty, fun and exciting.
Yamamoto's women's line is also
housed here in the main store.

Shopping

Clothing for women

There are a number of outstanding new Japanese designers, such as Issey Miyake and Rei Kawakubo, whose stylish clothes can be found in the following stores.

Alpha Cubic
From 1st Building, 1st floor, 5-3-10, Minami Aoyama, Minato-ku ☎499-4051. Map 7I5 AE ⓘ ⓒⓓ VISA

Smart, elegant and well-tailored uptown fashions for young women.

Boutique Junko Shimada
Aobadai Terrace, 1-1, Aobadai, Meguro-ku ☎463-2346. Map 2L3 AE ⓘ VISA

A Paris-based Japanese designer known for the sharp and sexy line of her clothes.

Boutique Kansai International
3-28-7, Jingumae, Shibuya-ku ☎478-1958. Map 6I4 AE ⓘ ⓒⓓ VISA

Brightly colored, theatrical sportswear with garish prints are Yamamoto Kansai's trademark. Best worn with high-topped sneakers, by youthful extroverts.

Boutique Yoshie Inaba
D1 Hillside Terrace, 29-9, Sarugakucho, Shibuya-ku ☎476-5856. Map 3L4 ⓘ ⓒⓓ VISA

The creator of the popular Bigi and Moga young fashion labels here presents her own label, composed of plain, simple and orthodox women's clothes. Thin lines, restrained browns and navy blues predominate, best exemplified in the uniforms Inaba has designed for female staff at the **Printemps Ginza** department store and usherettes at the Suntory Hall in Akasaka.

Comme Ca Du Mode
3-1-30, Jingumae, Shibuya-ku ☎478-6761. Map 6I4 AE ⓘ ⓒⓓ VISA

A popular Japanese fashion label featuring simple styles and basic colors in the new-wave style that is now facing mid-life crisis. Designer-concrete interior; helpful staff.

Comme des Garçons
From 1st Building, 2nd floor, 5-3-10, Minami Aoyama, Minato-ku ☎499-4370. Map 7I5 AE ⓘ ⓒⓓ VISA

Best known for her avant-garde baggy and monotonal designs, which took Paris by storm several years ago, Rei Kawakubo has had some difficulty lately in adapting her adventurous "Hiroshima chic" to the recent antithetic fashion for body-hugging femininity. Her latest clothes, although still maintaining new-wave credentials, such as asymmetric shapes and tonal austerity, now have a certain girlish prettiness, previously absent.

Hanae Mori
3-6-1, Kita Aoyama, Minato-ku ☎406-1021. Map 7I5 AE ⓘ ⓒⓓ VISA

On the chic Omotesando-dori, the Hanae Mori building, designed by renowned architect Kenzo Tange, with its reflecting glass walls and cool, opulent interior, mirrors the status of one of the world's leading couturières. "The Empress," as she is still respectfully known in Tokyo fashion circles, presents her entire collection here. The 1st-floor **Hanae Mori Boutique** offers an eye-catching array of silk scarves, accessories, children's dresses and household fabrics. Work by designer protégés is shown on the 2nd floor, and do not miss the gorgeous and exquisite kimonos in the **Masuiwaya Boutique**. On the floor above are Hanae Mori's *haute couture* (*closed Sun*), Paris prêt-à-porter and evening-wear collections, all testifying to her ideals of classic, well-tailored, feminine elegance. There is a branch of L'Orangerie de Paris on the 5th floor, one of the few places in Tokyo offering brunch (on Sun). A Belgian chocolate store and a smart café on the 1st floor strategically accentuate the pervasive aura of well-heeled refinement.

Issey Miyake
From 1st Building, 1st floor, 5-3-10, Minami Aoyama, Minato-ku ☎499-6476. Map 7I5 AE ⓘ ⓒⓓ VISA

Issey Miyake has been called "the greatest creator of clothing of our times" by a costume curator at the Museum of Decorative Arts in Paris, and trumpeter/composer Miles Davis unabashedly states, "He designs the way I think about music." Miyake's revolution was in creating clothes that make the body feel as loose and free as the fabric — they liberate rather than constrain the wearer. His name is also indissolvably linked with an entirely fresh approach to materials. "Anything can be clothing," he declared as a young rebel in the 1970s, and true to his word he has continued to excite and shock the fashion world with creations using everything from plastic, rubber and piping to Irish wool, Indonesian batik and Italian silk. This is Miyake's main showcase for women's clothing. However, be warned that "liberation" does not come cheap.

Jun Ashida
2-17-5, Minami Aoyama, Minato-ku ☎478-1611. Map 7/5 [AE] [⓪] [⓪] [VISA]

Outfitter to Japan's Crown Princess Michiko and Princess Takamado, Jun Ashida sells designs of suitably well-bred, conservative elegance.

Kenzo
6-12-3, Minami Aoyama, Minato-ku ☎498-2875. Map 7/5 [AE] [⓪] [⓪] [VISA]

One of Tokyo's few established designers to show a genuine love of color. Kenzo's bright palette can be seen to very striking effect in bold and beautiful floral prints in reds, yellows and greens as well as "ethnic" batiks.

La Boutique Junko Koshino
King Homes, 1st floor, 6-5-36, Minami Aoyama, Minato-ku ☎406-7370. Map 7/5 [AE] [⓪] [⓪] [VISA]

Best known for her knitwear and European-style sportswear Junko Koshino has sharp and simple designs. The menswear line, **Mr Junko**, is located diagonally opposite this store.

Nicole
Nicole Building, 3-1-25, Jingumae, Shibuya-ku ☎478-0998. Map 6/4 [AE] [⓪] [⓪] [VISA]

This boutique is worth a stop on the Aoyama fashion circuit, if only to admire the boutique's elegant and stylishly designed interior. No prizes, however, for clothing innovation, as Nicole designs draw heavily on retro-American influence. Women's fashions can be found on the 1st floor; "Monsieur Nicole" is on the floor above.

Oxford
4-4-1, Ginza, Chuo-ku ☎562-0021. Map 10/10 [AE] [⓪] [⓪] [VISA]

Genteel young ladies' fashions, showing a predominantly English sensibility.

Plantation
4-21-29, Minami Aoyama, 1st Basement, Minato-ku ☎423-1408. Map 7/5 [AE] [⓪] [⓪] [VISA]

Popular classics selected from more than a decade of eyebrow-raising designs by Issey Miyake.

Plantation Inn
Seed Fashion Building, 3rd floor, 21-1, Udagawacho, Shibuya-ku ☎462-3730. Map 6/J3 [AE] [⓪] [⓪] [VISA]

Issey Miyake's line of casual, more economical indoor wear. Free-flowing shapes and natural fabrics set the tone.

Saint Mark's
Inose Building, 1st floor, 2-12-31, Kita Aoyama, Minato-ku ☎479-1010. Map 7/5 [AE] [⓪] [⓪] [VISA]

Soft and feminine traditional clothes, popular with Japanese girls in their late teens and early twenties.

Tamaya
3-5-8, Ginza, Chuo-ku ☎563-4621. Map 10/10 [AE] [⓪] [⓪] [VISA]

Established in the early Edo period as a maker of nautical sextants, this company later switched to glasses and precious metals before settling on women's fashion in the 1970s. Imported lines include Yves St Laurent, Chloe and Renoma. Japanese dresses combine the elegance and fashion sense desired by so-called "Office Ladies."

Y's
For address see "Clothing for men" above.

One of the leaders of Japan's new wave in fashion, Yohji Yamamoto shares a taste for dark, plain colors with Rei Kawakubo of **Comme des Garçons**, but with a marked preference for sharper and more symmetric lines (his winter coats have a distinctly military flavor). Both Yamamoto's **Paris** and **Y's** boutique lines are displayed here in the main store.

Department stores

You can buy virtually anything in a Tokyo department store. As well as a comprehensive selection of merchandise, many of the large stores now have art galleries, theaters and even rooftop tennis courts.

Shopping

Ginza Core
5-8-20, Ginza, Chuo-ku ☎*573-4761. Map 10/10* AE ⊕ ◉ VISA

Mainstream and affordable women's fashions, shoes and accessories extend from the 1st Basement to the 3rd floor. The 4th floor is dedicated to both traditional kimonos and the new, easy-to-wear fashion variety, made of synthetic materials, that young girls like to wear at discos. Male trend-setters have their preserve on the floor above. On the 7th floor there is an audio, video and computer showroom for electronics maker National (Matsushita). Fine restaurants may be found in the 2nd Basement, as well as on the top two floors of the building.

Ginza Matsuzakaya
6-10-1, Ginza, Chuo-ku ☎*572-1111. Map 10/10* AE ⊕ VISA

Featured in Edo *ukiyo-e* prints by Hiroshige, Matsuzakaya remains a conservative bastion largely indifferent to expanding its clientele beyond middle-aged housewives. Standard fare, except for the kimono silks that the store has custom-dyed in Kyoto, and sold under Matsuzakaya's own brand.

Isetan
3-14-1, Shinjuku, Shinjuku-ku ☎*352-1111. Map 6F4* ⊕ ◉ VISA

More conventional than the Marui chain, by which it is becoming increasingly encircled, Isetan has managed to forestall retail menopause by successfully turning toward youth-oriented and designer clothes. Famous fashion houses are arrayed like exotic plants in glassy boutiques on the main building's 3rd floor. The connecting annex has four floors of men's clothing, and accessories can be found in the basement.

Marui
Fashion Building, 3-30-16, Shinjuku, Shinjuku-ku ☎*354-0101. Map 6F4* AE ⊕ ◉ VISA

Pioneers of the "buy-now-pay-later" craze among Japanese youth, the Marui formula has proved enormously successful, as the mushrooming of their stores testifies. The main colony is in Shinjuku, where **Techno, Fashion** and **Men's Marui** buildings confront Isetan across the street; **Interior Marui** (*5-16-4, Shinjuku*) looms at the rear; and **Young Marui** (*3-18-1, Shinjuku*) ensnares students just before they reach Kinokuniya bookstore. Characteristic "extras" usually

associated with department stores have all been stripped away to produce buildings and interiors of assembly-line nature. With three clothing stores in Shinjuku, Marui has a comprehensive collection of famous-name fashion boutiques, ranging from Bill Blass and Burberry to Kenzo, Issey Miyake and Tokio Kumagai. Techno Marui can be skipped in favor of Akihabara's electronic jungle. Interior Marui signals the long-awaited invasion of designer-mania into the Japanese home. There are eight floors of minimalist furniture, color-co-ordinated food mixers, streamlined air conditioners, as well as the ultimate designer extravagance: a plain *tatami* mat, bordered in red or black wood with four tiny legs, on which to unfold one's designer *futon* mattress.

Matsuya Ginza
3-6-1, Ginza, Chuo-ku ☎*567-1211. Map 10/10* AE ⊕ VISA

A long-time favorite among Tokyo residents, and with a more popular appeal than Yurakucho Seibu or Hankyu, Matsuya Ginza is more conscious of passing styles and generations than its dowdier forebears farther up the street. Frequent bargain sales are an obvious draw, and will remind foreign women of home. The 7th floor boasts one of Tokyo's sleekest and smoothest interior design collections, and there are a good selection of Western, Chinese and Japanese restaurants on the floor above.

Mitsukoshi
1-7-4, Nihonbashi Muromachi, Chuo-ku ☎*241-3311. Map 10G11* AE ⊕ ◉ VISA

Established in 1673 as a silk shop for kimonos, Mitsukoshi was the first in Japan to have a 2nd floor and glass display cases — both daring innovations at the turn of this century. Although no longer *the* place to see in Tokyo, for out-of-town Japanese this main store in Nihonbashi still has an aura of magnificence. Its imposing Renaissance facade, bronze lions guarding its entrances (replicas of those around Nelson's Column) and lofty-roofed atrium, are the epitome of retail grandeur. At three times during the day (10am, noon and 3pm) the pipes of the old Wurlitzer organ behind the tall statue of Magokoro (Goddess of Sincerity), a hideous riot of lurid color and intricate carving, summon the faithful, who sit transfixed in the central hall surrounded by Italian handbags and ladies shoes. Mitsukoshi still contrives to sell all kinds of goods to all sorts of people, despite a High Church conservatism and disdain for innovation. Fashion only occupies two floors, and partitioned designer boutiques have yet to catch on. The fine-arts and crafts section on the 6th floor (next to the Mitsukoshi Theater entrance) is well worth visiting, as is the gorgeous kimono corner on the 4th floor. The basement food hall, adjoining the marbled entrance to Mitsukoshi's own subway station (Mitsukoshi-mae on the Ginza line), has a mouthwatering selection. There is another branch in Ginza.

Printemps Ginza
3-2-1, Ginza, Chuo-ku ☎*567-0077. Map 10I10* ⊙ ꕤꕥ
The hordes of young Japanese women milling around Printemps Ginza soon confounded cynics who scoffed at the idea of a "foreign" department store opening in Tokyo. A joint venture between Printemps and Japan's Daiei supermarket chain, the Tokyo version bears as much relation to the French *grand magasin* as *sushi* to sole meunière. Less stuffy and conformist than its wholly Japanese counterparts, Printemps Ginza successfully effects an air of casual freedom and natural fashion flair, which dovetails with the romantic Japanese image of Paris. French touches, such as the branch of Brasserie Bernard, the Sylvie Vartan dance studio, French clowns who occasionally perform outside, French floor names and store announcements, all create a suitable atmosphere. Despite many French imports, most of the women's clothes and accessories are in fact Japanese. The 1st-Basement food hall does not do justice to the glories of both French and Japanese cuisine, and the teenage boutiques farther below can be missed. The **Café Bon Cinq**, next to the connecting housewares annex across the street, is a hastily improvised warehouse where Printemps habitués repair, to imagine they are in Paris.

Seibu
1-28-1, Minami Ikebukuro, Toshima-ku ☎*981-0111. Map 12B4* ꕤꗤ ⊙ ꕣꕢ ꕤꕥ
From lowly origins, as a mass dispenser of everyday items, Seibu has metamorphosed into the world's largest and most innovative department store. Seibu's Tokyo

empire radiates from this massive 12-story main store, with 346,000sq.m (84 acres) of floor space, squatting over Ikebukuro Station. As there are now more centrally located branches in Shibuya and Yurakucho specializing in fashion wear, the chief enticements for the trip N to Ikebukuro are the excellent pottery, ceramic, glass and crafts displays. **Seibu Art Museum** on the 12th floor can usually be relied upon for exciting and creative exhibitions.

Shibuya Seibu
21-1, Udagawa-cho, Shibuya-ku ☎*462-0111. Map 2J3* ꕤꗤ ⊙ ꕣꕢ ꕤꕥ
A relaxing place for shopping or browsing, this Seibu branch is less indebted to the wonders of Japanese electronics and interior design than its Yurakucho starship. Shibuya is increasingly the terrain of young Japanese materialists, so the store is inevitably geared toward fashion. There are five floors of women's clothing and three floors of menswear, in twin interconnecting buildings. Shopping in the many Japanese designer boutiques proves less tiring than a tour of their individual shops in Aoyama, and the second building has one of the best ranges of stylish menswear in Tokyo; the women's kimono corner also has some interesting new designs. The basement food halls, however, are incongruously plebeian, being more like neighborhood Tokyo supermarkets. Shibuya Seibu prides itself on an astonishing range of services: from necktie repair and silver polishing to laundry, pet storage and international delivery.

Takashimaya
2-4-1, Nihonbashi, Chuo-ku ☎*211-4111. Map 10G11* ꕤꗤ ⊙ ꕣꕢ ꕤꕥ
Just a short distance from Mitsukoshi's main Nihonbashi store, with which it is in perennial competition, Takashimaya invites comparison in classic opulence and nobility. Originally a silk draper in Kyoto (founded in 1831), Takashimaya's large selection of exquisite kimonos, on the 3rd floor, remains justly famous. More fashion and youth conscious than the *grande dame* over Nihonbashi Bridge, Takashimaya allows greater prominence, and latitude in display, to new Japanese designers for women. The 2nd floor has a peerless array of famous names, such as Gucci, Louis Vuitton, Chanel,

Hermes, Lanvin, Dunhill and Celine, for those who can afford the labels. The menswear here is impeccably mainstream, but uninspiring.

Wako
4-5-11, Ginza, Chuo-ku ☎*562-2111. Map 10/10* Ⓐ🄴 Ⓢ Ⓓ 🆅🄸🅂🄰

Relatively few of the multitude who pass by Wako's famous clock tower ever venture inside this most exclusive of Tokyo department stores. They are deterred perhaps, by its high prices, or the equally intimidating looks with which stiff-necked floorwalkers greet stray shoppers "of the wrong sort." Wako is a division of Seiko, the timepiece empire known before World War II as Hattori, after its founder. The first Hattori clock tower, Ginza's most famous monument, was erected here in 1894. The present building dates from 1932 and is one of the very few buildings in Ginza to have survived wartime bombing and the ravages of fire. In deference to its origins, luxury ranges of Seiko watches are sold on the 1st floor. Wako is noted for its almost snobbish indifference to the vagaries of high-street fashion, and its old-style interior complements the conservative

restraint of the mostly imported men's and women's clothing (on the 2nd and 3rd floors). It is worth visiting the 4th floor to see the exquisite Japanese ceramics, pottery and glassware. Mere mortals who meet in front of Wako's corner window on Ginza 4-chome Crossing are grateful for the famous artistry of its displays.

Yurakucho Seibu
2-5-1, Yurakucho, Chiyoda-ku ☎*286-0111 or 286-5682/3 for Foreign Customer Liaison Office. Map 9H9* Ⓐ🄴 Ⓓ 🆅🄸🅂🄰

A toast to high-tech Japan, the store features 177 video monitors transmitting views of cherry blossoms, snow scenes and breaking waves. Perhaps their purpose is to dispel the feeling of having materialized inside a 21stC space colony, inhabited by clones of new-wave Japanese fashion. There is a temptation to join these Japanese trend-setters and emerge a chic new being, but a glance at the futuristic price tags may restore terrestrial gravity. A Foreign Customer Liaison Office on the 5th floor, with polyglot staff and helpful brochures in English, is a feature that more staid Tokyo department stores should emulate.

Electrical goods
Japan is the acknowledged world leader in consumer electronics, but do not expect a Japanese electronic appliance to be automatically cheaper in Tokyo than back home. Some items were always cheaper in rock-bottom New York or Hong Kong discount stores, and the high yen has accentuated the difference, as manufacturers keep their export prices down to maintain market share. What Tokyo does offer is tremendous variety and innovation. Although the export lead time has been shortened considerably, you may still have to wait several months before the latest models seen in Tokyo surface outside Japan.

Showrooms
There are several leading makers' showrooms in Tokyo where you can calmly audition equipment before being hassled by salesmen.

Pioneer Showroom   1-4-1, Meguro ☎494-1111.

Panamedia Ginza   Ginza Core Building, 7th floor, 5-8-20, Ginza ☎572-3871. Map 10I10.

Sony Showroom   Sony Building, 3rd and 4th floors, 5-3-1, Ginza ☎573-2371. Map 10I10.

Victor Video Center   Kazan Building, 1st floor, 3-2-4, Kasumigaseki ☎580-4264. Map 9H9.

Stores
Akihabara has by now entered the international traveler's vocabulary as the Tokyo mecca of electronic discount stores. Price-slashing is a way of life here and, unusually for Japan, it is acceptable to "bargain" with sales staff. Don't forget that Japanese voltage (110V) is probably different from that at home, so insist on an "export model" if required. Also note when purchasing televisions or video equipment that Japan uses the American

NTSC broadcasting standard. If your country's system is PAL or SECAM, ask for the appropriate export model. It would be difficult to miss the following discount electronic "department stores" at Akihabara. Most stores below are open seven days a week, accept all major credit cards, and have duty-free sections for foreign visitors (remember to take your passport).

Hirose Musen 1-10-5, Soto Kanda ☎255-2211. Map **15**D10.
Ishimaru Denki 1-9-14, Soto Kanda ☎255-3111. Map **15**D10.
Laox Main Store 1-2-9, Soto Kanda ☎253-7111. Map **15**D10.
Laox Sound Shop 1-15-3, Soto Kanda ☎255-5481. Map **15**D10.
Nishikawa Musen 1-15-9, Soto Kanda ☎251-3891. Map **15**D10.
Yamagiwa Corp 4-1-1, Soto Kanda ☎253-2111. Map **15**D10.

Nearer the center of Tokyo, there are five tax-free/discount electrical stores in the **Nishiginza Electric Center** near the Imperial hotel (*2-1-1, Yurakucho* ☎591-0745, *map 9I9*).

Fashion buildings

A fashion building could be described as a cross between a department store and a shopping arcade, as it has a number of fashion boutiques all under one roof.

La Foret
1-11-6, Jingumae, Shibuya-ku
☎*475-0411. Map 6/4* AE ⓓ ⓒⓓ
Ⓥ(ISA)

This is the fashion citadel of Harajuku's teenage empire. Its seven floors have 159 different shops, mostly housing clothing and accessory boutiques, ranging from pubescent T-shirt and fad sticker vendors to polka dots and pearls. Adult boutiques are in evidence near the front of the store, but one soon crosses the bubble gum line as La Foret is heavily weighted toward the under twenties, reflecting the generation gap between Harajuku and the other nearby fashion centers in Shibuya and Aoyama. Not a place for claustrophobics on weekends and holidays.

Parco
15-1, Udagawacho, Shibuya-ku
☎*464-5111. Map 2/3* AE ⓓ ⓒⓓ
Ⓥ(ISA)

The Seibu-managed Parco chain was a pioneer of the fashion building concept, and comprises Parts 1, 2 and 3. Shibuya's **Parco 1**, though older than its twin progeny nearby, remains a popular meeting spot on Koen-dori. Inside are more conventional boutiques for young adult fashion, plus the **Seibu Theater** and many restaurants and cafés. **Parco 2** is dedicated to popular designer brands, including **Nicole, Kansai, Jun, Moga** and **Comme Ca Du Mode** boutiques. **Parco 3** embraces interior goods and "total fashion," although for the latter it may take a discerning eye to spot the difference.

Seed
21-1, Udagawacho, Shibuya-ku
☎*462-0111. Map 2/3* AE ⓓ ⓒⓓ
Ⓥ(ISA)

Seibu's newest and least successful experiment is a "conceptual department store," adjoining its conventional Shibuya parent. An intoxicated confusion of PR-hype and avant-garde boldness has led to outright pretentiousness. The result is ten floors with names such as "The Parts" and "The Next," containing unimaginatively displayed clothes and accessories of surprising blandness. Seed appears to have fallen on stony ground.

Vivre 21
5-10-1, Jingumae, Shibuya-ku
☎*498-2221. Map 6/4* AE ⓓ ⓒⓓ
Ⓥ(ISA)

A stroll round the first three floors offers an interesting cross section of both big names and aspiring designers of men's and women's fashion. Styles range from monotonal minimalism to elegant formal restraint and florid party-wear excess. The Adam and Eve Design collection on the 2nd floor offers something different in semi theatrical menswear, whether Nehru-inspired tunics or Al Capone double-breasters. The top two floors house a health and beauty club, an Italian patio restaurant and a professional recording studio. In the basement you will find an accessories section, as well as a French bakery/café, and an ice cream and cake shop. The street-level **Café-Haus** has quickly become one of the really chic places to feign drinking a coffee.

Pharmacies

Remember to bring along a doctor's prescription for any medication. Also bear in mind that certain drugs that do not require a prescription at home may require one here.

American Pharmacy   Hibiya Park Building, 1-8-1, Yurakucho ☎271-4034. Map 9H9. You may imagine that Tokyo's foreign community is plagued with hypochondria, judging by the number of American Pharmacy bags seen around. In truth many conceal imported confectioneries, biscuits and snacks that are sold here to satisfy *gaijin* cravings.

Hill Pharmacy   4-1-6, Roppongi ☎583-5044. Map 4J7.

National Azabu Supermarket Pharmacy   4-5-2, Minami-Azabu ☎442-3138. Map 4L6.

The Medical Dispensary   Mori Building 32, 1st floor, 3-4-30, Shiba-koen ☎434-5817. Map 5K8.

Shoes

Selfix
2-11-16, Kita-Aoyama, Minato-ku
☎478-2644. Map 7I5 AE ⓓ ⓖⓓ VISA
A small boutique selling handmade unisex shoes. Original "chunky" designs are heavy on leather and demanding on the wallet.

Tokio Kumagai
Cederstone Villa, 1st Basement, 15-5, Hachiyama-cho, Shibuya-ku
☎477-2613. Map 2L3 AE ⓓ ⓖⓓ VISA
Humorous and *très chic* pedestals to complement Japan's new-wave designer clothing. Here you can find glittering silver and gold slippers, shoes with protruding cat's whiskers, even a pair of shoes modeled on a motor car with a "grill" in front and four "wheels" at the side.

Washington
5-7-7, Ginza, Chuo-ku ☎572-5911. Map 10/10 AE ⓓ ⓖⓓ VISA
There are six floors of men's and women's shoes here in which to ponder your all-important purchase. They have a wide range of styles, prices and sizes, including a section for large feet and a computerized "made-to-order" department.

Yoshinoya
4-5-4, Ginza, Chuo-ku ☎562-3871. Map 10/10 AE ⓓ ⓖⓓ VISA
Established at the turn of this century, Yoshinoya's customers include dancers from the **Takarazuka** (see *Nightlife*) and members of the Imperial Family. The men's and women's shoes are well-made and conservative in taste.

Sportswear

Foot Jogger
4-2-11, Jingumae, Shibuya-ku
☎404-5045. Map 10/10 AE ⓓ ⓖⓓ VISA
A *must* for athletes and joggers who wish to stand out. Much of the large stock of fashionable sportswear and accessories is from the store's own original designs.

Seibu Sports Ikebukuro
1-28-1, Minami Ikebukuro, Toshima-ku ☎981-0111. Map 12B5 AE ⓓ ⓖⓓ VISA
Follow a marathon shopping spree with an invigorating sprint around the 100m indoor track here in Seibu Sports. Just the place to buy a racing bicycle, riding jodhpurs or skis.

Traditional Japanese arts and crafts

The endurance of Japan's enormously rich heritage of arts and crafts is due only in part to adaptation to modern tastes and methods of production. Export industries such as Kyoto silk and Arita porcelain flourished by meeting the demands of the mass market, but others were brought precariously close to extinction. Their survival was due to careful protection and nurturing by the government as well as a reaction which set in against the wholesale discarding of past cultural tradition. Since 1955 the government has granted the title of "Holder of an Important Intangible

Cultural Property" to artists and craftsmen outstanding in their traditional skills and dedication to keeping them alive for future generations. Only two doll makers are honored with this title (a.k.a. "Living National Treasure"), one of which is **Beishu Hara**.

These traditional objects have changed remarkably little over the years, and the uses to which they are put in modern Japanese society certainly have. Today the craftsman decorates his wares, rather than fulfils a daily need which has become outdated. For example, fans, which were once considered indispensable accessories, are now more likely to be displayed on a shelf or on a wall. As souvenirs, such works of traditional craftsmanship and artistry offer valuable fragments of life in old Japan.

Beishu Hara
Main shop, 2-3-12, Taito, Taito-ku
☎834-3501. Map **15D11**. *Ginza shop, 5-9-13, Ginza, Chuo-ku*
☎572-1397. Map **10I10** 🎴 VISA
Although the origin of *ningyo* (Japanese dolls) dates back more than 1,000yrs to their use as protective charms to ward off evil spirits, it was not until the Edo period that displaying dolls became part of the spring festival for girls (*Hina Matsuri*) on Mar 3. Examples of these *hina ningyo*, portraying idealized qualities of domestic grace and contentment expected of future Japanese wives and mothers, may be found either in the main Asakusabashi or Ginza showrooms of Beishu Hara, alongside the *musha ningyo* (samurai warrior dolls) for the old boys' festival (now called Children's Day) on May 5. Also note the *gosho ningyo* (palace dolls) of plump infants, and *kabuki* actors that Beishu Hara has been honored to present to the Imperial Family. The lovely white smoothness of the dolls' skin appears to be porcelain, but is made from *gofun* (chalk of ground seashells). Beishu Hara's skill in the difficult *gofun* technique earned him the title of "Intangible Cultural Property" from the Japanese government in 1966.

Buseki
3-13-5, Nishi Nippori, Arakawa-ku
☎828-1746.
Bamboo basketry has long been a recognized art form in Japan since it became imbued with the highly refined tastes of the tea ceremony, when a basket holding carefully arranged flowers became the visual centerpiece. The rich, dark patina of many of the baskets displayed in Suigetsu Buseki's small shop in Yanaka derives from *susu-dake* (bamboo taken from the smoke-darkened ceilings of old Japanese farmhouses). As *susu-dake* is highly prized for basket weaving and increasingly rare, Buseki often

invests more than his annual income in securing stock. Buseki's signed pieces — some deceptively simple, others ingeniously intricate — are woven according to the intrinsic character of the bamboo he is using. Members of Japan's Imperial Family and a US Ambassador are among his patrons, and his unique creations command high prices in Japanese department stores. His baskets are cheaper bought directly from his shop, where a welcome and a cup of Japanese tea are provided free of charge.

Fujiya
2-2-15, Asakusa, Taito-ku ☎841-2283. Map **16C13**.
Tenugui small cotton towels (literally, hand-cleaning cloths) were an essential accoutrement of the Edokko commoner. Even today, participants in traditional festivals, staff in *nomiya* bars and laborers indifferent to fashion still wind *tenugui* around their heads. At Fujiya, a tiny but famous shop in one of the side alleys near the *Asakusa Kannon Temple*, the printing design of *tenugui* has been elevated to an art form. Themes are taken from annual events at the temple, and from *kabuki* and *bunraku* drama. One of the Fujiya designs favored for its bold, dynamic simplicity is that of Gozen Tamate, passionate heroine of an 18thC *bunraku* masterpiece. Prices are very cheap, and Fujiya's *tenugui* make excellent gifts and souvenirs.

Haibara
2-7-6, Nihonbashi, Chuo-ku
☎272-3801. Map **10G11** VISA
The *washi* (Japanese paper) sold at Haibara is all made by a 1,300yr-old technique practiced in Japanese mountain villages. In other words, it bears even less resemblance to ordinary paper than, say, French loaves to bleached, pre-sliced bread. One of Haibara's specialties, since its founding in 1806, has been *gampi*, a soft, white paper used for the

calligraphy of *waka* and *haiku* poems; another has been the *uchiwa* (flat, circular summer fan), very popular in Edo times. More purist than Ginza's Kyukyodo, every wall of the old shop is lined with cabinets containing *washi* in a bewildering range of textures, colors and designs. Paper mobiles, miniature folding screens copied on ancient treasures, *uchiwa* and richly decorated folding fans are popular as gifts. Haibara also sells the best cards in Tokyo during the Christmas and New Year season.

Heiando
3-10-11, Nihonbashi, Chuo-ku ☎*272-2871. Map 10G11* `AE` `◆` `◆` `VISA`

From tiny cups and chopstick rests to *miso* soup bowls (lavishly decorated in gold and inlaid shell), chests and large vases, the lacquerware at Heiando is all of exquisite and lusterous finish — a quality befitting its cherished rank as a former purveyor to the Imperial Household. Prices are reasonable and appropriate to its high standard, but even browsing through the store can be enjoyable and rewarding. The best, and most expensive, lacquerware is on display upstairs.

Isetatsu
2-18-9, Yanaka, Taito-ku ☎*823-1453. Map 15C11.*

The *ukiyo-e* print and Edo-style signboards high up on the wall, the paper-covered lampstands and the red carpeted bench in front, together proclaim the highly traditional provenance of this charming shop in Yanaka. Founded in 1858, Isetatsu specializes in *chiyogami* (handmade Japanese decorative paper), its colorful designs evolved from kimono patterns and armor worn by court nobility and warriors. After lean postwar years when the Japanese paid little attention to traditional crafts, Isetatsu now finds a ready market for its abundant supply of beautifully printed paper *inuhariko*, or *papier-mâché* dogs (once used as good luck charms for children's health) and *chiyogami* kimono dolls.

Koyanagi
7-5, Ginza 1-chome, Chuo-ku ☎*561-3601. Map 10I10.*

This gem of a store is sufficient reason to extend your *Ginza-bura* (aimless stroll) on a tangent from the usual area around Ginza 5-chome Crossing to the far left side of Chuo-dori near Kyobashi. Established in 1854, Koyanagi's store front is crammed with traditional Japanese

household wares and, there are beautiful enameled plates and vases at the back. The beautifully designed interior of the 9th-floor exhibition gallery complements the exquisite creations of leading Japanese potters.

Kuroeya
Kuroeya Kokubu Building, 2nd floor, 1-2-6, Nihonbashi, Chuo-ku ☎*271-3356. Map 10G11.*

Established in 1689, Kuroeya nowadays sells lacquerware, which is generally simpler in style and more utilitarian than that sold at **Heiando**, with correspondingly cheaper prices.

Kyosen-do
2-4-3, Ningyocho, Nihonbashi, Chuo-ku ☎*666-7255. Map 10G11* `AE` `VISA`

First established in Kyoto by a Buddhist monk, Kyosen-do still stocks religious fans covered with sutra prayers, but has for some time been producing fans used on stage by *kabuki* and *Noh* actors, small fans to be tucked in the *obi* (silk kimono waistband) during the tea ceremony, and flat *uchiwa* (summer fans) for stylishly fending off the summer heat. The most stunning fans in this beautiful store are those hand-painted with cherry blossoms or flowers. These are not intended to cut a dash while watching *kabuki*, but for interior decoration.

Kyoya
2-12-10, Ueno, Taito-ku ☎*831-1905. Map 15D11.*

One of the few stores in Japan still producing traditional, Edo-style *sashimono* (nail-less furniture). Kyoya stocks *tansu* chests for storing clothing (very plain paulownia, ornately polished or lacquered), as well as much smaller boxes for sewing, letters and tobacco. Prices are expensive.

Kyugetsu
1-20-4, Yanagibashi, Taito-ku ☎*861-5511. Map 16E12* `◆` `◆` `VISA`

One of Asakusabashi's most famous doll stores, founded in 1830 in Ningyocho, and now housed in a large, black modern building (easily recognizable by its row of Japanese lanterns) on the other side of the JR line from the **Yoshitoku** and **Beishu** stores. Japanese dolls are all displayed on the 1st floor, with soft toys above. Most of the dolls have the same kitsch facial features as those in **Yoshitoku**, but the miniature kimonos are really exquisite.

Kyukyodo
5-7-4, Ginza, Chuo-ku ☎571
4429. Map 10/10 AE ◉ ◎ VISA

The Tokyo branch of Kyukyodo, opened after the Meiji Restoration, has remained remarkably true to tradition, given its occupancy of the most expensive plot of land in the world. Kyukyodo was founded in Kyoto in 1663 as a pharmacy dealing in herbs and "medicinal" incense, and by the sixth generation was supplying incense to the Imperial Family and members of the court. The Tokyo store still proudly boasts a license from the Imperial Family to make and sell six secret, mixed incenses, which for more than 1,000yrs had been used exclusively by the Imperial Family and court. The *Mukusa no takimono* (imperial mixtures) are sold in attractive containers in the hushed and reverential atmosphere reserved for the 2nd floor, where special quality paper, some 500 different ink brushes, ink stones and antique incense burners are displayed for discerning practitioners of *shodo* (calligraphy) and *kodo* (the way of incense). Less esoteric tastes are catered to on street level. Here, among battalions of pens, you will find flocks of young Japanese women browsing among prettily decorated writing pads and albums, decorative fans, exquisite mobiles, miniature dolls and ornaments made of paper.

Watanabe
8-6-19, Ginza, Chuo-ku ☎571-
4684. Map 10/10 AE VISA

Its prime location on one of Ginza's main shopping and entertainment streets understandably makes this long-established (1906) firm very popular with tourists. Do not be surprised if some original prints appear in dubious condition (peer closely and you may see wormholes). However, it is impossible to fault the gorgeously vivid and attractively priced reproductions.

Yonoya
1-37-10, Asakusa, Taito-ku
☎884-1755. *Map 16/10.*

One of only four stores still selling traditional combs in Japan, Yonoya was founded in 1673 and has been at its present location on Asakusa's Dembo'in-dori since the early 20thC. In its long history, many famous *kabuki* actors have entered its doors, but today's customers are usually housewives, and a few geisha, who cling to old ways of caring for their hair, plus the occasional passer-by entranced by the timeworn display cabinets and soft yellow glow of the combs. When Japanese women wore intricate, high-piled hair styles, Yonoya used to stock over 1,000 varieties of comb, and there are still 200 kinds to choose from. The lighter colored combs made of *tsuge* (boxwood) make beautiful presents, although there is still a lingering belief in Japan that giving a comb brings bad luck.

Yoshitoku Dolls
9-14, Asakusabashi 1-chome,
Taito-ku ☎863-4419 ◉ ◎ VISA

Founded in 1711, Yoshitoku has perhaps adapted too successfully to modern mass tastes. The 1st floor of its modern white-fronted store (unmistakable with its name written in large letters in English) is filled with Western soft toys and Japanese lamps. Upstairs, the hundreds of Japanese dolls, in all manner of size, style and price (but mostly *hina ningyo* for the girl's festival) share a common kitschness.

Ukiyo-e

These "pictures of the floating world" have leapt remarkably in artistic recognition since the 19thC when they were used to wrap ceramics exported to Europe. *Ukiyo-e* are usually *mokuhanga* (woodblock prints), although some were produced as paintings. Some of the most famous, such as the *Thirty-six Views of Mt. Fuji* by Hokusai (1760-1849), can now be seen not only on museum walls but on magazine covers, whenever an international symbol of Japan is demanded. Several factors determine the value of an *ukiyo-e*: the artist's name, the era in which it was printed, the beauty of the composition and subject matter, the quality of printing impression, and the state of preservation. *Ukiyo-e* should be protected from direct sunlight and excessive humidity, and mountings should be on acid-free backing paper. There are several expert picture-framers in Tokyo if you decide to have one mounted before leaving; **Sodosha** (*1-7, Kanda Ogawa-machi, Chiyoda-ku* ☎294-6411, *map 15F10*) is particularly recommended.

153

SPECIAL INFORMATION

Hara-Shobo

2-3, Jimbocho, Kanda, Chiyoda-ku ☎261-7444. Map 15F10 AE ⬤ VISA

One of a select circle of reputable dealers in antiques, original *ukiyo-e* and beautifully illustrated Japanese books of the Edo era can be found here. The framed *ukiyo-e* lining the stairway are but a small taste of the treasures stored in cabinet drawers on the 2nd floor. The prints are classified by artist, genre (for example, *bijin-ga* portraits of beautiful women; *yakusha-e* portraits of *kabuki* actors; and *fuzoku-ga* prints depicting daily city life) and era. Most recently in vogue are *Yokohama-e* prints (*c.*1860), showing the dramatic, and sometimes comical, changes wrought by Japan's opening to the West. You will probably see some of these prints hanging on the wall. Every print is tagged with its age, artist and subject.

Ohya-Shobo

1-1, Kanda Jimbocho, Chiyoda-ku ☎291-0062. Map 15F10.

Founded in 1882, Ohya-Shobo is a reputable dealer in *ukiyo-e*, antiquarian Japanese maps, Edo-era graphic art and old Japanese books. Stacked near the back of the store, many of the original *ukiyo-e* are somewhat pricey *Yokohama-e* and *Nagasaki-e* prints. Labels unfortunately are only in Japanese, but shop assistants can help in choosing. Cheaply priced reproductions are to be found by the door. Ohya-Shobo is located close to the **Sanseido** bookstore on Yasukuni-dori, and has its name written in English and an unmistakable signboard made of a *kabuki* print.

Watches and jewelry

Mikimoto Pearl

5-5, Ginza 4-chome, Chiyoda-ku ☎535-4611. Map 10/10 AE CB ⬤ VISA

The late Kokichi Mikimoto opened his first shop here in Ginza in 1899, just 6yrs after his "invention" of the cultured pearl. The store now stands out as a sleek and opulent jewel of granite and glass on Ginza's main street. The hushed floors with perfect pearls arranged by setting (for example, rings on the 1st floor) inspire reverence and lust in equal proportions. Mikimoto's valiant mission to save the oysters of Ise and make artificial pearls for rich women's necks is described in near religious terms in booklets available in the store. When they are in season, edible oysters may be savored in the basement French restaurant called **L'Ecrin**.

Nippondo

5-7-5, Ginza, Chuo-ku ☎571-5511. Map 10/10 ⬤ VISA

Nippondo boasts the largest selection of timepieces in Japan, ranging from cuckoo clocks and Mickey Mouse alarms to goldplated and fashion watches. Many are at bargain prices. They also stock jewelry, spectacles and telephones.

Tenshodo

4-3-9, Ginza, Chuo-ku ☎562-0021. Map 10/10 AE ⬤ ⬤ VISA

No-one is sure of the logical connections, but having started in 1879 with *inkan* (seals), Tenshodo later branched into selling quality timepieces, jewelry and model trains. Jewelry is displayed on the 1st floor with watches and clocks, both Japanese and imported, in the basement. Examples of Tenshodo's own brand of model steam locomotive can be seen in the store window on Harumi-dori. On the left side of the store is the special entrance to the 2nd floor display of HO-gauge train sets — popular with aging Peter Pans.

Sports and activities

The following guide to sport and leisure in and around Tokyo offers ideas for both spectators and participants.

Spectator sports

Sumo

The oldest martial art/sport in Japan, and today one of the most popular, with millions of fans following the professional sumo bouts throughout the year's 90 tournament days. Officially sumo is known as Japan's *kokugi*, or national skill. Dating back some 2,000yrs, many of its rituals are derived from Shintoism, such as the purifying sprinkling of salt by wrestlers before a bout begins, and the prohibition against women entering the ring.

The object of sumo is to lift, throw, trip, push or upset the opponent so as either to force him out of a 4.5m (14ft 10in) diameter circle of hard-packed clay (the *dohyo*) or make him touch down with some part of his body other than the soles of his feet. Grabbing of hair or "private parts" and punching are banned; however, slapping is allowed.

There are 6 annual *basho*, or sumo tournaments, each lasting 15 days. Three *basho* are held in Tokyo in Jan, May and Sept, at the new (1985) **Kokugikan**, also known as the **National Skill Hall** (*1-3-28, Yokoami, Sumida-ku* ☎*623-5111*). Sumo tickets go on sale about 3wks before each of the *basho*, and in Tokyo can be purchased either directly from the Kokugikan or from the various *Playguide* entertainment ticket offices in Tokyo (see *Nightlife*). The best seats are usually impossible to obtain without the right connections, but *isu* balcony seats are usually available on the day of the match (although there may be a long line). Tournaments last all day, but the hall only becomes crowded in late afternoon for the upper-ranked sumo wrestlers' contests.

An alternative is to watch sumo on television — NHK Channel 1 has live coverage in the afternoon during *basho*. The US Forces Far East Network (FEN) radio also gives simultaneous English commentaries (tune to 810 kHz).

Professional sumo wrestlers live and train in combined gymnasiums/dormitories called *heya* (stables). The following *heya* allow visitors to watch practice sessions (to get a good seat in the visitors' gallery go before the Tokyo tournaments are held or early in the morning).

Futagoyama Beya (*3-25-10, Narita Higashi, Suginami-ku* ☎*317-0018*)

Kasugano Beya (*1-7-11, Ryogoku, Sumida-ku* ☎*631-1871*)

Kokonoe Beya (*1-16-1, Kamezawa, Sumida-ku* ☎*621-1800*)

Takasago Beya (*1-22-5, Yanagibashi, Taito-ku* ☎*861-4600*)

Baseball

First introduced from the USA in 1873, baseball is the only Western team sport to have developed a mass following in Japan.

Two professional leagues, the Central and Pacific, play from Apr-Oct, and meet in final play-offs. The team belonging to Seibu Railway Company, the Seibu Lions, usually head the Pacific League, and the Yomiuri Giants team belonging to Japan's largest newspaper, the *Yomiuri*, normally top the Central League. The annual high school baseball tournament also receives extensive television coverage and is closely followed by the entire country. High school stars of winning teams are awarded lucrative contracts to join professional baseball teams after leaving school. Top professional players receive doting media coverage and are widely idolized. Listed below are Tokyo's three major baseball stadia.

Korakuen Kyujo (*1-3, Koraku, Bunkyo-ku* ☎*811-2111*)

Seibu Kyujo (*2135, Kami-yamaguchi, Tokorozawa-shi, Saitama-ken* ☎*(0429) 25-1151*). Take the Seibu line from Seibu department store in Ikebukuro, alighting at Seibu Kyujo-mae Station.

Meiji Jingu Kyujo (*13, Kasumigaoka, Shinjuku-ku* ☎*404-3130*)

Bicycle racing

As well as being a popular spectator sport, professional bicycle races are a major gambling activity in Japan. Average annual attendance at race meetings throughout the nation stands at 40 million people. Tokyo's main stadium is the **Kawasaki Keirin-jo** (*2-1-6, Fujimo-cho, Kawasaki-shi* ☎*(044) 233-5501*).

Horse-racing

There are two major racetracks in the Tokyo area, both of which hold year-round meets with excellent thoroughbreds. Betting is government controlled. Win, place and show bets can be placed as well as combination bets (win and place on any two horses in the race). Odds tend to be immensely long. Racetracks:

Oi Keibacho (*Samezu-machi, Ota-ku* ☎*763-2151*). 10km (6 miles) s of central Tokyo.

Tokyo Keibacho (*1-1, Hiyoshi-cho, Fuchu-shi* ☎*(0423) 63-3141*). 32km (20 miles) w of central Tokyo. Major Fucho racetrack purses: Oaks Race and Japan Derby (May), Autumn Tenno-sho (mid-Oct).

Powerboat racing

A peculiarly Japanese gambling mania. The take annually runs into trillions of yen, much of it controlled under government license by the philanthropic Japan Shipbuilding Foundation. The Foundation is headed by Ryoichi Sasakawa, who once described himself as the "world's wealthiest fascist" and was interned by the US Occupation as a suspected war criminal. (He also heads the World Union of Karate-do Organizations.) Contact the **Heiwajima Motorboat Race Association** (*1-1-1, Heiwajima, Ota-ku* ☎*761-9141*).

Volleyball

Japanese female squads have been spectacularly successful in international contests, and attract a large, loyal, mainly young, female following. Contact the **Nihon Volleyball Kyokai** (☎*467-3111, ext. 370*) for events information. Major Tokyo matches are often held at the **Komazawa Olympic-koen** (*1-1, Komazawa-koen, Setagaya-ku* ☎*421-6121*).

Participant sports
Basketball

Every ward in Tokyo has its own gymnasium, often within a multipurpose sports complex, where basketball can be played. The two major gyms in Tokyo are the **Tokyo Metropolitan Gym** or **Tokyo-to Taiikukan** (*1-17, Sendagaya, Shibuya-ku* ☎*408-6191*) and the **YMCA** (*7, Midoshiro-cho, Kanda, Chiyoda-ku* ☎*293-1911*).

Bicycling

Outside the major shopping/business districts, bicycling is allowed on the sidewalk, and in many areas there are special bicycle paths as well as special cycling courses. Rental outlets are increasing; consult the **Japan Cycling Association** (☎*582-3311*) or the **Tokyo Cycling Association** (☎*832-6895*). Inquiries in English are also handled by the **Tokyo Bicycle PR Center** (☎*586-0404: open Mon-Fri 10am-4pm, Sat 10am-2pm*). Listed below are three interesting cycle routes.

Imperial Palace Course   3km (2-mile) route encircling Palace outer moat (*open Sun only 10am-5pm, closed hols*). 500 bicycles rented free from police box in front of the Otemon entrance gate to the Imperial Palace Outer Garden, opposite the exit of Nijubashimae Subway Station.

Meiji Jingu Gaien Cycling Road   1.5km (1-mile) route (*open Sun, hols*). You can borrow a bicycle from near the Nihon-Seinenkan Hall. Treelined route around park's sports stadia. ☎*582-3311*.

Tamagawa Seishonen Course   18km (10-mile) route (*open daily*). Take the Tokyu Mekama rail line from Meguro to

Yaguchi-Watari Station. From the exit, cross to the other side of Tamayawa Ohashi (Tamagawa Bridge) and borrow a bicycle from the nearby service station. Foreigners must show their passports. The course traverses parks, tennis courts, playing fields and the Tamagawa River.

Bowling

After hitting heights of popularity in the 1960s, then the depths of neglect and bankruptcy in the 1970s, Japanese bowling is now successfully charting a middle course. Of the more than 60 bowling alleys in Tokyo, try one of the following:

Korakuen Bowling Center (*1-3, Koraku, Bunkyo-ku* ☎811-2111). Air-conditioned bowling from 7am-midnight with a choice of 62 lanes.

Tokyo Bowling Center (*2-8-9, Kita-Aoyama, Minato-ku* ☎401-1121). Open 7am-11.30pm.

Shinagawa Prince Hotel Bowling Center (☎400-1111)

Diving

Instruction in scuba diving is given by the **Aqua Diving School** (☎254-8855), **Asahi Bunka Center** (☎344-1941), **Do Sports Diving School** (☎346-2098), **Kanto Diving College** (☎329-1311) and **Tokyo Divers School** (☎204-0086/7). Many schools organize outings to diving spots near Tokyo.

Fishing

Although heavily polluted, Tokyo Bay still has large stocks of goby to be caught from late Sept. Less capricious and more convenient are the artificial fish ponds spawned around Tokyo to cater to the urban angler's growing demand. For guaranteed catches try the **International Trout Fishing Ground**, near Kawai Station, on the Ome line from Tachikawa. Serious anglers should contact the **Nihon Casting Kyokai** (☎886-3776) for information on more ambitious outings.

Golf

The multistory golf driving ranges you see dotted all over the city are a compromise between the game's enormous popularity in Japan and the extreme shortage of urban land. Membership fees of the best golf clubs in Tokyo are astronomical and being a member of one is treated as a tradeable blue-chip investment. The **Japan Gray Line** offers a full-day golf tour from Tues-Fri. Although expensive, it gives access to one of Japan's finest courses, the **Fuji Ace Golf Club** (☎433-5745/6).

Ice-skating

Skaters at the year-round **Koraku-en Ice Palace** (*1-3, Koraku, Bunkyo-ku* ☎811-2111) vary from skilled technicians and exhibitionists to toddlers and absolute beginners. Try also the **Ikebukuro Skating Center** (*2-5-26, Kami-Ikebukuro, Toshima-ku* ☎916-7171, from Sept 26-May 5) and the national rink, **Kokuritsu Yoyogi Kyogi-jo** (*2-1-1, Jinnan, Shibuya-ku* ☎468-1171, from Oct 9-Apr 25).

Japan's largest skating complex is the **Fujikyu Highland Skating Center**, with 5 separate rinks and all-night skating under the glow of multicolored lights (see *Mount Fuji* in *Excursions*).

Roller-skating

The boom has recently abated, but Yoyogi Park in summer still poses a hazard to nonwheeled pedestrians. The two most popular (and best) roller-skating rinks are the **Korakuen Amusement Center** (*1-3, Koraku, Bunkyo-ku* ☎811-2111) and the **California Skate Park** (*2-21-12, Shibuya, Shibuya-ku* ☎499-2468).

Rowboats

Available at Akasakamitsuke Bridge (☎261-2176), Chidorigafuchi moat (☎264-1943) of the Imperial Palace, Futago (☎412-1011) or

157

Maruko (☎750-4805) bridges, over the Tamagawa River in Setagaya-ku, or at Shinobazu Pond in Ueno Park (☎828-9502).

Running

The jogging craze never gripped Japan to the same extent as America, but nevertheless seeing Japanese huffing and puffing along streets has become a common sight in city neighborhoods. Tokyo's two best-known jogging/running courses are:

Imperial Palace Course A 5km (3-mile) run around the Palace moat has become so popular among office workers (many of whom one suspects are pressed into participating) that sidewalk traffic jams develop.

Yoyogi Park Course A 2.4km (1½-mile) run from Harajuku JR Station, around the NHK Broadcasting Center, Yoyogi National Stadium and into Yoyogi Park, to mingle with the roller-skaters, saxophonists, loving couples and peeping toms.

Swimming

During the Edo period, swimming (called *suijutsu*) was regarded as a martial art, and samurai swam holding flags and matchlocks. Modern-day congestion of swimming areas unfortunately cramps such feats of aquatic prowess. In the peak summer vacation months, crowds make swimming in public pools virtually impossible, and even on normal evenings, office workers "line up" in the water to take turns swimming a length. On beaches, in the hot weather, it is sometimes difficult to see the sand for the people.

National Gymnasium Pool (*2-1-1, Jinnan, Shibuya-ku (in Yoyogi Park)* ☎468-1171). One outdoor and two indoor pools. The Olympic Pool and small outdoor children's pool are open from July-Aug. The smaller sub-pool is open all year.

Tokyo Metropolitan Gymnasium Indoor Pool (*1-17, Sendagaya, Shibuya-ku* ☎408-6191). Open all year.

Meiji Jingu Pool (*5, Kasumigaoka, Shibuya-ku (Meiji Shrine Outer Garden)* ☎403-3456). Indoor and outdoor pools, open June-Sept.

Minato-ku Sports Center (*3-1-19, Shibaura, Minato-ku* ☎452-4151). Indoor pool open all year. Short walk from Shibaura exit of Tamachi JR Station.

Less crowded in summer months, but much more expensive, are hotel pools. The following allow visitors (see *Hotels* for addresses and telephone numbers): **Capitol Tokyu** (outdoor), **Century Hyatt** (indoor), **Keio Plaza** (indoor and outdoor), **Miyako** (indoor and outdoor), **New Otani** (indoor and outdoor), **Okura** (indoor and outdoor), **Shinagawa Prince** (indoor), **Tokyo Prince** (outdoor).

Demonstrations and classes

Strict adherence to that most exacting of religious disciplines, Zen Buddhism, may be on the wane in modern Japan but the popularity of the many traditional arts and skills it has helped form and shape continue to flourish: for example, *budo* martial arts, *kado* or *ikebana* (flower arranging), the *chado* tea ceremony and *shodo* (calligraphy).

The suffix *do* for each means "way of," an intimation of their spiritual and philosophical foundations. Zen, which arrived in Japan during the Kamakura shogunate in the late 12th and early 13thC, stressed harmony with the cosmos and oneness with nature. This was to be achieved by purging the mind of egoistic intellectualism through extreme discipline and concentration. Zen's anti-intellectualism and spartan training made it the ideal philosophical basis for the samurai warrior class, whose support gave it immense influence and prestige.

Few "masters" of the Zen-inspired arts and skills are capable of leading even the most dedicated and sincere of students to the ultimate goal of intuitive "enlightenment," and for many Japanese practitioners today such activities rank as little more than serious hobbies. However, a number of schools offer regular classes and demonstrations for the uninitiated or merely curious. For the martial arts, a greater commitment of interest and time is required.

Ikebana (Kado)

Originally developed to complement the tea ceremony, *ikebana* has developed into a completely separate art. The basic purpose is to create floral arrangements that subtly express the moods of nature and the changing seasons. For young Japanese women, skill in *ikebana* is still considered to be a particularly valuable accomplishment, but many men also enroll in classes. Over 20 schools, each offering certificates on completion of a course, teach the two main styles called *rikka*, or formal style, and *nageire*, or natural style.

Ikebana International (*2nd floor, Shufunotomo Building, 1-6, Surugadai, Kanda, Chiyoda-ku* ☎*293-8188*). Contact this organisation for further information.

Ikenobo (*2-3, Surugadai, Kanda, Chiyoda-ku* ☎*292-3071*). Classes 11am-12.30pm, 4-5.30pm (appointments one day in advance). The most traditional school.

Ohara (*2nd floor, Ohara Kaikan, 5-7-17, Minami-Aoyama, Minato-ku* ☎*499-1200*). Classes Mon-Fri 10am-noon (appointments 2-3 days in advance).

Sakura-kai (*3-2-25, Shimo-Ochiai, Shinjuku-ku* ☎*951-9043*). English-language classes Thurs, Fri 11am-3pm, each lasting about 40mins (by prior appointment).

Sogetsu (*4th floor, Sogetsu Kaikan, 7-2-21, Akasaka, Minato-ku* ☎*408-1126*). English-language classes Tues 10am-noon (appointments by preceding Mon). The most contemporary-style *ikebana* school.

Cha-no-yu (tea ceremony)

The elaborate etiquette and ritual of the tea ceremony originated in Zen monasteries. Zen monks first used tea to keep themselves awake during long *zazen* meditation sessions, and like every activity in the monasteries the serving of tea soon became systematized. Developing slowly (14thC annals indicate that tea-tasting "tournaments" were boisterous affairs), *chado*, or the "way of tea," reached a peak of elegance and refinement in the 16thC. Tea ceremonies were held in intimate, beautifully designed rooms and garden teahouses. These were sparsely decorated with a flower arrangement or *sumi-e* (ink painting), the microcosmic embodiment of a harmonious universe, and the aristocracy spent huge sums of money on tea utensils, the finest tea bowls, or *chawan*, being often most prized for their rough glazing and "deliberate" imperfections. The famous *chajin* (teamaster) Sen no Rikyu (1521-91) counted Hideyoshi Toyotomi, the unifier of Japan, as an ardent disciple.

The following places offer courses and demonstrations in the tea ceremony. Many Tokyo museums also have extensive collections of exquisite tea-ceremony ware (see *Sights and places of interest*).

Chosho-an (*7th floor, Okura hotel* ☎*582-0111*). Demonstrations 11am-noon, 1-5pm (by prior appointment).

Demonstrations and classes

Sakura-kai (*3-2-25, Shimo-Ochiai, Shinjuku-ku* ☎951-9043).
Lessons 11am-noon, 1-3pm.
Seisei-an (*7th floor, New Otani hotel* ☎265-1111). Demonstrations
Thurs, Fri, Sat 11am-noon, 1-4pm (by prior appointment).
Suntory Museum of Art Tea Room (*11th floor, Tokyo Suntory
Building, 1-2-3, Moto-Akasaka, Minato-ku* ☎470-1073).
Demonstrations Tues-Sun 1.30-4pm (☎ahead for appointment).
Toko-an (*4th floor, Imperial hotel* ☎504-1111, ext. 5858).
Demonstrations Mon-Sat 10am-4pm (☎ahead for appointment).
Yamatane Museum Tea Room (*8th floor, Yamatane Building,
7-12, Kabutocho, Nihonbashi, Chuo-ku* ☎669-3211).
Demonstrations Tues-Sun, 11am-5pm (☎ahead for appointment).

Budo

The "way of arms" developed with the rise of the *bushi* (samurai
military class), and with the spread of Zen Buddhism in the time of
the 12th-13thC Kamakura shogunate. By the Edo era (1603)
various early arts such as *iaido* (the way of drawing sword), *kyudo*
(the way of archery) and *jujutsu* (the art of unarmed combat — the
forerunner of judo) had become sufficiently formalized to be
taught in separate schools. The Zen influence is evident from the
emphasis laid on developing powers of concentration and on
physical and spiritual discipline. The goal, through constant
practice, is to develop "unconscious" and effortless mastery and
accuracy of the arts, and ultimately to achieve "inner truth." A
postwar ban on martial arts by the US Occupation forces was
revoked in 1950, but some revived *dojo* (schools) still retain a
distinctly militaristic atmosphere. Knowledge of Japanese is often
required for instruction, and some *sensei* (teachers) frown on
short-term students, so it is best to make prior inquiries at the *dojo*.

Aikido

A method of nonviolent self-defense, the "way of harmonious
spirit" originates from the *aikijutsu*, developed by Yoshimitsu
Minamoto, a member of the family that founded the Kamakura
shogunate. Modern *aikido*, incorporating elements from other
martial arts, was founded this century by Morihei Ueshiba. A
swift, smooth-flowing art, its purpose is to overcome an opponent
by using the minimum force necessary. Contact the **International
Aikido Federation** (*102, Wakamatsucho, Shinjuku-ku* ☎203-9236)
for further information.

Judo

Derivative of the old *jujutsu* skills of unarmed combat (themselves
a development from sumo wrestling), judo was first organized into
a school in 1882 by Jigoro Kano. Nowadays it is one of the world's
most popular martial arts and is included in the Olympic
Games — in which Japan, not surprisingly, usually takes the gold.
Kodokan (*1-16-30, Kasuga, Bunkyo-ku* ☎811-7151). The oldest
and largest judo institute in Japan. A full range of lessons and
courses are offered, and the public is also free to watch from the
spectators' gallery during practice hours. The **All-Japan Judo
Federation** is also based here.

Karate

A system of empty-handed fighting developed in Okinawa, China,
several hundred years, and introduced into Japan only in 1922 by
Gichin Funakoshi. Unlike *kendo* and judo, it has split into more
than 20 different styles.
International Karate League (*3-3-9, Nishi-Ikebukuro, Toshima-ku*

☎984-7421/4). Kyokushin-kai style.
Japan Karate Association (JKA) (*2nd floor, Rose Center, 1-6-1, Nishi-Ebisu, Shibuya-ku* ☎462-1415). Shotokan style.
World Union of Karate-do Organizations (*4th floor, Sempaku Shinkokai Building, 1-15-16, Toranomon, Minato-ku* ☎503-6637). Umbrella organizion for the Wado-kai, Goju-kai, Shito-ryu, Rembu-kai and Rengo-kai styles of karate.

Kendo

Together with judo, this is one of the two major martial arts in Japan. It is practiced in schools, in the police and armed forces and by many amateur enthusiasts. *Kendo*, or the "way of the sword," developed from *kenjutsu*, the "art of swordsmanship" that was a crucial part of a samurai's training. *Kendo* practitioners use only bamboo staves or sometimes solid wooden swords, plus protective clothing.
Japan Kendo Federation (*c/o Nippon Budokan, 2-3, Kitanomaru Koen, Chiyoda-ku* ☎211-5804/5).
Metropolitan Police Board(*PR Center, 3-5-1, Kyobashi, Chuo-ku* ☎561-8251). Even-numbered Tues, Wed and Fri 6-7pm; Sat 1.30-3.30pm; Sun 10am-noon. One of the best places to see and practice *kendo* (or judo) free of charge, with policemen!

Kyudo

The "way of archery" probably has a closer relationship to Zen than any other martial art, especially among its upper ranks. *Kyudo* stresses intense concentration and meditation, with the actual releasing of the arrow being of secondary importance to the ritual beforehand. In Japan almost as many women as men practice the art. Contact the **All-Japan Kyudo Federation** (*4th floor, Kishi Memorial Hall, 1-1-1, Jinnan, Shibuya-ku* ☎467-7949).

Shintaido

Literally meaning the "New Art of Movement," it is questionable as to whether *shintaido* can be classed as a form of *budo*. To outsiders it resembles an amalgam of abstract *aikido* and avant-garde dancing exercises, rather than a combative method of self-defense originally cultivated for the battlefield. However, as a means of removing tension and revitalizing mind and body it appears highly effective and is rapidly gaining in popularity. Shintaido's originator, Hiroyuki Aoki, is a man of impeccable *budo* credentials, for he is a student of one of the great exponents of *shotokan* karate. Contact the **Shintaido Association** (*2-10-16, Kasuga Bunkioku* ☎818-2421).

Zen meditation

Several temples in the Tokyo area offer interested foreigners the chance to experience *zazen* meditation and even to sample life in a Zen monastery, although the spartan severity and discipline of the latter should not be undertaken lightly.
Taisoji Temple (*7-1-1, Komagome, Toshima-ku* ☎917-4477). Visiting times announced in *Japan Times* newspaper. Relaxed and friendly *zazenkai*. (Classes only in Japanese.)
Nishijima Group (*7th floor, Nippon Shimpan Building, 3-33-5, Hongo, Bunkyo-ku* ☎235-0701 *during office hours*). Zen lectures in English and *zazen* meditation practice by Rev Roshi Nishijima, a noted Zen priest. *Zazen* from 1-1.30pm, followed by lecture and more *zazen* on odd-numbered Sat. Rev Nishijima also organizes five annual *sesshin* intensive training courses at a Zen mountain temple sw of Tokyo.

Demonstrations and classes

Buddhist English Academy (*802, Diamond Palace, 3-5-3, Nishi-Shinjuku, Shinjuku-ku* ☎342-6605). Organizes a wide variety of *zazen* sessions, lectures and field trips, as well as serving as an information center.

Zenyoji Temple (*4-8-25, Nishi-Sugamo, Toshima-ku* ☎915-0015 *for Rev Masao Ichishima c/o Taisho University*). Monthly seminars, including lectures in English by Tendai sect priest and *zazen*.

Toshoji Temple (*4-5-18, Yutakacho, Shinagawa-ku* ☎781-4235). A modern, no-frills Zen temple squeezed between ordinary buildings, which offers rooms for anyone wishing to experience regular *zazen* without a full-time commitment. (All residents must get up at 5am for exercises and meditation, followed by sutra chanting and room cleaning.)

Shodo (calligraphy)
The "way of the brush" requires not just a dexterous and fluid hand but intense concentration and practice. Schools require enrollment for at least one month (usually 4 lessons).

Edo Language and Culture Center (*1-26-30, Higashi, Shibuya-ku* ☎486-7745). English spoken.

Cooking and cuisine
Akahori Cooking School (*2-17-6, Koishikawa, Bunkyo-ku* ☎811-0698). Private lessons offered in English.

Sushi Daigaku (Sushi University) (*4th floor, Yuki Building, 3-10-44, Minami Aoyama, Minato-ku* ☎479-1425). Classes for foreigners twice a week.

Ningyo (Japanese doll making)
Ozawa Doll Academy (*202, Akasaka Central, 9-2-13, Akasaka, Minato-ku* ☎408-8232, 404-3694 and 403-3535). 2hr lessons given in English by prior appointment.

Tokyo Doll School (*1-57-3, Yoyogi, Shibuya-ku* ☎375-4041). Visitors allowed to observe by prior appointment. One-day enrollment also possible.

Origami
The Edo Language and Culture Center (see *Shodo* above) offers weekly English-language lessons on the intricate Japanese art of paper-folding, for a fee.

Origami-kan (*2nd floor, Crystal Vessel, 2-34-3, Kitazawa, Setagaya-ku* ☎469-9715) Try for a free lesson.

Pottery
The following organizations offer lessons in English.

Asahi Culture Center (*4th floor, Sumitomo Building, 2-6-1, Nishi-Shinjuku, Shinjuku-ku* ☎344-1941).

Nippon Togei Club (*1-5, Jingumae, Shibuya-ku* ☎402-3634). Located in precincts of Togo Shrine, near the Harajuku JR Station.

Thread-weaving
Seikatsu-to Shugei-no Kai Headquarters (*2-14-5, Kami-Ikedai, Ota-ku* ☎729-8576). Free observation possible; also tuition with English-language interpreters.

Mokuhanga (woodblock prints)
S. Watanabe Color Print Co. Ltd (*8-6-19, Ginza, Chuo-ku* ☎571-4684). Visitors are welcome to observe once a week, by prior appointment.

Excursions

Tokyo compensates for its own lack of spectacular natural scenery and great historical treasures by having abundant supplies of both on its doorstep. The Hakone mountains with their famous spas, the splendor of Nikko's shrines and temples in forested landscape, the national symbol of Mt. Fuji and the site of Japan's first shogunate in Kamakura are all within easy reach of the capital. Kyoto and Nara, the ancient capitals and wellsprings of Japanese Buddhism, and Hiroshima, victim of the world's first atomic bombing, are farther away from Tokyo, but ought not to be missed.

Hakone

100km (62 miles) SW of Tokyo. Getting there: by train, to Hakone-Yumoto Station, 1½hrs from Shinjuku Station by Odakyu Railway's "Romance Car"; to Odawara Station, 40mins from Tokyo JR Station by "Kodama" Shinkansen. From Odawara or Hakone-Yumoto take the Hakone-Tozan mountain railroad into the heart of the region.

Hakone's beautiful scenery, wealth of hot springs, and salubrious climate have made it one of the most popular resorts in the Tokyo area for over a century. The Hakone Ropeway, ice skating, museums and convenient transportation have enhanced this area's natural attractions for both foreign and Japanese visitors seeking easy relief from the pressures of life down on the Kanto plain.

Although frenetic one-day trips from Tokyo are feasible, an overnight stay is preferable so as not to miss one of Hakone's chief delights, which is a long and soothing soak in the *onsen* hot spring water that bubbles and steams out of subterranean volcanic vents and is channeled into many of Hakone's fine hotels and *ryokan*.

Exploring the region

To begin your exploration of the region, take the Hakone-Tozan mountain railroad either from Odawara or Hakone Yumoto to Miyanoshita.

Odawara's chief attraction is its **castle** (🔒 *open 9am-4.30pm, closed New Year*), which was originally built in 1416 and reconstructed in 1960. Odawara was the castle-town of the powerful Hojo clan who once held sway over the Kanto plain. The successful siege of their reputedly impregnable castle in 1590 by Hideyoshi Toyotomi overcame the last stumbling block to Toyotomi's military unification of Japan. His general and ally Ieyasu Tokugawa was granted the Kanto domain of the Hojos as reward for his help in the campaign. Instead of Odawara, Tokugawa made the momentous choice of Edo as his new seat. The castle contains an interesting historical **museum**, and the rebuilt 4-story keep commands a fine view over the surrounding area. Odawara also has a large selection of souvenir shops, many specializing in the region's own Hakone-Zaiku inlaid and mosaic marquetry ware.

Hakone-Yumoto is the oldest and largest of Hakone's famed **Twelve Spas**, which were first mentioned in the 8thC *Manyoshu* poetry anthology. In the Tokugawa era, bathers from Edo would walk here in 2-3 days, or if they could afford it they would travel by *kago* box-palanquin. Several *ryokan* both in the town and nearby, such as **Hatsuhanaso** in Oku Yumoto (*5mins by bus from Hakone-Yumoto*), allow the public to relax in their *onsen* waters (🔒 *before 5pm*). One can also bathe at one of the famous *senninburo* (thousand people baths) in the town center (🔒). On Nov 3, a *daimyo* procession is held in the town when 400 local men and women re-create in old costumes the fanfare of the feudal lord's processions along the Tokaido, the ancient highway to Edo.

On your way to Miyanoshita, as the train toils slowly up the hill, pausing several times to reverse directions in switchbacks, you will be reminded of an earlier and more relaxed age of travel. A century ago travelers to Miyanoshita had to be brought up the mountain on litters carried by hired "coolies" all the way from Yumoto. As the train grinds upward, you can appreciate the breathtaking views of wooded slopes on either side of the Hayakawa River.

Miyanoshita town, 5mins' walk down the slope from the station, dates from the Meiji era when everything Western was in vogue. Its heritage has left Miyanoshita with quaint, old-world art and antique shops to browse through, and several *onsen ryokan* to relax in for the night. The chief place of interest is the venerable **Fujiya Hotel** (1878), the oldest in Hakone and one of the first Western-style hotels in Japan. After Miyanoshita was "discovered" in the 18thC by French and Englishmen, it became a highly fashionable resort. The Fujiya and the **Naraya Ryokan** opposite became engaged in a commercial war for custom, which was settled by typical Japanese compromise; the Fujiya was given the concession for foreigners, and Japanese visitors were to stay at the Naraya (the Fujiya, however, also had to pay compensation to the Naraya every year for lost patronage).

The Fujiya is as nostalgically redolent of the days of "tiffin" as Singapore's Raffles, but has thankfully escaped the same ruthless exploitation of its heritage. British and Japanese royalty, Charlie Chaplin, Helen Keller and General Douglas MacArthur are listed among its distinguished guests. The indoor terrace café, overlooking the carp pool and garden at the back, is an especially pleasant place to stop for refreshment.

From Miyanoshita, buses can be taken directly to **Hakone-machi** (Hakone town) on Lake Ashi, but you may find it more interesting to continue up the Hakone-Tozan railroad. If you alight at the stop before Gora, turning left on leaving the terminus, and taking a 5min stroll up the hill, you will come to Hakone's famous **Open-Air Museum** (see below), or, as the Japanese call it, Chukoku no Mori (Forest of Sculpture).

Next, take the train to Gora, then transfer to the cable train, which will take you up the mountain to Soun Zan (Mt. Soun). Here you transfer once again to the Hakone Ropeway, the longest cable car ride in Japan (lasting 33mins). As the car crests the pass you will be taken over the aptly named **Owakudani** (Great Boiling Valley), also colorfully known as Ojigoku (Great Hell). The entire gorge reeks of sulfurous fumes spurting from rock crevices or the bare earth, and the hovering clouds of steam add to the impression of a demonic inferno. Signal to the operator at the Owakudani cable station (the highest point of the pass) that you wish to disembark here.

A 600m (1,970ft) concrete nature walk begins here, beyond the boiling pools and steam vents. At the top is a vendor for eggs boiled in the hot spring water, and by tradition each one eaten grants the visitor seven more years of life. Below and to the left of the cable car station stands the **Owakudani Natural Science Museum**, with georamas, color film panels, mechanical exhibits of Hakone's natural history, and an aquarium. The basement is devoted to volcanoes, with a dramatic diorama of nearby Mt. Kamiyama's eruption, and operating seismographs that record the imperceptible tremors that still shake the Hakone area.

Complete the cable car descent to Togendia on the edge of **Lake Ashi** (also known by foreigners as Lake Hakone). Then transfer to

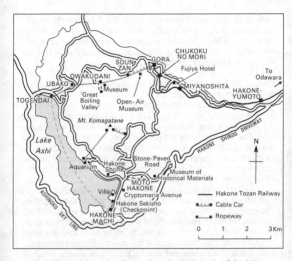

one of the large sightseeing boats that ply the length of the lake (some of which are motorized replicas of Spanish galleons) and ask for a ticket to Hakone-machi. From the middle of the lake you will see a cable car on the left that ascends Mt. Komagatane to the indoor and outdoor **Hakone Skating Center** on the summit. Loudspeakers on board the ship will broadcast, both in Japanese and English, all the points of interest along the lake (including a mass of statistics).

Disembark at the first port of call, Hakone-machi. Walk past the restaurants and food stalls to the main street and turn left, past the lake-shore **Hakone Hotel**, as far as a T-intersection. Then turn left again for the **Hakone Sekisho** (Hakone Barrier Gate) and checkpoint (see below).

Clustered around the checkpoint are souvenir shops selling local crafts and the region's renowned Hakone-Zaiku marquetry ware. Proceed along the shoreline to a promontory jutting out into the lake. An 1887 villa for the Imperial Household was built here, and in 1946 the garden was opened to the public. From Apr-July when azaleas are in bloom the garden is especially beautiful; it offers fine views of the lake and Mt. Fuji in the distance.

Rejoin the lake-shore road, heading left toward Moto Hakone. Here, on the right, you will come to **Cryptomeria Avenue**, with trees originally planted in 1618 to offer protection to travelers on the Tokaido highway. Continue through Moto Hakone town, and at a fork in the road veer right, which will bring you to a portion of the original stone-paved Tokaido that stretched 448km (276 miles) from Edo to Kyoto. Transport was by foot, horse or palanquin; for commoners the trip took 10-12 days on foot. Post stations (these are the "53 stations" immortalized by *ukiyo-e* master, Hiroshige) maintained fresh porters and horses, and there were inns for the night. The stretch of road over the Hakone mountains was the most arduous, and not until 1862 did the shogunate pave the well-traveled road with stones. The **Museum of Historical Materials** on the Tokaido lies at the end of the short trail.

Returning to the shore road, the **Hakone Shrine** (see below), a little farther along the lake, is also noteworthy.

The **Hakone-en Aquarium** lies still farther along the shore of

Lake Ashi, just before the cable car up Mt. Komagatake to the ice-skating center. Those feeling weary by this time should retrace their steps to Moto Hakone, where regular bus services run on a spectacularly scenic and breathtaking route downhill to Hakone-Yumoto or Odawara, for the return to Tokyo.

Hakone Sekisho

During the Edo era this was the *kan* (barrier) of Kanto, and passing through it brought travelers E of the barrier; hence the name "Kanto." (Likewise the "Kansai" region of Kyoto-Osaka-Kobe means W of the barrier.) The Tokaido highway that during the Tokugawa shogunate connected Edo and Kyoto came down from the NE through the pass formed here by the mountains and the lake. At the neck of this pass stood a gate and checkpoint. A strict control of people and goods moving in and out of Edo was part of the shogun's defense against rebellion by *daimyo* feudal lords (see also *Introduction*).

The **checkpoint** was erected in 1619, but eventually closed and dismantled in 1869, one year after the downfall of the shogunate. The present one is an exact replica built in 1965 but situated on the opposite side of the road. Official papers had to be presented to pass the barrier, and any man caught trying to cross on the hills behind risked crucifixion here at the station. Women offenders were shorn of their hair and sent back to Edo in disgrace. An admission ticket is necessary to get into the grounds, and on passing through the guardhouse you will see life-size mannequins of guards, examples of weaponry, and in one room a mannequin of a female guard searching the hair of a woman traveler for any smuggled items. The same ticket will allow entry to a fascinating **museum**, a little farther down toward the lakeshore. Although there is little explanation in English, especially worth noting are the records of early foreign travelers along the Tokaido, the samurai suits of armor, and particularly the shocking early photographs depicting the fate awaiting those who tried to sneak past the barrier — men crucified, and severed heads stuck on poles as a warning to others.

Hakone Shrine

This shrine was reputedly founded in 757, and in its forecourt a huge *sugi* cedar, encircled by sacred rope, is called *Yatate no sugi*, or Standing Arrow Cedar, as the place where generals are said to have offered arrows to the gods before battle. Yoritomo Minamoto, who went on to found the Kamakura shogunate, took refuge here after his defeat near Odawara by the Taira clan in 1180. The shrine is also famous for the celebrated 12thC vendetta of the Soga brothers, whose father was treacherously slain by a high vassal of Yoritomo Minamoto. One of the two sons, Goro, was sent to be a priest at this shrine, and he and his brother Juro waited for years for their revenge, when they assassinated their father's murderer as he was out hunting with Minamoto near Mt. Fuji. The two brothers died for their act, but later their action became glorified as a supreme act of filial piety, and generations of pious samurai came to worship at Hakone Shrine and venerate their spirits. Beside the shrine's main hall (on the left at the top of the stairs) there is a treasure house displaying the sword Goro is said to have used in avenging his father's death, a scroll depicting the origin of the shrine, and a wooden image of the shrine's 8thC founder, Priest Mangan.

Open-Air Museum

Open Mar-Oct 9am-5pm, Nov-Feb 9am-4pm.

Founded in 1969 by the Fuji-Sankei TV and newspaper group, the museum has over 300 sculptures (from Rodin to Henry Moore and

Yodoi Toshio) displayed in garden settings. The museum has recently opened a new Henry Moore Collection, and after acquiring another 18 of his sculptures, the total number now on display is 21. This comprises one of the world's most extensive Moore collections. The Main Hall houses about 200 paintings and smaller sculptures, including works by Giacometti, Hepworth and Léger. A large new **Picasso Gallery**, opened in 1984, houses 300 of his works, including 188 ceramic pieces from the collection of his eldest daughter, Maya. Kinetic pieces, and mazes in which visitors are free to play and climb, will also be fun for children.

Hiroshima

895km (566 miles) w of Tokyo. Population: 920,000. Getting there: by air, 1½hrs from Tokyo's Haneda domestic airport; by train, 5hrs from Tokyo Station or 2hrs 20mins from Kyoto Station by JR Sanyo Shinkansen.

This so-called "City of Peace" would like to be known for more than the "Bomb." The ineffable tragedy of the world's first atomic bombing has been countered by Hiroshima's renewal as a thriving and prosperous modern city.

The destruction of Hiroshima heralded the monstrous birth of the atomic age, and was even worse than in Nagasaki where there were hills to cushion the blast. At 8.15am on Aug 6 1945 the city was completely flattened, and 200,000 people died. Thousands more died later from appalling injuries inflicted by the blast and radiation-induced diseases; and more than 40yrs later many are still hospitalized, and some are still dying.

Nowadays, Hiroshima boasts one of Japan's most famous baseball teams, the Hiroshima Carp, to which citizens are slavishly devoted. The city also has impressive boulevards, attractive parks, an excellent art museum, as well as Japan's most beautiful island — Miyajima — on its doorstep.

Sights and places of interest

Most of the modern monuments in memory of the bombing were erected in the **Peace Memorial Park** (*Nakajima-cho* 🏢 ♿ 💺 ◄€), in the city center, after World War II. The exhibits in the **Peace Memorial Museum** (*Nakajima-cho 1-3, Naka-ku* ☎(082) 241-4004 🏢 ✍ ◄€ *open May-Nov 9am-5.30pm, Dec-Apr 9am-4.30pm, closed Dec 29-Jan 3*) catalog with numbing objectivity and detail all the horrors of the bombing; the photographs of charred bodies and grotesquely disfigured victims are not for the squeamish. Nearby stands the **Peace Memorial Hall** where conferences and meetings to promote disarmament are held. The **Memorial Cenotaph** dedicated to the A-bomb victims is shaped like the *naniwa* figurine clay saddles found in Kofun burial tumuli, and was designed by the renowned architect, Kenzo Tange. Underneath its huge vault a stone chest has been placed containing the names of those killed by the bomb. The cenotaph is designed so that by standing in front of it you can see the A-Bomb Memorial Dome and, by turning around, the Peace Memorial Hall.

The **A-Bomb Dome** stands on the E bank of the Motoyasu River, overlooking the N end of the park. Formerly the Industry Promotion Hall, its once majestic dome was completely gutted by the bomb's explosion overhead, which totally devastated everything within a 3km (2-mile) radius. The steel skeleton of the dome's frame is the only bombed building in Hiroshima allowed to stand, as a grim reminder of the tragedy.

Hiroshima Castle (*Motomachi 21-1, Naka-ku* ☎(082) 221-7512 🏢 ✍ ✱ ◄€ *open Apr-Sept 9am-5.30pm, Oct-March 9am-4.30pm,* closed Dec 29-Jan 2), situated NE in the city's Central Park, was one of the most famous castles in Japan, and considered a National Treasure until its destruction by the A-bomb. In 1958 the central keep of the original 1593 castle was reconstructed, and its interior houses a local museum. The **Hiroshima Museum of Art** (*Motomachi 3-2, Naka-ku* ☎(082) 223-2530 ▤ ⓗ ▨ ▣ ◀€ *open Tues-Sun 9am-5pm (last entry 4.30pm), closed Mon, Dec 28-31*), opposite the bus parking lot in front of the castle, has a large and exceptionally well-displayed collection of paintings by European masters, as well as by Japanese artists.

Shukkei-en Garden (*Kaminoborimachi 2-11, Naka-ku* ☎(082) 221-3620 ▨ ◀€ *open Apr-Sept 9am-6pm, Oct-Mar 9am-5pm, closed Dec 29-Jan 3*), situated to the E of the castle on the Ota River, was originally laid out in 1620 by Lord Asano, and its name literally means Landscape Garden in Miniature. Modeled on Si Hu (West Lake) in Hangzhou, China, the garden has many islets, bridges and picturesque ponds brimming with carp.

Hijiyama Park (*Hijiyama-koen, Naka-ku* ◀€) is set on a small hill in the E part of the city, with fine views over the city, and is crowded with cherry trees. The park also contains radiation research laboratories.

◎ Hiroshima's two major hotels are the **Hiroshima Grand** (*4-4, Kami-Hatchobori, Naka-ku* ☎(082) 227-1313 ☻ 652666 ℗ (082) 227-6462, 386 rms ▭ ⒶⒺ ⓪ ⓪ ⓋⒾⓈⒶ) and the **Hiroshima ANA** (*7-20, Nakamachi, Naka-ku* ☎(082) 241-1111 ☻ 652751 ℗ (082) 241-9123 ▭ ⒶⒺ ⓪ ⓪ ⓋⒾⓈⒶ). Both are of international standard and are conveniently located, the Grand being near the JR Shinkansen station and the ANA being well placed for reaching the airport.

Kamakura

51km (32 miles) SW of Tokyo. Population: 175,500. Getting there: by train, 62mins from Tokyo JR Station by Yokosuka line.

Kamakura occupies a special place in Japanese history as the birthplace of 700yrs of military rule (known as *bakufu*, or literally "tent government") by the shoguns and samurai warriors. The Kamakura period (1192-1333) also witnessed an artistic and religious renaissance, patronized and partly inspired by the new warrior society. The legacy of more than 50 historic Buddhist temples and over a dozen Shinto shrines can easily be visited today, in a day's outing from Tokyo.

The origins of Japan's first *bakufu* in Kamakura lay in the growing enfeeblement of the Imperial Court in Kyoto in the 12thC, and the struggle for national supremacy that ensued between the two leading warrior clans, the Taira and Minamoto. (This was known popularly as the War of the Heike and Genji, from alternate readings of their family names, and it has provided fertile soil for endless works of Japanese literature and drama.)

The head of the Minamoto clan and two of his sons were killed in a shattering defeat by the Taira in 1159, but two other sons — Yoritomo and Yoshitsune — were spared death and exiled. Growing up in his native Kanto region in E Japan, Yoritomo gathered support for the Minamoto among other local warrior families, and in 1180 selected Kamakura as his headquarters. The small fishing village had the defensive advantage of being surrounded on three sides by hills and by the sea on the other; also, Yoritomo was determined to distance himself and his warriors from the distractions of life in the imperial capital. After two great victories against the Taira in 1184 and 1185, Yoritomo became undisputed military leader of Japan.

The dashing Yoshitsune had played a major role in the Minamoto victories, and in a bid to drive a wedge between the two brothers the Emperor lauded him with honors, thus feeding Yoritomo's suspicions. When Yoshitsune attempted to enter Kamakura in 1185 with Taira captives, he was turned back. Yoritomo dispatched a band of men to murder him. For the next 4yrs he was a fugitive from his brother, until he was trapped and, at 30yrs of age he committed suicide to avoid capture. The saga of this fratricidal conflict and Yoritomo's hounding of his brother became a common theme in Japanese *Noh* and *kabuki* drama, poetry, folk tales and movies.

Yoritomo's career ended abruptly in 1199 when he was thrown off a horse and died shortly after. His widow Masako entered a convent, but continued to wield power through her Hojo family, earning the nickname of "Nun Shogun." Two of Yoritomo's sons who succeeded as shoguns were assassinated on Hojo orders, and from 1219 until 1333 the Hojo family exercised real power as regents of puppet shoguns.

The 5th and 6th Hojo regents were lavish patrons of Buddhism, particularly of the Zen and Jodo (Pure Land) schools, which fit the austere code of the samurai. Kamakura's history is also intertwined with the fiery Buddhist prophet Nichiren (1222-82), who taught that the single path to salvation lies through belief in the Lotus Sutra and whose sect now claims millions of adherents and is linked to the Komei political party, the third largest in Japan. After being expelled from his home province near Tokyo for blistering attacks on Zen and Jodo, Nichiren moved to Kamakura in 1254 but was banished 6yrs later for teaching that the samurai would face national destruction if they allowed other "degenerate" sects to undermine his teaching. Within 3yrs he was pardoned, but after further exasperating the Hojo with his subversive evangelism, he was sentenced to death and held on nearby Enoshima island. According to legend, a bolt of lightning split the executioner's sword in two, and instead he was banished again in 1271.

Nichiren's prophecies of doom were fulfilled with the Mongol invasions of Japan by Kublai Khan's armies in 1274 and 1281, the latter miraculously repulsed with the help of a typhoon, which Japanese called *kamikaze*, or divine wind. However, the cost of national defense against Kublai Khan had sapped the strength and energy of the *bakufu*, and after a 3yr campaign, forces loyal to the Emperor Go-Daigo finally overthrew the Hojo regency in Kamakura. The Ashikaga warrior clan who led the anti-Hojo campaign on behalf of the Emperor had contrived to have his energetic son Prince Morinaga banished to Kamakura in 1335 where he was promptly murdered, and the Emperor himself was overthrown within 1yr by an Ashikaga who declared himself the new shogun. Ashikaga shoguns ruled Japan from Kyoto until they were eventually ousted by Nobunaga Oda in 1573.

From being the greatest city in Japan, Kamakura lapsed back into being a sleepy fishing village littered with monuments of past grandeur, until it became connected to Yokohama and Tokyo by the Yokosuka train line in 1889. Kamakura has since grown into a prosperous "dormitory" town for commuters to both the above cities, and is a favorite residence of artists and writers (including the late Nobel prizewinning novelist Yasunari Kawabata). Fine sandy beaches to the s, and a slower, more carefree pace of life have enhanced Kamakura's historical draw for Tokyoites.

Sights and places of interest

The main historical sights w of the JR line are about 2km (1 mile) from Kamakura Station and can be reached by Enoden local rail line, bus or bicycle. Sights E of the JR line may be covered on foot or by bicycle (for rental, inquire at the Tourist Information Center, on the left of the main JR station entrance).

Disembark at Kamakura Station, one stop after Kita-Kamakura, and take the Tsurugaoka Shrine exit to emerge on a busy square. Proceed straight across the square. One block later you will reach Wakamiya Oji (Great Road of the Young Prince). The road was completed in 1182, in time for the procession of Yoritomo Minamoto's newborn son Yoriee to his dedication ceremonies at the Tsurugaoka Hachimangu Shrine. The road begins at the **Yuigahama Beach** (a popular bathing resort once used for riding and archery practice by Yoritomo and his successors), at which point it was once 9m (29ft) wide, tapering to 2.7m (9ft) at its N end. This was designed, through contrived perspective, to make the road appear longer and grander than it actually was. Turn left and you will see a *torii* arch marking the entrance to a raised footpath, called Danzakura, lined with azaleas and cherry trees. As you proceed toward the shrine, you will see many antique and craft shops specializing in Kamakura bori lacquerware, which attains its renowned deep-red lustre from seven or eight coatings of lacquer.

Hachimangu Shrine (*open 5am-9pm*) was founded in 1063 by Yoritomo's ancestor Yoriyoshi Minamoto (988-1075) in gratitude for a military victory in the N. In 1191 Yoritomo moved it from its original site by the seashore to this more imposing site on Tsurugaoka (Stork Hill). It is dedicated to the Emperor Ojin (said to have reigned from 270-310) and his parents; Ojin was later deified as the Japanese god of war, Hachiman, tutelary deity of the Minamoto clan.

Crossing from the end of Dankazura to the entrance of the shrine precincts one encounters the **Drum Bridge**, first built here in 1182. Crossing its steep and slippery surface unassisted is said to assure one of long life; it is also said that only the shogun was permitted passage. Since the shogun would certainly risk his dignity if not a serious fracture in the attempt, both claims should be treated with skepticism. Note the three islands in the large lotus pond on the right and the four islands in the smaller pond to the left, constructed according to a suggestion by Yoritomo's wife Masako. The Japanese word for "three" can also mean birth and prosperity and "four" can mean death and downfall. Hence the pond on the right represented the triumph of the Minamoto, and the pond on the left the demise of the Taira.

Proceeding along the main avenue running through the shrine grounds you will soon come to a dirt track, running off at right angles, where a display of *yabusame*, or mounted archery, takes place (*on Sept 16 each year*). Yoritomo was constantly keeping his men in prime condition, through hunting expeditions on the slopes of Mt. Fuji, archery practice on Yuigahama Beach, and, from 1187, mounted archery, here in the shrine, which is celebrated with the popular annual display (mentioned above).

Farther along, in the middle of a wide open space below a broad flight of steps, you will see the **Maiden**, a red-painted dancing pavilion, commemorating one of the most famous and dramatic dances in Japanese history. After the gallant Yoshitsune fled to N Japan to escape being murdered by his brother, his mistress Shizuka was captured by Yoritomo's men and taken to Kamakura for interrogation. She refused to reveal her lover's whereabouts.

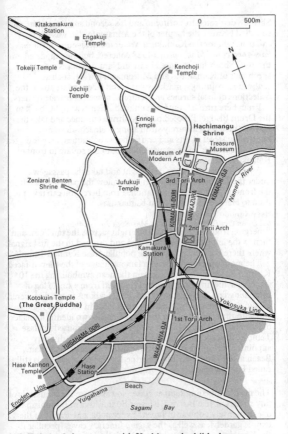

Although 4mths' pregnant with Yoshitsune's child, she was compelled to dance in the shrine's colonnade (thought to be on the site of the Wakamiya, or Junior Shrine, just to the right) to entertain Yoritomo and his wife Masako. The dance touched Masako, but Yoritomo later had Shizuka's newborn son executed.

Ascending the stone steps, you will notice on the left a gigantic, hoary old ginkgo tree, girded with sacred rope. In 1219 the shrine's chief priest Kugyo leapt out from behind the trunk of an even more ancient forebear that grew on the same spot, to chop off the head of his uncle Sanetomo, the third Kamakura shogun, who was returning from a visit to Hachimangu.

The vermilion **main hall** of the shrine, renovated in 1828 after numerous fires and other calamities, comes as an anticlimax; its interior, like most Shinto shrines, is almost bare and devoid of decoration. To the left is a gate to the shrine's **Treasure House** (🏠 open 8.30am–4pm), which possesses many ancient swords, armor, masks, etc.

Returning to the top of the stairs, turn left and descend a small shaded footpath, with a forest stream and ancient evergreen at the bottom (designated a National Monument). Cross the bridge, and on the left of a T-intersection is **Shirahata Jinja** (White Banner

Shrine), dedicated to Yoritomo and his second son Sanetomo, and so-called because the banner of the Minamoto clan was white.

Turn right for the **Kamakura Municipal Museum** (🖼 *open 9am-4pm, closed Mon, hols*), a 1928 concrete building modeled on the 8thC Shoso-in Treasure House in Nara. It houses many fine specimens of Kamakura- and Muromachi-era art, such as sculptures, paintings, masks, swords and lacquerware, from the collections of local shrines and temples, as well as private owners.

From here turn left onto a main road, then bear right, back to the Drum Bridge. Proceed past the shrine entrance and take the first left turn for a leisurely stroll along Komachi-dori, a flourishing street of arts and crafts shops, boutiques, crêperies, tea and coffee houses and restaurants, back to the square in front of Kamakura JR Station.

As you enter the square, turn right and take the passageway under the JR lines. On the other side follow the path on the left to the front of the Enoden line station. From here, you can take the train to Hase (three stops from Kamakura).

Hase Kannon Temple
🖼 *Open Oct-Feb 7am-4.40pm, Mar-Sept 7am-5.40pm.*

Emerging from Hase Station, turn right, across the rail lines, and then to the left side of the boulevard and proceed to the first signal, where there is a small sign for the popular Hase Kannon Temple.

The **main sanctuary** houses a famous image of the Eleven-faced Kannon Bosatsu (the 10 visages on the head symbolizing the 10 stages of achieving Enlightenment) carved from a single log of camphor wood. Legend has it that in 721 a pious monk discovered a large camphor tree near the village of Hase in the Nara region, and with the support of the Empress Gensho two identical images of Kannon were carved from the tree. One was housed in Hase Temple, the other set adrift in the Pacific to find its divinely appointed resting place. The statue finally reached Yuigahama Beach in 736, and was duly enshrined at this place, which is still called Hase in memory of its origin.

Hase

The most compelling sight at Hase, however, are the thousands of tiny statues of Jizo Bosatsu, a lesser Bodhisattva of Buddhism but one immensely popular in Japan. Every nook and cranny of the temple gardens, as well as the *yagura* funerary caves (peculiar to the Kamakura era, being dug into the hillside), seem to overflow with Jizo statues, bedecked with offerings of toys, candy, dolls and other items to amuse a child. These are displayed because Jizo is a protective deity of children, and in recent years the statues have been placed in the garden to comfort the souls of children who died in infancy or at birth, or who were aborted by mothers who could not raise them. Abortions for "economic reasons" officially total hundreds of thousands every year in Japan. Hase's Jizo garden offers a poignant reminder.

Kotokuin Temple
🖼 *Open in winter 7am-5.30pm, in summer 7am-6pm.*

Return to the main road, turn left and follow the avenue up to the Kotokuin Temple, which houses the famous **Kamakura Daibutsu** (Great Buddha). This giant statue (a National Treasure) of the Amida Buddha was cast in bronze in 1252 and is the second largest in Japan after the Daibutsu housed in Nara's Todaiji Temple (though as a work of art the Kamakura Daibutsu is undoubtedly superior); it is a superb example of the individualized expression Japanese artists could achieve even within the rigidly prescribed confines of iconography. The facial expression, with half-closed eyes, subtly expresses the ideal of perfect repose and passionless calm that underlies Buddhist teaching. This serenity is ironically enhanced by the camera-clicking tourists perennially swarming around the Buddha's base.

The statue was originally encased in a great hall, and the foundation stones that supported its pillars may still be seen around it. The hall was first damaged by a storm in 1369 and was finally carried away by tidal waves in 1495, thus leaving the Buddha exposed, where it has been ever since. The statue is 11.4m (37ft) tall and, though hollow, weighs 93 tons. The boss on the forehead, representing the light of wisdom, is made of silver and weighs 13.6kg (30lbs). A staircase leads from a door below the left knee up to the Buddha's shoulders, should you desire a close-up view of the cavernous, roughly-finished interior (🔊 *open 8am-4pm*).

Behind the statue and to the right, there is a delightful **garden**, where you can rest on the giant foundation stones of the hall that once encased the Daibutsu.

From here you can either return to Kamakura (on the Enoden line), or continue along the avenue to **Yuigahama Beach**. The sand here is barely visible on a hot summer's day because of the large crowds it always attracts.

Visitors with more time should take the Yokosuka line to Kita-Kamakura to visit the 13thC **Engakuji Temple**, with its great bell, cast in 1301, and its celebrated Shariden relic hall built in 1285. Nearby **Kenchoji** (1253) and **Tokeiji** (1285) are also worth visiting, the latter known as the "Divorce Temple" for its ancient right of sanctuary for Japanese wives escaping ill-treatment by their husbands.

Kyoto

514km (318 miles) w of Tokyo. Population: 1,473,000.
Getting there: by train, 2hrs 40mins from Tokyo Station by
JR Sanyo Shinkansen super-express.

Kyoto remains the cultural and spiritual heart of Japan, a legacy of more than 1,000yrs as the nation's capital, from 794 to 1868. Kyoto's pride in its role as font and trustee of Japanese tradition has been unmoved by the shift of effective government to Edo in 1603 by Ieyasu Tokugawa, and the Emperor's relocation there in 1868 (when it was renamed Tokyo, or Eastern Capital). Spared from bombing during the Pacific War due to intercession by American scholars, Kyoto today offers a unique cross section of Japanese history, with more than 2,000 temples, shrines, palaces and villas.

It must be said that Kyoto is not a museum, but a major city that is thriving, thanks to its industry (mainly on the s outskirts), a large student population, and the millions of tourists who flock here every year. Inevitably progress has robbed the city center of many of its old wooden buildings (themselves rebuilt after successive internal wars and fires), yet the living fabric of tradition is more intact here than anywhere else in Japan, in back-street inns, shops and elegant restaurants.

For the Japanese, Kyoto is justly synonymous with exquisite taste and refinement, exemplified in the *kaiseki* dishes of Kyo-ryori (Kyoto cuisine), as well as in its Kyo-yaki (fine ceramics), silk weaving and dyeing, lacquerware, doll and fan making, and confectionery.

As one of the world's great cities, Kyoto deserves as much time as possible to explore its many sights. The best times to visit are spring and autumn, thus avoiding the Kyoto extremes of winter cold and stiflingly hot summers, though in high season be prepared to jostle with crowds at the major sights. And despite deep pride in their rich heritage, visitors will find most Kyotoites are open, gracious and unpretentious.

History

Japan's first permanent capital was established at Nara in 709, but in 784 the Emperor Kammu (737-806) abandoned the city, probably to escape the growing power of the Buddhist temples, and set up a new capital in Nagaoka. 10yrs later he decided to move his capital again, a little farther E to a site optimistically named Heian-kyo (Capital of Peace), later referred to as Miyako (Imperial Capital) or simply Kyoto (Capital City). The new city, completed in 805, was modeled after the Chinese T'ang dynasty (618-907) capital of Chang-an (modern Xian) with nine large streets running from E to W beginning with Ichijo (First Street) and ending with Kujo (Ninth Street), intersected by a series of broad avenues. (This original rectangular grid plan is an invaluable aid in getting around modern Kyoto.) The Imperial Palace (Shinsen-in), between Ichijo and Nijo, burned down in 960, and its successors suffered the same fate both in 1177 and 1227. Today all that remains of the original Shinsen-in is a small pond just s of Nijo Castle.

During the relatively peaceful Heian era, known as Japan's "Golden Age," which produced the *Pillow Book* and *Tale of Genji*, the emperors initially wielded great influence, then progressively retired to a life of indolence, luxury and elegance. The Fujiwara clan wielded power by marrying into the Imperial House and assuming the role of regents. After a reassertion of imperial authority in the 11thC, the Taira clan rose to brief prominence before being overthrown by Yoritomo Minamoto in 1185, who established a shogunate in Kamakura.

After arriving from China in the early 13thC the influence of Zen Buddhism spread quickly, and the great Zen temples built in Kyoto in the next century became centers of culture patronized by the Ashikagas, who seized power in Kyoto in the early 14thC. The Muromachi period, named after the place where the Ashikaga shoguns built their palace in Kyoto, witnessed a renaissance in the arts coupled with unremitting social, political and natural catastrophes. The 4th shogun Yoshimitsu was the first to reveal the esthete strain in his family, and during his reign, when Japan was ravaged by plague, drought and famine, the sumptuous Flower Palace in the Muromachi quarter was built, and in 1397 the Gold Pavilion. His grandson Yoshimasa inherited even greater chaos: the warrior priests of Enryakuji on Mt. Hiei had frequently stormed down into the city and forced their demands on the Imperial Court, and plagues, earthquakes, famine and riots were rampant. At the height of these calamities Yoshimasa, aged 35, retired as shogun and handed over power to his 9yr-old son, and pined away the rest of his life in esthetic pursuits such as tea ceremonies, incense parties and tree and moon viewing, behind the walls of his new Ginkakuji (Silver Pavilion).

Yoshimasa's indifference to government was blamed for the outbreak of civil war, which continued almost constantly for the next century until Nobunaga Oda (1534-82) forcibly reunited the nation and overthrew the decrepid Ashikaga shogunate (in the process burning down over 400 temples at Enryakuji, in 1571, and massacring the priests who had opposed him). Oda's successor was Hideyoshi Toyotomi (1536-98), who did most to restore Kyoto to its former grandeur from the ruin wrought by constant war.

Although usurped by Edo after 1603 as the new political, and later commercial, center of the nation, Kyoto prospered under the peace brought by the Tokugawa (although a great fire in 1788 burned down most of the city center), and its rising merchant class became generous patrons of traditional arts. But then, in the plotting that preceded the Meiji Revolution of 1868 that overthrew the Tokugawa shogunate and restored the Emperor, Kyoto was once more the scene of a national power struggle before returning to dreams of its past.

Sights and places of interest

Many of Kyoto's major sights are clustered together. In the following text they are grouped by area, and the more important sights are described individually.

The best way to see Kyoto is on foot. Taxis are also an easy way to get around, although with most sights charging admission fees this can get expensive. The bus system is excellent and simple to use, but the subway is limited with currently one line running directly N. The **Tourist Information Center** (☎*(075) 371-5649, 1st floor, Kyoto Tower Building, located in front of Kyoto Station*) has an easy-to-follow city map with bus routes to major sights clearly marked. The adventurous might try bicycling (rental shops may be found on Kawabata-dori on the E bank of the Kamo River, N of Sanjo Keihan Station).

East of the Kamo River

Although the most eccentric of Kyoto's Buddhist temples, **Sanjusangendo** (Hall of Thirty-three Bays) is a convenient starting

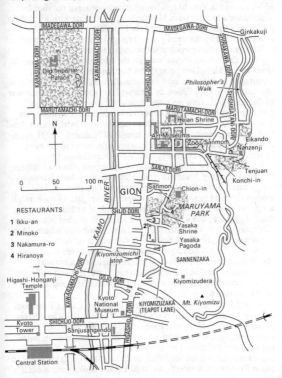

point for the historical sights of E Kyoto (see below). Directly N of Sanjusangendo, the 1897 **Kyoto National Museum** (*Higashiyama Shichijo, Higashiyama-ku* ☎(075) 541-1151 ■■ ◀€ *open Tues-Sun 9am-4.30pm (last entry 4pm), closed Mon, Dec 26-Jan 3*) is a fine example of Meiji-era Japanese architecture in its own right, as well as containing more than 1,000 art treasures from Kyoto's temples, shrines and private collections.

Next, catch bus 206 to the Kiyomizu-michi stop, or walk N on Higashioji-dori, and proceed E up Kiyomizu-zaka Hill, known as Teapot Lane for the number of shops selling ceramics. **Kiyomizudera** (see below), one of the most famous sights in Japan, is one of the compulsory pilgrimage stops for Japanese school parties to Kyoto and Nara, so from here you may well be joining a human torrent. Now retrace your steps to the entrance of the temple and walk down Kiyomizuzaka, but turn right down the steps on Sannenzaka and head for Yasaka Jinja and Maruyama Park. Passing along the back of **Yasaka Pagoda** (erected 1440, repaired 1618), the route passes many traditional Kyoto-style houses. The area also has many famous Japanese restaurants: **Ikku-an**, **Minoko**, **Nakamura-ro** and **Hirano-ya** (see *Restaurants*, below).

Yasaka Shrine (*Shijo-dori, Higashioji Higashi-Iru, Gion-machi, Higashiyama-ku* ☎(075) 561-6155 ▣ ◀€ *open 24hrs*), commonly called Gion San, dates on this site from 876, but with the exception of the older 2-story W gate most of the present buildings date from 1654, erected in the old residential style by order of the shogun. The shrine's famous Gion Matsuri festival, ending with a parade of large floats through the city on July 17, celebrates the 9thC procession led by the head priest through the city to seek divine aid in halting the plague epidemic that raged at that time.

From the Yasaka Shrine's W gate the alluring delights of Gion's main street (Shijo Dori) eagerly beckon, but postpone the temptation and instead take a short walk uphill, skirting Maruyama Park, to **Chion-in Temple** (see below). After returning to the main gate, turn right and follow the street to Sanjo Dori, cross over and take a 5 or 27 bus to reach **Nanzenji Temple** (see below). If you have run out of time (and energy) by this stage, head back to Gion. However, the Zen temple of Nanzenji (1293), set in a wooded area at the foot of the eastern hills, is one of the most beautiful in Kyoto and really should not be missed.

Returning to the front precincts of the temple, the road forming the N perimeter of Nanzenji, called **Shishigatani-dori**, is famous for its many fine *yudofu* temple restaurants (see **Okutan**, below). Follow the road past **Eikando Temple**, turn right and walk uphill until you reach a gravel path along the bank of a canal. This is the start of **Philosopher's Walk**, named after philosopher Ikutaro Nishida (1870-1945), who took his daily constitutional here. Many coffee houses (one of the better is **Nyakuoji**, near the beginning of the walk), chintzy boutiques and souvenir houses are found along the path, now more favored by young couples than *penseurs*. Eventually emerging at the foot of a hill, turn right and walk past some tourist-trap souvenir shops to **Ginkakuji** (see below).

Gion to central Kyoto

The most famous entertainment area in Kyoto, **Gion** covers both sides of the main Shijo-dori road on the E side of the Kamo River. Thanks to successful promotion, the area has become, to foreigners, almost synonymous with Gion Corner, with its twice nightly tourist shows of traditional arts in the Yasaka Kaikan. A nocturnal walk S from Shiji-dori along Hanamikoji, taking time to meander down side streets, as far as Yasaka Kaikan and Kenninji

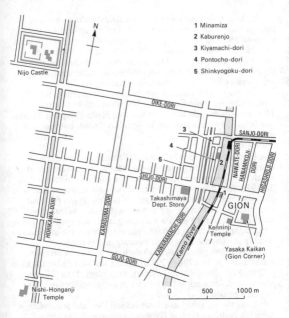

1 Minamiza
2 Kaburenjo
3 Kiyamachi-dori
4 Pontocho-dori
5 Shinkyogoku-dori

temples, takes you past discreet *machi-ai* restaurants (to which geisha are summoned) and expensive *ryotei* each a perfect harmony of wood, water, texture and design, and quintessentially Japanese. To the N of Shijo, "entertainment" tends to run to flashy nightclubs, seedy cabarets and modern bars that could be found in almost any Japanese city; however, scattered in between there are some excellent Japanese restaurants, and particularly on Nawate-dori some fine antique, curio and crafts shops.

The Gion section of Shijo-dori is where Kyoto most openly displays to visitors its famed *furyu* elegance and refinement. The street abounds with shops selling Japanese umbrellas, boxwood and tortoiseshell combs, hair ornaments, lacquerware, cakes and exquisite *wagashi* candies to accompany the serving of Japanese tea. On the left, just before Shijo Bridge, stands the **Minamiza Theater**, built in 1929 to house *kabuki* as well as Western-style drama. Established in early Edo, it claims to be the oldest existing theater in Japan.

After crossing the bridge, the first narrow lane on your right, off Shijo-dori, is an area famous for its amazing number of tiny bars and many excellent restaurants, their often highly discreet entrances lit only by lantern at night. The area called **Pontocho** extends all the way N to Sanjo-dori, where it merges onto a lively (at times raucous) quarter of cheaper drinking halls and discos frequented by students. Just before this, on the right, you will pass the **Kaburenjo Theater**, where geisha perform the Kamogawa Odori dance (*from May 1-24 and Oct 15-Nov 7*).

The next turning on the right from Shijo-dori is **Kiyamachi-dori**, divided into E and W sides by the Takase River. E Kiyamachi-dori is mainly composed of small Japanese inns, with some exclusive ones S of Shijo-dori, and on the W side there are bars, restaurants and nightclubs; a colorful place to stroll at night.

The main **Kawaramachi** thoroughfare extending N and S of the intersection by the Takashiyama and Hankyu department stores, is a good place for shopping. Shinkyogoku-dori, the first street on the right after Shijo-Kawaramachi intersection, is sometimes called Theater Street and is brimming over with theaters, movie theaters, restaurants, dance halls and tearooms. Bright, large, noisy and garish, it is the antithesis of Gion-machi.

From Shijo-Kawaramachi intersection you can either walk the short distance to **Nijo Castle** (see below) or take bus number 12. The other major sight in central Kyoto is **Nishi-Honganji Temple** (see below), which is less well known, less visited, but probably more interesting.

Northwest Kyoto

You have probably seen or heard of the rocks and gravel in **Ryoanji's** garden even if you have no idea of the Zen temple to which they belong (see below). Since the garden's "discovery" in the 1930s the 15 stones have been exhaustively photographed and discussed as the essence and enigma of all Zen. If you can clear your mind of the barrage of publicity and numerous "solutions" offered to explain the garden's meaning, and close your ears to the commentary that blasts through loudspeakers and the incessant clicking of cameras, the garden's beauty may reveal itself.

From Ryoanji proceed to **Kinkakuji** (see below). A further 5mins' ride E by bus 204 or 205 from here will take you to the front of **Daitokuji** (Great Virtue Temple), a rambling, 11ha (27-acre) pine-shaded Zen complex rich in art treasures and beautiful, secluded gardens.

Passing through the S gate from Kitaoji Dori and proceeding N along the path, stop first at **Ryogen-in** subtemple (the second entrance on the left). The tearooms near the entrance overlook the first of five classic rock, gravel and moss Zen gardens. One room contains the oldest gun in Japan, and the *go* Japanese chess set that Toyotomi Hideyoshi and Ieyasu Tokugawa used when they played chess together. The 1502 **Hojo** (quarters of the chief priest) is one of the oldest Zen structures in Japan and embodies the Zen ideals of spartan simplicity (however, note the dreamlike dragon painting on the sliding doors).

Leaving Ryogen-in, turn left and proceed to the main buildings of Daitokuji (*entry to these buildings is only allowed with prior permission*). You will see first **Chokushimon** (Gate of Imperial Messengers), built in 1590 as the S gate of the Imperial Palace but given to the temple in 1640. The 2-story Sanmon (Main Gate) was erected in 1598 by tea-ceremony master Sen-no-Riyku (1522-91). Among the Buddhist images contained in the upper story is one of Rikyu that he sculpted himself, and which so enraged patron Hideyoshi that he threatened to destroy the whole temple. The 1665 **Buttsu-den** (Buddha Hall) and 1636 **Hatto** (Lecture Hall) are noted for their ceiling paintings of the Kano school. The interior of the 1636 Hojo contain sliding screens decorated in ink painting by Tan'yu Kano and, outside, two beautiful Zen gardens laid out by Enshu Kobori. From the side of the Hatto you can see the **Karamon** (Chinese Gate) to the larger W garden of the Hojo. It came from Hideyoshi's Fushimi Castle and is carved with typical Momoyama-style ornateness.

Eight of Daitokuji's 22 subtemples are open for sightseeing, though some require prior permission to enter, and solicit "contributions" in preference to flat admission fees. Each has its own characteristics, and Daisen-in, behind the Hojo although one of the more famous, has recently become crassly commercial. So instead, follow the avenue heading W from the Hatto, and turn left at the first intersection. The first subtemple on the right, **Koto-in** (*Daitokuji-cho, Murasakino, Kita-ku* ☎(075) 492-0068 ▣ ◁€ *open 9am-4.30pm*) should restore your faith in Zen tranquility. Koto-in was founded in 1601 by Tadaoki Hosokawa (1563-1645), a warrior who fought with Hideyoshi in Korea and later with Ieyasu Tokugawa in the campaign that brought him to national supremacy. Hosokawa was tutored in the tea ceremony by Sen-no-Rikyu, became a tea master himself and, on his retirement, a Zen monk. His grave, together with members of his family, lies next to a far wall of the temple. Rikyu used to live in one of the temple buildings. Note the "wriggling in" garden entrance to one of the tearooms, and the tiny 4½-mat tearoom in one corner. Koto-in's chief beauty is its marvelous maple tree garden, so spare some time for restorative contemplation from the terrace.

Imperial sights

There are four sights in Kyoto that require written permits from the Kyoto office of the Imperial Household Agency. These are Shugakuin and Katsura Imperial Villas, Gosho (Kyoto Imperial Palace) and Sento-Gosho (Ex-Emperor's Palace). Applications to join a guided tour (only in Japanese), should be made at least 24hrs in advance at the Agency's office in the grounds of the Imperial Palace (*Kamigyo-ku* ☎(075) 211-1211, *open Mon-Fri 8.45am-noon, 1-4pm, Sat 8.45am-noon, closed Sun, hols, Dec 28-Jan 4*). You may need your passport.

Visits to the Gosho and Sento-Gosho should be passed up unless you are spending a lot of time in Kyoto. All that remains of the 17thC **Sento-Gosho** is one tea pavilion and a beautiful garden laid out by Enshu Kobori; the buildings of the "old" **Gosho** palace date back only to 1855 and many are shuttered or barred to visitors. **Katsura Villa**, constructed over 50yrs, beginning in 1590, is one of the crowning achievements of Japanese architecture. Its logic, economy, harmonious use of natural materials and abstract beauty have been the inspiration for much modern design, and fodder for an evergrowing corpus of admiring and explanatory literature. Unfortunately the guided tour, conducted with great solemnity is restricted to the "strolling garden" and its teahouses. The villa itself may not be entered, but only tantalizingly glimpsed as the tour procession winds along the garden paths.

In contrast to Katsura's rigid and studied formality, the more relaxed tour of **Shugakuin** is tailored to its more open and natural quality. Built by the Tokugawa shogunate in 1659 as a retreat for ex-Emperor Gomizuno-o, the extensive 26ha (65-acre) grounds occupy a spectacular position on a foothill of Mt. Hiei. Shugakuin consists of three gardens with their own pavilions, each simply and airily designed so as not to intrude on the beauty of the natural scenery. The Upper Garden is the largest and most impressive, a large lake with bridges, islands, waterfalls and winding paths accentuating the "borrowed" grandeur of its commanding views over Kyoto and surrounding mountains. The Kyuisui-ken pavilion, standing on an island in the lake, has been unchanged since the 1650s. The window, which swings out from the bottom, and the raised mats beside it, were intended to aid the Emperor in composing classical *waka* poetry inspired by the view.

Chion-in ★

Shinbashi-dori, Yamato-oji, Higashi-iru, Hayashishita-cho, Higashiyama-ku ☎(075) 531-2111 ▣ ▨ *inside temple buildings* ▣ ◁€ *Open 9am-4pm.*

The elevated 2-story, 23m-tall (75ft) **Sanmon** dates from 1619 and is the most imposing temple gate in Japan. Three steep flights of 72 stone steps lead up to the main precincts (for the less energetic the gentle Nyonin-zaka, or Slope for Women, which runs on the s side, is recommended.

The huge **Miedo** (Statue Hall) that faces you across the large courtyard enshrines an image of the revered monk Honen (1133-1212) who founded the Jodo (Pure Land) Buddhist denomination of which Chion-in is the headquarters. The aspiration of Jodo members is to be reborn in the Western Paradise of Amita Buddha by relying upon faith in him and endlessly invoking his name. Jodo was the faith of the Tokugawa shoguns, which helps explain the temple's grandeur and its rich endowments (from 1619 until 1868 the sect's archbishop was always an imperial prince). The back of the hall has an elaborate central shrine, containing a seated statue of Honen, surrounded by rich ornaments that re-create the paradise awaiting true believers after death. The platform on the left side shows other statues of Ieyasu Tokugawa, (who dedicated the building) and his mother and son.

Stepping out into the corridor that encircles Miedo, follow it around to the rear of the hall and over the connecting passageway. The wooden planks are cleverly constructed (like those at Nijo Castle) to emit the call of a *uguisu* (nightingale) as you walk over them. Next you will see the Shuedo (Assembly Hall), built in the same year as the Miedo (1639), but it is of little interest apart from the statue of Amida Buddha, probably carved by Eshin (942-1017), in the central sanctum. Chion-in's large guesthouse to the right is decorated with beautiful paintings of the Kano school and has a front garden that was designed in 1644 by Enshu Kobori (both are now regrettably off limits to the public).

Ginkakuji ★

Ginkakuji-cho, Sakyo-ku ☎ *(075) 771-5725* ▦ ◁ *Open 8.30am-5pm (last entry 4.45pm).*

In 1483 the 8th Ashikaga shogun Yoshimasa had Ginkakuji (known to Westerners as the Silver Pavilion) and its surrounding grounds built as a retirement villa, modeled on his grandfather Yoshimitsu's Kinkakuji (Gold Pavilion) on the other side of the city. The Onin War (1467-77) had left Kyoto in ruins, and in 1480 82,000 citizens died of starvation, at which time the reclusive Yoshimasa engaged in esthetic pursuits behind the walls of his villa; its exquisite pavilion symbolically faced the Higashiyama mountains, rather than the city (the arts that prospered under his patronage are hence known as Higashiyama Bunka, or Culture of the Eastern Mountains). After his death the villa was turned into a Buddhist temple (officially called Jishoji).

In the delightful moss-covered garden, with its artificial pond and island and crystalline cascades of water, it is easy to imagine Yoshimasa ambling around in silk kimono with Nero-like indifference to the fate of the city outside. The intriguing sandpiles in the main courtyard are designed for moonlit viewings, and are said to represent famous mountains in China. The extreme simplicity of the pavilion itself, which visitors are not permitted to enter, is another testament to Yoshimasa's refined tastes.

Kinkakuji ★

Kinkakuji-cho, Kita-ku ☎ *(075) 461-0013* ▦ ◁ *Open Oct-Mar 9am-5pm, Apr-Sept 9am-5pm.*

This is the Gold Pavilion of third Ashikaga shogun Yoshimitsu (1358-1408), which he constructed in 1397 for his retirement. Successor Yoshimochi followed his father's will by turning the villa into a Buddhist temple (Rokuonji). After passing through two gates you will first reach the temple's main hall, with screens decorated by Tan'yu Kano and statues of Buddhist deities,

Yoshimitsu and other paintings. The garden is entered through the Karamon (Chinese Gate), and the wooded grounds and ramps around the pond are beautiful. The present Gold Pavilion is a 1955 replica of the original, tragically burned down by one of its priests in 1950. The late Yukio Mishima based his novel *Kinkakuji* on the story of the deranged young priest who set fire to the pavilion, which was to him a symbol of absolute beauty.

Kiyomizudera ★
Kiyomizu 1-chome, Higashiyama-ku ☎(075) 551-1234 🖾 🏤 inside temple buildings ◁ Open 6am-sunset.

Kiyomizudera (Clear Water Temple) was founded in 780 by Enchin, a priest from Nara, who had been told in a vision to search for the clear water source of the Kizu River. During its 1,200yr history the temple was repeatedly destroyed, and most of the present buildings, including the Main Hall, were rebuilt in 1633.

Noting the Muromachi-era **Horse Stalls** on the left at the foot of the stairs where upper-class visitors to the temple would hitch their mounts, pass through the attractive 1478 **Niomon Gate**, guarded on either side by fierce statues of Deva Kings and the oldest structure in the temple. The belfry facing you was built in 1596, the bell itself cast in 1478. After passing through the unusual Momoyama-era **Saimon** (West Gate), you will soon be solicited by temple officials for a "contribution" to the renovation of the grand 1633 3-story pagoda: this is in effect a compulsory admission fee. The twin-roofed Zuigu Hall to the left is a subtemple where Hideyoshi Toyotomi frequently worshiped and owns many of his personal effects. The path branching farther to the left leads to **Joju-in** (Achievement Temple), now used as priests' quarters, which has a beautiful Momoyama-era Japanese garden.

The magnet for visitors to Kiyomizudera is the **Hondo** main hall. It is not the dimly lit interior with its statue of Senju-Kannon and its 50-odd historic *ema* votive tablets hung on the walls under the eaves that draws the crowds but the large platform in front called Butai (Dancing Stage) and its famous view over the city. The Butai and its wings are built on wooden scaffolding that juts out almost 11m (40ft) over the edge of the cliff. "To leap from Kiyomizudera Butai" has passed into the Japanese language as meaning a momentous decision or act requiring great courage.

At the foot of the stone steps leading down from the Hondo is the **Otowa-no-Taki** (Sound of Feathers Waterfall), which enshrines an image of Fudo Myoo (God King of Fire) and is the source of the "pure water" that monk Enchin discovered in 780, after which the temple was named. The devout sometimes even stand in the waterfall while worshiping. The small pagoda on a hill to the right is called Easy Childbirth Pagoda, as it is said the consort of Emperor Shomu (699-756) prayed to the Kannon inside, at the time of her delivery in 718, of the future Empress Koken (749-759).

Nanzenji ★
Fukuchi-cho, Sakyo-ku ☎(075) 771-0365 🖾 inside Sanmon and Seiryo-Den ◁ Open Mar 6-Nov 15 8am-4.30pm, Nov 16-Mar 5 8.30am-4pm.

At its s end, Nanzenji's Konchi-in subtemple has a famous landscape garden that was laid out in 1632 by Enshu Kobori; the Tenjuan subtemple to the right of the impressive Sanmon also has a Zen garden *(open to the public)*.

It is well worth climbing the steps to the 2nd floor of the 1628 Sanmon (🖾) to see the marvelous views of Kyoto and the Higashiyama mountains from all four sides of the corridor. Ceiling paintings of phenixes and angels, and pillars adorned with waves, by the Tosa and Kano schools, can be glimpsed in the dimly lit interior, which houses a sitting Buddha sculpture surrounded by attendants. The gate is famous as the hiding place of outlaw Goemon Ishikawa, lionized in *kabuki* drama. When captured he and his son were boiled alive in an iron vat (*c.*1632), but Ishikawa bravely held the boy above his head until he expired.

On the right, as you approach the Hojo, and behind the aqueduct carrying water from Lake Biwa, lies the **Nanzen-in** subtemple. This was once the temporary residence of Emperor Kameyama (1249-1305), and it has an ancient landscape garden first laid out in the 14thC. The main attraction of Nanzenji, however, is the Hojo. It is reached through a modern entrance, and consists of two buildings, the **Seiryo-den**, once part of the Imperial Palace but removed here during reconstruction in 1611, and a smaller suite of chambers, which once formed part of Toyotomi Hideyoshi's Fushimi castle. The terrace overlooks a lovely Zen garden (called Leaping Tiger because of its suggestive shape) laid out by Enshu Kobori. Unfortunately, the serenity is marred (as at Ryoanji) by a PA system informing visitors what to admire. The sliding screens are beautifully decorated by artists of the Kano school; the painting of *Tigers in a Bamboo Grove* by Tan'yu Kano (1602-74) is particularly famous.

Nijo Castle ★

Horikawa Nijo, Nijojo-cho, Nakagyo-ku ☎ (075) 841-0096 ■ ☜ ♣
Open 8.45am-4pm.

Despite its moats and battlements, this castle was originally built in 1603 as a luxurious residential palace for Shogun Ieyasu Tokugawa whenever he visited Kyoto from Edo. Ironically it was here in 1868 that the Emperor Meiji issued the edict abolishing the shogunate. After belonging to the Imperial House, it was handed over to the city in 1939 and has been open to the public ever since. The castle buildings are registered as National Treasures, and are noted for the opulent and profuse interior painting by Tan'yu Kano (1602-74) and his school. The Third Building, which contains the Great Hall where the shogun sat on a raised dais while granting audience to the *daimyo* lords far below, is particularly impressive. The floorboards are built to emit a "nightingale" chirping (as those at Chion-in Temple). It is said that those at Nijo were to warn of the approach of potential assassins. The garden, sw of the Great Hall, was meticulously laid out by Enshu Kobori. Originally it had no trees, as falling leaves were a reminder of impermanence, deemed unpleasing to the shogun.

Nishi-Honganji Temple ★

Nishi Rokujo, Shimogyo-ku ☎ (075) 371-5180 ◎ ✗ *compulsory for inner temples and rooms. Application must be made at least one day in advance from temple offices; tour times Mon-Fri 10am, 11am, 1.30pm, 2.30pm, Sat 10am, 11am; no tours on Sun. Open Nov-Feb 9am-5pm, Mar-Aug 5.30am-6pm, Sept-Oct 5.30am-5.30pm.*

Visitors are free to enter the temple's large front courtyard and see inside the Goeido and Amidado halls of worship, but the main artistic treasures at the back may only be seen in a tour group where the guide speaks only Japanese.

The Jodo Shin denomination is the most popular in Japan, but as a result of a schism partly engineered by Ieyasu in 1602 to split Jodo Shin's growing power, it now has two main branches, with their headquarters here, in the Nishi (West) Honganji Temple and in Higashi (East) Honganji (immediately N of Kyoto Station). The buildings of the breakaway Higashi-Honganji were repeatedly destroyed by fires and currently date from 1895; and unfortunately they are not so appealing.

Entering through the **Seimon Gate** (1645), one of the most impressive in Kyoto, you will immediately be struck by the majestically sweeping roofs of the **Goeido** (Founder's Hall) to the left and **Amidado** on the right. The original Nishi-Honganji buildings were completed in 1592, but burned down in 1617. The Goeido, rebuilt in 1636, enshrines a sitting image of Jodo Shin's founder carved by St Shinran (1173-1262) himself, and flanked by portaits of successive abbots. The tablet above the sanctuary bears the characters for the posthumous name granted to Shinran, written by the Emperor Meiji. The Amidado, completed in 1760, enshrines a standing figure of Amida Buddha with portraits of Prince Shotoku (573-621) and Priest Honen (1133-1212) to the right and left of the altar. The *naijin* chancel is elaborately decorated, especially the sliding screen paintings of phenixes and peacocks by the Kano school, representing the Pure Land paradise promised to believers.

The treasures at the rear of the temple came from Toyotomi Hideyoshi's Fushimi Castle when it was broken up and distributed among other temples, in 1632. The **Daishoin Hall** is divided into various gorgeously decorated chambers named after their dominant motif, such as the Sparrow Chamber, Wild Geese Chamber and Chrysanthemum Chamber. The largest and most sumptuously adorned is the Stork Chamber, 33m (108ft) long and 25m (84ft) wide, where the abbot holds audience and once Hideyoshi held councils. The smaller Shiroshoin, once a state chamber of Hideyoshi and later used by the abbot to receive special guests, is perhaps the most beautiful. Most of the paintings in the Daishoin Hall are of the Kano school.

Another acquisition from Hideyoshi's Fushimi Castle is the **North Noh Stage** facing the Shiroshoin. Built in 1581, it is the oldest in Japan and is counted a National Treasure. The stones in the courtyard are said to have been specially laid out to dampen echos from *Noh* performances. The **Hiunkaku** (Flying Cloud Pavilion) built by Hideyoshi in 1588 as part of his Jurakudai Palace and like the Katsura Imperial Villa a model of elegant simplicity, is not included in the tour. The ornate **Karamon** (Chinese Gate) brought here from Fushimi Castle stands to the s of Nishi-Honganji and must be reached from outside.

Ryoanji ★
Ukkyo-ku ☎ (075) 463-2216 ▪ ◀€ Open Jan-Nov 8am-5pm, Dec 8.30am-4.30pm.

This was originally an estate belonging to a Heian-era nobleman of the Tokudaiji, a powerful branch of the Fujiwara family. His legacy included the large pond at the back of the temple, and the tombs of seven Heian-era emperors to be found on the hills N of the Hojo. The estate passed into the Hosokawa family and eventually Katsumoto Hosokawa (1430-73), one of the main protagonists in the 10yr Onin Civil War sparked off by a dispute over Shogun Yoshimasa's succession. After his death, he willed it to become a Zen temple. The Hojo (Superior's Quarters), immediately facing the rock garden, contains a life-size statue of Hosokawa in the altar. The origins of the rock garden are as mysterious as its meaning is elusive — it "appeared" around 1500.

Sanjusangendo ★
Higashi Shichijo-dori, Higashiyama-ku ☎ (075) 561-3334 ▪ ☆ Open Mar 16-Oct 31 8am-5pm, Nov 1-Mar 15 8am-4pm.

The 119m-long (390ft) hall derives its popular name (Hall of Thirty-three Bays) from the 33 spaces between the pillars in front of the main altar: the Kannon Bodhissatva (Buddhist Personification of Mercy or Compassion) enshrined here is believed to assume 33 different forms. The original hall, ordered by the Emperor Goshirakawa (1126-91), who became a monk and fervent devotee of Kannon after he abdicated, was built in 1164. 85yrs later it burned down, and the present hall dates from 1266.

A breathtaking army of one thousand Senju-Kannon (One-Thousand Armed Kannon) gilded wooden statues are arrayed along the entire length of the hall on tiered platforms, with a much larger Senju-Kannon statue in the center (carved by Tankei, a master sculptor of the Kamakura era, at the age of 82). The smaller statues are joint works by 70 sculptors under the command of Tankei and his father Unkei. Look above and you will see many *ema* votive paintings. After the striking uniformity of the Kannon statues' beatific poses, the physical vigor and dynamic individual expressiveness of many of the 28 statues of lesser spirits and deities in the rear (w) corridor comes as a double surprise. These are also presumed to be works of the Tankei school.

The outside veranda has been used since 1606 for a celebrated archery contest (*held annually on May 2*). The archers, who squat on the s end, aim to shoot as many arrows as possible to the far N end without hitting the building (note the protective metal casing around some of the pillars).

Nearby sights

Not all Kyoto's treasures are within the city's confines. Farther afield, but within easy reach, are at least three important sights.

Byodo-in ★

Uji Renge, Uji City ☎ *(0774) 21-2861* 🔳 🎟 *inside Phenix Hall* ◀
Open Mar-Nov 8.30am-5pm, Dec-Feb 9am-4pm.

Situated at Uji, 18km (11 miles) from Kyoto, Byodo-in can be reached by the JR Nara line local train service, stopping at Uji Station. It is well worth a detour to see this, one of Japan's most celebrated and historic buildings (depicted on one side of every ¥10 coin in your pocket).

From Uji Station entrance turn left and descend a main street of dispiriting grayness to Uji Bridge at the bottom. Next take the small street on the left side, lined with stores selling famous Uji green tea (reputedly the best in Japan), and you will come to the entrance of Byodo-in on the right, around the next corner. (As the area has few restaurants, you would be wise to stop for refreshment at a coffee shop in a converted private residence, or a Japanese inn opposite.)

Originally a villa of chief minister Michinaga Fujiwara, Byodo-in was converted into a monastery by his son in 1052. The temple's main hall, **Ho-odo** (Phenix Hall), built in 1053, is the only original building to have escaped destruction and is designated a National Treasure. The hall was designed to represent a phenix descending to earth — the central hall is the body, the lateral corridors its wings, and the rear corridor its tail. On either side of the roof of the main hall are a male and female phenix cast in bronze. The overall effect, best seen from the far end of the pond in front, is of amazing lightness, grace and perfect symmetry. The hall enshrines a famous statue of Amida, sitting cross-legged on a lotus pedestal. The carving on the halo and canopy are of marvelous intricacy. Note the 52 Bodhissatva statues hanging on the walls, and the early Buddhist frieze paintings (now very worn and faded).

The **Kannondo** building to the left of the precinct entrance was rebuilt in the Kamakura era and is known as Angling Hall because in former days the Uji River ran underneath and fishing was possible from inside. Behind the Kannondo is a tiny garden bordered by a fan-shaped stone fence. Legend has it that this

marks the spot where Yorimasa Minamoto committed *seppuku*
(ritual disembowelment) in 1180 while sitting on his fan, after his
army suffered a crushing defeat across the Uji River in a battle
against the Taira (see *Kamakura*). Minamoto's tomb can be found
in the far left corner of Saisho-in subtemple diagonally behind the
Phenix fan.

Leaving Byodo-in, turn right and follow the path up to the Uji
River, then turn right and cross the first footbridge to the
Tonoshima islet. On your right you will see a stone tablet
commemorating the site where in 1184 two warriors of Yoshitsune
Minamoto competed for the honor of being first to cross the river
on horseback. Taking in the beautiful view upriver, cross the next,
gracefully curved bridge to the other side. Proceed through the red
torii arch that marks the entrance to **Uji Shrine**. The Lower Shrine
buildings are from the Kamakura era; the Upper Shrine buildings,
situated on a slope on the left, were built in the early 10thC and are
said to be the oldest surviving in Japan.

Enryakuji ★
*Mt. Hiei, Sakamoto Honmachi, Ohtsu, Shiga Pefecture ☎(0775)
78-0551 ▨▨ ▨▨ inside temple buildings ▣ ◁≡ Open Mar-Nov
8.30am-4.30pm, Dec-Feb 9am-4pm.*

One of the most important temples in the history of Japan,
Enryakuji (a 1hr 10min bus ride from Kyoto Station) was founded
on top of Mt. Hiei in 788 by a monk, Saicho, founder of the
Tendai sect, on orders from Emperor Kammu to protect the new
capital from evil spirits thought to come from the NE. The temple
soon became more of an affliction than a blessing. From the 11thC,
Enryakuji, having fought frequently with rival temples in Nara
and with a schismatic Tendai sect who had a temple nearby, had its
own army, one of the most powerful in Japan. Whenever the
bonzes (monks) disagreed with the Emperor, they would pick up a
sacred Shinto palanquin, scramble down the mountain and march
on Kyoto. In a famous statement the Emperor Shirakawa
(1056-1129) admitted, "There are three things which I cannot
bring under obedience, the waters of Kamo River, the dice of the
sugoroku game, and the *bonzes* on the mountain." Although the
founders of all the new sects which sprang up in the 12th and
13thC had all studied on Mt. Hiei, Enryakuji's army did not
hesitate to raid their temples, burn their literature and kill their
priests (as late as 1536 Enryakuji forced the Nichiren sect out of
Kyoto by razing 21 of its temples to the ground and slaughtering
most of its priests). The temple monks' fatal mistake was taking
sides against Nobunaga Oda, whose army in revenge stormed the
mountain in 1571, burned its temples (more than 3,000 of them)
and killed its priests. Hideyoshi later allowed Enryakuji to be
rebuilt, and although much reduced in size, it is still one of the
largest monasteries in Japan.

It is Enryakuji's superb mountain setting of towering *sugi*
(cryptomeria trees) more than its temple architecture that provide
compelling reasons to make the short trip from Kyoto. Entering
from the Enryakuji bus terminal, the path leads first to the
Daikodo (Great Lecture Hall), rebuilt after a fire in 1956. On the
right is the belfry, and farther down is the heart of the temple,
which should be left until last. From Daikodo turn left and take
the path farthest right, leading up the hill. On the corner (right)
you will pass the **Kaidan-in** where ordination ceremonies for
Tendai priests have been held ever since AD827. The present
Momoyama-style building dates from 1604.

The mountain path leads through a hushed forest of *sugi* that are
centuries old, past a small *jizo* statue. Arriving at a road on the

right, cross the pedestrian bridge past the small Sanno-in (Mountain King Temple), which can be ignored, then turn left and walk down the steep flight of steps lined with stone lanterns. The *Jodo-in* (Pure Land Temple) at the bottom was originally erected by Saicho to house a statue of Amida that he had carved, now kept in the **Amidado Hall** to the w of the main building, which houses an image of the founder. Saicho's tomb lies behind a stone fence N of the main building. Priests staying at Jodo-in have to perform an ascetic training practice called "sweeping hell" (you will notice how the grounds are kept spotlessly clean and the gravel meticulously raked). Monkeys who inhabit Mt. Hiei can often be seen clambering over the roofs and swinging in the nearby cherry trees. The N precinct, which has the oldest extant building in Enryakuji, can be reached after a long walk farther along the path in front of Jodo-in, but unless you have much time it is better to retrace your steps as far as the belfry, to the right of Daikodo.

Proceed down the steps to the courtyard in front of **Kompun-chudo** (Fundamental Central Hall). The site is thought to be where Saicho built the first hut for meditation, when he climbed Mt. Hiei in 788. Growing vastly in size, the last hall was burned down in 1571 by Oda's troops. The present building dates from 1642, and combines Momoyama boldness with the traces of excessive Edo ornateness. The coffered ceiling is decorated with flower paintings provided, at Tokugawa's command, by all the *daimyo* of Japan. In front of the majestic altar are three large lanterns bearing the 16-petaled chrysanthemum crest of the emperor; only Enryakuji claims the crest was originally its own, and was granted by Enryakuji to the Emperor Kammu who founded Kyoto.

Opposite the entrance to Kompon-chudo, ascend the steep steps to **Monju-ro** gate. Originally built in 866, this used to be the formal entrance to Enryakuji. The present building is contemporary with the rebuilt Kompon-chudo. Climbing the steps inside to the upper level, you will see a statue (*c.* 1700) of Monju, Buddhist god of wisdom, enshrined. From the foot of Monju-ro there is a fine view of Lake Biwa.

Nishijin

Nishijin is the silk-weaving district that stretches E of the Kitano Shrine to Horikawa-dori, and from around Daitokuji s to Imadegawa-dori. The name means Western Camp and derives from the Onin War in Kyoto during the 15thC. During the Tokugawa era (1603-1867) all the silk for the court and nobility was produced in this area. Most of the weaving is still done in homes or neighborhood workshops, and Kyotoites still call the old wooden row houses in Nishijin *unagi-no-nekodo*, or bedrooms of eels. 1-story front wooden grills are for privacy, and far in the back there is an inner garden. As you walk past you will hear the whir of looms, and in summer you can usually take a peek inside. The **Nishijin Textile Center** (*Imadegawa Minami Iru, Horikawa-dori, Kamikyo-ku* ☎(075) 451-9231 ▣ ▨ *for kimono shows and museum* ♿ 🍴 ≈ 🖥 ➡ *open 9am-4.30pm, last entry 4pm*) offers demonstrations of silk-weaving techniques, in addition to a **museum** tracing the history of the industry, kimono shows for tourists, and the inevitable shops.

☞ The **Kyoto Hotel** (*Kawaramachi-Oike, Nakagyo-ku, Kyoto* ☎(075) 211-5111 ☎ 5422126 ℻ (075) 221-7770 ⅢⅢ 507 *rms* ≈ Ⓐ Ⓒ Ⓓ Ⓥ), situated opposite the City Hall, has excellent food and service, though its room rates are overpriced. The **Miyako Hotel** (*Sanjo Keage, Higashiyama-ku, Kyoto 605* ☎(075) 771-7111 ☎ 5422132 ℻ (075) 751-2490 ⅢⅢ 480 *rms*

≋ AE CB D D VISA), although not in such a prime location as the Kyoto, is of comparable standard, with cheaper room rates and some interesting interior details. The **Kyoto Royal Hotel** (*Kawaramachi-Sanjo, Nakagyo-ku, Kyoto 604* ☎(075) 223-1234 ● 5422888 ℗(075) 223-1702 ≋ AE D D VISA) occupies a prime spot farther down Kawaramachi-dori. The **Kyoto Park Hotel** (*644-2, Sanjusangendo Mawari-machi, Higashiyama-ku, Kyoto 605* ☎ 5422777 ℗(075) 551-4350 ▯ 270 rms ≋ AE D D VISA), next to Sanjusangendo, has good views over the Kyoto National Museum; one drawback is its dreadfully kitsch lobby area.

🛏**Tawara-ya** (*Anekoji-agaru, Fuyacho-dori, Nakagyo-ku, Kyoto City* ☎(075) 211-5566 ● 5423273 ℗(075) 211-2240 ▮▮▮ 19 rms AE VISA) has accommodated royalty, as well as the Rothschilds and Rockefellers, and is very choosy about its guest list. **Hiiragi-ya** (*Oike-kado, Fuyacho-dori, Nakagyo-ku, Kyoto City* ☎(075) 221-1136 ● 5422045 ℗(075) 221-1139 ▮▮▮ 33 rms AE D D VISA) next door is in the same class. Midtown **Daimonji-ya** (*Kawaramachi Nishi-iru, Sanjo-dori, Nakagyo-ku, Kyoto City* ☎(075) 221-0603 ℗(075) 241-4704 7 rms ≋ AE D) is somewhat less expensive but boasts an excellent restaurant. **Kinmata** (*407, Shijo-agaru, Gokomachi, Nakagyo-ku, Kyoto* ☎(075) 221-1039 7rms ≋) is an old family-run *ryokan* with traditional interior, also in the center.

Shiraume (*Shirakawa-hotori, Gion-shinbashi, Higashiyama-ku, Kyoto* ☎(075) 561-1459 ▮▮▮ 8 rms) was once an *o-chaya* "teahouse" for geisha parties in the Shinbashi area of Gion. **Iwanami** (*Higashioji Nishi-iru, Shinmonzen-dori, Higashiyama-ku, Kyoto* ☎(075) 561-7135 ▯ 8 rms) is another precious old inn with more reasonable rates.

Heihachi-jaya (*8-1, Kawagishi-cho, Yamabana, Sakyo-ku, Kyoto City* ☎(075) 781-5008 ℗(075) 781-6482) ▮▮▮ 8 rms D D VISA) a little N of Shugakuin, is a rustic old inn, ideal for unwinding in. **Kikaku-tei** (*55, Higashiyama-cho, Kamitakano, Sakyo-ku, Kyoto* ☎(075) 781-4001 ℗(075) 701-0051 ▮▮▮ 7 rms D D VISA), farther N, at the foot of Mt. Hiei, was once an elegant villa belonging to the magnate who founded the Miyako Hotel. It has beautiful gardens and, like Heihachi-jaya, a relaxing *kamaburo* steambath.

For travelers on a shoestring, the **Hiraiwa Inn** (*314, Hayao-cho, Kaminoguchi-agaru, Ninomiyacho-dori, Shimogyo-ku, Kyoto City* ☎(075) 351-6748 16 rms AE), by the old canal in central Kyoto, offers unbeatable value.

≋Kyoto was the birthplace of *kaiseki* haute cuisine, which elevates the simple act of eating into an elaborate artistic ritual. Ideally, *kaiseki* should combine three elements: the spiritual surroundings of the tea ceremony; perfectly fresh morsels of food with the flavor of each course complementing the last and garnished so as to accent the seasonal color; and a serene harmony of food and utensil. Such a banquet of 7-12 courses at a fine *ryotei* will, of course, be expensive.

For the full experience, reserve a private room at **Nakamura-ro** inn (*Yasaka-jinja-uchi, Gion, Higashiyama-ku* ☎(075) 561-1016/8 ▮▮▮ ▬ ◁€ *last orders 6pm, closed last Thurs in each mth*), probably Japan's oldest restaurant (its front teahouse at the entrance to Yasaka Shrine dates back at least to the early 17thC). After the meal you may be lucky enough to be shown the rooms used by the Imperial Family in the 19thC, with sliding screens painted by Korin Ogata. Nakamura-ro also serves reasonably priced *o-bento* lunch-box samplings of the day's cuisine.

Even more formal is *cha-kaiseki*, served at nearby **Minoko** (*480, Kiyoi-cho, Shimogawara-dori, Gion, Higashiyama-ku* ☎(075) 561-0328 ▮▮▮ ▬ ◁€ D D VISA *last orders 8.30pm, closed second and fourth Wed in each mth*) in Gion, where tiny morsels are served to accompany the drinking of thick green tea. In this kind of *kaiseki* the character *cha* means tea, *kai* a pocket or fold and *seki* a stone, from the practice of Zen monks folding warm stones in their garments to stave off the cold. For delicious *kaiseki*-style cuisine in relaxed but tasteful surroundings overlooking the Kamo River, head for Pontocho and try **Izeki** (*Pontocho Shijo Agaru, Nakagyo-ku* ☎(075) 221-2080 ▮▯ ▬ *last orders 8.45pm, closed Wed*) for a reasonably priced lunch. **Yagenbori** (*Sueyoshi-cho Kiritoshi-kado, Gion, Higashiyama-ku* ☎(075) 551-3331 ▮▯ ▭ ▬ *last orders 10.30pm*), in the heart of Shinbashi, offers similar value.

Although *kaiseki* is most often associated with Kyoto cuisine (or *Kyo-ryori*), simple dishes such as potatoes and salted fish are even more traditional to the city: try the well-known **Hirano-ya** (*Maruyama Koen-uchi,*

Excursions

Higashiyama-ku ☎(075) 561-1603 🍴 🖥 ◁ *last orders 7.30pm*), in the approach to Chion-in.

Kyoto sauces are also much lighter and more delicate than you will find in Tokyo, as you will immediately discover from even a simple but delicious bowl of noodles; ask for *kama-age udon* at **Gombei** (*Gionkiridoshi, Higashiyama-ku* ☎(075) 561-3350 ☐ ☐ *last orders 10.30pm, closed Thurs, Jan 1-2*), a restaurant in the Gion district just off the N side of Shijo. In hot summers Japanese eat calorie- and vitamin-rich *unagi* (eel) to relieve fatigue. One Gion restaurant nearly always crowded in this season is **Umenoi** (*Nawate Shijo Agaru, Higashiyama-ku* ☎(075) 561-1004 🍴 ☐ 🖥 ◑ 💳 *last orders 8.30pm, closed Wed*): ask for the delectable *unagi-don toku-jo* broiled eel on a bed of rice, or the more expensive *unagi kaiseki* course.

For temple food, **Okutan** (*86-30, Fukuchi-cho, Nanzenji, Sakyoku* ☎(075) 771-8709 🍴 🖥 ◁ *last orders 5.30pm, closed Thurs*), in the grounds of the subtemple of Nanzenji, offers an unforgettable taste of *yudofu* (simmered *tofu*) in rustic *tatami* rooms overlooking a garden; and the famous **Ikkyu-an** (*Kodaiji Minami-monzen, Higashiyama-ku* ☎(075) 561-1901 🍴 🖥 ◁ 💳 *last orders 6.30pm, closed Tues*) has been serving delicious *fucha ryori* (an 8-course Chinese-style Zen meal) for 15yrs and is highly recommended (reservations essential).

For cheap *kushikatsu* kebabs in an old *kura* treasure house on Kiyamachi, try **Oiwa** (*Nijo-sagaru, Kiyamachi-dori, Nakagyo-ku* ☎(075) 231-7667 ☐ ☐ 🖥 ◁ *last orders 9.30pm, closed Sun, hols*); for the same, plus inexpensive *tempura* in a 100yr-old teahouse on Pontocho, head for **Fujino-ya** (*Shijo-agaru, Pontocho, Nakagyo-ku* ☎(075) 221-2446 ☐ ☐ 🖥 *last orders 9.30pm, closed Mon*). *Tempura aficionados* should seek out **Takasebune** (*188, Sendo-cho, Shijo-sagaru, Shimogyoku* ☎(075) 351-4032 🍴 ☐ 🖥 *last orders 6.30pm, closed first and third Wed during Jan-Sept*) for affordable tongue-tingling. The impressive (English) menu at **Minokichi** (*Sanjo-agaru, Dobutsuenmae-dori, Sakyo-ku* ☎(075) 771-4185 🍴 ☐ 🖥 ◁ 🅰🅴 ⓓ ◑ 💳 *last orders 9pm*), established in 1735, is especially popular with tourists who cannot decide what they want to eat, and has a large, attractive garden.

Kyoto is not rich in Western-style restaurants. **Manyo-ken** (*Higashi-iru, Fuya-cho, Shijo dori, Shimogyo-ku* ☎(075) 221-1022 🍴 🖥 🅰🅴 💳 *last orders 8.30pm, closed Tues*), serving French *cuisine bourgeoise*, is the oldest and has a good reputation. **Ashiya** (*Kiyomizu 4-chome, Higashiyama-ku* ☎(075) 541-7961 🍴 🖥 🅰🅴 💳 *last orders 10pm, closed Mon*), in the Kiyomizu area, is renowned for expensive but mouthwatering Kobe beef.

Shopping

Japanese enjoy shopping in Kyoto for the peerless elegance and refinement of its crafts, an elusive quality called *miyabi*, missing from the grander establishments in Tokyo.

Aizen Kobo   Omiya Nishi-iru, Nakasuji-dori, Kamigyo-ku ☎(075) 441-0355. Traditional *aizome* indigo-dyed garments are sold here, in this Meiji-era building in the Nishijin textile district.

Asahi-do   1-280, Kiyomizu, Higashiyama-ku ☎(075) 531-2181 🅰🅴 ⓓ ◑ 💳 Before 1945 a purveyor to the Imperial Household, Asahido has the best choice of Kiyomizu ceramic ware in Kyoto.

Fuji Kei Shoten   Shinbashi, Nawate-dori, Higashiyama-ku ☎(075) 561-7863 🅰🅴 ⓓ ◑ 💳 A beautiful old shop situated on Nawate-dori, just below Shinbashi, selling both antique and new Japanese dolls, *netsuke* carvings and *kanzashi* hair ornaments.

Jusan-ya   Otabi-cho, Shinkyogoku, Higashi-iru, Shijo-dori, Shimogyo-ku ☎(075) 221-2008 ◑ 💳 Here, farther along Kawaramachi from the Takashimaya department store, you will find boxwood combs handcrafted by a 5th-generation maker.

Kasagen   284, Gion-machi Kitagawa, Shijo-dori, Higashiyama-ku ☎(075) 561-0672 🅰🅴 ⓓ ◑ Handmade, oiled-paper umbrellas have been sold here since 1861. Next door is the **Kazurasei**.

Kazurasei   285, Gion-machi Kitagawa, Shijo-dori, Higashiyama-ku ☎(075) 561-0672 🅰🅴 ⓓ ◑ One of many shops in Kyoto selling *kanzashi* hair ornaments, this one is on the N side of Shijo-dori in Gion.

Kungyokudo   Nishi Honganjimonmae, Horikawa-dori,

Shimogyo-ku ☎(075) 371-0162. Japanese prefer to use the verb to "hear" rather than "smell" when referring to incense.

Kungyokudo, located at the E gate of Nishi Honganji, sells most of its incense for religious use but also to a dedicated band of *kodo* (way of incense) practitioners who try to guess the different kinds of incense they "hear."

Kyoto Craft Center   Gion Shijo Hanami Koji Higashi, Higashiyama-ku ☎(075) 651-9660 AE ⊙ ⊙ VISA There are a variety of crafts such as cloisonné, leather, jewelry and ceramics available on the 1st floor, with changing exhibitions on the floor above. Unfortunately the quality is not consistent.

Kyukyodo   Anekoji-kado, Teramachi-dori, Nakagyo-ku ☎(075) 231-0510 VISA This famous dealer in incense, stationery and ink brushes was founded in 1774 and has a license from the Imperial Family to produce secret incense recipes. It is more old-fashioned and relaxed than its Ginza branch in Tokyo.

Maronie Crafts and Gallery   Kawaramachi Shijo Agaru, Nakagyo-ku ☎(075) 221-0117 VISA Centrally located on the main Kawaramachi shopping street, Maronie's selection of crafts is of a higher quality than the **Kyoto Craft Center** in Gion.

Miyawaki Baisen-an   Tominokoji Nishi-iru, Rokkaku-dori, Nakagyo-ku ☎(075) 221-0181 AE VISA Fans of every description, from ordinary *sensu* (for making a cooling breeze) to those used in tea ceremony and *Noh* drama, are to be found in this 1823 shop.

Nishimura   Teramachi-kado, Sanjo-dori, Nakagyo-ku ☎(075) 211-2849. Most of the owner Nishimura's large stock of *ukiyo-e* prints are stored in a cabinet, but he is always willing to spread them on the floor of his tiny shop for perusal. Although well-acquainted with the eclectic tastes of foreigners, it would help if you first gave Nishimura a rough idea of what you are seeking.

Rakushi-en   4-chome, Gion-bashi Higashi, Higashiyama-ku ☎(075) 541-1161 AE ⊙ A limited selection of work by noted individual potters.

Tachikichi   Tominokoji-kado, Shijyo-dori, Shimogyo-ku ☎(075) 211-3141 AE ⊙ ⊙ VISA This is the main shop of the Ginza Tachikichi you may have browsed through in Tokyo. Selling fine *Kyo-yaki* (Kyoto ceramic ware) since 1752, Tachikichi ships to anywhere in the world.

Tazawa Kobijutsu-ten   Sanjo-Sagaru Nishi-gawa, Higashioji-dori, Higashiyama-ku ☎(075) 561-3009. One of several interesting antique shops of Higashioji just N of Shinmozen, specializing in Meiji-period Japanese glassware.

Yamato Mingei-ten   Takoyakushi-agaru, Kawaramachi, Nakagyo-ku ☎(075) 221-2641 AE VISA Reasonably priced handmade *mingei* (folk craft ware) from all over Japan.

Yamazoe Tenkodo Sanjo-sagaru, Yamatooji-dori, Higashiyama-ku ☎(075) 561-3064. Fine scroll paintings are sold here, on Nawate-dori, but you will find the choicest examples stored at the back of the shop.

Mount Fuji and the Five Lakes region

Getting there: by bus, 2½hrs by Fuji Kyuko Express Bus (Fuji Kyuko Travel Center ☎376-0311), runs from mid Apr-early Nov. Bus leaves from W side of Shinjuku Station, goes up "Subaru Skyline Driveway" to the Go Go-me (Fifth Station) on the mountain's N face. Also 1hr from Kawaguchiko Station.

Fuji is the highest mountain in Japan, standing at 3,776m (12,385ft), and is the most beloved by the Japanese people. Its superb conical form, with a 40-50km (25-31 mile) diameter base, which is almost as distinctly circular as the 500m (1,640ft) crater, has inspired countless poems, paintings and prints since ancient times and has become an international symbol of Japan. Hokusai, the celebrated *ukiyo-e* artist, was moved to produce *Thirty-six Views of Mt. Fuji* in 1831. The volcano's awesome violence — 18 recorded eruptions, including one that blanketed Edo in 15cm (6ins) of ash in 1707 — has also contributed to its spiritual potency. Although pilgrims still make the ascent (a Shinto shrine, as well as a weather observatory, is maintained at the summit), most of the climbing nowadays is done for pleasure.

Religious worshipers of Mt. Fuji began the custom of dividing the climb into ten different stations, or stages. A Skyline Driveway now extends to the halfway mark, or *Go Go-me* (Fifth Station), from which the summit crater can be reached in about 5hrs on foot. From July 1 to Aug 26, when Mt. Fuji is officially "open" for climbing (winter ascents are possible but dangerous), every trail to the top is crowded with long lines of hikers from the base to the summit. Fuji Kyuko buses also run from July-Aug from Gotemba and Mishima stations to the "New Fifth Station" on the s side (the ascent to the summit from here takes about 5½hrs on foot). Those who wish to join the line are advised to take food and water, a sweater, raincoat, walking stick and strong boots.

A recommended alternative for the less energetic, during summer or autumn, is the Ochudo-meguri (Halfway Trail Encircling Mt. Fuji). Starting from the Fifth Station, a walk along this route, in summer, offers fine views of the summit across huge spills of volcanic cinder, at little cost in feet blisters.

You alight from the bus in a parking area and can then take a 2hr stroll, in either direction, on generally level and well-marked paths. Encircling the mountain by this path would require a full day, and with difficult scree on the w side this is not advisable. Instead, walk for a short distance and then turn back to the parking lot for a similar stroll along the opposite path.

An easy way to tour many of the scenic spots around the base of Mt. Fuji is by sightseeing bus. The round trip from Tokyo takes about 8½hrs (see *Tour operators* in *Basic information*, or ask at your hotel travel desk for details).

Alternatively, Kawaguchiko, on the SE shore of **Kawaguchiko Lake** may be reached in 2hrs by either Fuji Kyuko or Keio Teito (☎343-1801) express bus from the w side of Tokyo's Shinjuku Station, or in 2hrs 20mins by JR Chuo line express, from Shinjuku to Otsuki, changing to the Fuji Kyuko Railway for Kawaguchiko. (There are also a few through train services from Shinjuku to Kawaguchiko depending on the season, so check ahead.)

Kawaguchiko is a bustling town of *ryokan* inns, hotels, restaurants and souvenir shops. Kawaguchiko Lake vies with **Lake Yamanaka** as a favorite summer resort for Tokyoites. A superb view of Mt. Fuji and the lake, with its thickly wooded islet called Unoshima (Cormorant Island), where there is a shrine dedicated to Benten, a goddess of beauty and music, can be seen from the observation tower on top of Mt. Tenjo. This is reached by a cable car boarded at the lakeside near Kawaguchiko Station. The flat road that encircles the lake is dotted with numerous parks, rest areas, shrines and temples. Close to the town, rowboats and motorboats may be rented, and along the s shore there are many restaurants and teashops. Bicycles are a good way to tour around the lake, and may be rented from an establishment on a side street, directly opposite the front of Kawaguchiko Station. The **Fujikyu Highland Amusement Park** is only a brief train ride from Kawaguchiko Station and is a delight for restless children.

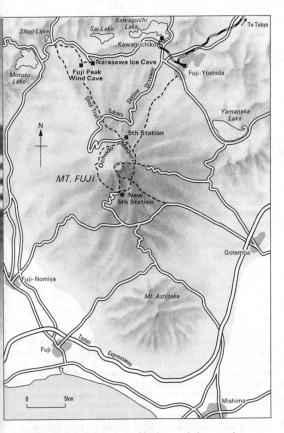

Lake Shoji, secluded on three sides by wooded mountains, which open toward the SE facing Mt. Fuji, is arguably the prettiest of the Fuji Go Ko (Fuji Five Lakes) and can be reached in 50mins by bus, from Kawaguchiko Station. From the village of Shoji on its N shore a 1hr 30min hike of 2.5km (1 mile) takes you to Mt. Eboshi's summit between Lake Shoji and **Lake Motosu**, with a magnificent view of Mt. Fuji over the **Jukai** (Sea of Trees) clustered in front. (**Lake Saiko** is unremarkable but makes up the numbers.)

For the more adventurous, take the bus from Platform 6 in front of Kawaguchiko Station and alight at **Narasawa Hyoketsu** (Narasawa Ice Cave) after a 40min journey. A 3-5hr hike will lead you to Lake Shoji. To reach the ice lava cave, cross the street and walk for 5mins until you come to a small parking lot and the entrance to the cave. Both this and the **Fukagu Fuketsu** (Fuji Peak Wind Cave) are formed by pockets of trapped gas in the immense lava field created centuries ago by eruptions from the NW flank of Mt. Fuji. After visiting the ice cave, walk to the rear of the parking lot and follow the trail leading into the woods, to the right. After 20mins' walking, turn right at a T-intersection to the wind cave.

Returning to the trail, you can turn here and start a 1hr walk through the Jukai along the N fringe of the **Aokigahara Forest**, where trees subsist on a thin layer of organic matter covering the brittle lava underneath. This forest is a 25sq.km (10sq. miles) protected natural wilderness, and is a notorious place both for suicides and for getting lost in, as wanderers are unable to see for more than a few meters off the trail, and the magnetic properties of the cooled lava underneath makes compasses unreliable.

Within a few minutes of returning to the trail from the wind cave, the path veers right, back toward the highway; a little farther on at a fork in the road, bear left. Walk for a further 10mins, and you will be parallel to the highway. After less than an hour's easy walking you will descend some earthen steps, pass through a barrier of logs and step out onto an intersection. Turn right here and you will soon descend to the highway; then turn right again and 10mins later you will arrive at the entrance of Lake Shoji.

Lake Yamanaka is a playground for affluent Tokyoites (as is Lake Kawaguchi), with a fine golf course and excellent trout fishing nearby. The lake shore has been heavily developed and Yamanaka boasts the three finest hotels in the Fuji Five Lakes region. To reach Lake Yamanaka from Tokyo, take one of the four Odakyu line express trains that run every day from Shinjuku Station to Gotemba (1hr 45mins). From here the main town of Asahigaoka on the S shore can be reached by bus in 45mins.

Nara

553km (342 miles) W of Tokyo. Population: 330,000. Getting there: by train, 33mins from Kyoto Kintetsu Station by Kintetsu Kyoto line "tokkyu" limited express, or 60mins from Kyoto JR Station by JR Nara line i Nara City Tourist Center ☎(0742) 22-3900. Open 9am-9pm.

Although historically juxtaposed, Nara and Kyoto are completely different in character. Nara stands like a grave dowager beside the frivolous young prince that is Kyoto. In the grandeur and importance of its temples, in its lush greenery and parks, Nara may even outmatch Kyoto, yet it seems to lack its neighbor's *joie de vivre*, sophistication and refinement. You may also find its citizens have a provincial wariness of outsiders.

In ancient Yamato (precursor of the modern Japanese state) the practice was to move the capital every time the ruler died, to preserve Shinto ritual purity. The growing size of the state and administration finally made this impossible, and in 710 the Empress-Regnant (reigning Empress) Genmei settled the first permanent capital slightly W of the present city of Nara and called it Heijokyo. For the next 74yrs Japan underwent astonishing development in every field of art, culture, government and religion under the strong influence of T'ang China. Buddhism in particular exerted a powerful hold over the Imperial Court and nobility, producing some remarkable temples and monuments. After the capital moved to Nagaoka, then to Kyoto in 794, Nara fell into decline, despite briefly recovering its prosperity during the Kamakura period. Growth has only restarted in the past 30yrs as Nara became a residential suburb of Osaka, 42km (26 miles) away, but its population is still only one-third larger than it was in the 8thC.

Sights and places of interest

Many of the main sights are in green and wooded Nara Park where nearly 1,000 sacred tame deer, "guardians" of Kasuga Shrine, roam about. The best way to reach these sights is on foot or by bicycle (the Nara Hotel rents by the day or 4hr period).

To the w of the Nandaimon main gate of Todaiji you will find the only Japanese-style garden in Nara, named **Isui-en**, where you can escape the crowds. **The Neiraku Museum** (*74, Suimon-cho* ☎ *(0742) 22-2173* ■ *joint fee for museum and garden* ✿ ◁€ *museum open 10am-4.30pm, closed on Tues during Jan-Mar, June-Sept, Dec; garden open 10am-5pm, closed as museum*) is inside the garden and has a large collection of ancient Chinese bronzes, seals and mirrors, as well as ancient Korean pottery.

A 15min walk sw of the Kasuga Shrine takes you to **Shin-Yakushiji Temple** (*1352, Takabatakefukui-cho* ☎ *(0742) 22-3736* ■ ◁€ *open 8.30am-5pm*), founded in 747 by Empress Komyo to pray for the recovery of Emperor Shomu from an eye disease. The main hall, paved with tiles and built in the typical style of the Nara era, has a circular dais of white clay holding a seated wooden image of Yakushi-Nyorai flanked by an 11-headed, painted wooden statue of Kannon. It is surrounded by 12 extremely fine images of the Divine Generals, 11 of them made of clay.

Worth a visit too is the **Yamato Bunka-kan Museum** (*1-11-6, Gakuen Minami* ☎ *(0742) 45-0544* ■ ✿ *open Tues-Sun 10am-5pm (last entry 4pm), closed Mon*), near Kintetsu Gakuenmae Station, noted for its large collection of *netsuke* carvings and special exhibitions of Chinese ceramics. The great **Tenri Museum** (*Furu-cho 1, Tenri-shi* ☎ *(07436) 3-1511* ▣ ᖴ ✿ *open 9am-4pm (last entry 3pm), closed Dec 28-Jan 4*) of the Tenrikyo Shinto sect has a huge collection of 20,000 pieces of classical art from the Far East, Middle East, Egypt and Mediterranean, and an equally large number of ethnological exhibits.

Kasuga Shrine ★
160, Kasugano-cho ☎ *(0742) 22-7788* ▣ *for Homotsuden and Botanical Gardens. Discount on joint ticket* ◁€ *Homotsuden open 9am-4pm. Man-yo Botanical Gardens open 8.30am-4.30pm.*

The most impressive approach to the shrine is from Sanjo-dori, running E from Nara JR Station, through the large *torii* arches in the Deer Park, and along the famous avenue lined with 1,780 stone and 1,012 bronze lanterns (*lit on the nights of Feb 3 and Aug 15*). Kasuga Shrine was founded in 768 as the tutelary shrine of the Fujiwara family. Passing through the s gate, go down a long corridor to the floorless Heiden (where offerings are made) with the Naoriden (Entertainment Hall) on the left; both buildings date from 1650. The Honden sanctuary itself comprises four separate shrines (all National Treasures), each with its own Shinto deity. The Honden used to be rebuilt every 20yrs, but this now only applies to the roofing, and the current Honden dates from 1863. The Homotsuden (Treasure Hall), NW of the Honden, displays armor, swords, *bugaku* dance masks and other heirlooms of the Fujiwara family. The **Man-yo Botanical Garden**, on the left of the shrine approach, contains hundreds of plants mentioned in the ancient *Manyoshu* anthology compiled in the Nara period.

Kofukuji ★
48, Noborioji-cho ☎ *(0742) 22-7755* ▣ *for pagoda* ▣ *for Tokondo and Hoku-endo* ■ *for Kokuhokan Treasure House* ✿ *inside Kokuhokan, Tokondo and Hoku-endo* ◁€ *Pagoda open 24hrs, Tokondo and Kokuhokan open 9am-5pm, Hoku-endo open Apr-May, Oct-Nov (exact dates change annually) 9am-5pm.*

This impressive 5-story pagoda is Nara's central landmark. Its name means Happiness Producing Temple, and it dates back to 669, when it was originally a tutelary temple of the great Fujiwara family, who dominated political life in Japan from the 9th to early 11thC. The temple (comprising 175 buildings) was moved here in 710 and greatly prospered under Fujiwara patronage. However, its

1 Five-storied Pagoda
2 Tokondo
3 Nanendo
4 Three-storied Pagoda
5 Hokuendo
6 Kokuhokan

fortunes correspondingly declined with those of the Fujiwara.
During the 11th and 12thC its army of warrior monks frequently
fought with those from Enryakuji, on Kyoto's Mt. Hiei. Having
backed the vanquished Yorimasa Minamoto in 1180 Kofukuji was
burned down by the avenging Taira. Although the victorious
Yoritomo Minamoto later helped to reconstruct its temples,
Kofukuji never regained the leadership it had wielded in the Nara
and early Heian periods. Successive fires destroyed most of the
buildings, culminating in a huge conflagration in 1717. None of
the original Nara structures remain: the pagoda (a National
Treasure) was rebuilt in 1426 and is the second highest in Japan.

The **Tokondo** immediately N of the 5-story pagoda was founded
in 726 by Emperor Shomu and rebuilt in 1416. Enshrined here is
Yakushi Nyorai (Buddha-as-healer), flanked by other skillfully
carved Buddhist statues. The octagonal **Nanendo Hall** (1741),
situated directly W of the pagoda, contains a gilded statue of
Kannon, carved in 1181, and some notable statues of the Four
Heavenly Guardians. Often crowded, Nanendo is one of 33 sacred
pilgrimage destinations in W Japan. Behind here, and to the SW, is
a 3-story pagoda dating from the early Kamakura period. In the far
N corner from the pagoda can be seen another octagonal building,
the **Hoku-endo**, which contains some beautiful Buddhist images
by Unkei, the most noted sculptor of the Kamakura period. To the
N of the Tokondo stands the **Kokuhokan Treasure House**, which
contains the cream of the Buddhist masterpieces belonging to
Kofukuji (of which many are National Treasures).

Nara National Museum
*50, Noborioji-cho ☎ (0742) 22-7771 🖃 ♿ 🚻 ◀ Open Tues-Sun
9am-4.30pm (last entry 4pm). Closed Mon, Dec 26-Jan 3.*
This museum, opposite Kofukuji, is known for its extensive
Buddhist sculpture, painting, calligraphy and archeological
collection. The 1894 Annex, representative of the Western style in
vogue during the Meiji period, and itself an Important Cultural
Property, mainly houses temple plans, Buddhist tiles, urns and

tomb inscriptions. The 1972 Main Building divides Buddhist art into Mahayana, Jodo, Zen etc. Among the collection are richly illuminated 11thC-12thC handscrolls and mandalas and a 9thC seated sculpture of Yakushi (Healing) Buddha. A special exhibition on a particular theme of Buddhist art is held in May, and for two weeks in Oct priceless treasures from the Shoso-in are exhibited.

Todaiji ★

406-1, Zoshi-cho ☎ (0742) 22-5511 ▒ for Daibutsu-den, Sangatsudo, Kaiden-in ▓ inside Sangatsudo and Kaiden-in ▒ ▒ ★ ◁ Open Apr-Sept 7.30am-5.30pm, Oct-Mar 8am-5pm. Shoso-in open only Apr 29-May 5, Oct 23-Nov 6 9.30am-3.30pm, or at other times by arrangement with your embassy in Japan.

With its famous Daibutsu (Great Buddha) statue, this temple is the foremost sight in Nara. It was founded in 745 by Empress Shomu to head all the temples in Japan.

You will first come to **Nandaimon**, the huge main gate, which dates in its present form from 1199. The brackets supporting the twin roofs are unusually simple and open, suggestive of Indian architecture. The outside niches contain two giant wooden statues of Deva Kings dating from 1203: A-gyo, on the left, has his mouth and left hand open; Un-gyo, on the right, has them both closed. *A* and *Un* are the first and last letters of the Sanskrit alphabet. Thus they signify in Buddhism the inseparability of inhale-exhale, heaven-earth, positive-negative and male-female in the universe. In both vigor and animation these statues are probably unmatched anywhere else in Japan; they are thought to be the work of Unkei and Kaikei, master sculptors of the Kamakura period. The statues are currently undergoing extensive repair work. The inside niches contain guardian lions made in 1196 by Chinese artist, Chin Nankei.

It is difficult to decide which is the more powerful and imposing — the **Daibutsu-den Hall** or the **Daibutsu statue** it encloses, for both are superlative. The hall was burned down twice, and the current building dates from 1709. Although in restoration its size was reduced by one-third, it is still the largest wooden structure in the world, with a height of 48m (156ft). Given its colossal size and the structural limitations of wood, the building is an impressive feat of engineering. In front of the hall is an 8thC octagonal bronze lantern, famous for its reliefs.

Your first sight of the vast, looming presence of the Daibutsu inside the hall is liable to leave a deep impression. This is Vairocana Buddha, which the temple's Kegon sect regards as the original, or spiritual, body of Sakyamuni. The casting was finally completed in 745, after years of failed attempts, although much has had to be recast since to replace damage from earthquakes and fires. It is, at 21m high (71ft), the largest bronze statue in the world, weighing 551 tons. The dedication ceremony in 752 was attended by Empress-Regnant Koken, her parents, the entire court and 10,000 priests and nuns.

To the w of the Daibutsu-den, in a little-visited corner of the grounds, is the **Kaidan-in Ordination Hall**, the oldest in Japan. It was first built in 754 for the Chinese priest Ganjin, who ordained more than 500 Buddhists (including retired Emperor Shomu and Empress-Regnant Koken), and later founded the Toshodaiji temple in Nara. The present building dates from 1731; inside, on a raised platform, four famous 8thC clay statues of the Four Heavenly Guardians are exhibited. These masterpieces are famous for their ferocious and solemn expressions as they vanquish the enemies of Buddhism underfoot.

Proceeding N behind the Daibutsu-den you will pass a fenced-in park housing the **Shoso-in** repository of treasures of Emperor

Shomu. The original Shoso-in (756) is a wooden storehouse in the
azekura style, resembling a log cabin on stilts (its style has since
been widely copied, as in the *Meiji Treasure Museum* and the
National Theater in Tokyo). Nearby are two more modern
storehouses added in 1962. The Shoso-in houses a unique and
priceless collection of ancient ceramics, textiles, jewelry, musical
instruments, glassware and metalwork, examples from which are
removed and displayed in the Nara National Museum during Oct.
Both at this time and for five days at the beginning of Feb, the
grounds of the Shoso-in are open to the public (*9.30am-3.30pm*).
However, entrance to the buildings is still prohibited.

Following the path N and bearing E you will come to a
stone-paved lane that curves up the hillside. Behind the baked
mud walls are the houses of the Todaiji priests. The path leads to a
flight of steps, at the top of which is the **Nigatsudo** (February
Hall), named after the *o-mizutori* (water-drawing ceremony) held in
the second month of the old lunar calendar (the festival is still held
between Mar 1-14, with an enchanting torchlit procession through
the gallery on the night of Mar 12). The hall was founded in 752,
although the present building dates from 1669 and enshrines two
secret images of Kannon. The veranda commands a fine view over
the Nara Basin and Daibutsu-den rising from the trees.

Below this is **Sangatsudo** (March Hall), named after the custom
of holding an annual sutra service here in the third month of the
lunar calendar. This is the original building founded in 733, except
for the Raido (Oratory), added in 1200 and the oldest surviving
building in Todaiji. Inside, the central object of worship is
Fukukenjaku Kannon; made of dry lacquer, its diadem is of
perforated silver bedecked with agate, crystal and some 20,000
pearls surrounding a 23cm (9in) silver Buddha. The two clay
images of Nikko-Bosatsu and Gakko-Bosatsu (on the right and left
respectively) are also of exquisite workmanship.

Leaving the front of the Nigatsudo, proceed down the stone
staircase to another courtyard, where you will find a belfry
enclosing the 8thC temple bell. In the far left-hand corner of the
courtyard nearest the front of Daibutsu-den there is a pleasant
teashop that serves *amazake* (sweet rice wine).

Nearby sights

Horyuji ★
Ikaruga-cho, Ikoma-gun ☎ *(07457) 5-2555* ■ *Open Mar 11-Nov 19
8am-5pm, Nov 20-Mar 10 8am-4.20pm.*
The oldest existing temple in Japan, Horyuji, is situated 11km (7
miles) E of Nara, and houses the most ancient wooden buildings in
the world. It was founded in 607 by Prince Shotoku (554-628),
who like Charlemagne made his court a center of learning and
civilization for the whole country. Horyuji is justly regarded as the
fountainhead of Japanese art and culture. (Understandably it is
nearly always inundated with Japanese school tour groups, with
teachers and guides blaring instructions through megaphones.)

Horyuji is divided into two parts: the **West Temple**, containing
the Kondo main hall and pagoda, and the **East Temple**, mainly
comprising the Yumedono pavilion and the Chuguji convent. At
the end of an avenue of pine trees you will pass through the
Nandaimon (Great South Gate), rebuilt in 1439 into the precincts
of the West Temple. Next comes the **Chumon** (Middle Gate),
which dates from the year of the temple's construction. Unusually,
it is supported by pillars in the center, so that the entrance has two
parts. The Deva Kings in the outside niches (one painted red, the

other black, to symbolize light and darkness) date from 711.

The **pagoda** on your left still has its original timbers (607), and a vault under the central pillar may contain a bone of the historic Buddha. On each of the four sides of the pagoda you can just see Buddhist scenes represented in clay. The **Daikodo** (Lecture Hall), at the far side of the courtyard, contains the *Yakushi Trinity*, sculptures of clay and wood. The interior of the Kondo (on the right of the pagoda) houses the bronze *Sakya Trinity*, cast in 623 in memory of Prince Shotoku on the anniversary of his death, and the bronze *Yakushi-Nyorai*, cast in 607 on the order of Empress-Regnant Suiko and Prince Shotoku. Unfortunately, the natural light, as elsewhere in Horyuji, is so dim that these masterpieces are scarcely visible. Before leaving the West Temple be sure to visit the two buildings of the new **Treasure House**. Of special note is the 2m-high (6.5ft) Kudara Kannon, carved from a single piece of camphorwood, and the two famous miniature shrines formerly housed in the Kondo: Lady Tachibana's Miniature Shrine and the Tamamushi-no-Zushi.

The 8-pillared **Todaimon** gate leads to the East Temple where the palace of Prince Shotoku once stood (after his death it was destroyed by his political enemies and the East Temple built on its ruins). Its main hall, in the center of the courtyard, is the octagonal **Yume-dono** (Hall of Dreams), where it is said the prince would withdraw for meditation on the sutras. The Kannon statues inside the Yume-dono can just be made out through the windows.

The **Chuguji** convent, NE of the courtyard, was originally built by Prince Shotoku for his mother, some 500m (1,640ft) E of the present site. The current buildings are unremarkable, but it is worth entering just to see the exquisite beauty and grace of the black Nyoirin Kannon statue (probably Korean work) inside the modern main hall, as well as the collected fragments of the *Tenjukoku-Mandala* (Tapestry of Heaven), the oldest existing embroidery in Japan, framed on a stand by the altar.

On the way back to Nara, the **Yakushiji** and nearby **Toshadaiji**, are worth visiting.

Toshodaiji ★

Gojo-cho ☎ *(0742) 33-7900* 🚫 🈲 *inside Treasure House* ◁€ *Open 8.30am-5pm (last entry 4.30pm). Treasure House open Mar 21-May 19, Sept 15-Nov 8 9am-4pm. Mieido open June 5-7.*

Founded in 757 by Chinese priest Ganjin (688-763), this is one of the most rewarding of Nara's temples. The **Kondo** (Main Hall) has a delightful lightness, harmony and graceful simplicity, and the most beautiful colonnade in Japan. Built shortly after Ganjin's death, the unusual row of rounded pillars along the front porch possibly betray a Greek influence. Looking inside from the porch, note the halo around the monumental dry-lacquer statue of Vairocana Buddha in the center; of the original 1,000 tiny Buddhas that made up the halo, 864 still remain. Nearby, on the left, is a breathtaking dry-lacquer statue of Thousand-Handed Kannon. Unlike the symbolic statues in Sanjusangendo in Kyoto, this one was actually made with 1,000 arms, of which 954 are still attached.

The **Kodo** (Lecture Hall), behind the Kondo, was originally the audience hall of the Nara Imperial Palace, but has since been substantially modified. Passing through the center of a long temple building on the right flank of the Kondo and Kodo, you will see, on the same side, two 8thC *azekura* storehouses. The smaller one on the right is said to be even older than the Shoso-in in the grounds of Todaiji. The **Treasure House** ahead, open in spring and autumn, houses valuable Buddhist statuary. The **Mieido** (Founder's Hall), lying NE of the Kodo and briefly open in June, enshrines a beautifully serene, painted dry-lacquer sitting statue of Ganjin dating from 763.

Yakushiji ★

457, Nishinokyo-cho ☎ *(0742) 33-6001* 🚗 ◁€ *Open 8.30am-5pm.*

The original (AD730) pagoda of Yakushiji is of exceptionally beautiful proportions. The **Kondo** (Main Hall), rebuilt in 1600, contains the famous *Yakushi Trinity*, completed in 697, and the 2.6m-high (8.5ft) statue of *Yakushi-Nyorai*, Lord of the Eastern Paradise, seated on a dais set on a marble platform, flanked by attendants Nikko- and Gakko-Bosatsu. The **Toindo Hall** (rebuilt in 1285) also contains a bronze masterpiece Kannon, said to have been a gift to the Imperial Court from the Korean King of Paekche.

≈ One of the treats of visiting Nara is to stay in the rambling **Nara Hotel** (*1096, Takabatakecho, Nara City 630* ☎ *(0742) 26-3300* ☎ *5522108* ⊗ *(0742) 23-5252, 132 rms* ➡ AE 💠 ⊙ VISA), with its high rooms, coffered wooden ceilings and Meiji-era Japanese paintings hanging in the entrance hall. The service is formal to the point of stiffness, but this suits its old-world air. As a Western hotel it is second only to the Fujiya in Hakone, and it is where most foreign heads of state stay while in Nara; however, the cheerless modern wing should be avoided at all costs.

The centrally placed **Fujita Nara** (*47-1, Shimo-Sanjocho* ☎ *(0742) 23-8111* ☎ *5522137* ⊗ *(0742) 22-0255), 118 rms* AE 💠 ⊙ VISA) is international rather than charming, and the **Hotel Yamatosanso** (*24-1, Kawakamicho, Nara City* ☎ *(0742) 26-1011* ⊗ *(0742) 26-1016, 51 rms* ➡ AE 💠 ⊙ VISA), in a well-appointed location, with beautiful entrance and garden, offers both Western- and Japanese-style rooms.

≈ **Uosa Ryokan** (*Imamikado 15, Nara City* ☎ *(0742) 23-6035* ⊗ *(0742) 23-6039, 34 rms* ➡), although more expensive than some, is well located, being on the s side of Sarusawa Pond, overlooking Kofukuji Pagoda; it serves good Japanese food. **Kikusuiro** (*1130, Takabatakecho, Nara City* ☎ *(0742) 23-2001* ⊗ *(0742) 23-2001, 13 rms* ➡) is a first-class *ryokan*, with room-rates to match. Situated near Kofukuji, it is housed in an elegant mansion with a lovely garden, and has two excellent restaurants.

≈ Gourmets jaded by Kyoto may suffer from lack of choice here, but there are still some good restaurants to be found. For Japanese *kaiseki* haute cuisine try **Tsukihitei** (*158, Kasugano-cho* ☎ *(0742) 26-2021* 💴 ◁€ *last orders 7pm*), set deep in an ancient forest 3km (2 miles) E of Todaiji Temple. The Japanese restaurant of **Kikusuiro** ryokan (💴 ◁€ *last orders 8.30pm*) also offers excellent but expensive *kaiseki*, as well as more affordable *sukiyaki* and *shabu-shabu*. There is also a modern French restaurant annex called **Kikusui** (💴💴 ◁€ VISA *last orders 8.30pm*), overlooking the same lake as the Nara Hotel. In the **Nara Hotel's** old-fashioned dining room (💴 ▭ 💴 AE 💠 ⊙ VISA *last orders 10pm*), reasonably priced French cuisine and pricey steaks, as well as some Japanese standbys, are available; the hotel's new grill menu is comparable, but its interior lacks character and ambience. The **Kasuga Hotel Grill** offers inexpensive lunches and good, moderately priced dinners (*last orders 8pm*).

Nikko

120km (75 miles) N of Tokyo. Population 23,885. Nikko town is in the center of the 1,407sq.km (543sq. miles) Nikko National Park. Getting there: by train, approximately 1hr 45mins by Tobu line-limited express, from Matsuzukaya department store in Tokyo's Asakusa district.

Nikko National Park (a 2hr train journey from central Tokyo) is a supreme synthesis of natural and manmade beauty. Lofty mountains clad with fir trees, maples ablaze in autumnal reds, crystalline lakes, cascades and dramatic waterfalls vie in splendor with opulent architectural jewels from the age of the Tokugawa shoguns, which sparkle in the ethereal gloom of ancient forests.

Nikko has been a religious center since the 8thC when the Buddhist priest and ascetic Shodo (735-817) founded temples here, but Nikko attained national grandeur only after the death of Ieyasu, founder of the Tokugawa shogunate in 1616. In his will Ieyasu left instructions that he should be buried first at Mt. Kuno, in his native Mikawa province (now Shizuoka prefecture), then 1yr later that his remains were to be transferred to Nikko for permanent internment. In the same year the Emperor conferred upon Ieyasu the posthumous title of Tosho Daigongen, or Great East-Illuminating Incarnation of Bodhissatva. No expense was spared on the construction of the **Toshogu Shrine** (see below), which began in 1634, as the finest artists and craftsmen in Japan competed in groups. It is estimated that the timber used in the buildings, if extended, would stretch from Tokyo to Kyoto; some 37,500kg (38 tons) of rich, red *urushi* lacquer were applied; with each piece of wood receiving 40 coatings; nearly 2.5 million sheets of gold leaf — equivalent to 2.4ha (6 miles) — were used in their gilding; and altogether 15,000 men were employed in the 2yr task of the shrine's construction.

Iemitsu's successor Ietsuna granted the shrine its own surrounding lands to finance upkeep and the constant repair required, and an imperial prince served as its chief priest until the fall of the shogunate in 1868. Worship of Ieyasu's spirit was assiduously cultivated by Tokugawa shoguns, until some 100 Toshogu shrines were built in his honor throughout Japan (one of the earliest may be seen today in Tokyo's Ueno Park).

The shrine structures, many designated as National Treasures, narrowly escaped destruction in the Meiji Restoration after being seized by Tokugawa loyalist troops in preparation for a siege. However, a leading statesman persuaded the *Shogitai* to leave, thus sparing the monuments.

Lake Chuzenji

Shortly before arriving at Nikko's Tobu-line station, note the towering *sugi* (cryptomeria trees) as the train makes a brief stop at Imaichi. *Daimyo* Masatsuna Matsudaira (1576-1648) is said to have planted more than 200,000 *sugi* along the major paths to Nikko as his contribution to the Toshogu mausoleum, in lieu of silver or gold, which he could not afford; some 13,000 still survive.

From the bus terminal near the station board one of the buses leaving from platforms 1, 2 or 3. The buses all go to Lake Chuzenji; if you just wish to see the shrines and temples, disembark at either the Nishi Sando or Sogo Kaikan Mae stop.

After passing through the generally uninspiring town, the bus rounds hills and valleys to the NW before starting the spectacular climb to the lakeside, at an altitude of 1,270m (4,167ft), along a toll road with numerous hairpin curves and precipitous overhangs, as it crosses the Daiya River. (There are two roads, one for ascent and the other for descent. The return is even more thrilling.) From the top of the hill the bus descends quickly to the town of Chuzenji, at the E end of the lake where the Daiya River forms the **Kegon Falls**. Alight from the bus, walk down on the right following the path veering away from the lake, and look out for the sign to the Kegon Falls. Once there, a pay elevator carries visitors to the bottom of the gorge for the best view.

From the elevator entrance, go past the bus terminal toward the lake on the left side of the road along the banks of the Daiya. Where the river joins the lake, you will see a large 8thC red *torii* that is the main entrance to the **Futaarasan Shrine** (see below). The name Futaarasan is the old name for Mt. Nantai; the graceful volcanic cone of this 2,484m-high (8,150ft) mountain can be seen on the right. The head shrine of Futaarasan is down below, next to the Toshogu mausoleum, but the inner **Futaara Shrine** is on the SE edge of the summit crater. Every Aug thousands of pilgrims make the arduous climb up the sacred peak.

Just before the *torii*, turn left over an ornamental bridge for a stroll of 1-1.5km (¾-1 mile) s, along the lake shore. On your right you will pass the **Chuzenji Temple** (⚐ *open 9am-4pm, free English brochure available*); an underground passage from the parking lot leads to the temple grounds. Founded by Shodo in 784, Chuzenji belongs to **Rinnoji Temple** (see below) and originally stood on the N shore of the lake until removed here following a landslide in 1902. The temple's main treasure, a statue of a thousand-handed Kannon called Tachiki Kannon Bosatsu survived the disaster and remains the chief object of worship. This is the oldest Buddhist image in the Nikko area, and according to legend, Shodo saw the reflection of Kannon Bosatsu in the lake from the top of Mt. Nantai, and on his descent carved this 5.5m (18ft) statue from a living *katsura* (Japanese Judas) tree; the ax marks made by Priest Shodo may still be seen around its base.

Several coffee shops and restaurants bordering the lake-front road, on the way back to the bus terminal, offer respite for lunch or snacks.

Sights and places of interest in Nikko

From Chuzenji take any bus bound for Nikko Station and alight at Sogo Kaikan Mae stop. Ascend the staircase at the back of the large parking lot, and walk straight on until you reach the broad Ote Dori avenue that leads up to the Toshogu Shrine main gate.

Rinnoji Temple ★
2300, Sannai ☎ *(0288) 54-0531* ⚐ 🏛 *inside temple buildings* ◁€

At the gatehouse of **Rinnoji Temple** (on the lower right side of the avenue) buy a complete strip of tickets, which is much cheaper than buying them separately, for admittance to Rinnoji Temple's Sanbutsu Do, the Treasure House and the Shoyo En abbot's garden, and for Toshogu, Futaarasan Shrine and Daiyuin Mausoleum (*all open Apr-Oct 8am-5pm, Nov-Mar 8am-4pm*).

The Tendai Buddhist temple of Rinnoji was founded in 766, and the present **Sanbatsu Do** (Three Buddhas Hall) was first built in 848 by the pioneer monk Jikaku Daishi (797-864) and reconstructed by Shogun Iemitsu, grandson of Ieyasu Tokugawa, as part of a general facelift in 1648 following the creation of nearby Toshogu. Ascending the steps to the Sabutsu Do, you will see on your right a 400yr old cherry tree that bears yellow blossoms. Entering the main doorway, turn right and follow the E wall; in the first corner stands a statue to the ubiquitous monk Shodo, who is also credited with having founded Rinnoji. You will soon find yourself at the feet of three enormous gilt statues made in 1621, said to be the largest Buddhist sculptures in Japan: to the right, the Senju (Thousand Armed) Kannon, or Goddess of Mercy; in the center the Amida Nyorai Buddha; and on your left, the Bato Kannon, with the head of a horse, symbolizing the links between all living things in the cycle of Buddhist rebirth (Karma).

The **Shoyo En Garden** adjoining the Hombo (abbot's residence), and the Treasure House are at the opposite end of the temple precincts. The garden is a classic example of Edo-era landscaping, a meticulous composition of trees, plants and boulders collected from all around the Nikko area to suggest a microcosm of natural beauty. As you proceed along the path, to the right you will pass the old residence of the abbots, where in

1879 General Ulysses Grant stayed for eight days on a formal visit to Japan after retiring from the US presidency. E of the Hombo is the **Spirit Hall** (*visits allowed, with prior permission*), which enshrines the mortuary tablets of the imperial princes, who once served as Rinnoji's chief abbots.

The **Treasure House**, entered near the garden gate, has a fine collection of richly illuminated Buddhist scrolls, carvings, screen paintings, lacquer and bronzeware. An iron staff dated 770 is said to have belonged to the monk Shodo.

Toshogu ★
2301, Sannai ☎ (0288) 54-0560 📷 📖 inside shrine buildings ◁⊑

From Rinnoji, rejoin the main Ote Dori and proceed to the mausoleum, ascending the broad stairs called Sennin Ishidan, or Thousand-Person Stone Steps, which during the shogunate was the closest point commoners were allowed to approach Toshogu. At the top of the steps is the largest stone *torii* arch in Japan; the granite was shipped here from southern Kyushu in 1618 as a contribution from one of Ieyasu's *daimyo*. The bronze inscription of the name of the shrine is in the handwriting of Emperor Gomizuno-o (1596-1680), who married the daughter of Ieyasu's successor, Shogun Hidetada. The 5-story **pagoda** on the left, normally found only in temple grounds, is an example of the then officially sanctioned syncretism of Shinto with Buddhism. This 150yr-old reconstruction replaced the original, which was burned down in 1815, and bears the Tokugawa crest on all but the 1st story.

Passing through the elaborately carved **Niomon** front gate, with images of the Deva Kings on either side, you enter the lower courtyard of the **Sacred Storehouses**. Opposite the Middle Storehouse is the **Sacred Stable** for the shrine's white horse. The only unlacquered building in the Toshogu grounds, it is famous for its lintel carvings of the Three Wise Monkeys, whose "Hear No Evil, Speak No Evil, See No Evil" poses are derived from tenets of the Tendai Buddhist sect. Turning around, peer below the upper eaves of the Upper Storehouse to see two carved elephants, executed from drawings by Tan'yu Kano (1602-74). Only a very few elephants had been brought to Japan, and Kano probably never saw them himself, which may account for the fantastic shapes of the carvings.

Proceeding toward the next flight of stairs, you will pass on your left a cistern for holy water used by Shinto worshipers for purification, and at the foot of the stairs the **Rinzo Sutra Library** (*closed to the public*), which contains a 6m-high (20ft) revolving bookcase holding 7,000 copies of Buddhist sutras (even though this is a Shinto shrine!). In front are the wooden images of Fudaishi (497-596), the reputed Chinese inventor of the revolving library and those of his two sons. The rows of stone, bronze and iron lanterns in the courtyard were presented by *daimyo* of the 185 fiefdoms recognized by Ieyasu, as well as others created after his death. Ascending the steps, note the Leaping Lions carved in the solid stones, which serve as main pillars of the balustrade.

This is now the Middle Court, and before you is one of the most famous sights in Japan, the **Yomeimon Gate**, entrance to the Inner Shrine. First, however, take in the courtyard on your right, and the belfry and the drum tower on the left. A freestanding bell, also on the right, was presented by the King of Korea, and the ornate Western-style bronze candelabrum under a giant *sugi* tree was sent by the Dutch government, when it was most anxious to maintain its monopoly on foreign trade with the shogunate through Nagasaki. The huge revolving bronze lantern on the left is

NIKKO SHRINES AND TEMPLES

another gift of the Dutch to the shrine, in 1636; the lantern bears the Tokugawa crest, but positioned upside down — presumably a mistake of Dutch artisans.

Farther along on the left, the **Yakushido** can be seen, a purely Buddhist-style building, which enshrines the 12 gods of war and the Yakushi Buddha (Physician of Souls). However, the Yakushido's real claim to fame rested with its *Naki Ryu* (Crying Dragon) ink drawing by Yasunobu Kano (1613-85) on the ceiling of the nave. When visitors clapped their hands beneath the drawing, the echo sounded like a groan from the dragon — hence the name. The present Yakushido is a careful reconstruction of the original, which was destroyed by fire in 1961.

Yomeimon

Ascending once more toward the Upper Court, you will directly confront the **Yomeimon,** or Gate of Sunlight. Lower-ranked samurai were once permitted only as far as this gate, and higher ranks had to remove their swords before passing through.

This National Treasure is popularly called Higurashinomon, or Twilight Gate, implying that a visitor needs from dawn to dusk to appreciate all its amazing detail. A riotous and florid excess of color, gold leaf and intricate carving, Yomeimon is not merely a grandiose testament to the absolute power of the shoguns, but a unique embodiment of all the finest applied arts of the exuberant Momoyama era (as 80 percent of its craftsmen came from Kyoto and Nara, and the new Edo style had yet to make its mark).

Every facet of Yomeimon bears close study. See especially the drawings of two dragons on the portico ceilings, the one nearer the entrance by Tan'yu Kano and the inner, descending dragon by Yasunobu Kano. Passing through the gate itself, note also the shoulder-high carving of two tigers on the white-painted pillar in the exact left-hand center of the gate: the natural grain of the wood is cleverly used to represent the fur (hence their name, Mokume no tora, meaning wood-grain tigers). One of the 11 inside pillars (Mayoke no hashira, or evil-averting pillar) has a pattern purposefully carved upside down — the Toshogu craftsmen feared that creating something of perfect beauty would invoke the wrath of jealous gods.

From the Mikoshigura to the Honden

Inside the gate to the left is the **Mikoshigura** (Sacred Palanquin House), used for portable shrines for the annual spring festival, Sennin Gyoretsu (*May 17 and 18*). On the ceiling are large Buddhist angels painted by Ryotaku Kano. The **Kaguraden** (Sacred Dance Stage) to the right is notable for the basket of Japanese flowers in the gilded panel in the right-hand corner,

Mausoleum of
Ieyasu Tokugawa

1 Sacred Stable for White Horse
2 Upper Storehouse
3 Middle Storehouse
4 Lower Storehouse
5 Shinto-worshippers Cistern
6 Rinzo Sutra Library
7 Yomeimon Gate
8 Belfry
9 Drum Tower
10 Mikoshigura
11 Kaguraden
12 Karamon Gate
13 Haiden (Oratory)
14 Honden (Main Hall)
15 Sakashitamon Gate

**TOSHOGU
SHRINE**

COURT

LOWER COURT

Niomon Gate

ve-
Pagoda

Large Torii Arch

Sennin Ishidan
(Thousand person steps)

OTE-DORI

Sambutsodo

RINNOJI TEMPLE

Abbots Palace

Treasure House

*Shoyo En
Garden*

Hombo

Shodo Statue

Sogo Kaikan-mae
Bus Stop

To Shinkyo →

carved from a design by Korenobu Kano (1753-1808). The pattern
on the basket is thought to have been influenced by the style of
baskets used by Dutch traders in Nagasaki, and is the only carving
in the precincts to show any Western influence.

Directly before the Yomeimon stands a much smaller gate,
Karamon or Chinese Gate, named because of its debt to Chinese
architecture and inlay technique. Presiding over the gate is a
tsutsuga, which protects buildings; note also the ascending and
descending dragons in inlaid imported wood in the main pillars,
and the plums and bamboos, all symbols of felicitation.

Next is the **Haiden** (Oratory), where you must remove your
shoes before entering. The middle chamber is replete with
carvings of Chinese phenixes, pheasants, bamboo, apricots, pines
and paulownia, and over the lintels are portraits of 36 poets by
Mitsuoki Tosa (1617-91), with poems in the calligraphy of
Emperor Gomizuno-o. The mirror at the back is said to represent
the spirit of the deity enshrined, Ieyasu Tokugawa. The E
antechamber was formerly reserved for the shogun and the three
Tokugawa houses of Owari, Kii and Mito, and the w antechamber

was intended for the chief abbot of Rinnoji Temple, an imperial prince.

Leading from the Haiden to the Honden (Main Hall) is a passage called Ishi-no-Ma (Stone Room). The **Honden**, up five more copper-plated steps, bears similar frieze work and carving to the Haiden. The paneled door in front is closed to general visitors.

Gokuden

A succession of chambers leads to the "sanctum of sanctums," the **Gokuden** (Sacred Palace), housing the resplendent gold-lacquer shrine dedicated to Ieyasu and two other great warrior leaders, Yoritomo Minamoto (see *Kamakura*) and Hideyoshi Toyotomi. In 1873 it was decided to also enshrine Minamoto and Toyotomi here in an attempt by the new Meiji government to undermine the cult-worship of the overthrown Tokugawa shoguns, but the remains of the two other men lie in their original graves. The tomb of Ieyasu actually lies some way distant.

Leaving the Haiden and retrieving your shoes, head toward the Sakashitamon gate, passing under a gateway with a small carving of a cat on top. This is the famous **Nemuri-neko** (Sleeping Cat), tiny and simple compared to the rest of the grandiose sculpture in the shrine and probably for that reason best-loved by the Japanese. It is said to have been carved by Hidari-Jingoro, who may be apocryphal and whose other work was seen in the Karamon of the smaller Toshogu in Tokyo's Ueno Park. Passing through the highly decorated Sakashitamon (Bottom of the Slope) Gate, ascend the 200 steps to reach a bronze *torii*, with a copper-covered storehouse and another oratory alongside. Behind the oratory stands a solid cast-bronze gate, 3.5m (11ft) tall, and inside is the bronze sarcophagus, replacing the original stone tomb damaged in a 1683 earthquake, wherein lie the ashes of Ieyasu. Until 1868, nobody was allowed through Sakashitamon to climb the steps to the tomb except the shogun's family, imperial messengers and high priests.

Futaarasan Shrine

Retrace your steps to the entrance of Toshogu, and after passing through Niomon gate, turn right at the foot of the steps and follow a path lined with 37 stone lanterns to the large *torii* marking the entrance to Futaarasan Shrine. The Honsha, or Head Shrine of Futaarasan, was erected by order of Shogun Hidetada, son of Ieyasu and father of Iemitsu. On the left of the Honden are some inner gardens (**◼**), and to the right beside the oratory stands an ancient gnarled *koyamaki* umbrella pine said to have been planted by the Buddhist saint Kobo Daishi (774-835). Beyond it, in a corner of the shrine fence, is a small wooden enclosure housing an antique bronze lantern called Bake-doro (Goblin Lantern). Legend has it that at night the lantern assumed supernatural shapes, and samurai guards slashed at the evil apparition in terror. The scratches left by their swords are still visible on the rim of the bronze lamp. Beyond the second Treasure House (which contains a famous sword of the Kamakura period) is a delightful garden with a rustic teahouse beside a small spring and pond.

Leaving the shrine through its front gates opposite the Honden, note the venerable *sugi* on either side. Both are about 450yrs old, and grew from the same roots; the one on the left is called Meotosugi (Man and Wife Cedar), the one on the right is Oyako Sugi (Parents and Child Cedar). Descending the stone steps, you will see before you the **Jogyodo** and **Hokkedo Twin Halls** belonging to Rinnoji Temple, founded in 848 in imitation of similar buildings at Mt. Hiei near Kyoto. A large number of Buddhist images were removed from Nikko shrines after a nationalist purge in 1869.

A possible diversion here is to follow the path running s from the Twin Halls leading to **Jigendo Hall**, of the Rinnoji Temple, erected in honor of Tenkai (1536-1643), chief abbot of the Nikko temples and the great Kan'eiji Temple in Edo. His massive granite tomb lies behind its oratory.

Daiyuin Mausoleum

Facing the Twin Halls, turn right and follow the broad walkway through the first gate (**Niomon**) to the **Daiyuin Mausoleum**, where Toshogu's builder, Shogun Iemitsu, is enshrined and buried. Inside the gate on the right is a massive granite cistern, under a roof supported by 12 granite pillars. On the ceiling is a famous, but faded, painting of a dragon by Yasunobu Kano.

A flight of 21 stone steps leads to the second gate (**Nitenmon**); on passing through, pause to admire the statues of the Gods of Wind and Thunder, on guard from inside niches. The third gate, called **Yashamon** for the images of Yasha Buddhist demons that stand in its niches, is a miniature counterpart to Toshogu's Yomeimon. It is also popularly known as Botanmon (Tree-peony Gate) because of their abundant gilded carvings. The fourth **Karamon** gate — modeled on Toshogu — leads to the gorgeous **Haiden** oratory, the **Ai-no-Ma** connecting chamber, and the **Honden**, all of which are classed as National Treasures.

The bronze candlesticks and flower vases arranged along the walls of the Haiden were donations from the three principal subhouses of the Tokugawa; the tortoiseshell lanterns represent more gifts from Holland. To the right of the entrance to the Ai-no-Ma is a glass case containing a full suit of armor belonging to Iemitsu. The gold lions on panels in the Ai-no-Ma are by Tan'yu and Yasunobu Kano. The Buddhist-style Main Shrine's profusion of elaborate carving — dragons, arabesques, tree peonies and lion heads — are almost as overwhelming as those in Toshogu, yet more skillfully balanced in such a way as to accentuate the richly lacquered shrine to Iemitsu, superbly decorated with paintings of animals, birds, and flowers and housing a 1m-high (3ft) seated figure of the shogun himself.

Outside (on the right behind the walled enclosure) a flight of stairs leads upward to Iemitsu's tomb (now regrettably closed to the public). However, the tiny **Kokamon** gate, on the way from the Honden to the tomb, merits a diversion. The gate is distinguished by the Chinese Ming masonry of its lower section and its rounded ivory-colored arch of plaster, painted with ground seashells. Its airy fancy, so different to the cloyingly rich wonders of Toshogu, has led Japanese to call it Ryugumon, or Dragon's Palace Gate, as it reminds them of the fantastic palace of the Dragon King that according to children's folk tales lies at the bottom of the sea.

Shinkyo

Retrace your steps to the start of this walk, at the foot of Ote Dori. Turn left past Rinnoji's Shoyo En garden and then right at the intersection, to descend the stairs that emerge at the foot of the **Shinkyo** (Divine Bridge). According to legend, this is where two huge serpents rose from the river to form a bridge with their backs by which Shodo crossed the Daiya on his pilgrimage up Mt. Nantai. The original red-lacquered bridge was built in 1636 for the exclusive passage of visiting shoguns and imperial messengers, but was lost in a flood in 1906. This replica was built the following year. Just below here, cross the traffic bridge (which affords the best view of Shinkyo), and on the left side of the street is a bus stop for the return to Nikko.

Index

Individual hotels, restaurants, shops etc. are only included in the index if they are mentioned in the *Excursions* or *Planning and walks* sections; otherwise they are in alphabetical order within their appropriate sections and can easily be located.

Page numbers in **bold** type indicate main entries. Page numbers in *italic* type refer to illustrations or plans.

Index

Index

209

Index

Index

Index

Index

TOKYO

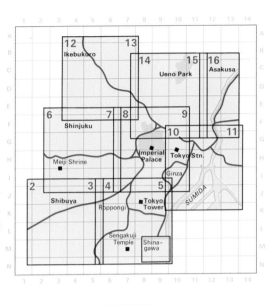

LEGEND

```
0              500            1000 m
```

▨ Major Place of Interest	⅃	Information Office
▨ Other Important Building	⊠	Post Office
▨ Built-up Area	✋	Police Station
▨ Park	✈	Parking Lot
† † Cemetery	—	Japanese Railway
卍 Temple	Ⓢ	Subway Station (Teito)
卐 Shrine	Ⓜ	Subway Station (Toei)
† Church	◀9	Adjoining Page No.
⊞ Hospital		

5 YOYOGI-UEHARA

2 3
5 YOYOGI-KOEN

6

Yoyo
Natio
Stadi

I
J
UEHARA

2

SHIBUYA-KU

TOMIGAYA

N.H.K. Japan
Broadcasting Corp.

NHK
Hall

JINNAN-C

Toba
Salt M

Shibuya
Tobu Hotel

YAMATE-DORI

Komaba
Park

Japan Folk
Crafts Museum

Tokyo Dept
Store

Ga
V

DOGENZAKA

SHOTO

YAMATE-DORI

J

K

Tokyo
University
Annex

KOMABA

TAMAGA

OHASHI

K

L

EXPRESSWAY   No. 3

AOBADAI

HIGASHIYAMA

YAMATE-DORI

IKEJIRI

NAKA
MEGUR

L

M

Setagaya
Park

KAMIMEGURO

SHIMOUMA

YUTENJI

M
N

GOHONGI

KOMAZAWA-DORI